Living on the Edge of the Gulf

Living with the Shore *Series editors, Orrin H. Pilkey and William J. Neal*

The Beaches Are Moving:
The Drowning of America's Shoreline
New edition
Wallace Kaufman and Orrin H. Pilkey

Living by the Rules of the Sea
David M. Bush, Orrin H. Pilkey, and
William J. Neal

Living with the Alabama-Mississippi Shore
Wayne F. Canis et al.

Living with the Coast of Alaska
Owen Mason et al.

Living with the California Coast
Gary Griggs and Lauret Savoy et al.

Living with the Chesapeake Bay and
Virginia's Ocean Shores
Larry G. Ward et al.

A Moveable Shore: The Fate of the
Connecticut Coast
Peter C. Patton and James M. Kent

Living with the East Florida Shore
Orrin H. Pilkey et al.

Living with the Georgia Shore
Tonya D. Clayton et al.

Living with the Lake Erie Shore
Charles H. Carter et al.

Living with Long Island's South Shore
Larry McCormick et al.

Living with the Louisiana Shore
Joseph T. Kelley et al.

Living with the Coast of Maine
Joseph T. Kelley et al.

Living with the New Jersey Shore
Karl F. Nordstrom et al.

The North Carolina Shore and Its Barrier
Islands: Restless Ribbons of Sand
Orrin H. Pilkey et al.

The Pacific Northwest Coast: Living with
the Shores of Oregon and Washington
Paul D. Komar

Living with the Puerto Rico Shore
David M. Bush et al.

Living with the Shore of Puget Sound and
the Georgia Strait
Thomas A. Terich

Living with the South Carolina Coast
Gered Lennon et al.

Living on the Edge of the Gulf:

The West Florida and Alabama Coast

David M. Bush   Norma J. Longo   William J. Neal   Luciana S. Esteves

Orrin H. Pilkey   Deborah F. Pilkey   Craig A. Webb

Duke University Press   Durham and London 2001

Living with the Shore Series
Publication of 21 volumes in the Living with the Shore series has
been funded by the Federal Emergency Management Agency.

Publication has been greatly assisted by the following individuals
and organizations: the American Conservation Association, an
anonymous Texas foundation, the Charleston Natural History
Society, the Office of Coastal Zone Management (NOAA), the
Geraldine R. Dodge Foundation, the William H. Donner Foundation, Inc., the George Gund Foundation, the Mobil Oil Corpo-
ration, Elizabeth O'Connor, the Sapelo Island Research Foundation, the Sea Grant programs in New Jersey, North Carolina,
Florida, Mississippi/Alabama, and New York, The Fund for New
Jersey, M. Harvey Weil, Patrick H. Welder Jr., and the Water Resources Institute of Grand Valley State University. The Living with
the Shore series is a product of the Duke University Program for
the Study of Developed Shorelines, which was initially funded
by the Donner Foundation.

Contents

8 Living with Coastal Construction: Buying, Building, or Retrofitting Your House   245

Figures, Tables, and Risk Maps

Figures

Tables

Risk Maps

Alabama

Florida

Preface

In the 1980s we produced *Living with the West Florida Shore* and *Living with the Alabama-Mississippi Shore*—two simple summaries of coastal hazards, the human response to such hazards, and guides to help citizens reduce vulnerability of their property to coastal risk. Of the more than 20 volumes in the Living with the Shore series, the West Florida volume was one of the more popular ones and went out of print. The Alabama-Mississippi book was a different story. The lower population density and somewhat lower risk for damage added up to poor sales and little interest. Much has changed along the Gulf coast in the last 15 years, in part because of Hurricanes Elena, Erin, Opal, Danny, Georges, and Mitch. Development has increased, regulations have changed, and risk mapping has improved. As a result, we decided to combine the open Gulf shoreline portion of Alabama with the west Florida shore into one, new and revised, book. We do not anticipate releasing a revised Mississippi book in the near future. This new volume is largely concerned with west Florida and may seem in places to overlook Alabama. Most of the examples of living with the shore, good and bad, are drawn from west Florida, but the same rules and cautions apply to Alabama and all other coastal states.

The huge losses this area experienced in Hurricanes Andrew and Opal, as well as the cumulative losses from lesser hurricanes, tropical storms, and southwesters, provided new insights into how construction techniques could be improved to reduce property losses, how to better manage protective beaches and dunes, and the need for new approaches to property damage mitigation. During the same 15-year period, our knowledge of coastal evolution, especially barrier island dynamics, has grown. Our approach to evaluating coastal development risk has progressed and expanded as a result of new storm experiences. Risk-mapping techniques have grown from a narrow focus on the shoreline and the obvious property at risk to a whole-island or "coastal zone" approach. Even the philosophy of shoreline stabilization has changed from an emphasis on shore-hardening structures to beach nourishment, and the next mitigation option of choice: relocation. Coastal regulation has changed as well, moving in the direction of resource management and risk reduction.

Unfortunately, not all of the changes have been positive. The population concentrated in the coastal zone continues to increase, putting more and more people and property at risk. And the majority of these coastal dwellers are unaware, inexperienced, or complacent toward the dangers they face in living on the coast. The recovery period after storms has not been a time of prudent corrections of past mistakes; rather, the reconstruction has followed a "bigger is better" philosophy, replacing beach cottages with beach mansions and single-family dwellings with condominiums. The result is that more property is at risk after the storm than before it! And the development continues to spread from the barrier islands and sandy beaches to the mainland shores that a generation or two ago were considered wastelands. Much of this development, old and new, is in flood-prone areas where each disaster places a growing burden on taxpayers at large, who must pick up tabs that have grown from millions of dollars to billions. Natural habitat is still being destroyed and water quality sacrificed in the name of development. Generations of shore-hardening structures are still contributing to beach degradation and downdrift erosion problems. And people are still asking the universal question, "When is *someone* going to do something about *my* eroding beach?" Rarely a day goes by without a media story that centers on some coastal issue. And the sea level continues to rise. So the time is appropriate to provide a new examination of life on the edge of the Gulf.

Two of the original authors, Orrin Pilkey Jr., of Duke University, and William Neal, of Grand Valley State University, are joined by lead author David Bush, of the State University of West Georgia; Norma Longo, a graduate of Duke University; Luciana Esteves, formerly at Florida Atlantic University; Deborah Pilkey, a professional engineer; and Craig Webb, a former Duke graduate student who is currently a professor at Mount San Antonio College in Walnut, California.

Dave Bush is an authority on coastal hazards, risk assessment mapping, and property damage mitigation. He has experience with the U.S. Atlantic, Caribbean, and Gulf coasts, and was a member of the National Academy of Sciences postdisaster field study teams after Hurricanes Gilbert and Hugo. He was involved with planning the U.S. Decade for Natural Hazard Reduction and is the senior author of *Living with the Puerto Rico Shore* and *Liv-*

ing by the Rules of the Sea. At West Georgia, Dr. Bush teaches courses in risk assessment, geomorphology, and oceanography, and he has published numerous papers on coastal hazards.

Norma Longo, an avid naturalist, traveler, and beach lover, is a graduate of Duke University who has worked in the Program for the Study of Developed Shorelines. Her video analyses of the Gulf shoreline and her 1997 Duke University honors thesis, "Quantitative Evaluation of Shoreline Armoring on the Florida Gulf Coast," provided a continuous coastal overview, summaries of armoring and development, and important input for coastal conditions before and after Hurricane Opal.

Luciana Esteves's 1997 master's thesis at Florida Atlantic University, "Evaluation of Shore Protection Measures Applied to Eroding Beaches in Florida," provided an updated summary of the sandy shorelines of 13 counties in west Florida. Luciana was our most distant author, providing her input all the way from the Fundação University of Rio Grande, Brazil, where she teaches courses on shore erosion and protection, marine sediments, and depositional environments in the Department of Geosciences. She is an invited consultant on coastal problems in Brazil.

The late Orrin Pilkey Sr. contributed a construction chapter to each of the earlier Living with the Shore books. His granddaughter, Deborah, maintains the family tradition. She authored the construction chapter in this volume, including concepts and design recommendations based on the lessons of Hurricanes Andrew, Fran, Hugo, Iniki, and Opal. She received her Ph.D. in engineering from Virginia Polytechnic Institute and State University in 1998.

Craig Webb's Duke University master's thesis, "Risk Mapping of North Carolina's Barriers," provided him with great experience in coastal risk mapping and the hazards of coastal living. His thesis work provided the inertia behind *Living with the North Carolina Coast.* He was part of the Program for the Study of Developed Shorelines team that investigated and published reports on such events as the impact of Hurricane Emily (1993) on sound-side shorelines in North Carolina and property damage mitigation lessons from Hurricane Opal (1995) in Florida.

The Living with the Shore series has been supported by the Federal Emergency Management Agency. The conclusions of this book, however, are those of the authors, based on various published reports and studies of record, and are not meant to reflect the views of FEMA or any other agency. The Natural Hazards Research and Applications Information Center in Boulder, Colorado, supported immediate poststorm field investigations after Hurricane Opal.

We are indebted to the positive feedback and support of many individuals without whom this book would not have been completed. Special thanks are due to our FEMA colleagues, especially Jane Bullock, Dick Krimm, and Gary Johnson. Thanks also are due to several people in various offices and departments involved with Florida's coast and environmental protection for providing assistance and materials over the years, especially Mike McDonald, Michael Loehr, Frank Koutnik, Don Collins, Heidi Recksiek, Paden Woodruff, Jim Balsillie, Ralph Clark, Mark Leadon, Tom Waters, and Phil Flood. Several students at our respective institutions helped with fieldwork, map preparation, typing, and countless other thankless tasks. A special thank-you to John Congleton and Amy Daniels at West Georgia for sharing their digital know-how to do the actual mapping. Thanks to Scott Smith, Nicole Cover, Donald Vick, Karen King, Chester Jackson, Matt Pennington, Jason Smith, Kris Nolan, and Graham Bates.

We thank also the authors of the previous west Florida and Alabama-Mississippi books for laying the groundwork, especially Larry Doyle, Al Hine, and Wayne Canis. Skip Davis generously provided several photographs from his vast west Florida collection. We are indebted to him and hope we returned all his slides to him. We also thank Tracy Rice for supplying photographs and insights from her post–Hurricane Georges field inspection. Special thanks are due Rob Young for his post-Opal reconnaissance report and photographs.

We acknowledge the superb assistance of several agencies during the field inspection after Hurricane Opal, including several Florida county sheriff's departments, especially in Bay, Okaloosa, and Escambia Counties, for their help with access; the National Guard, especially Spc. Gary Bégin of the Florida Army National Guard Public Affairs Office for a guided tour of Fort Walton Beach and a detailed description of the damage in Navarre Beach; and Michael Simmons and Brandon Richberg, four-wheel-drive volunteers who provided safe transportation and their insights on the storm damage on Pensacola Beach.

Amber Taylor is a major contributor to the book, having drafted all the line drawings and risk maps while refusing to sacrifice quality. Thanks, Amber.

We thank all of the coastal residents who shared their knowledge, experiences, and concerns gained from living on the coast, as well as the authors of the earlier *Living with the West Florida Shore,* who established a model for the outline of this book.

Finally, a special thank-you to Carmen, Mary, and Ray for their continuing support and for putting up with us.

William J. Neal
Orrin H. Pilkey
series editors
September 3, 1999

A rising tide of growth imperils the beaches of Florida. So went the headline of a recent article by *Miami Herald* environmental writer Juanita Greene. A lot of other Florida newspaper headlines over the past two decades have said the same thing. Yet nothing seems to halt the relentless push to the sea by Florida builders and Florida dwellers.

Take Panama City Beach, for example. According to Deborah Flack, director of the Florida Division of Beaches and Shores, "You can't talk about destroying Panama City Beach because it already is destroyed." Buildings were jammed up against a beach that was retreating landward, and the inevitable happened. The beach disappeared.

Take Walton County, for example. A couple of years ago developers bulldozed dunes on land they were not even ready to develop, just to prevent application of a new state building control (setback) line.

Take Captiva Island, for example. Acres of mangroves on the lagoon side fell victim to bulldozers operating on a weekend when legal steps to prevent this destruction could not be taken.

Now thousands of buildings ranging from simple beach cottages to 20-story condominiums hug the beautiful west Florida shore. In Pinellas County and to the south, these buildings are often located at elevations of no more than 5 feet, too low for residents to safely ride out a storm. The quality of building is variable. Some structures are built well, but many others will be damaged in the high winds and seas that will accompany the next big storm. Escape from the next storm is not feasible for thousands of inhabitants because most evacuation routes are across drawbridges that cannot be depended upon during power outages and rising seas. A more immediate but non-life-threatening problem is the disappearing beachfront in many communities. Repair of costly seawalls and the pumping up of new beach sand promise to add significantly to community tax bills in coming years.

But the future of living on the west coast of Florida has its bright spots, too. For example, there are some sites along the shoreline with relatively high elevations and rows of protective dunes. Furthermore, wise and informed coastal dwellers can take a number of steps to reduce the hazards they face. Most important, concerned residents can be a major political force in the promotion of a rational coastal zone management policy to help save the beautiful west Florida shore for generations to come.

These are the reasons we wrote this book: to help those who already live on the shore, to aid others who may wish to do so, and to preserve the beauty of the west Florida coastline for our grandchildren.

When we began to think about the person to head up this project, Larry Doyle, professor of marine science at the University of South Florida, was a natural choice. Larry has lived near the shore for a number of years and is widely recognized for his studies of the marine environment, on and off-shore, of the Gulf of Mexico. He is the author of many technical papers and several books. Co-author Al Hine, also a USF professor, is a coastal geologist with experience on the coasts of Massachusetts, North Carolina, South Carolina, and Florida. Daniel Belknap, who now teaches geology in Maine, has worked on coastal problems in both Delaware and Florida. Dinesh Sharma is an environmental consultant living in Fort Myers, Florida. He has long been a highly visible power in the struggle for a sound statewide coastal zone management policy. David Martin is a student in maritime science at the University of South Florida. Bill Neal and Orrin Pilkey Jr. (professors of geology at Grand Valley State Colleges and Duke University, respectively) are editing the state-by-state book series of which this title is one entry. And last but not least, Orrin Pilkey Sr. is a retired civil engineer, living in Charlottesville, Virginia. The senior Pilkey's interest in shoreline construction problems stems from the time his house was severely damaged when Hurricane Camille struck the Mississippi coast in 1969.

This book is one of some 20 projected volumes in the Living with the Shore series. Eventually there will be a book for each coastal state as well as for Lake Erie and Lake Michigan.

As an umbrella book to the series the Duke Press has reprinted with an updated appendix the classic *The Beaches Are Moving: The Drowning of America's Shoreline*, by Wallace Kaufman and Orrin H. Pilkey Jr. This book covers the basic issues dealt with specifically in the state-by-state books.

The series editors have published with Van Nostrand Reinhold Company a construction guide, *Coastal Design: A Guide for Builders, Planners, and Homeowners* (1983), giving detailed coastal construction principles. The prudent coastal dweller should own both *Coastal Design* and the individual shore volume.

A lot of people helped us produce this book. Larry Doyle was supported by Florida Sea Grant. This is Florida Sea Grant College Program Report #63. The Florida Department of Community Affairs, through a grant to coauthor Dinesh Sharma, provided funds to cover some research and printing costs. We would like to extend special thanks to Dr. Asish Mehta and Dr. T. Y. Chia of the Coastal Engineering and Oceanographical Engineering Department at the University of Florida for providing a great deal of information for the compilation of the hazard profiles of individual counties. Lucille Lehman at the coastal engineering archives secured several hundred reports and documents during our research, and the Jacksonville District Headquarters of the U.S. Army Corps of Engineers was extremely helpful in providing us with hard-to-get reports. County and regional planners provided copies of technical reports and ordinances for our review and research.

The overall coastal book project is an outgrowth of initial support from the National Oceanic and Atmospheric Administration through the Office of Coastal Zone Management. The project was administered through the North Carolina Sea Grant Program. Most recently we have been generously supported by the Federal Emergency Management Agency (FEMA). The FEMA support has enabled us to expand the book into a nationwide series including Lake Erie and Lake Michigan. Without the FEMA support the series would have long since ground to a halt. The technical conclusions presented herein are those of the authors and do not necessarily represent those of the supporting agencies.

We owe a debt of gratitude to many individuals for support, ideas, encouragement, and information. Doris Schroeder has helped us in many ways as Jill-of-all-trades over a span of more than a decade and a dozen books. Doris, along with Ed Harrison, compiled the index for this volume. The original idea for our first coastal book (*How to Live with an Island*, 1972) was that of Pete Chenery, then director of the North Carolina Science and Technology Research Center. Richard Foster of the Federal Coastal Zone Management Agency supported the book project at a critical juncture. Because of his lifelong commitment to land conservation, Richard Pough of the Natural Area Council has been a mainstay in our fundraising efforts. Myrna Jackson of the Duke Development Office and the

President's Associates of Duke University have been most helpful in our search for support.

Mike Robinson, Jane Bullock, and Doug Lash of the Federal Emergency Management Agency have worked hard to help us chart a course through the shifting channels of the federal government. Richard Krimm, Peter Gibson, Dennis Carroll, Jim Collins, Jet Battley, Melita Rodeck, Chris Makris, and many others opened doors, furnished maps and charts, and in many other ways helped us through the Washington maze.

We also received a lot of help from Tallahassee officialdom. We would like to particularly note Jorge Southworth of the Department of Commerce and James Stoutamire of the Department of Environmental Regulation. Along the way we received help and encouragement from many of our fellow geologists. We particularly wish to mention our gratitude to Charles Finkle.

Orrin H. Pilkey Jr.
William J. Neal
series editors

Wednesday, October 4, 1995, really *was* a dark and stormy night along the Gulf coast. Residents had been focused on the national news, but not the weather. On Tuesday, life had come to a momentary standstill as Americans waited to hear the verdict in the O. J. Simpson trial. Far less attention was being paid to Hurricane Opal, which had been a lingering threat at sea: first as a category 3 storm with winds exceeding 110 mph, then strengthening to a strong 3, and, while still at sea, reaching the category 4 level with 150 mph winds! How big would Opal grow? Where would it strike? Many people began to pay attention, but only just in the nick of time.

At about 6:00 P.M. on October 4, 1995, Opal struck Florida near the Okaloosa–Santa Rosa County line. Fortunately, as tragic as the damage caused by Opal would be, the storm had by then weakened back to a category 3 hurricane with maximum sustained winds of 125 mph and gusts to 144 mph. In the hours before landfall and in the days and weeks that followed, the lives of the residents of a long stretch of the Panhandle and beyond would change dramatically. Some would be seeing the dark side of living at the shore for the first time.

At least 100,000 people experienced the dislocation of the prestorm evacuation — a displacement that probably saved their lives. The area of coast where they had been just a few hours before was ravaged by a storm surge that raised the sea level as much as 20 feet, topped by storm waves and associated flood currents! From Gulf Shores, Alabama, to Tampa, Florida, coastal flooding changed the landscape. In the landfall zone, sand dunes that had stood 20 feet above sea level were flattened, and beach and dune sands were washed through lobbies and living rooms into pools, driveways, and streets. Sand was deposited in some beachfront businesses and houses

1.1 Hurricane Opal (1995) damage in Mexico Beach, Florida. Photo by Craig Webb.

to depths of 3–5 feet. But that was the least of the destruction the returning residents would find in Opal's wake (fig. 1.1).

Oceanfront property over the five-county area (Escambia, Santa Rosa, Okaloosa, Walton, and Bay; see fig. 1.2) extending in both directions from the eye landfall was laid waste by Opal. The National Climatic Data Center's summary lists approximately 3,300 structures destroyed and more than 18,000 damaged. Some of those houses were still under repair from Hurricane Erin, a category 1 storm that had swept along southern Alabama and the Florida Panhandle earlier that summer. Opal's impact was far greater. Hundreds of boats were destroyed in marinas, and the businesses serving the coastal tourism industry shared in the disaster. More than a million people in a three-state area were without power, and all services on the coast were interrupted. Roads were flooded, eroded, buckled, buried in sand, or completely gone in some locations. Water and sewer lines were damaged, phone lines and utility poles were down, and gas leaks were reported. More than three miles of total armoring — so-called shoreline protection — had been damaged and destroyed, rendered ineffective by the overtopping storm surge and waves.

Virtually every building at Navarre Beach was damaged, and a high percentage of them were completely destroyed. One resident was quoted in a newspaper article as saying, "I have a house on the Gulf. You can't see where it even was." The poststorm landscape of Fort Walton Beach was described as surreal. Destin and Okaloosa Island's 13,000 residents returned to scenes of destruction ranging from total loss to minor water and wind damage and loss of services. Niceville, Miramar Beach, and Mexico Beach experienced extensive destruction and damage; Pensacola Beach and Panama City Beach properties were hard-hit as well (fig. 1.3). And the damage extended well beyond the five-county eye zone. Houses and structures along the barriers of Gulf and Franklin Counties, farther east, were also damaged.

The Alabama Gulf coast, which took only a glancing blow, suffered similar dune erosion, extensive washover of sand, and severe damage to some beachfront houses, hotels, and the state's convention center. Most of these buildings were in high-hazard zones that had been wiped clean by Hurri-

1.2 Index map of Alabama and Florida coastal counties.

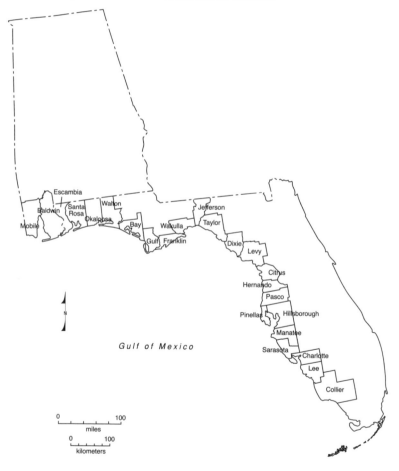

1.3 Little was left of this Pensacola home after Hurricane Opal
passed over on October 4, 1995. Photo by David Bush.

cane Frederic in 1979. Dauphin Island was far enough beyond the core of
the storm to escape major damage, but 70 mph winds, 10-foot waves, and
overwash left their mark. When the final tally was in, Opal's bill of destruction was $2.1 billion in insured losses, and another billion dollars of un-
insured losses!

If Hurricane Andrew (1992) was the storm that demonstrated the power
of the wind, Opal exemplified how devastating the process of storm surge
can be. The storm-generated rise in sea level, topped by waves, smashed
some beachfront houses and lifted others off their pilings and out into the
sound, carried large boats and stranded them inland, ripped facades off of
two-story buildings, washed over and deposited sand on a wide area, flattened dunes, eroded a new inlet (a pass was opened east of Navarre Beach),
removed the sound-side beach on the back of part of Santa Rosa Island
(parts of which were completely submerged during the storm), and eroded
gullies and scarps into the beaches. And Opal was only a category 3 (and
weakening) storm.

Almost immediately afterward, fundamental rules on how this devastation could have been avoided or reduced (mitigated) were being rediscov-
ered. The *Mobile Register* ran a front-page article on October 8 titled "Dunes
Would've Saved the Beaches." What was really meant was that dunes would
have saved the buildings. The beaches were still present after the storm; they
had simply migrated inland over the yards, foundations, parking lots, and

streets! The observation was that high, wide dunes, and multiple rows of dunes (two and preferably three) protected buildings and roads, while areas without dunes or with poorly developed dunes suffered destruction. The same facts had been driven home by Camille in 1969, and Frederic in 1979, and by hurricanes in other areas as well (e.g., Hugo in South Carolina), but the protective dunes had been replaced by cottages, condos, and seawalls, setting the stage for Opal and the coming storms.

A post-Opal assessment of destroyed and damaged buildings (appendix C, ref. 16) concluded that most of the severe damage occurred within 200–300 feet of the shoreline, coinciding closely with the zone defined by Florida's coastal construction control line (CCCL). Nearly half of the CCCL-nonpermitted structures in the storm area were seriously damaged or destroyed, while only two permitted structures were seriously damaged. This strongly suggests that storm damage can be mitigated (but not eliminated) through the use of setback controls and building codes. Ironically, while Opal was meandering offshore, its course not yet determined, the drafters of the Standard Building Code were meeting in Atlanta. Among the revisions they were considering was one that would have required houses built in the coastal zone to be more resistant to high winds. Incredibly, the proposal was turned down because it would have added an estimated $2,400 to the cost of a house. If you were to ask survivors of Hurricane Andrew or Opal if they would have been willing to spend an extra $2,400 to have kept the roof on their house and the contents dry during the storm, what do you suppose they would say?

That is the point of this book: to consider how to live *with* the coast as opposed to living *at* the coast and being a potential victim of its natural hazards. The aftermath of Opal, previous storms, and storms yet to come sends an age-old message: "Better safe than sorry." If we are to live with the coast, we must understand and plan for its dynamics, for it has a life of its own — perhaps nine lives if the effects of nature, humans, and the interaction of the two are combined.

Climatic Life: The Dynamic Coastal Zone

We give hurricanes people's names (e.g., Andrew, Erin, Georges, Mitch, Opal) and talk about them as if they are living beings. "She decided to head north" or "she's a fickle storm and can't decide her course" are descriptions that humanize nature. Of course, storms can't think, but they have an origin, an evolution or development, and a history — a life of sorts. On a grander scale, climates change through time, altering the land and the ocean, and life in those environments. Climate is a fundamental component of the human environment, a fact that coastal residents sometimes forget or ignore.

Hurricanes, southwesters, droughts, El Niño and La Niña effects, and changing weather in general provide frequent reminders that the Alabama-Florida coast spans nearly 8 degrees of latitude across three climatic belts between two oceanic expanses — prime real estate in the middle of a cauldron! Living conditions on the Gulf coast range from temperate to tropical in environments as diverse as the sandy shores of Alabama, the Panhandle, and the central barrier islands; the marshy hummocks, savannas, and flatwoods on the Big Bend coast; and the salt marshes, mangrove coasts, and great Everglades swamp transition between fresh and salt waters. Perhaps the most significant climatic factor on the Gulf coast, however, is that the region is in a zone of frequent ocean storms, hurricanes, and southwesters. And, as we will see, while all of Florida is subject to hurricanes, the Gulf coast has the higher frequency.

Above all else, the region's climatic life teaches us that the coastal zone is dynamic. It is subject to almost constant natural change that does not recognize static buildings or structures placed in the paths of storms, waves, currents, or the resulting shoreline retreat.

Geologic Life: Geologic Origins, Time, and Change

The Gulf coast illustrates the principle that geology is a fundamental component of our environment. We need not go back into the mists of earliest geologic time or to a Jurassic Park to illustrate this concept, but it is interesting to note that the rocks deep beneath the state were once part of an earlier African plate. That continental landmass had merged with North America and other landmasses to form a supercontinent, Pangea, which subsequently broke up into the present continents (fig. 1.4). After the breakup, a fragment of ancient Africa remained attached to North America and became the base on which the Florida Platform grew. The distinct Florida peninsular outline is the emergent portion of this much larger Florida Platform, a mass of buried limestones (carbonates) that formed in persistent shallow marine environments like those found today in the Bahama Banks and the Florida reef tract. These limestones began forming as much as 145 million years ago, and continued to form into the Pleistocene in south Florida.

The great carbonate bank was separated from North America by a trough, the Suwannee Channel, which effectively prevented the sands and muds eroded off the Appalachian Mountains from reaching Florida (fig. 1.5). Later in time the trough filled with sediment and the platform became attached

Quaternary	Holocene	0.01 Ma	Modern sea level rise
	Pleistocene		Ice Age sea level changes
		2 Ma	
Tertiary	Pliocene	5 Ma	Terrigenous sediments from Appalachians move along emergent platform
	Miocene		
		25 Ma	
	Oligocene	38 Ma	Suwannee Trough fills. Limestones accumulate over the area of the Florida Platform.
	Eocene		
		55 Ma	
	Paleocene		
		65 Ma	
Cretaceous			Florida Platform
		140 Ma	
Jurassic			Opening of Atlantic

Ma: Million years before present

1.4 Geologic time scale with selected Gulf coast events.

1.5 Paleogeographic map of Florida about 45 million years ago showing the Suwannee Channel separating quartz-sand-dominated deposition to the north from carbonate bank to the south. The channel was an actively flowing marine seaway that prevented quartz-rich sediments from reaching the carbonate bank. From R. A. Davis Jr. and A. C. Hine, *Quaternary Geology and Sedimentology of the Barrier Island and Marshy Coast, West-Central Florida, U.S.A.*, 1989 (appendix C, ref. 19).

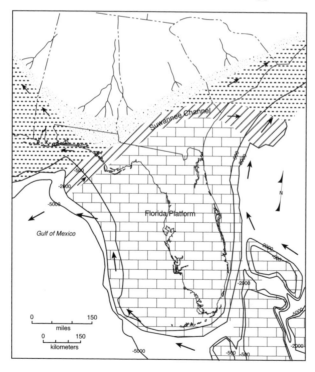

to the mainland, allowing quartz-rich sands to move south along both the Atlantic and Gulf shores.

Richard Davis Jr., of the University of South Florida, notes in his "Barriers of the Florida Gulf Peninsula" (appendix C, ref. 18) that this Gulf coast sediment supply was cut off for good at the end of the Pleistocene Ice Age. Thus, at the present time, the marshy Big Bend coast is devoid of northerly-derived sands. This geologic fact — that the peninsular Florida coast is receiving no new land-derived sediments, either from longshore drift or from rivers draining Florida's uplands — has serious implications for coastal management. Given that the continental shelf has very limited sand reserves, the peninsular barrier islands depend for their existence largely on the reworking of their own sands and sands from the associated tidal deltas. Prudent sand management is dictated by the region's geology.

On the Gulf Coastal Plain, sands derived from the Appalachians made it as far as the Alabama-Florida Panhandle and were incorporated into the barrier island coast, but less of this sand was carried farther south onto the platform. Yet beaches still formed in west-central Florida, supplemented by the abundance of shells and carbonate skeletal fragments that broke up into sand-sized particles. The coarser shelly beaches are usually steeper than the beaches comprised of fine quartz sand. These differences in the composition of beach sands between east and west Florida, and from north to south along the Gulf coast, reflect a long history of changes through time that may seem to be of little consequence, but the availability, composition, and behavior of the sand in today's beaches is the result of that history. We rely on limited ancient sand resources, i.e., fossil sand. The Gulf's waves and currents are working on a wide variety of deposits from these earlier times.

The geologic record of the Gulf coast illustrates that climate and sea level are in a constant state of flux. Whether one accepts the premise of the greenhouse effect or not, the climate and the level of the sea are unquestionably changing over both the short and the long terms. We need to go back only to previous interglacial warm periods to find that the sea level was 150 feet higher than at present, inundating well over half of the present land area of Florida.

At the end of the Pleistocene Ice Age some 18,000–15,000 years ago, the sea level was 300–400 feet below its present level and the shoreline was out at the edge of the continental shelf. The great sea-level rise that followed, known as the Holocene transgression, was one of the most significant predetermining events relative to the origin of the present shorelines. Large amounts of water were tied up in the massive glacial ice caps (e.g., as in present-day Antarctica and Greenland) that covered parts of North

America, Europe, and Asia at the end of the Pleistocene Ice Age. As the ice caps melted, the postglacial sea-level rise caused the Gulf coast shorelines to migrate across the continental shelf as much as 130 miles to their present positions (fig. 1.6).

Climatic warming and melting of those ice caps was well under way by 10,000 years ago, and the sea level was rising at a rate of 3–4 feet per century until 5,000–4,000 years ago when the rate decreased (fig. 1.6, inset). Although scholars disagree about the details, the sea level has continued to rise since then, although at a much slower rate, perhaps on the order of 4–8 inches per century. This slower rate of sea-level rise favored the formation and development of the barrier islands.

The geologic life of the Gulf coast teaches us that the earth is constantly changing. With the sea level falling and rising, and sediment supplies changing, we should not expect the shorelines to remain forever as they are today. Opal, like hurricanes of the past, reshaped beaches, dunes, shorelines, and inlets, obliterating buildings with their feet in such mobile fea-

1.6 Position of the Alabama and Florida portions of the Gulf shoreline 15,000–18,000 years ago. Inset is sea-level change over the past 15,000 years. Melting of the great ice caps formed during the ice ages caused the sea to rise and the shoreline to migrate landward.

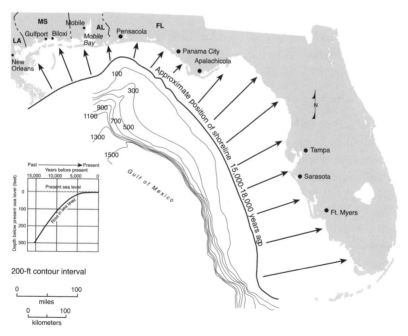

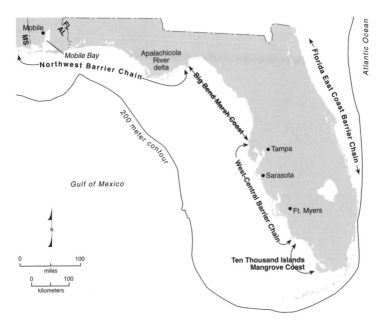

I.7 Regional coastal types in the eastern Gulf of Mexico vary because of geologic and oceanographic controls. From R. A. Davis Jr. and A. C. Hine, *Quaternary Geology and Sedimentology of the Barrier Island and Marshy Coast, West-Central Florida, U.S.A.*, 1989 (appendix C, ref. 19).

tures. More of the same can be expected from future hurricanes. Repeated Opals over time will leave platted lots behind in the surf while accreting new ephemeral shores in your former fishing spot!

Coastal Life: Regional Coastal Types

If a coast could think, it would want to be straight. When processes create irregularities in the coastline, nature works to straighten the shore. The present coastal condition is part of a continuum of such change, and the variations in the coast that we see today are the result of the differences in geology, oceanography, and climate of the various reaches. Figure 1.7 shows this regional coastal variation. The distinction of coastal types and how they function is fundamental to understanding and mitigating coastal hazards.

Barrier islands are magnets for coastal development. The beauty of their beaches, the serenity — even starkness — of their sand and water, and their multi-recreational opportunities are a prime attraction of the Gulf coast. The Northwest Barrier Chain of Alabama and the Florida Panhandle and the West-Central Barrier Chain of Florida are the centers of the coastal population. In contrast, the marsh and mangrove coasts have been obstacles to coastal settlement. Life at the coast is controlled by the regional coastal types, and coastal management must be structured on the basis of such differences.

Physical Life: Processes, Sediments, Environments

Living with the shore requires an appreciation of physical processes and how they shape sediments and create unique environments. Beaches, for example, attain their shape in response to the sea level, wave energy, and sediment supply. The beach evolves toward a natural balance or equilibrium (fig. 1.8), but as sea level rises, wave conditions change, or sediment supply fluctuates, the beach shifts, flattens, steepens, narrows, or widens. Nature doesn't remain the same long enough to allow the beach any permanence in terms of being a suitable footing for a hotdog stand, cottage, or condominium.

The physical rhythm of the shore incorporates wind, waves, currents, tides, and the associated sand flow. Storms are the acme of such processes, and Opal demonstrated the vigor of this physical life. Again using barrier islands as an example, the entire island system is much like the beach, moving to reach equilibrium with the same controls. As the sea level rises, the barrier must adjust by building its elevation and shifting landward. Dunes and overwash are examples of both cross-island sediment transport and mechanisms by which the island builds its elevation. These processes and

1.8 Dynamic equilibrium of beaches. When one factor changes, all others adjust accordingly.

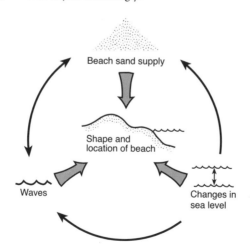

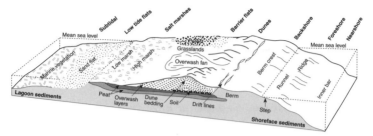

1.9 Typical barrier island cross section, adapted from work by Paul Godfrey. Environments change quickly both laterally and across the island, and storm impacts vary between environments.

resulting landforms control the environments that we commonly associate with the coast (fig. 1.9).

Biologic Life: Plants and Animals

The range of climatic zones, coastal types, and geologic settings and processes lead to a great diversity of environments within the coastal zone. Reefs, salt marshes, and mangrove swamps are among the most productive ecosystems on earth. They are the nurseries for sea and land, and the loss of marshes and mangroves can spell disaster for future fishing stocks that are found far beyond these key environments.

Beaches and dunes, maritime thickets and forests, coastal grasslands, marshes, and tidal flats (fig. 1.9) all have their own biota (fig. 1.10). From microscopic organisms that live between sand grains in the beach to coquina clams and beach burrowers to wading birds and nesting turtles and all the variety of coastal plants, biologic life is living in a balance with the physical environment. This diversity of life in the onshore/offshore environments of the Gulf coast is one of the attractions of the coastal zone, one of the golden eggs that nature's goose has provided to the Alabama-Florida coast. How can we live with, enjoy, and conserve these living resources?

1.10 A number of ecosystems may coexist on a barrier island, depending on the island's width, elevation, sediment supply, climate, and vegetation types. From *Purchasing Paradise: Things to Know and Questions to Ask When Buying Coastal Property in Florida*, Florida Department of Community Affairs, Florida Coastal Management Program brochure (June 1997).

Prehistoric Life: Early Humans

Ten thousand years ago, or perhaps earlier, when the first humans ventured into the Florida-Alabama province, they found an environment far different from the one we know today. The sea level was 100 feet lower, and the Gulf shores were far seaward of their present position. The inner continental shelf was dry land and the climate was temperate. Freshwater resources probably were more restricted, limited to rivers and deep sinkholes that intersected a deeper water table. Animals were abundant because the Florida peninsula was a refuge for animals that migrated south during the severe Pleistocene Ice Age climate. The fossil record in the region's Pleistocene and younger sediments includes a wide range of marine and nonmarine animals and plants. The vertebrate animal record is an impressive list of species that are now extinct or are rare or absent from the region. Mammoths and mastodons, giant sloths, bears, beavers, camels, saber-toothed cats, horses, lemmings, llamas, tapirs, dire wolves, and others may have greeted the early hunters who ventured into the Southeast.

The record of early humans in North America is sparse, but over the generations these early people witnessed the retreating shoreline and climatic change that brought subtropical to tropical conditions to the Alabama-Florida coast. Kitchen middens, the shell heaps left by people who took advantage of the coastal food resources, provide some of the oldest evidence of the human presence in the coastal zone. Because the clamshells contain the element carbon, the c-14 dating method can be applied to establish the age of these middens. The oldest, at Tenshaw Lake, Alabama, are 4,100 years old, and a midden on St. Vincent Island is at least 3,500 years old. By that time the climate was approaching conditions more like the present and humans were well established in the area, leaving as their record fired-clay pottery and stone tools. No doubt the elements sometimes treated these peoples harshly, but no evidence exists that they tried to build and maintain villages at the edge of the rising sea, or to hold back the inundation.

The lesson we must learn from them is to utilize and enjoy resources while minimizing environmental risk.

Historic Life: The First Resorts, Development, Storms

Ponce de León is credited with the European discovery of Florida in 1513. There is some irony in his supposed search for the fountain of youth and the reality of the modern migration of seniors (both high-school class year and citizens) to Florida and the Gulf coast. Ponce de León returned in 1521 in an attempt to colonize the vicinity of Charlotte Harbor, but the Spanish never could overcome the bad weather and natives' resistance. Hurricanes disrupted their expeditions and colonization attempts through the sixteenth century, and they left the Pensacola area in 1561 and did not return until the late seventeenth century, when they were again frustrated by storms and Indians. When Don Alejandro Wauchopee took possession of the Pensacola area in 1723, he abandoned the site of an earlier fort because it had been undercut by water and overtaken by sand dunes. His new town on Santa Rosa Island was destroyed 29 years later by a 1752 hurricane. Eight years after that, in 1760, the same area was struck by another destructive hurricane. Earlier, in 1702, the French had established early Mobile on a bluff upstream on the Mobile River. A flood swept away the settlement in 1711, and the French relocated the town to its present site. From 1493 to 1870, Florida, the Gulf, and the Caribbean region experienced close to 400 hurricanes (appendix C, ref. 8), so the early European explorers were among the first to learn the lessons that nature repeats at the shore.

Well over 300 years would pass after Ponce de León's first visit before tourism would become an industry. Florida and southern Alabama were under several flags and experienced several wars before real settlement came to the area. And ports, lumber, agriculture, and fishing were long established before the lure of the coast made it a popular vacation site.

Tourism paralleled access, which the railroads brought in the 1880s and roads brought in the twentieth century. The railroad entrepreneurs were also hotel builders, and the numbers of tourists grew from hundreds to thousands. By 1920 the Florida frontier had been conquered, and the land boom of the 1920s brought a surge of tourism and coastal development. Although dampened by the hurricanes of 1926 and 1928 and the Great Depression, the population growth continued, nearly doubling between 1920 and 1940. Tourism was an important stimulant to the coastal economy during the depression, and World War II brought a new generation to Florida who would return again and again in the years to come. By the early 1940s approximately 2.6 million tourists per year were visiting Florida. At the same time, a shift from rural to urban living was occurring. The 1950s saw a postwar building boom, and in 1953, 5.1 million tourists spent an estimated $930 million — one-third of Florida's total income!

Given the rapid population growth both past and present, the collective memory of the Gulf coast's population is less than a generation, and probably less than a decade. The lessons taught by Andrew and Opal are the same as those taught by a host of earlier disasters, which also went unheeded. In this great age of communication we seem to have gained little knowledge from the past, and development in high-risk zones continues.

Present Life: Population Explosion and Impact

Population growth in the coastal counties of Alabama and Florida reflects the national trend of the post–World War II population shift into the coastal zone, although Florida's growth rates are phenomenal. Fewer than 600,000 people lived in all of Florida's coastal counties in 1920. By 1950 the number was above 2 million, and the population had doubled again by the decade of the 1960s. The rate of population growth peaked at over 90 percent in 1960 and has since declined, although it is still very high. From 1980 to 1990 the state's population grew by nearly 33 percent, far higher than the national average. By 1995, 7.8 million people — more than 60 percent of Florida's entire population — were living within 5 miles of the coast, and the estimated population of the Gulf coastal counties was approximately 4.4 million.

Florida's growing economy attracts increasing numbers of people, especially in the coastal zone (fig. 1.11). The coastal counties with sandy shores generate about 50 percent of the state's income. By the 1990s more than 20 million people were visiting Florida's beaches each year, pumping $15 billion per year into the economy. There can be no denying that Florida's beaches are its most important assets. W. B. Stronge stated in 1994 that

> these beaches are important economic assets, and their maintenance is necessary to preserve the economic health of one of Florida's most important industries. . . .
>
> An important part of tourist development is maintenance of the

1.11   More tourists can crowd onto Clearwater Beach near the jetty on the north side of Clearwater Pass than on the north end of Sand Key across the pass. Sand is being trapped here to help widen the beach and keep the pass open for boaters. Photo by Ray Longo.

state's barrier island beaches. (*Beaches, Tourism, and Economic Development: Shore and Beach,* vol. 62, no. 2, pp. 6–8)

By the state's own estimate, however, approximately 560 miles of Florida's sandy coasts is eroding or critically eroded!

In west Florida, the coastal population is concentrated on the sandy barrier island coasts of the Panhandle, the West-Central Barrier Chain, and around Tampa Bay and other embayments. These are the same areas in which tourists concentrate to swell the number of people and properties at risk from coastal hazards. Clearance times needed to evacuate such populations in the face of a hurricane now exceed 20 hours in some areas, well above the maximum warning time that the Weather Service may be able to give for some storms. This present pattern of coastal overdevelopment is also true of Alabama. The pejorative name "Redneck Riviera" downplays the significance of Alabama's beach resources, but the post-Frederic building boom concentrated more property and people at risk in extreme-to-high-hazard zones.

The erosional loss of beaches and the increasing property losses associated with even low-rank hurricanes has led to increased pressure to build coastal stabilization structures. The record of shoreline engineering, particularly shore-hardening structures, shows short- to intermediate-term protection of property, but accelerated beach loss. Unless the two states, coastal communities, and individual property owners conserve beaches and take actions to mitigate storm impacts, the future of Alabama's and Florida's beach-based economies is in question.

The lesson of the present is that more and more people and property are being put at risk daily, so the price of each storm is greater. Our eyes and actions should be toward the immediate future.

Future Life: Prospects

It would be comforting to conclude that the phenomenal population growth in the coastal zone will not continue, but that is not the case. By the year 2020, the population of Florida's coastal counties is projected to be over 15 million, twice the 1980 population. Even under the best management, this level of growth and the momentum of development will disrupt physical processes, degrade coastal ecosystems, and increase vulnerability to natural and human-induced hazards.

The lesson for the present is that future storm damages will routinely be in the billions of dollars, matching and possibly dwarfing losses associated with hurricanes such as Opal and Andrew. Loss of lives in major storms

Under water after 15-foot rise in sea level

Under water after 25-foot rise in sea level

High ground

1.12 Coastal changes in Florida under two sea-level rise scenarios. From *Florida's Geological History and Geological Resources,* 1994 (appendix C, ref. 2).

will increase as population density exceeds the government's ability to warn and evacuate large numbers of people in a relatively short time, reversing a long trend of declining fatalities in storms. The sea level will continue to rise, and for the low-sloping coasts of the eastern Gulf, this spells a long-term pattern of impact for all coastal development (fig. 1.12).

The lesson for the future is that the coastal carrying capacity has been exceeded. If we cannot collectively make prudent decisions on how to live with the coast, then individual property owners and coastal dwellers must make informed choices to protect themselves and their property. Guidance in making such choices, particularly on barrier islands and sandy shores, is the goal of this book.

Living with the coast requires an overview that goes beyond the focal point of the beach. Knowledge of the suitability of a particular coastal type for development, and how it might change during the lifetime of a cottage or condominium, is essential. Understanding the beach requires some knowledge of the type of coast that the beach is fringing. Coastal types change in response to even subtle changes in the equilibrium-controlling factors.

The regional divisions discussed below provide a first measure of a site's vulnerability to coastal hazards and explain why beaches are present or absent, and what to expect in terms of storm response. Figure 1.7 introduced the regional coastal provinces of the eastern Gulf of Mexico. From north to south the divisions are: the Northwest Barrier Chain, the Big Bend Marsh Coast, the West-Central Barrier Chain, and the Ten Thousand Islands Mangrove Coast and Everglades. Each division is introduced below.

Northwest Barrier Chain

The Gulf Coastal Lowlands of southern Alabama and the Florida Panhandle provide the ideal coastal plain setting in which barrier islands, barrier beaches, spits, and estuaries form. The steeper offshore slope in the central Panhandle has precluded barrier island formation, although this mainland shore is still characterized by sandy beaches. The Alabama reach has both barrier islands and mainland segments. Barrier island coasts are common throughout the Gulf and along the Atlantic seaboard, and in this province the islands attain considerable length (e.g., Perdido Key, Santa Rosa). Their original wide sandy beaches were the primary reason for their recreational development, and the Sun Coast has earned its fame for the combination of beaches and pleasant climate it features.

As noted in chapter 1, the sand on the Panhandle coast derives from rivers as far away as the southern Appalachians and Piedmont. This original abundance of sand is reflected in both the beaches and their associated dunes. The geologic relationship between this coast and rivers, and between the influx of sediment and the opposing sea-level rise, is also reflected in the Apalachicola delta, drowned river and creek mouths, and the marsh wetlands. The delta region has a robust set of barrier islands (e.g., St. Vincent and St. George) and the related St. Joseph Peninsula. Evidence of a good sand supply can be seen in the St. Joseph spit, which was formed by the buildup of several dune ridges. The sand forming the ridges is carried northward by the longshore currents in the surf zone (fig. 2.1). Over the last century these islands have been erosional on both sides, but particularly on the southeast-facing shorelines. The province's response to Opal (de-

2.1 St. Joseph spit has been formed by the buildup of several dune ridges. The sand forming the ridges is carried northward by the longshore currents in the surf zone.

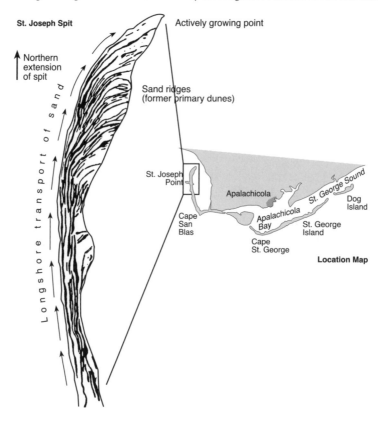

scribed in chapter 1) can be taken as an example of its typical response to a category 3 storm.

Big Bend Marsh Coast

The Big Bend Marsh Coast of Florida is a mainland coast extending from Apalachee Bay (Wakulla County) south to Anclote Key in Pasco County. In contrast to the barrier island coasts of the Panhandle and west-central Florida, this reach of the Gulf Coastal Lowlands' shore is sand starved and free of barrier islands. Beaches are small and very localized. Streams such as the Suwannee River carry no sand to the coast. The gentle shelf, more than 90 miles wide, effectively dissipates waves, and the shore is described as a very low-energy coast, although this is misleading if you expect never to see waves, erosion, or flooding! The low wave energy cannot drive currents along the shore to bring in sand from more distant sandy shores. Low wave energy also means little reworking of sand and low potential for barrier island formation.

This coast is not without complexity, however, again relating to its underlying geology. The bedrock consists of soluble limestones, the deposits of former seas from the time of the great carbonate bank that gave birth to Florida. During the Pleistocene Ice Age, conditions fluctuated between times of land emergence, during sea-level low stands, and flooding, when the rising sea level would drown the mainland. When Florida was above sea level, the limestone bedrock was exposed to weathering by chemical solution, producing sinkholes and irregular topography (a karst terrain). When the ice caps melted and the sea level rose, this irregularly weathered surface was planed by combined erosion and sediment infill of the solutional depressions. This kind of topography is seen in the Woodville Karst Plain (Wakulla County) and the drowned karst of Citrus County. As the drowned karst coast was flooded in the last sea-level rise, a low-elevation, seaward-sloping plain fringed by coastal swamps and marshes developed (fig. 2.2).

This wetland coast has not been attractive to development, but the concentrated population associated with the developed barrier island coast to the south is pushing northward into this hazardous region as suburbia expands (e.g., Holiday and Gulf Harbors, New Port Richey, Jasmine, Hudson). And hazardous the region is! If you have trouble visualizing the short-term results of the sea-level rise, you have only to look at a marsh or swamp and imagine how far a 1-foot rise would carry a flood. Storm surge causes flooding for miles inland, and erosion is a problem except where bedrock is exposed at the surface.

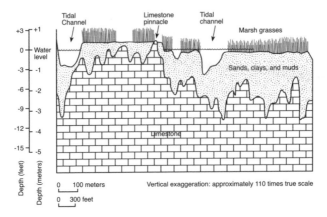

2.2 The present-day land surface of Florida is formed on a highly eroded lime-stone platform, as seen in this cross section of the underlying geology. Taken from R. A. Davis Jr. and A. C. Hine, *Quaternary Geology and Sedimentology of the Barrier Island and Marshy Coast, West-Central Florida, U.S.A., 1989* (appendix C, ref. 19).

West-Central Barrier Chain

This diverse system of 29 barrier islands and 30 inlets extends for about 180 miles from Anclote Key to Kice Island (Cape Romano) and reflects the interaction of tides, waves, and sediment supply. Island shape is highly variable, but the barriers here tend to be shorter than the Panhandle barriers, with frequent tidal inlets. Typical for some islands is the so-called drum-stick shape, which derives its name from the island's tendency to be wider at the ends, adjacent to inlets, and narrow in the middle. The shape results from complex erosion/accretion patterns that develop in association with wave patterns around tidal deltas at the mouths of inlets. The tidal inlets are also variable in size and behavior. Inlet size is related to the tidal range and to the area of water in back of the island that drains through the inlet on the ebb tide. No two inlets behave the same; some are more or less permanent, others open and close with time, and some inlets follow a pattern of lateral migration — bad news for developed areas downstream of them. New inlets (often called *passes* in the Gulf) have cut through many existing barrier islands in historical storms, and they will cut through islands in the future (fig. 2.3). The islands vary in elevation and in dune and beach ridge development, and, correspondingly, in how frequently they are flooded and overwashed during storms.

Like all barrier islands, the west Florida chains are highly susceptible to rapid change, including shoreline retreat, overwash, dune development or reduction, and inlet formation and migration. Few areas are really suitable for development, but this coast has some of the densest development to be found on the U.S. shore. Likewise, the associated development on bay shores and the low-lying mainland is often at risk. Although the region has a record of hurricanes, most of this development has not been tested by a great hurricane, or even by an Opal equivalent. The limits of South Florida's storm evacuation effectiveness may be severely tested in the next major hurricane.

Ten Thousand Islands Mangrove Coast and Everglades

Florida's southwest mangrove coast extends from behind Cape Romano to Cape Sable and the mangrove keys of north Florida Bay (see figs. 1.2 and

2.3 Potential sites of washover and inlet formation for two stretches of the Florida shore near Hollywood Beach and Laguna Beach.

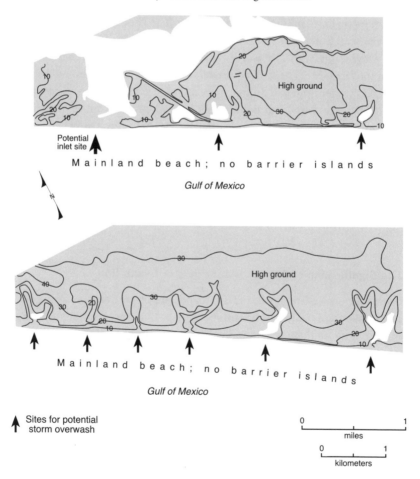

1.7). The northern Ten Thousand Islands segment consists of mangrove islands, at or barely above sea level, separated by numerous tidal channels and creek mouths. A low slope, slow sea-level rise, limited sandy sediment supply, and the presence of mangroves account for this particular coastal type. Dense stands of mangroves have colonized shoals and topographic highs, including those produced by the growth of vermitid reefs (worm-secreted calcareous buildups), and shell mounds. The mangroves trap mud and produce organic matter that accumulates to build the low sedimentary islands.

To the south, where tidal currents weaken and more mud reaches the coast through the drainage of the Everglades, the small islands give way to a continuous mangrove coast broken only by the stream channels coming out of the swampland and Everglades. In Florida Bay, small mangrove islands appear again, and carbonate muds are common on the floor of the bay. Shelly carbonate sands occur locally (e.g., Cape Sable).

With the exception of a couple of settlements to service the Everglades, the entire region is part of the Cape Romano Ten Thousand Islands Aquatic Preserve and Everglades National Park and is out of the development loop. The province illustrates, however, that hazards in the coastal zone can arise from the land side. The long controversy over land reclamation, diversion of surface water flow, and human impact on the Everglades system are part of Florida's economic and political history. Attempts to out-engineer nature through drainage projects over the decades have resulted in bad debts, significant loss of life due to dike failures during hurricanes (e.g., in the Lake Okeechobee area in the 1920s), imbalances in water supply accentuating the impacts of flood and drought, invasion by alien species, and major saltwater incursion into the groundwater under the Everglades (appendix C, ref. 1).

The Significance of Barrier Islands in Risk Evaluation

Of the various coastal types, barrier islands are of greatest concern in our consideration of Gulf coast hazards because of the concentration of people and property on these fragile and vulnerable strips of sand. Barrier islands are perhaps the world's most dynamic real estate, for they are capable of actually migrating landward when the sea level rises. The islands are also some of the world's most sought-after real estate. As noted above, barrier islands make up the two significantly populated segments of the eastern Gulf coast: the Northwest Barrier Chain (Alabama and the Florida Panhandle), which also includes sandy mainland shores, and the West-Central

Barrier Chain. Barrier islands dominate the upper Gulf coast from Cat Island, Mississippi, east along the Alabama shore and Florida Panhandle, and down through the Apalachicola coast. This extensive barrier chain is interrupted by mainland shores such as the Fort Morgan Peninsula and Gulf Shores, Alabama, area, a 51-mile stretch east of Santa Rosa Island (from Destin to Panama City Beach), and short reaches of Bay, Gulf, and Franklin Counties, Florida. Even these nonbarrier coasts, however, are fronted by sandy beaches and are subject to most of the same processes and hazards as the associated barriers.

By definition, barrier islands are elongate bodies of sand bounded on either end by inlets that allow salt and fresh water to flow to and from the sound or embayment behind the island. In front of, or seaward, of the island is the shoreface, a steeply dipping surface usually extending to a depth of 30 or 40 feet, at which point the slope of the continental shelf becomes more gentle.

Barrier islands form in response to four common factors:

1. A rising sea level
2. A large sand supply
3. A gently sloping mainland coast (a coastal plain)
4. Sufficient wave energy to move sand

All four requirements must be met before islands will form. Changes in one or more of these factors will upset the balance of an existing island. Perhaps of greatest concern to development are the effects of diminished sand supplies and rising sea level, whatever its cause.

The Big Bend coast lacks barrier islands because the shoreline normally receives only small waves, making this coast essentially one of zero energy. Thus, although this shoreline reach has a gentle mainland coast and is experiencing a rising sea level, barrier islands are absent. The absence of barriers is also due in part to the low sand supply; however, sand is not completely deficient and small beaches are present locally. The lack of energy results from a continental shelf that is so broad and gently sloping that wave energy is effectively dampened. Without the wave energy component, barrier islands cannot form. In contrast, barrier islands are probably absent in the Panama City–Destin reach because of the steep shoreface there.

Once an island does form, it almost immediately begins to change its shape, vegetation, and landforms (fig. 2.4), and in some cases even to migrate. No two islands evolve at the same rate and in the same way, but an understanding of general island-evolution mechanisms is particularly important for those who wish to live in harmony with these ephemeral, dynamic features. The siting, design, and construction of houses must be

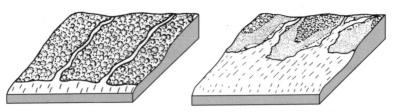

Stage 1: Low sea level at peak of glaciation

Stage 2: Flooding of river valleys

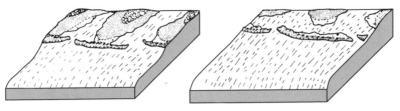

Stage 3: Formation of spit along headlands

Stage 4: Separation of barrier from mainland

2.4 Barrier island formation during a rising sea level. Stage 1: Straight coast forms during lower sea level. Stage 2: Sea level rises and floods valleys on land, transforming a straight coast into a sinuous coast. Stage 3: Sand eroded from preexisting ridges forms spits. Stage 4: The spits are breached by storms, making them into islands.

based on knowledge of coastal processes in order to prevent structure loss or damage.

Barrier Island Evolution

Barrier islands form in response to rising sea level (see fig. 1.6). Although the experts' opinions differ regarding the exact time, by 3,000 years ago or even earlier, barrier islands were probably a common feature along the ancestral Gulf coast, although in some cases lying offshore from their present positions. Once a chain of barrier islands forms, a whole new set of processes takes over. The islands begin to move landward and/or to build upward in response to sea-level rise. This process, called island migration, is a remarkable mechanism by which the islands can escape drowning by an encroaching sea. If the ancestral barrier islands formed early in the postglacial sea-level rise, their first few thousand years were marked by rapid landward retreat because the sea level was rising at a fairly high rate. When the sea level was rising rapidly, the islands may have been only small, low spits or even completely absent for periods of time.

As the rate of sea-level rise slowed around 3,000–4,000 years ago, these islands slowed in their migration. This was also a time of new island formation. The barrier islands of the West-Central Chain and some of the northern barriers probably formed at this time. According to research by Ervin G. Otvos, these barrier islands may have grown in place as embryonic islands emerging from shoals (appendix C, ref. 23). No evidence has been found on the adjacent continental shelf of former barrier islands that would infer migration. Migration depends on open water landward of the islands and on the nature of the surface over which the migration takes place. Islands in the West-Central Barrier Chain are grounded on older topographic highs, and Dauphin Island grew from a flooded topographic high as a spit. On the other hand, the barrier islands associated with the Apalachicola delta are likely to have migrated in the past, and the existing islands may do so in the future.

The slower rate of sea-level rise — perhaps less than 2 inches per century — that followed allowed the barrier islands to stabilize and grow into the barrier chains that make up the present coast.

Another way in which barrier islands may form is by spit detachment. When river mouths were flooded to form estuaries, the shores of the seaward ends of the upland drainage divides eroded, and attached sandbars or spits built out across the bay entrances (fig. 2.4). The spits grew in elevation as dunes formed, but ultimately they were breached, or cut off from their land connection, during storms. When inlets formed to detach the spits, barrier islands were born. Then a new combination of natural processes began reshaping them, including the day-to-day erosion and transport of sediment by waves and currents as well as less frequent powerful storms and hurricanes.

By 2,000 years ago the islands were close to their present position and were growing in area and elevation. The rate of shoreline retreat and island migration was a function of the slope of the inundated land and the rate of sea-level rise (fig. 2.5). This applies to mainland shores as well. For example, the slope of the lower coastal plain and shelf off of west Florida

2.5 Ratio of horizontal barrier island migration to the vertical sea-level rise. A very small vertical increase in sea level will lead to a much larger horizontal island migration because the slope of the land surface is very gentle.

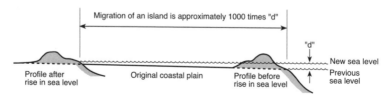

ranges from 1:1,200 (expressed as vertical change over horizontal distance) at Indian Rocks, Pinellas County, to 1:4,000 near the Crystal River (appendix C, ref. 19). This means that for every foot of sea-level rise, the amount of shoreline retreat theoretically should be somewhere between 1,000 and 4,000 feet (fig. 2.5)!

One type of evidence that your island has or has not migrated is the kind of seashells you find on the ocean-side beach. On some beaches you will find shells of oysters, clams, or snails that once lived in the bay or sound behind the barrier island. How did shells from the estuary get to the ocean side? One possibility is that the island migrated over the back marsh and estuary, and open-ocean waves eroded the old estuary sands and muds, now exposed on the shoreface, and threw the shells onto the present-day beach. If the beach has been artificially nourished, however, the shells may have arrived in the nourishment sand. Sometimes salt marsh peats that formed in back of the island at some earlier time are exposed on the ocean-side beach after a storm. Tree stumps exposed on beaches (e.g., Captiva, Sanibel, and Mullet Key) are the remains of forests that once grew well back from the beach (fig. 2.6).

Each island responds to its surrounding marine environment in a dif-

2.6 These tree stumps on the beach at Stump Hole on St. Joseph Peninsula are remnants of a forest that once stood well back from the shore. They are certain evidence of severe erosion. Overwash from storms like Hurricanes Opal and Earl is a common occurrence in Gulf County. The entire southern end of St. Joseph Peninsula is susceptible to erosion. Photo by Norma Longo.

ferent fashion and at differing rates. The reasons for this variability can be attributed to differences in the amount and type of sand; island orientation; the type, direction, and size of the waves that strike the beach; and the nature of the rocks underlying the barrier island. Each island's unique behavior should be a crucial consideration for residents and potential residents. Unfortunately, those who set the price of real estate on barrier islands do not recognize these differences.

Even among adjacent barrier islands, differences can be significant. Dr. Richard Davis Jr., professor of geology at the University of South Florida, describes Florida's West-Central Barrier Chain as "the most geomorphologically diverse barrier island system in the world" (appendix C, ref. 18). He recognizes three fundamental types of barriers: those associated with mainland headlands; long barriers that are wave dominated; and shorter, drumstick-shaped islands. Even parts of a single island may show great differences in origin and dynamics. For example, the west end of Dog Island (Franklin County) has long, narrow beaches that are very susceptible to breaches and inundation during even moderate storms, while the eastern end is wider and is characterized by sand accumulation.

Regardless of how they form, change is always the rule on barrier islands, and the shorelines we see today are the products of the most recent set of variables affecting the islands (e.g., the latest hurricane, changes in sand supply, impacts of engineering modifications). Some evidence suggests that the rate of sea-level rise has increased in the last several decades. If such is indeed the case, it is bad news for communities on barrier islands.

Stationary or Grounded Barrier Islands

Islands that have formed by emergence, or upward in-place growth, and those that have migrated onto a topographic high or obstruction on the seafloor such as a bedrock ridge may be held in place (e.g., some of the West-Central Barrier Chain). Such islands either cannot migrate or are less likely to migrate. In order to persist as islands in the face of a rising sea level they must build vertically at a rate equal to or greater than the sea-level rise. The two mechanisms of dune growth and overwash buildup, discussed below, are important in maintaining elevation above sea level. Under natural conditions stationary islands widen and narrow, are breached by inlets, and reorient in position as the equilibrium controls fluctuate. When densely developed, however, such islands lose their flexibility, and even their capability of upward growth. When such an island is altered by a hurricane or by day-to-day beach erosion, its residents are faced with maintaining the beach and island artificially.

Rolling Sandbars: How Islands Migrate

In order for an island to migrate, four things must happen:

1. The front (ocean) side must move landward through shoreline retreat.
2. The back (sound) side must do likewise by landward growth (island widening).
3. The island must continually build up in order to maintain its elevation above a rising sea level.
4. The mainland shoreline must retreat to keep pace with island migration.

On the Gulf coast, all of these things are happening and true island migration is occurring in the low-lying, narrow, and mobile islands of northern Collier County, Florida.

The current sea-level rise of about 1 foot per century is a principal worldwide cause of beach erosion, although other local factors, such as the lack of sand supply, also cause landward retreat of beaches. Along specific shoreline segments, humans are responsible for a great deal of the shoreline retreat in recent decades. The shoreline of the Nile Delta in Egypt, for example, is eroding at an unprecedented rate because the Aswan Dam on the Nile River has cut off the supply of new beach sand. The blockage of river sand by dams on the Rio Grande and the Brazos River is causing barrier islands in Texas to erode rapidly. Similarly, loss of Columbia River sands because of dams is causing the barrier spits of Oregon and Washington to retreat.

On the other hand, the shoreline may move seaward in areas where river sediments reach the shore. This seems to have happened along the mainland shoreline of the Florida Panhandle where beaches are wider than in adjacent shoreline segments and there are several outlets draining the water from upland freshwater lakes to the Gulf coast. The surplus sand results in beach accretion and supplies sediment for dune growth. Storms such as Opal, however, rearrange the sand distribution, destroying dunes and altering beaches, so the sand budget may move into the negative column.

Everywhere in the world, construction of seawalls, groins, and offshore breakwaters and deepening of channels within inlets significantly reduce sand supply and lead to shoreline erosion. Such engineering contributes to erosion along the lower Gulf coast as well, where extensive development has resulted in shore-stabilization efforts. The numerous man-made structures interrupt the low littoral-drift sand supply, contributing to the overall erosion and combining with the low-lying elevations of this coastal segment to increase its vulnerability to storm impacts. The effects of shoreline engineering on beaches are discussed in more detail in chapter 4.

Back-side widening on the sound sides of Gulf islands is the result of two mechanisms: tidal delta incorporation and overwash. Tidal deltas are the bodies of sand that form outside (seaward) and inside (landward) inlets. The open-ocean tidal delta is called the ebb delta; the tidal delta inside the sound is referred to as the flood delta (fig. 2.7). When a new inlet forms, usually by water pouring from the estuary to the ocean in response to a

2.7 Flood-tidal and ebb-tidal deltas are found at all barrier island inlets. These bodies of sand are moved into and out of the inlet by tidal currents. Flood-tidal deltas, the bodies of sand formed in the estuary side of the inlet, are often incorporated into the island once the inlet closes. (a) Natural ebb-tidal deltas are capable of transporting sand across the inlet from one island to the next. (b) The ebb-tidal delta moves offshore when jetties are built to improve navigation, and its sand is lost forever from the island.

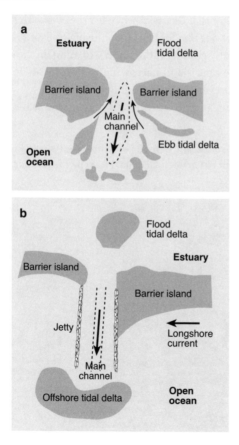

major storm surge, these tidal bodies of sand build up (the sand is moved primarily by tidal currents). If the inlet closes or migrates away, the flood-tidal delta eventually becomes part of the island (fig. 2.8). As the inlet migrates, sand continues to pour into the estuary, and a series of new flood-tidal deltas form along the entire zone of inlet migration. In this way the island is widened over the full distance that the inlet shifted. Such a pattern was followed by Captiva Inlet.

Tidal delta incorporation widens only a portion of an island. Other portions of islands migrate via storm overwash. This mechanism is at work today on low islands such as parts of Dauphin and Santa Rosa Islands. Overwash sand widens an island when it is carried completely across the island and deposited in the sound. This happens on narrow island segments where there are no dunes to block the overwash, such as on St. George and Santa Rosa Islands. Marsh colonization of overwash sands can be seen on Sanibel Island. Old overwash deposits can be identified by looking at sediment types and ages (fig. 2.9).

Most eastern Gulf islands are too wide for the overwash migration mechanism to work as it does on St. Joseph Peninsula or Santa Rosa Island. These islands are currently eroding rather than widening on the sound side. Some geologists believe that island narrowing is a precursor to renewed migration. Is your island getting ready to migrate?

Islands maintain their elevation and bulk as the sea level rises through

2.8 The extensive marshland behind Dunedin Pass, Pinellas County, Florida, is the remnant of an old flood-tidal delta. Photo by Richard A. Davis Jr.

2.9 Hurricane Opal caused several areas of overwash such as this one on Santa Rosa Island. The Gulf is to the right, front in this photo. Lobes of overwash sand extend across the road and island and into the sound. Photo by Rob Young.

two processes: dune formation and overwash fan deposition. Both processes obtain their sand from the beach. In fact, every grain of sand on an island came from the beach at some point in its history.

Dunes are formed by the wind, and if a sufficiently large supply of sand comes to the beach by alongshore drift or is pushed up by the waves from the continental shelf, a high-elevation island can be formed. A good example of this type of island is St. Vincent Island in Franklin County, Florida, with its dune-and-swale topography. Dunes cannot form if the adjacent shoreface does not supply sand or if the prevailing wind direction cannot take advantage of the sand supply. The resulting low-elevation island is then more susceptible to the overwash process.

Figure 2.10 illustrates how overwash can build the elevation of the interior or back side of an island. Hurricane Georges, for example, carried frontal sand across Santa Rosa Island and deposited it in overwash fans. Such fans coalesce laterally into an elevated terrace and extend the island's back side into the sound.

Unfortunately, developers often reduce island elevation by removing or scalping dunes, trucking away overwash sand after storms, or removing vegetation that is stabilizing the sediment. Development discourages natural growth in island elevation by blocking sand flow across the island and

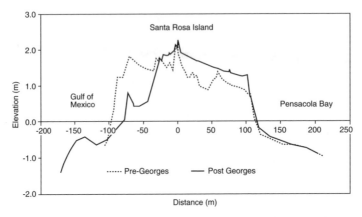

2.10 Cross-section comparison of Santa Rosa Island before and after Hurricane Georges, 1998. Sand removed from the front of the island was deposited as an overwash terrace on the back side to build the island's elevation. Note that the vertical scale is exaggerated 50 times the horizontal for illustration purposes. After G. W. Stone et al., 1999, *EOS*, vol. 80, no. 27, p. 305.

by paving over the sand supply. The widespread attempts to rebuild the dunes after Hurricane Opal are a reminder of how important these features are in both the short and long terms.

The mainland shore must retreat if open water is to persist in back of the island and allow its continued migration (fig. 2.5). Again, such retreat will occur as sea level rises and in proportion to the slope of the land. The Big Bend Marsh Coast is the result of marine flooding of the low-gradient mainland, and the mainland marsh coasts behind barrier islands retreat in the same fashion. Erosion of the mainland shore also contributes to beach retreat, and the processes of inundation and erosion show no consideration for houses in their path.

If the mainland shore does not retreat or retreats at a rate slower than that of the offshore barrier, the sound will narrow and the island may attach to the mainland. If the sea level falls, the barrier island will be left as a ridge on the emergent coastal plain. Such features from the former high stands of Pleistocene sea levels are common on the southeastern U.S. coastal plain.

The Role of the Shoreface in Barrier Island Evolution

The shoreface plays a major role in determining how a barrier island behaves. The shoreface in the eastern Gulf is a relatively gentle surface extending from the shoreline to the innermost continental shelf at a depth of around 30 feet. In effect, the entire shoreface is the active beach; the portion we walk on is really only the tip of the zone of active sand movement. The rate of shoreline retreat, the way an island responds to and recovers from a storm, the size of the dunes, and even the size of the island are all greatly affected by the nature of the shoreface.

The character of the shoreface is also a central element in the models used by engineers to predict beach behavior when they design coastal engineering projects such as beach nourishment. Most coastal engineers assume that all shorefaces are composed of a loose pile of sand that forms a predictable "profile of equilibrium." In this view, the shoreface has a profile produced entirely by ocean waves, and the shape of the shoreface is determined by the grain size of the sand. This simplistic characterization is the reason why coastal engineers generally have a poor record in predicting beach behavior, particularly the behavior (that is, life span) of nourished beaches. In fact, because storms are usually responsible for the demise of nourished beaches, no one can accurately predict how long such beaches will last. As will become clear in the following discussion, the shoreface is much more complex than a loose pile of sand.

Geologic Framework of the Eastern Gulf Coast: Know Your Shoreface

The geologic framework underlying Alabama and west Florida consists of sediment and rock units that range in age from 90 million years to the present (fig. 1.4). The complex variability in this underlying geologic framework, in consort with the physical dynamics of each specific barrier island, ultimately determines the three-dimensional shoreface shape, the composition of beach sediments, and shoreline erosion rates. Old drainage systems formed on the continental shelf when it was standing as the coastal plain during the lowered Ice Age sea level filled with sediment as the sea level rose. Coastal segments underlain by this less-resistant sediment fill erode faster than areas underlain by bedrock. Former interstream divides composed of older and harder geologic units may form headland segments of the coast. These rocks may crop out on the beach in features such as the Quaternary coquina rocks found on Lido and Siesta Keys. More commonly, however, the rocks crop out on the shoreface below sea level. These resistant shoals modify incoming waves and affect the rates of shoreline erosion on the adjacent beaches. For example, prehistoric valley fill sequences are reported at the mouth of Tampa Bay off Sand Key, in large sand ridges off Indian Rocks Beach, and in hard bottom and/or coarse carbonate shell material off Sarasota (appendix C, ref. 23).

The shoreface of a barrier island underlain by the fill of either historical or prehistoric inlets is composed of unconsolidated sand that backfilled the inlets as they migrated or closed. And in areas where narrow and low barrier islands are actively migrating up and over the back-barrier estuary, the shoreface is composed of peat, mud, and clay. The young sediment units may extend from the estuaries, under the barrier, and out the other side, and crop out within the surf zone and shoreface. In other words, the shoreface is not a simple pile of sand and often does not perform as simple models predict.

One good rule to follow when locating on the coast is to know the type of shoreface because it is one predictor of future island changes. And when a barrier island changes, as in a hurricane, the appropriate "solution" to mitigate the impact of the changes should also be based on the type of shoreface.

Beaches: The Shock Absorbers

The beach is one of the earth's most dynamic environments. On barrier islands, the beach is the source of sand for the entire island. And the beach, defined as the zone of active sand movement, is always changing. Most beaches are retreating in a landward direction, and as this gradual migration goes on, the beach changes its shape on almost a daily basis.

The natural laws of the beach control a beautiful, logical environment. The beach builds up when the weather is good and strategically (but only temporarily) retreats when confronted by big storm waves. As noted in chapter 1, beach behavior depends on four factors: wave energy (proportional to wave height), the quality and quantity of beach sand, the shape and location of the beach, and the rate of sea-level change. The beach behaves through a natural balance or dynamic equilibrium of these four factors (see fig. 1.8). When one of the four factors changes, the others all adjust accordingly to maintain a balance. When humans enter the system in opposition to the status quo of natural processes, as they often do, the dynamic equilibrium continues to function in a predictable way, but a way that damages or destroys buildings and infrastructure. Answers to the following often-asked questions may clarify the nature of the dynamic equilibrium.

How Does the Beach Respond to a Storm?

Old-timers and storm survivors from Gulf islands have frequently commented on how beautiful, flat, and broad the beach is after a storm. The flat beach can be explained in terms of the dynamic equilibrium: as wave

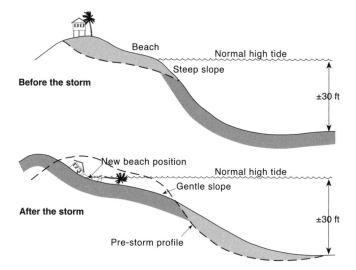

2.11 Beach flattening in response to a storm. This is nature's way of dissipating the wave energy over a greater surface area (wider beach) and to reduce the impact of the waves.

energy increases and sea level rises (as part of the storm surge), materials move about to change the shape of the beach. The flattening is a logical move that causes storm waves to expend their energy over a broader and more level surface. On a steeper surface storm-wave energy would be expended on a smaller area, causing greater change. Beaches do such logical and predictable things, they almost seem to be alive!

Figure 2.11 illustrates the way in which the beach flattens. Waves take sand from the upper beach or from the first dune and transport it to the lower beach. In major storms this surf-zone sand is sometimes transported beyond the base of the shoreface and is lost to the beach forever. An island can lose a great deal of sand during a storm. The sand that remains on the shoreface, however, may return, gradually pushed shoreward by fair-weather waves. This is known as beach recovery. Beaches with coastal engineering structures (such as seawalls) and nourished beaches generally recover much less sand after a storm than natural beaches.

How Does the Beach Widen?

Beaches grow seaward principally by the addition of new sand carried laterally by the so-called longshore (surf-zone) currents (fig. 2.12) or by the addition of new sand from the shoreface by the shoreward movement of sandbars. These two methods of beach widening often occur simultaneously.

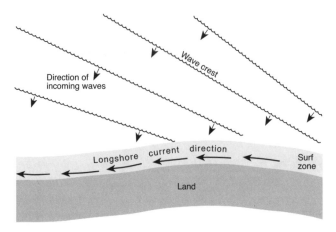

2.12 Longshore currents, sometimes referred to as longshore drift, are formed by waves approaching the shoreline at an angle. The longshore current transports sand parallel to the shore.

Longshore currents are familiar to anyone who has swum in the ocean; they are the reason you sometimes end up far down the beach from your beach towel. Such currents result from waves approaching the shore at an angle, causing a portion of the breaking waves' energy to be directed along the beach. When combined with breaking waves that put sand into suspension, the current is capable of carrying large amounts of sediment material for miles along a beach. Sand will move in either direction on beaches depending on the direction of the winds that produce the waves. Most beaches have a dominant or net direction of sand transport that is called "downdrift" or "updrift" depending on the direction, and is analogous to downstream and upstream in rivers.

During the summer you can frequently see a sandbar within a few tens of yards offshore on many (but not all) Gulf beaches. This offshore bar or ridge is usually where the better swimmers and surfers congregate to catch the big wave. The trough between the beach and the ridge or sand bar is called the runnel (fig. 2.13). Ridges and runnels are typically formed during small summer storms. In the quiet weather between storms, the ridges virtually march onto the shore and are "welded" to the beach. The next time you are at the beach, observe the offshore ridge for a period of a few days and verify this movement for yourself. You will find that each day you have to swim out a slightly shorter distance in order to stand on the sandbar. The beach between the low and high tide lines frequently has a runnel filled or partly filled with water. This trough is formed by a ridge that is in the final stages of filling the runnel and welding onto the beach.

2.13 Ridge-and-runnel system on south Bunces Key, Florida. The ridge is a sand-bar and the runnel is a trough. Ridges are actually bodies of sand that will move ashore and widen the beach. Photo by Richard A. Davis Jr.

Where Does Beach Sand Come From?

As noted in chapter 1, most of the sand in the system was derived long ago from sources that are no longer adding new sand to the overall system. New sand does come from the breakdown of shells that contribute new sand grains and from older sedimentary deposits that are eroded to provide small quantities to the sediment budget.

The reservoir of sand in the shoreface, barrier islands, tidal deltas, and mainland beaches is constantly being recycled. Sand is supplied to the beaches from the adjacent shoreface and laterally from inlets, deltas, capes, and updrift beaches. Additional sand is carried parallel to the beach by longshore currents. Such laterally moved sand moves into and across inlets, which is why the dredging of navigation channels often leads to sand starvation and increased erosion on downdrift islands.

Why Are Our Shorelines Retreating?

Beach loss or erosion due to natural processes accounts for approximately 30–50 percent of the total erosion along the Gulf coast of Florida. Anything that influences sand supply to the beaches can change the rate of erosion, and humans are often the major cause of changes in the sand supply. Activities such as shoreline armoring, construction too close to the shore, and inlet dredging and/or stabilization have significantly contributed to shoreline changes over the past 100 years. Add sea-level rise and the previously discussed differences in the erosion potential of shorefaces and you have it all. Shoreline erosion is here to stay, and in fact, it is likely to increase in the future as more navigation channels are dredged and as the sea-level rise accelerates.

It is important, however, to distinguish shoreline erosion from a shoreline erosion "problem." There is no erosion problem until buildings, roads, and services are built close to the beach. Natural coastlines without buildings and infrastructure do not have erosion problems.

If Most of the Ocean-Side Shorelines Are Eroding, What Is the Long-Range Future of Beach Development?

Much of the Gulf coast is eroding, although locally sands do accumulate and temporary beach growth may occur. As the frequency of storms and storm tracks vary through time, the local patterns of erosion will vary as well, often depending on the type of shoreface, as described above. Erosion rates should definitely be expected to increase because:

1. Human impacts on barrier island sand supplies are increasing, leading to increasing shoreline retreat rates.
2. The greenhouse effect will cause an increase in the rate of sea-level rise, leading to increasing shoreline retreat rates.
3. Storminess is expected to increase as a result of the greenhouse effect.

For responsible Gulf coast coastal property owners, the prospects for the future are not happy ones. Current state construction setback regulations requiring buildings to be set back from the shore simply put the long-term erosion problem off to the next generation. But they don't postpone the threats to life, limb, and property from hurricanes and storms! And the same three factors of human impacts, sea-level rise, and increased storminess also affect the back shores of the islands and the mainland shores of the associated estuaries and low-lying Big Bend coast. Every current and potential coastal property owner should consider his or her site's storm history and the coastal response.

In the light of the sunny days that followed Hurricane Opal in 1995, the devastation the storm had left behind seemed impossible to comprehend (see figs. 1.1 and 1.3). Newcomers may have believed that the release of such destructive energy by nature was a rare event, but for a few old-timers and some long-term residents this was a recurring nightmare (fig. 3.1). The horror of 1979's Hurricane Frederic was reawakened for some people in Alabama. Others only had to think back to 1985 when Hurricane Elena, a category 3 hurricane, hit northwestern Florida, Alabama, and Mississippi causing $1.25 billion in damage (in 1985 dollars). As recently as 1994, Tropical Storm Alberto caused 30 deaths and about $500 million in damage and made the list of the 30 costliest and deadliest hurricanes to hit the U.S. mainland since 1900 (table 3.1). Although Alberto was a relatively weak storm, it was slow moving and a heavy rain producer. Most of Alberto's damage was from flooding. Similarly, Hurricane Danny in 1997 dumped a tremendous amount of water on lower Alabama, causing severe flooding across Dauphin Island.

Hurricanes and tropical storms have always been an integral part of the Gulf coast experience, and the danger these massive storms pose cannot be overstated (table 3.2). Unfortunately, growth rates in the coastal zone constantly renew the population with inexperienced coastal dwellers. Opal and its cousins should not just awaken our memories of the past; they can also provide us with a glimpse of the future.

Although hurricanes are responsible for most of the storm-related coastal property damage in the United States, other types of storms, particularly northeasters along the East Coast and southwesters on the Gulf coast, are undeniably important as well (fig. 3.2). The 1993 "Storm of the

Table 3.1 The 30 Costliest Hurricanes in the United States (1900–1996) Adjusted to 1996 Dollars

Ranking	Hurricane	Year	Category	Damage (U.S.) [a]
1.	Andrew (SE FL, SE LA)	1992	4	$30,475,000,000
2.	Hugo (SC)	1989	4	$8,491,561,181
3.	Agnes (NE U.S.)	1972	1	$7,500,000,000
4.	Betsy (FL, LA)	1965	3	$7,425,340,909
5.	Camille (MS, AL)	1969	5	$6,096,287,313
6.	Diane (NE U.S.)	1955	1	$4,830,580,808
7.	Frederic (AL, MS)	1979	3	$4,328,968,903
8.	New England	1938	3[b]	$4,140,000,000
9.	Fran (NC)	1996	3	$3,200,000,000
10.	Opal (NW FL, AL)	1995	3[b]	$3,069,395,018
11.	Alicia (N TX)	1983	3	$2,983,138,781
12.	Carol (NE U.S.)	1954	3[b]	$2,732,731,959
13.	Carla (TX)	1961	4	$2,223,696,682
14.	Juan (LA)	1985	1	$2,108,801,956
15.	Donna (FL, E U.S.)	1960	4	$2,099,292,453
16.	Celia (S TX)	1970	3	$1,834,330,986
17.	Elena (MS, AL, NW FL)	1985	3	$1,757,334,963
18.	Bob (NC, NE U.S.)	1991	2	$1,747,720,365
19.	Hazel (SC/NC)	1954	4[b]	$1,665,721,649
20.	FL (Miami)	1926	4	$1,515,294,118
21.	N TX (Galveston)	1915	4	$1,346,341,463 [c]
22.	Dora (NE FL)	1964	2	$1,343,457,944
23.	Eloise (NW FL)	1975	3	$1,298,387,097
24.	Gloria (E U.S.)	1985	3[b]	$1,265,281,174
25.	NE U.S.	1944	3[d]	$1,064,814,815
26.	Beulah (S TX)	1967	3	$970,464,135
27.	SE FL, LA, MS	1947	4	$810,897,436
28.	N TX (Galveston)	1900	4	$809,207,317 [e]
29.	Audrey (LA, N TX)	1957	4	$802,325,581
30.	Claudette (N TX)	1979	T.S.[f]	$752,864,157

[a] Adjusted to 1996 dollars on basis of U.S. Dept. of Commerce Implicit Price Deflator for Construction.

[b] Moving more than 30 mph.

[c] Damage estimate was considered too high in 1915 reference.

[d] Probably higher.

[e] Using 1915 cost adjustment base; none available prior to 1915.

[f] Only of tropical storm intensity but included because of high damage.

Source: The Deadliest, Costliest, and Most Intense United States Hurricanes of This Century (and Other Frequently Requested Hurricane Facts), by Paul J. Hebert and Glenn Taylor, 1988 (appendix C, ref. 11).

Table 3.2. The Deadliest Hurricanes in the United States, 1900–1996

Ranking	Hurricane	Year	Category	Deaths
1.	TX (Galveston)	1900	4	8,000[a]
2.	FL (Lake Okeechobee)	1928	4	1,836
3.	FL (Keys), S TX	1919	4	600[b]
4.	New England	1938	3[c]	600
5.	FL (Keys)	1935	5	408
6.	Audrey (SW LA, N TX)	1957	4	390
7.	NE U.S.	1944	3[c]	390[d]
8.	LA (Grand Isle)	1909	4	350
9.	LA (New Orleans)	1915	4	275
10.	TX (Galveston)	1915	4	275
11.	Camille (MS, LA)	1969	5	256
12.	FL (Miami), MS, AL, Pensacola	1926	4	243
13.	Diane (NE U.S.)	1955	1	184
14.	SE FL	1906	2	164
15.	MS, AL, Pensacola	1906	3	134
16.	Agnes (NE U.S.)	1972	1	122
17.	Hazel (SC, NC)	1954	4[c]	95
18.	Betsy (SE FL, SE LA)	1965	3	75
19.	Carol (NE U.S.)	1954	3[c]	60
20.	SE FL, LA, MS	1947	4	51
21.	Donna (FL, E U.S.)	1960	4	50
22.	GA, SC, NC	1940	2	50
23.	Carla (TX)	1961	4	46
24.	TX (Velasco)	1909	3	41
25.	TX (Freeport)	1932	4	40
26.	S TX	1933	3	40
27.	Hilda (LA)	1964	3	38
28.	SW LA	1918	3	34
29.	SW FL	1910	3	30
30.	Alberto (NW FL, GA, AL)	1994	T.S.[e]	30

[a] May actually been as high as 10,000–12,000.
[b] More than 500 of these lost on ships at sea; 600–900 estimated deaths.
[c] Moving more than 30 miles an hour.
[d] Some 344 of these lost on ships at sea.
[e] Only of tropical storm intensity.
Source: The Deadliest, Costliest, and Most Intense United States Hurricanes of This Century (and Other Frequently Requested Hurricane Facts), by Paul J. Hebert and Glenn Taylor, 1988 (appendix C, ref. 11).

3.1 Destruction by Hurricane Elena at Indian Rocks Beach, Florida, September 1985. Photo by Richard A. Davis Jr.

Century," which necessitated middle-of-the-night evacuation of people from the low-lying marshy coast communities, should still be fresh in the minds of both year-round coastal residents and snowbirds caught in the flooding. Properly referred to by meteorologists as extratropical cyclones (cyclones that form outside the Tropics), southwesters are associated with large, intense low-pressure systems that move offshore along the coast and are accompanied by winds and waves out of the southwest. Such storms are severe enough to cause some degree of coastal damage along the shoreline. Rarely a year goes by without a hurricane or southwester eroding some part of the Gulf shore.

Hurricanes

The actual processes that affect the coastal zone are similar in all storms, but they are most intense in hurricanes. During the relatively hurricane-free period from the 1960s to 1992, the majority of Gulf coastal residents and property owners had never experienced the full force of a hurricane. Even though some major hurricanes hit during this period, including the great Camille (1969), the devastating Frederic (1979), and Elena (1985), overall it was a time of relative hurricane quiescence in the region. This lull led to an apathetic disregard of the hurricane menace and increased development in high-hazard zones. Recovery efforts from the large storms that

3.2 This storm scarp at Ft. DeSoto Park, Pinellas County, was formed in the spring of 1987 by a passing winter storm. Photo by Richard A. Davis Jr.

did strike during this period, such as Camille and Frederic, were looked on as opportunities to come back "bigger and better" rather than as times to plan new development better able to weather the next storm (you never see a poststorm slogan that says, "We'll come back smaller and safer"). In rapid succession, Elena, Andrew, Alberto, Allison, Erin, Opal, Danny, and their smaller cousins changed all that. The odds are evening out; time is not on the side of coastal development.

Each year on June 1 the official hurricane season begins. For the next five or six months, conditions favorable to hurricane formation can develop over the tropical and subtropical waters of the Western Hemisphere. Early-season tropical cyclones form mostly in the Gulf of Mexico or the Caribbean Sea, where the waters heat up faster than the Atlantic Ocean. The monster hurricanes that strike the East and Gulf coasts of the United States usually originate later in the season (August, September, and October) in the eastern North Atlantic, and intensify on their long, slow trek across the ocean. Of the 24 most severe hurricanes that have hit Alabama and Florida since 1900, two-thirds occurred in September.

Hurricanes begin as tropical depressions that develop into tropical storms. Once formed, the storm mass begins to track westward and into higher latitudes and may continue to grow in size and strength. Hurricane status is attained when wind velocities reach 74 mph or greater. The velocity of the storm's tracking movement can vary from nearly stationary to

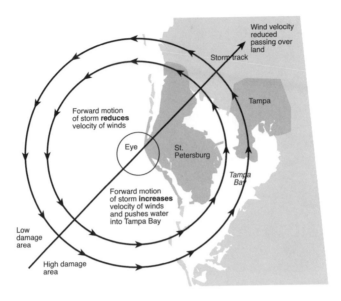

3.3 The most dangerous potential hurricane track. If such a storm occurs, a great deal of flooding will result in St. Petersburg and Tampa; hundreds of thousands of people will have to evacuate.

greater than 60 miles per hour. When a hurricane makes landfall, the destructive forces are at their maximum in the area to the right of the forward motion of the eye (fig. 3.3), but the entire landfall area will experience the severity of the storm, and significant destruction can be generated even by a storm that passes offshore. Do not feel secure in the knowledge that you are to the left of the eye or that the eye is passing offshore! Even in areas where the tidal range is small, if the hurricane strikes during a high tide, especially a spring high tide (the highest high tide), the effects of storm surge flooding, waves, and overwash will be magnified.

Coastal residents of the eastern Gulf of Mexico face a double whammy. Not only must they be concerned about hurricanes that form in the Gulf, they must also worry that storms that strike the east coast of Florida will cross over to the west side of the state. Some of these storms regain their hurricane strength once over the Gulf and strike again. In 1995, Hurricane Erin made landfall on August 2 near Vero Beach, Florida, as a category 1 hurricane with maximum wind speeds of 75 knots, and then weakened to a tropical storm. On emerging into the eastern Gulf of Mexico, Erin reintensified and made landfall near Pensacola as a category 2 hurricane on August 3 (fig. 3.4). The National Weather Service office in Melbourne, Florida, estimated that Erin generated a 2–4-foot storm surge during the Florida east coast landfall and a storm surge of about 6–7 feet just west of Navarre Beach on its second landfall. A total of six Erin-related deaths (all drownings) occurred in the Atlantic and Gulf of Mexico waters off Florida. The 234-foot gambling and cruise ship *Club Royale* sank 90 miles east of Cape Canaveral and three crew members were lost. A 15-year-old surfer drowned in a rip current off Palm Beach County. And a man and his daughter in an inflatable boat were swept from the Cape San Blas area into the Gulf of Mexico where they presumably drowned. Erin caused total U.S. damage estimated at $700 million, including wind damage over east-central and northeastern Florida, thousands of homes and businesses damaged in Brevard County, freshwater flooding from rainfall in the Melbourne and Palm Bay areas, beach erosion along the central Florida east coast (with damage mainly to boardwalks, beach accessways, and the dune system), and significant structural damage on Pensacola Beach, Navarre Beach, around Mary Esther near Fort Walton Beach, and in northeastern Pensacola (with more than 2,000 homes damaged and crop losses reported).

3.4 Landfalling hurricanes in the eastern Gulf of Mexico, 1885–1998. Modified from *Geology of Holocene Barrier Island Systems*, 1994, edited by Richard A. Davis Jr. (appendix C, ref. 18).

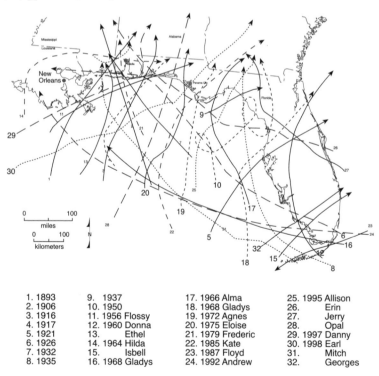

1. 1893	9. 1937	17. 1966 Alma	25. 1995 Allison
2. 1906	10. 1950	18. 1968 Gladys	26. Erin
3. 1916	11. 1956 Flossy	19. 1972 Agnes	27. Jerry
4. 1917	12. 1960 Donna	20. 1975 Eloise	28. Opal
5. 1921	13. Ethel	21. 1979 Frederic	29. 1997 Danny
6. 1926	14. 1964 Hilda	22. 1985 Kate	30. 1998 Earl
7. 1932	15. Isbell	23. 1987 Floyd	31. Mitch
8. 1935	16. 1968 Gladys	24. 1992 Andrew	32. Georges

The probability that a hurricane will make landfall at any given point along the coast in any one year is low, and the probability of a great hurricane occurring is even lower (fig. 3.5). But low probabilities give a false sense of security because the lesson of hurricane history tells us that in the lifetime of a structure such a storm is almost a certainty. For example, the National Hurricane Center's summary for west Florida shows that from 1900 to 1996, 57 hurricanes made landfall in Florida, 24 of which were major hurricanes. Twenty-four hurricanes hit the northwestern coast and 18 the southwestern coast of Florida (fig. 3.4). Furthermore, the occurrence of a great hurricane one year does not reduce the likelihood that a similar storm will strike again the next year. And several storms can strike the

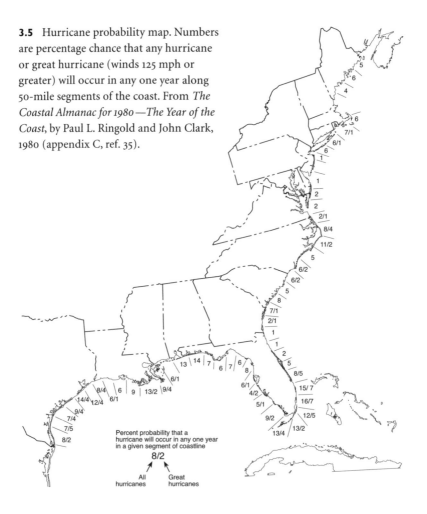

3.5 Hurricane probability map. Numbers are percentage chance that any hurricane or great hurricane (winds 125 mph or greater) will occur in any one year along 50-mile segments of the coast. From *The Coastal Almanac for 1980—The Year of the Coast*, by Paul L. Ringold and John Clark, 1980 (appendix C, ref. 35).

Percent probability that a hurricane will occur in any one year in a given segment of coastline

8/2

All hurricanes   Great hurricanes

Table 3.3. Evacuation Clearance Times for Selected Gulf of Mexico
Metropolitan Areas

Location	Median Clearance Time (hrs)	Maximum Clearance Time (hrs)
Mobile, AL	14	17
Pensacola, FL	14	19
Panama City, FL	9	12
St. Petersburg–Tampa, FL	16	22
Ft. Myers, FL	12	31 [a]

[a] Clearance time for Ft. Myers would exceed 50 hours for a category 4–5 hurricane because of evacuees from neighboring counties.

Source: Coastline at Risk: The Hurricane Threat to the Gulf and Atlantic States, 1992 (appendix C, ref. 50).

same area in a single year (e.g., Hurricanes Earl, Georges, and Mitch in the Caribbean in 1998)!

Death tolls from modern hurricanes have been greatly reduced thanks to National Weather Service warnings, radio and television communications, and evacuation and sheltering plans. Nevertheless, we must not grow complacent; our storm response can be improved. The hurricane watchers of the National Oceanic and Atmospheric Administration (NOAA) track hurricanes and provide advance warning for the evacuation of threatened coastal areas. Yet as little as 9–12 hours of advance warning may be all that is possible, given the unpredictable turns a hurricane can take. These short warning times are alarming in view of the fact that the estimated evacuation clearance times for many communities exceed the warning lead time (table 3.3).

Clearly, portions of the Alabama and west Florida coast are at population densities that stretch the system's capacity for storm evacuation. A 1992 study indicated that three of the five worst evacuation problem areas in the United States were in Florida, and southwest Florida was ranked number 1! A major hurricane approaching the Tampa Bay region would require more than 810,000 people to be evacuated! In many parts of west Florida (e.g., the Big Bend coast, Marco Island) the evacuation routes leading inland cross miles of flood zones, adding to the travel time needed to reach safety. The more people on the coast, the longer the time needed to evacuate; and the less likely it becomes that all will make it to safety. For example, a hurricane approaching the southeastern Florida coast will trigger the evacuation of tens of thousands of residents and visitors from the

Florida Keys into the Miami metropolitan area. These people will then need to be evacuated or sheltered along with the metropolitan area population. Add to this the large number of retired, elderly, and special-needs people living in the area, and the emergency preparedness and response teams will certainly be taxed to the limit or beyond. If we are to prepare for such storms and attempt to reduce their impact in terms of property losses and potential loss of life, we must understand how our coast and storms interact, and the potential for conflict between nature and development.

Ranking Hurricane Intensities

The National Weather Service has adopted the Saffir/Simpson scale (table 3.4) for communicating the strength and damage potential of a hurricane to public safety officials of communities in the storm's potential path. The scale ranks a storm on three variables: wind velocity, storm surge, and barometric pressure. Although hurricane paths are still unpredictable, the scale quickly communicates the nature of the storm — what to expect in terms of wind, waves, and flooding. Risk for property damage and property damage mitigation recommendations discussed throughout this book are based on moderate category 3 hurricane conditions. Category 4 and 5 storms will cause massive property damage or destruction in spite of mitigation efforts.

Do not be misled by scales, however. A hurricane of any size and strength is still a hurricane. The scale simply defines how bad is bad. When the word comes to evacuate, do it. Furthermore, the category rank can change quickly and unexpectedly. As an example take Allison, a category 1 hurricane that struck the less-developed shores of the Big Bend (Dixie, Levy, Taylor, and Wakulla Counties) on June 5, 1995. Most of Allison's damage was caused by storm surge, which reached maximum heights of 6–8 feet and resulted in 60 houses and businesses damaged, 5,000 people evacuated from the coast, minor beach erosion, damage to seawalls and coastal roadways, and the sinking of several small boats. Total damage in Florida was estimated at $860,000, and a related tornado near St. Marys, Georgia, caused about $800,000 in damage, bringing Allison's overall U.S. damage figure to $1.7 million. If a weak hurricane like Allison were to make landfall along more developed shores, the damage would be much greater.

Hurricane History: A Stormy Past

No one knows what is in store for the twenty-first century, but more Camilles, Frederics, Andrews, and Opals will occur, and your house may go

Table 3.4   The Saffir/Simpson Hurricane Scale

Scale Number (Category)	1	2	3	4	5
Central Pressure:					
millibars	980	979–965	964–945	944–920	919
inches of mercury	28.94	28.91–28.50	28.47–27.91	27.88–27.17	27.16
Winds:					
miles per hour	74–95	96–110	111–130	131–155	>155
kilometers per hour	119–153	154–177	179–209	211–249	>249
meters/ second	32–42	42–49	50–57	58–68	>69
Surge:					
feet	4–5	6–8	9–12	13–18	>18
meters	1.2–1.5	1.8–2.4	2.7–3.7	4.0–5.5	>5.5
Damage	Minimal	Moderate	Extensive	Extreme	Catastrophic
Recent Gulf Examples	Erin 1995	Alma 1966	Betsy 1965 Elena 1985 Eloise 1979 Frederic 1979 Opal 1995	Andrew 1992	Camille 1969

down in even a category 1 storm if it is poorly sited or poorly built, or if your neighbor's house is poorly built and the wreckage smashes into your house. Today, anyone on the Gulf coast, particularly on a barrier island, during a hurricane is almost certainly there by choice. In the past, however, people could not be warned of a hurricane's approach, and thus were not always able to flee beforehand. The absence of warning made hurricanes even more feared than they are today and accentuated the need for safe development. Figure 3.4 shows the tracks of several hurricanes that have struck Alabama and west Florida. According to the National Hurricane Center, 6 of the 30 costliest Atlantic and Gulf storms to strike the United States hit the Florida Gulf coast: Opal and Erin in 1995, Alberto in 1994, Elena and Kate in 1985, and Eloise in 1975. This list also includes Frederic (1979) and Camille (1969), which hit the coast of Alabama.

Early Hurricanes

The effects of seventeenth-, eighteenth-, and even nineteenth-century storms on the eastern Gulf coast are generally not well documented because so few people lived on the barrier islands then. Although few detailed measurements exist for early hurricanes, personal accounts and reports reflect storm intensities and impacts. The following information, taken largely from *Florida Hurricanes and Tropical Storms,* by John M. Williams and Iver W. Duedall (appendix C, ref. 8), and the National Climate Data Center Internet web site (www.ncdc.noaa.gov), summarizes some historical tropical storm and hurricane data for the region.

Among the many storms that have struck West Florida and Alabama are the following: August 1, 1889, Carrabelle-Apalachicola area, 6 deaths, more than 50 ships destroyed, $500,000 damage; September 19–29, 1906, Mobile-Pensacola area, landfall in Alabama, 164 deaths, storm surge 8.5 feet, $3–4 million damage; July 1916, Mobile-Pensacola area, 92 mph winds, $1 million damage, landfall in Mississippi; October 1916, Pensacola, 120 mph winds recorded when instrument broke; September 1917, Pensacola-Valparaiso (north of Fort Walton Beach) area, 103 mph winds, peak at 125 mph; October 20, 1921, Tarpon Springs, much damage to Tampa and surrounding area, 10.5-foot storm surge and winds greater than 100 mph; and November 30, 1925, the latest-season tropical storm to affect the United States, landfall near Tampa.

Before 1941, storms were not named or were referred to by the dates they hit or the areas they affected. From 1941 to 1950 storms were named using the World War II phonetic alphabet: Able, Baker, Charlie, Dog, Easy, etc. Hurricane Easy, which struck Cedar Key, Florida, in September 1950, was the worst hurricane there in 70 years. The fishing fleet was destroyed, and Tampa Bay experienced a storm surge of 6.5 feet, 125 mph winds, and 38.7 inches of rain at Yankeetown.

Beginning in 1953, hurricanes were given female names. In 1960, Donna caused $300 million damage and struck Naples, Florida, with winds gusting up to 150 mph. Donna affected the Florida Keys and both the east and west coasts and caused minor damage in northwestern Florida. In September 1964, Hurricane Dora struck nearly head-on near St. Augustine, Florida, then crossed the peninsula and hit the Florida Panhandle. Hurricane Isbell crossed Cuba and the Florida Straits in October 1964 and affected the Ten Thousand Islands area of Florida, only to turn to the northeast, cross the peninsula, and pass near Fort Lauderdale. Alma struck northwestern Florida on June 9, 1966. Until Hurricane Allison in 1995, Alma was the earliest-season storm to hit Florida. Hurricane Gladys (October 18–19, 1968) hit between Bayport and Crystal River along Florida's marshy west coast. Maximum wind gusts of 100 mph were recorded.

The period between 1971 and 1980 saw the lowest number of storms for a 10-year period in Florida, with only three hurricanes and one tropical storm; however, the hurricanes were memorable ones. Although Agnes (1972) was only a category 1 hurricane, it caused tremendous flooding, death, and destruction. Agnes made landfall near Apalachicola and traveled more than 1,000 miles on its path of destruction through Florida and up the entire eastern section of the United States.

Hurricane Eloise struck in September 1975 as a category 3 hurricane and followed a path very similar to a more recent hurricane, Opal in 1995. Eloise made landfall between Fort Walton Beach and Panama City, the first major hurricane to affect that area in the twentieth century. Storm surges ranged from 12 to 16 feet. Eglin Air Force Base experienced winds of 81 mph before instrument failure. Rainfall totaled almost 15 inches. Maximum sustained winds during Eloise were estimated at 125 mph with gusts to 156 mph. Heavy coastal damage was reported from Fort Walton Beach to Panama City. Eloise was responsible for 21 deaths in the United States and more than $1 billion in damage.

In 1979, the National Hurricane Center integrated male names into the lists of female names for hurricanes. On September 11 of that year, a memorable "guy" hurricane, Frederic, hit the Gulf coast.

Recent Hurricanes

The twentieth century closed with an upswing in hurricanes, beginning in the 1980s with several smaller storms, and continuing in 1989 with Hugo, which made landfall at Charleston, South Carolina, and moved inland to Charlotte, North Carolina, and beyond. Then came Andrew in 1992, and the very active 1995 and 1998 seasons, along with predictions of more frequent and more intense hurricanes in the years to come.

Along the Gulf coast, Elena (1985) stalled off Cedar Key for 24 hours and caused high waves from Venice to Pensacola, but did not cause significant damage. On November 21, 1985, the latest date for any hurricane striking that far north in Florida, Hurricane Kate struck the coast near Port St. Joe as a category 2 storm. Storm surge and waves from Kate caused more than $300 million in damage. In 1988, Tropical Storm Keith affected the coast between Fort Myers and Tampa on November 22, but did most of its damage as a hurricane after it passed over the peninsula to the east.

Fourteen named storms developed in 1990, but only Tropical Storm Marco was of note as it slightly affected the northwestern portion of Florida.

In 1994, Tropical Storm Alberto crossed over the panhandle of Florida near Fort Walton Beach. Maximum sustained winds were around 65 mph, and the highest storm surge, near Destin, was about 5 feet. Alberto stalled over west-central Georgia, dumping 10–20 inches of rain. It did not cause significant wind damage, but flood damage in the Florida Panhandle, southeastern Alabama, and west-central Georgia totaled nearly $1 billion, mostly in Georgia. River floods that exceeded the 100-year storm levels in Florida occurred on the Apalachicola River at Blountstown and at Woodruff Dam at Chattahoochee.

One of the most active hurricane seasons on record occurred in 1995; in fact, it was the most active storm season since 1933, the second busiest hurricane season since 1871! Of the 19 named storms that formed, 11 reached hurricane strength. The coastal residents of the Florida Panhandle bore the brunt of Hurricane Opal in October of that year.

Five of the 11 hurricanes that formed in 1995 reached category 3 or higher on the Saffir/Simpson hurricane scale (table 3.4) with sustained winds of 110 mph or greater. Five made landfall in the continental United States, including Hurricanes Erin and Opal. Hurricane Allison, a marginal hurricane with top winds near 75 mph, made landfall over Alligator Point, Florida, on June 4, 1995.

Erin, the second hurricane of the 1995 season, made landfall on Florida's east coast near Vero Beach on August 1 at about 10:00 A.M. with sustained winds of 86 mph. Erin crossed the peninsula and strengthened over the warm Gulf of Mexico waters late on August 2, then came ashore on August 3 near Fort Walton Beach with winds of about 98 mph. Erin caused six fatalities and $700 million in damage.

Opal was the third hurricane to strike the Florida Gulf coast in 1995, and the most destructive hurricane to hit the U.S. mainland since Hurricane Andrew. A separate section below deals with Opal.

After the extremely active 1995 season, Alabama and Florida welcomed the relative inactivity of 1996, when only Tropical Storm Josephine made landfall on the Gulf coast. Josephine's maximum sustained winds were around 69 mph (60 knots) as it moved over Apalachee Bay on the evening of October 7. The storm had a minor impact on Taylor County, Florida, before weakening and moving northward.

The inactive 1997 tropical storm system was attributed to a very strong El Niño. Danny, the only hurricane to form in the Gulf of Mexico that year, made landfall just northwest of the Mississippi River delta and then moved back over the Gulf of Mexico. Danny was a very slow mover and a great rain producer. It wobbled slowly over Mobile Bay, near Fort Morgan, Alabama, early on July 19, then battered Dauphin Island with torrential rains and hurricane-force winds. Danny's rainfall totals exceeded 30 inches in some areas, with 36.71 inches recorded at the Dauphin Island Sea Lab. Danny was directly responsible for four deaths, and overall damage totaled $100 million.

Hurricane Opal

On October 4, 1995, at about 6:00 P.M., Hurricane Opal struck the Florida Panhandle shore along the Okaloosa–Santa Rosa County line near Pensacola Beach as a category 3 hurricane. Opal was the first major hurricane to strike the Florida Panhandle since Eloise in 1975. (Hurricane Frederic caused millions of dollars of damage on the Florida Panhandle in 1979, but made landfall in Alabama.)

According to the National Hurricane Center, Opal was moving north-northeast at 22 mph with maximum sustained surface winds estimated at 115 mph in a narrow swath at the coast near the extreme eastern tip of Choctawhatchee Bay about midway between Destin and Panama City (fig. 3.4). The strongest winds reported by a land station were 84 mph with gusts to 144 mph at Hurlbert Field, Florida, near Fort Walton Beach. It should be emphasized that the strongest winds were in a very limited area and most of the coastal areas of the Panhandle experienced winds equivalent to a category 1 or category 2 hurricane, between 75 and 109 mph. Although the winds were diminishing at the time of landfall (Opal was a category 4 hurricane before it struck the coast), extensive damage due to storm surge and breaking waves occurred over most of the Panhandle shore. Significant storm surge was reported from southeastern Mobile Bay and Gulf Shores, Alabama, east all the way to Cedar Key, Florida. Still-water-mark elevations inside buildings and tide gauge maximums, which damp out breaking wave effects and are indicative of the storm surge, ranged from 5 to 14 feet above mean sea level. Outside water marks on buildings and debris lines on sand dunes within 200 feet of the Gulf of Mexico shoreline generally ranged from 10 to 21 feet. The tide gauge at the Panama City Beach pier recorded a maximum of approximately 8.3 feet above mean sea level; however, at the end of the pier a debris-line elevation of approximately 18 feet above mean sea level was recorded. Thus, the breaking waves on top of the storm surge added approximately 10 feet to the flood level. Many structures in this combined storm surge and breaking wave zone were not elevated high enough and suffered major structural damage. Nine deaths were associated with Opal.

The total cost assessment was more than $3 billion, including losses due to damage or destruction of houses and structures and the cost of cleanup. Most of the severe structural damage occurred at the shore, where the storm surge crushed piers, demolished homes, and eroded or submerged highways. Additionally, the storm's strong winds caused inland damage. Opal downed trees and knocked out power to nearly 2 million people in Florida, Alabama, Georgia, and the Carolinas. Many people in Florida were without water for several days. Opal ranks fourth on the list of costliest twentieth-century U.S. hurricanes (table 3.1). Furthermore, the loss or narrowing of dunes (e.g., east of Fort Walton beach) set the stage for future overwash and flooding.

Opal shocked residents who were unaware of the power of a hurricane. Hurricane Erin had come through earlier that year, but Erin, packing only a 2–4-foot storm surge and wind gusts only on the order of 76 mph, was barely a category 1 hurricane. Its wind, water, and wave damage was minimal. In contrast, Opal was the first major hurricane to hit the Florida Panhandle since Hurricane Eloise in 1975, Hurricane Frederic notwithstanding. Opal's storm surge of 5–14 feet caused extensive overwash and flooding, and waves on top of the storm surge added an additional 10 feet! Tremendous amounts of overwash occurred along Santa Rosa Island, and breaching occurred along Norriega Point, a low-elevation spit east of East Pass and south of Destin. Opal destroyed dunes, overtopped seawalls, and cut swashes, while storm-generated waves and currents smashed and undercut buildings. The wind damage was actually more severe inland than at the shore, and areas as far north as northern Alabama and Georgia were affected because the irregular land surface contributed to swirling winds and tornadoes. Near the coast the wind damage was highest in Okaloosa County. Hardest hit were the beaches from Pensacola to Fort Walton Beach, where stretches of buildings were completely destroyed. Sand up to 10 feet thick covered much of Santa Rosa Island. Returning storm surge caused scouring, and a half-mile segment of Highway 98 was washed out, forming a temporary inlet into Choctawhatchee Bay.

And Opal was a much less powerful storm than Andrew. What is the message to those who redevelop and expand development on barrier coasts? Should taxpayers help to underwrite such development by paying for infrastructure? Is the high value of coastal property real or artificial?

Southwesters and Winter Storms

Although only a few southwesters affect the eastern Gulf coast each year, they are often larger and more persistent than hurricanes. Hurricanes are typically 300–400 miles in diameter, with the greatest winds concentrated around an eye wall 50–60 miles in diameter. A hurricane's exposure to any given area of the coast is usually measured in hours. Winter storms are not so concentrated or so quick to leave. A winter storm may be spread over 1,000 miles and may remain in the eastern Gulf for days.

Southwesters typically form as low-pressure cells over the Gulf of Mexico or the Pacific Ocean. The rotating air circulation that creates a southwester results in winds that blow onto the Gulf coast from out of the southwest when the storm center is out over the Gulf, hence the name. These are the same storms that are called northeasters when they affect the East Coast of the United States. Most often these cells track to the northeast, gaining strength from the warmer ocean waters of the Gulf of Mexico or the Atlantic Ocean. Once the storm tracks to the north, the counterclockwise rotating winds pull moisture from the Atlantic onto the heavily populated eastern seaboard, and the winds arrive from the northeast, hence the name northeaster.

Destructive winter storms require the presence of a strong, stable high-pressure system over eastern Canada that prevents the storm from moving quickly to the north or northeast and ensures that it will remain over the Gulf for a longer period, often several days. The longer the storm remains offshore, the more powerful it can become. The result is that storm surge and waves are the most destructive processes along the coast during a southwester.

The northeaster/southwester of March 12–15, 1993, named the "Storm of the Century," was not a record-breaking coastal storm in terms of strength or duration, but its damage was widespread. It caused storm surge and wave erosion along the Florida Panhandle, record-breaking snow cover inland along the East Coast, and cosmetic but costly wind damage to coastal buildings from Florida to Maine. Total damage was estimated to exceed $6 billion.

The storm was blamed for 44 deaths in Florida and 16 in Alabama, but several of the deaths were indirect results of the storm (for example, heart attacks while shoveling snow). Every major airport on the East Coast was closed at one time or another by this massive storm. Florida was struck by 15 tornadoes. A 12-foot storm surge in Taylor County, Florida, caused at least 6 deaths. Up to 6 inches of snow fell in the Florida Panhandle. Mobile, Alabama, and Pensacola, Florida, were among the many cities that experienced record low temperatures.

The Storm of the Century had associated hurricane-strength winds; the Dry Tortugas, west of Key West, Florida, recorded gusts of 109 mph. In fact, on the Saffir/Simpson hurricane scale (table 3.4), the storm equated to a category 3 hurricane based on storm surge and minimum pressure attained.

Coastal Storm Processes

Storm processes are natural forces that often result in environmental impact and property damage. These energy agents include wind, waves, coastal and inlet currents, storm surge flooding, and storm surge flood and ebb currents. Wind, waves, and rising water account for most storm damage. Currents are responsible for moving vast amounts of sediment during storms. Storm surge causes flooding and may induce scouring currents around and behind structures. The rising water level allows the zone of wave attack to move inland, and sediment to wash over onto the land. Storm surge ebb, or the seaward return of storm surge, is a less familiar storm process that may erode new inlets and contribute to the overall erosional damage.

Natural Processes: Energy in Motion

Storm processes rarely act separately. That is, wind, waves, and currents are all active at the same time and combine to form secondary processes. Storm surge, for example, is formed by several processes acting together, any one of which may be dominant during any given storm or for a given period during a certain storm. Wind pushes water toward shore, waves push water toward shore, low pressure allows doming of the sea surface, and the rotating winds of a hurricane actually cause the shallow water near shore to spiral higher. Consider the following individual storm processes, but keep in mind their combined actions during storms.

Wind

The most common, and often the most costly, of storm hazards causing damage to buildings is direct wind impact on structures, including damage from flying debris (known as *missiling*). In addition, strong winds can destroy vegetation by uprooting and knocking over trees, defoliating trees and other vegetation, blowing down shrubs and grasses, and by damaging leaves directly, either by blasting them with airborne sand or by carrying damaging salt spray inland. The same salt-spray pruning effect that produces the nearshore sloping profile of maritime vegetation will kill or damage inland vegetation that is not salt-tolerant. Strong winds can also be responsible for transporting sediment onto and off of the shore.

Storm Waves

Storm waves damage property both by direct wave attack on structures and when structures are pummeled by floating debris, a process called

3.6 Winds from Hurricane Opal are thought to have tilted the St. George Island Lighthouse to 17 degrees, making it Florida's own "leaning tower." This photo was taken in September 1998 after Hurricane Earl knocked the lighthouse off its foundation. At this writing, a move is under way to save the lighthouse, but a hurricane could cause it to fall beforehand. The beaches at this location are suffering erosion and may also contribute to the fate of the lighthouse. Note the destroyed houses landward of the lighthouse. Photo by Ralph Clark, Florida Department of Environmental Protection, Bureau of Beaches and Coastal Systems.

ramrodding. Probably the only buildings capable of surviving direct wave assault unscathed are concrete pillboxes. Even lighthouses have toppled under wave attack (fig. 3.6). Waves are also responsible for shoreline erosion (on bay and lagoon shores as well as ocean shores), dune erosion, overwash, and destruction of vegetation.

Storm Surge

Storm surge (fig. 3.7) is technically defined as "the super-elevation of the still-water surface that results from the transport and circulation of water induced by wind stresses and pressure gradients in an atmospheric storm" (appendix C, ref. 10). "Pressure gradient" refers to the lowered atmospheric pressure in storms, which by itself can cause a rise in local sea level, extending the zone of wave impact inland and causing flooding and damage to structures. The initial flow over and around obstructions (for example, pilings) may cause scouring and sediment transport. Storm surges that overtop barrier islands may transport beach sand onto the island, forming overwash deposits, and into the adjacent sound. Storm surge may also float

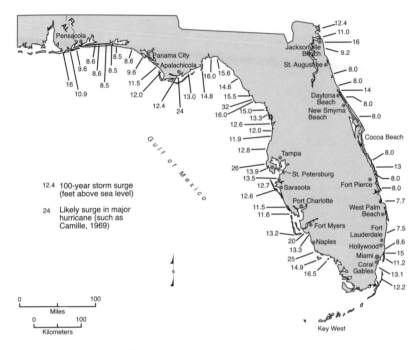

3.7 Storm surge map for Florida. Taken from NOAA data.

Map labels:
12.4
11.0
16
9.2
Jacksonville Beach
St. Augustine
8.0
8.0
14
Daytona Beach
8.0
New Smyrna Beach
8.0
Cocoa Beach
8.0
Tampa
13
St. Petersburg
8.0
Sarasota
Fort Pierce
8.0
7.7
Port Charlotte
West Palm Beach
Fort Myers
Fort Lauderdale
7.5
Naples
Hollywood
8.6
Miami
15
Coral Gables
11.2
13.1
12.2
Key West

Pensacola
Panama City
Apalachicola
8.6 8.5 8.8
9.6   8.8
8.6 8.5 9.6
16   8.5 11.5
10.9   12.0
12.4
24
15.6
16.0
14.6
13.0 14.8 15.5
16.0 15.0
13.3
12.6
12.0
11.9
12.8
26   13.9
13.5
12.7
12.6
11.5
11.6
13.2
20
13.3
25
14.9
16.5
32
16.0

Gulf of Mexico

12.4 100-year storm surge
      (feet above sea level)

24   Likely surge in major
      hurricane (such as
      Camille, 1969)

0   100
      Miles

0   100
      Kilometers

structures off their foundations, carry debris inland — sometimes with ramrod force — and damage inland plants that are not saltwater tolerant.

Storm surge effects were observed at East Pass on the Florida Panhandle after Opal: a narrow overwash fan was formed near the west end of the highway bridge (at the same place as the 1928 breach that formed the present East Pass), and half of west jetty was overwashed with sand transported from Santa Rosa Island into the channel.

While a hurricane is in deep water, storm surge is minimal because converging water and the subsequent piling up are compensated for by currents at greater depths moving water away. As the hurricane moves onto the continental shelf and makes landfall, the slope of the shelf and the shoreline eliminate the compensating currents and the converging water rises. In many cases, maximum storm surge heights measured relative to mean sea level have been recorded at the head of bays or even inland away from the shoreline. Generally, storm surge gradually rises to a peak and then returns to normal within 6–12 hours. Storm surge, which has been recorded reaching heights of 20–30 feet, has been responsible for some of the largest losses of life associated with hurricanes.

Currents

Storm-generated currents transport water, sediment, and storm debris both parallel with and perpendicular to the coast. Waves usually approach the coast at an angle and create a longshore current, moving parallel with the shore, after they break. This current can move sediment (and storm debris such as trees, sand fencing, and dune crossovers or walkways) for great distances. The sediment loss may be temporary or permanent, depending on many factors. In some cases, rip currents may be intensified during a storm, making conditions even more dangerous for those foolhardy enough to try to surf or swim.

Changes in channel positions during storms may cause erosion of one island and deposition on an adjacent island. East Pass, an inlet stabilized by two jetties, had its main inlet channel moved toward the west when overwash sand was deposited near the east jetty after Opal's landfall. Historic trends suggest that the future migration of the channel will be to the east, eroding the sand deposited by Opal.

Storm Surge Ebb

As the storm passes, the "piled up" storm surge water flows back to sea, either by the force of gravity alone or when driven by offshore-blowing winds, generating an erosive ebb current. This type of current occurs while the storm is moving out of the area or diminishing. Storm surge ebb can cause an existing inlet to change shape, create a new inlet, scour shallow cross-island channels (breaches), transport storm debris (including houses) offshore, and cause permanent removal of sand from the beach-dune system to the deeper offshore area. Prior to Opal, Hurricane Eloise (1975) struck the Florida Panhandle near Destin, producing a dune retreat of about 54 feet in Walton County and a maximum surge height of 5 feet. After landfall, the water piled up in Choctawhatchee Bay caused a surge that overwashed Holiday Isle, flooding some condos but causing little damage to the dunes. The 14-foot surge caused by Opal at East Pass pushed a huge volume of water through the inlet into Choctawhatchee Bay. The elevated bay water (plus the freshwater runoff of the Choctawhatchee River) drained out to sea, generating a strong ebb current that carried sand out of the inlet and onto the ebb shoal, and formed a scour depression in the inlet throughout the ebb shoal.

Human Modification of the Coast

Construction in the coastal zone may enhance or alter the natural processes discussed above and increase their resulting impacts. Roads and access paths perpendicular to the shore that penetrate the dune line will become overwash passes or focal points for storm surge flood or ebb currents. Seawalls may redistribute wave energy or obstruct sediment movement. Jetties may block sand from being transported along the coast, resulting in deposition of sand and beach widening on the updrift side and a long-term sand deficit and erosion on the downdrift side. Groin fields and breakwaters have the same effect of interrupting alongshore sediment transport. Ground-level houses and closed-in ground floors of houses on stilts obstruct the passage of overwash sand, which is then lost to front-side erosion. Where vegetation cover has been removed, erosion by wind or water may occur.

Loss of beach sand increases a community's vulnerability to future storms. The protective role of a heavily nourished beach such as Treasure Island, Upham Beach, or Pensacola is as yet unclear. Claims that islands with replenished beaches sustained less damage during Opal than neighboring islands may be unfounded. The lesser damage may have been due more to geological variability or storm processes than to the mitigative effects of beach replenishment.

Studies conducted after Opal demonstrated that Florida's coastal construction control line (CCCL; see chapter 9) had a positive effect in reducing damage by the storm along the Panhandle shores. About one quarter of the major habitable structures seaward of the CCCL were permitted buildings. Almost half of the nonpermitted structures were seriously damaged or destroyed, while only two permitted structures were seriously damaged.

Understanding your shore type, whether barrier island, mainland beach, or marshy shore, is important to avoiding property loss. Unfortunately, the picture is complicated by humans' attempts to out-engineer nature.

Everyone living in the coastal zone today knows or will come to know coastal engineers. Between 80 and 90 percent of the American open-ocean shoreline, including much of the Alabama and west Florida shore, is retreating landward because of the rise in sea level and coastal erosion. Because more and more static buildings are being sited next to this moving and constantly changing line in the sand, it follows that beach communities face major problems, one being how to keep the buildings from falling into the sea!

And that is not at all a simple problem. More than a century of experience with seawalls and other engineering structures in New Jersey and with other coastal developments has shown that the process of holding the shoreline in place leads to the loss of the beach. So the real problem is how to save both buildings and beaches, and that turns out to be a most difficult task.

Four collective approaches address this problem. First, we can be proactive and zone areas to keep people and buildings out of harm's way. But there are few "safe" areas for development on most barrier islands and along the low-lying west Florida mainland coast. In addition, barrier islands will continue to change in size and shape over the coming decades, so areas that were once relatively suitable for development will become unsuitable. Second, we can engineer the shoreline with armoring in an attempt to stabilize it or hold it in place (hard stabilization). Third, we can apply soft stabilization methods, typically beach replenishment, to hold the line and maintain a beach. And fourth, we can move buildings back from the shore, demolish them, or allow them to fall into the sea.

Three of these four approaches involve some aspect of engineering. And

4.1 This shoreline near Mexico Beach is littered with pieces of broken roadway, pilings, and groins, all evidence of the forces of nature combating human designs. Hard structures armor more than half of the developed beaches in Bay County, the most of any county along the Panhandle. Photo by Norma Longo.

4.2 Hefty concrete seawalls with boulder toe armoring front large condominiums along Sand Key in Pinellas County. No recreational beach is present and waves are sending salt spray over the walls during a regular tide cycle. The property behind is barely being protected now. If a storm were pounding the area, just imagine how much water would surge over these rocks and walls! Photo by Norma Longo.

4.3 Bulkheads such as these are built to retain the sand or soil behind them. The soil here is supporting palm trees and other landscaping materials in front of a hotel in Bay County. At high tide, there is no beach in front of the bulkheads. This photo was taken after the passage of Hurricane Earl over the Panhandle. Photo by Norma Longo.

even the other, zoning, is likely to include requirements that will call for input from construction engineers.

Shoreline Armoring

The presence of hard structures continues to have a negative impact on Florida's beaches (fig. 4.1). Property owners should be aware that seawalls, groins, and offshore breakwaters are all associated with continued shoreline retreat and beach loss. Those with property within inlet zones should be aware of the effects of jetties as well as natural inlet dynamics.

Seawalls

Seawalls include a family of coastal engineering structures built on land at the back of the beach, parallel to the shoreline. Strictly defined, seawalls are freestanding structures near the surf-zone edge. The best examples are the giant walls of the northern New Jersey coast, the end result of more than a century of armoring the shoreline. But Florida has some hefty examples as well (fig. 4.2). When such walls are filled in behind with soil or sand, they are referred to as bulkheads (fig. 4.3). Revetments, commonly made of large rock in poured concrete (fig. 4.4), are walls built up against the lower

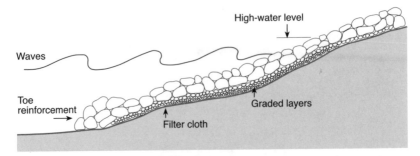

4.4 A typical rock revetment, shown here, is plastered against the slope of the dune or upper beach (as opposed to standing as a free wall like a seawall). When waves break against a rock revetment, some of the water is absorbed in the interstices, reducing backwash.

dune face or land at the back of the beach. For most purposes the distinction between the types of walls is unimportant, and we will use the general term *seawalls* for all structures on the beach that parallel the shoreline.

Seawalls are usually built to protect the property behind them, not to protect the beach. Sometimes they are intended only to prevent shoreline retreat. Virtually every seawall within the reach of Hurricanes Opal, Frederic, and Camille was overtopped by waves and storm surge. The seawalls failed to protect the buildings they fronted, and the fair-weather shoreline was prevented from moving inland. Almost every seawall eventually deteriorates into an eyesore (fig. 4.1).

Seawalls are successful in preventing property damage if they are built strongly, high enough to avoid being overtopped, and kept in good repair. The problem is that such protection comes at a very high price: the eventual loss of the recreational beach. Several states (e.g., Maine, Rhode Island, North Carolina, South Carolina, Texas, and Oregon) prohibit or place strict limits on shoreline armoring. There are strong reasons for doing so. Senator Phil Graham, a former governor of Florida, put it this way: "This generation does not have the right to destroy the next generation's beaches."

Seawalls Cause Beach Loss

Three mechanisms account for beach degradation by seawalls (fig. 4.5). *Passive loss* is the most important. Whenever a fixed, immovable object such as a seawall or highway is built adjacent to an eroding beach, the beach eventually retreats up against the wall. The forces causing the shoreline to retreat are unaffected by the wall, and erosion continues until the beach is gone. *Placement loss* refers to the emplacement of a wall on the beach seaward of the high-tide line, thus removing part of the beach on the day the wall is constructed. Such walls on Miami Beach led to the need for the largest beach nourishment project in North America, completed in 1981. *Active loss* is the least understood of the beach degradation mechanisms. It is generally assumed that interaction of the seawall with the surf during a storm enhances the rate of beach loss. This interaction could occur in a number of ways, including reflection of waves and intensification of surf-zone currents.

A 1990 state study indicated that 147 miles of the total 710 miles, or 18 percent, of the east and west Florida shores regulated by the coastal con-

4.5 Seawalls degrade recreational beaches in three ways: (A) Passive loss occurs when the beach and dune line migrate over time (time 1 to time 2) but the seawall blocks beach migration. (B) Placement loss occurs immediately because the seawall is built seaward of the dune line, narrowing the beach. (C) Active loss occurs when waves reflect off a seawall to scour and erode sediment in front of the wall.

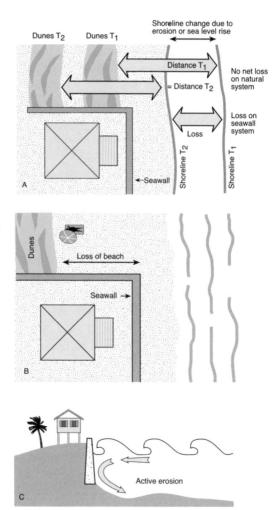

struction control line (CCCL, chapter 9) was armored. This percentage is misleading, however, because the regulatory zone includes undeveloped shoreline. When one considers only developed shorelines, with development driving the perceived need to build seawalls, groins, and breakwaters, the percentage of armored shoreline on the west Florida coast jumps to 50 percent; the same as the New Jersey coast! Similarly, 45 percent of the developed east Florida shoreline is armored, in contrast to 27 percent for South Carolina and only 6 percent of the developed North Carolina open-ocean shoreline. These figures represent the armored percentage of developed shoreline and generally do not include parks and national seashores. The message is clear: parklands that do not allow shore-hardening structures and states that have adopted regulations discouraging engineering structures are maintaining their beaches for future generations. The 1990 state study projected significant future armoring, much of it in areas that are important sea turtle nesting sites.

Shoreline stabilization is a difficult political issue because its effects are not immediately visible. Seawalls may take as long as five or six decades to destroy beaches, although the usual time range for the beach to get to the point where it is entirely gone at mid to high tide may be only one to three decades. Thus it takes a politician of some foresight to vote for prohibition of armoring. Another issue of political difficulty is that there is no room for compromise. Seawalls, once in place, are rarely removed. The economic reasoning is that the wall must be maintained and even itself protected, so most walls grow higher and longer (fig. 4.6). What politician likes an issue with no room for compromise?

The emplacement of many seawalls and revetments in Pinellas and Sarasota Counties and elsewhere must be considered an irreversible act. As any long-term observer of Gulf beaches knows, the beaches in front of the walls are gone or going except where nourishment has replaced them. And many of the original walls have been replaced by "bigger and better" walls.

On Dauphin Island, Alabama, the U.S. Army Corps of Engineers built a small rock revetment to protect a small pier at the public park. This is an extreme example of over-engineering: protection of a minor and easily lengthened pier by use of a structure that will greatly increase downdrift erosion in coming decades.

Groins and Jetties

Groins and jetties are walls or barriers built perpendicular to the shoreline. A jetty, often very long (thousands of feet), is intended to keep sand from

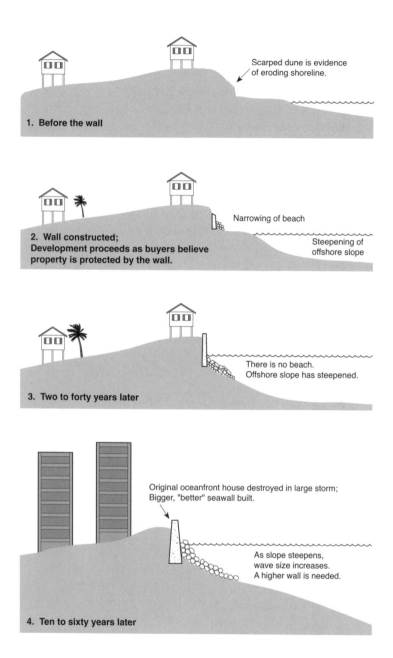

4.6 The saga of a seawall. This process, which may take several decades, is the ultimate fate of walled shorelines.

flowing into a ship channel within an inlet. Groins, much smaller barriers built on straight stretches of beach away from channels and inlets, are intended to trap sand moving in longshore currents. Groins are present on many west Florida beaches, including Honeymoon Island, Sand Key, Madeira Beach, Treasure Island, Longboat Key, Anna Maria Key, and the Manasota Peninsula. Groins can be made of wood, stone, concrete, steel, or fabric bags filled with sand. Some newer designs are referred to as T-groins because the end of the structure terminates in a short shore-parallel segment.

Both groins and jetties are very successful sand traps. If a groin is working correctly, more sand should be piled up on one side of it than on the other. The problem with groins is that they trap sand that is flowing to a neighboring beach. Thus, if a groin on one beach is functioning well, it must be causing erosion elsewhere by "starving" another beach (fig. 4.7). Per Bruun, the retired director of the Coastal Engineering Program at the

4.7 Map view diagram of downdrift erosional effect of groins and the typical proliferation of groins into a groin field. Beach retreat typically continues and groins become detached, leading to rapid erosion shoreward of the detached groins.

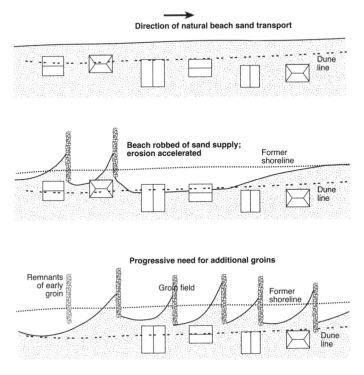

4.8 On Dauphin Island, Alabama, shoreline retreat has stranded at sea the groins that once "protected" the beach.

University of Florida, has observed that, on a worldwide basis, groins may be a losing proposition; that is, more beaches may be lost than gained by their use.

Miami Beach, Florida, and many New Jersey beaches illustrate the end-point of groin usage. After one groin is built, the increased rate of erosion on adjacent beaches has to be addressed. So other groins are constructed in self-defense. The result is a series of groins sometimes extending for miles and called a *groin field* (fig. 4.7). Prior to the 1981 beach nourishment project, Miami Beach looked like an army obstacle course; groin after groin obstructed both pedestrian and vehicular traffic.

Groins fail when continued erosion at their landward end causes the groin to become detached, allowing water and sand to pass behind the groin. When detachment occurs, beach retreat continues and the groin becomes a useless obstruction in the water. The small groin field at the eastern end of Dauphin Island adjacent to the old fort is an example (fig. 4.8).

Jetties are walls built next to inlets (fig. 4.9). Usually much longer than groins, jetties are constructed to stabilize inlets to make them safer for navigation and cheaper to maintain (less dredging). On the east coast of Florida, where 17 out of 18 inlets are jettied, these structures are considered to be the principal cause of beach erosion. West Florida examples include Crooked, Shell, and Honeymoon Islands; Clearwater Beach Island; Doctors

4.9 Jetties are built to stabilize inlets for navigation, but they also interfere with the longshore sand transport system. Notice in this photo of Blind Pass taken in 1995 that the updrift side of the inlet (to the left) has a much wider beach than the downdrift side (to the right). Photo by Richard A. Davis Jr.

Pass; and Gordon Pass (Naples). Perdido Pass in Alabama is also jettied.

Sand-bypassing systems are sometimes included in the design of jettied inlets to prevent the jetties from blocking longshore sand transport. In order to get sand to the downdrift beaches, the trapped sand must either be pumped or periodically dredged and placed on the opposite side of the inlet.

Offshore Breakwaters

Offshore breakwaters are also features of the west Florida shore. Breakwaters are walls, usually built parallel to the shoreline but at some distance offshore, typically a few tens of yards seaward of the normal surf zone (fig. 4.10). These structures dampen the wave energy on the "protected" shoreline behind them, interrupting the longshore current and causing sand to be deposited. Sometimes the sand deposits accumulate all the way out to the breakwater, creating a feature like a natural tombolo. As in the case of groins, the sand trapped by breakwaters is removed from the longshore transport system, causing a shortage of sediment downdrift and leading to additional shoreline retreat. A boulder breakwater constructed at Redington Shores was quite successful in trapping sand, but beaches to both the north and the south narrowed as a result. Another unexpected problem was the death of five swimmers near the structure in the months after its construction, apparently because they were knocked into the rocks by waves or currents generated around the structure. Swimming is no longer allowed there.

Snake Oil Devices

Invention is the mother of false promises at the shore. The ultimate crises faced by communities and individuals in the path of shoreline retreat create a repeated scenario. Faced with the knowledge that walls, groins, and

4.10 The Redington Shores, Florida, breakwater was quite successful at trapping sand, but in a little more than a year five swimmers were killed on the rocks. The trapped sand may be responsible for the narrowing downdrift beach visible at the top of the photo.

breakwaters have not held back the sea, and that building a truly effective protective structure would be very costly, the seawall shopper is an easy mark for those who sell alternative or "nontraditional" engineering structures guaranteed to prevent shoreline retreat. These devices carry a fascinating variety of names, including Beach Builder, Wave Buster, Wave Shield, Sand Grabber, Surge Breaker, Sta-beach, PEP Reef, Seascape, and speed bumps. A claim that a particular novel device will protect or save any beach, anywhere (one size fits all), should raise the first red flag.

Although such structures may not have the appearance of seawalls or groins, and thus may sometimes slip under the "no armoring" regulations, they are only variations on the same fundamental shoreline-hardening schemes. For example, fishnet stretched perpendicular to the beach, as proposed for Keewaydin in 1999, is the same as a groin and will have the same effects, although the netting is less likely to be stormworthy.

A review of more than 40 such devices found no hard evidence of successes but did reveal a few glaring failures. Furthermore, a disturbingly high percentage of companies promoting such structures had gone out of business. Some of the structures may temporarily protect property, but they are no different from traditional seawalls and groins in that they cause downdrift erosion or the eventual loss of the beach associated with them.

In almost every case, the inventors of the devices claim that their "inventions" (and, yes, many are patented) have worked somewhere else, usually far enough away that potential buyers aren't likely to visit the "successful" site. The inventors of a shoreline stabilization device being promoted in Norfolk, Virginia, claimed success in Australia and New Guinea! A device promoted in Florida was said to have worked in Denmark. Any prudent community group will go to the expense to check out "somewhere else" very carefully before buying.

Another problem is that most claims of success consider only the short term; and more often than not, the claimed "success" is nothing more than normal seasonal changes in the beach. Success must be viewed over the intermediate to long term, that is, beach accretion and sustained property protection for at least 5 years, and preferably for a decade. The majority of victory claims for these too-good-to-be-true inventions are premature, some after only a few weeks!

In 1997, the state of South Carolina allowed the emplacement of Stabler Disks, claimed by the manufacturer to cause beach sand accumulation, on Myrtle Beach. State bureaucrats said, incorrectly, that the device, which consists of concrete disks, was not shoreline armoring. Personnel in the city manager's office claimed to have researched the device and were certain that it would solve the local erosion problem. But apparently they researched it by reading the company's literature! Coastal managers in New Jersey, where the device had previously been used, were unimpressed with its effectiveness, but the word hadn't reached South Carolina. The device was removed for the given reason that a beach user was injured on it, but in truth it was not working.

The one advantage of most of these structures is that they can be removed at a lower cost than a more massive structure if the community is unhappy with them. An alternative type of breakwater at Palm Beach provides a good example. Breakwater units consisting of heavy triangular concrete prisms, approximately 6 feet in height, were placed in a line just off the beach. Although the "reef" structure was designed to dissipate wave energy and reduce shoreline erosion, it introduced a new set of offsetting problems. The structures halted the beachward flow of new sand during fair weather and deprived the beach of one source of its sediment. In addition, the artificial reef caused erosion rates to increase because water volumes between the beach and the breakwater increased. The Palm Beach reef was removed within 2 years of its emplacement.

By law, Florida allows alternative technologies for coastal protection to be emplaced on an experimental basis, but the permit usually requires that the structure be removed if it becomes deformed, dislodged, a nuisance, or a public hazard. A "new technology" is any method about which there is insufficient available information to predict its performance under a range of operational conditions and its potential environmental impacts. The regulation that such structures must be removable is important, and the state has required removals; for instance, the PEP reef at Vero Beach on the east coast and the underwater stabilizers at Captiva Island. The manufacturer of the latter sand- or concrete-filled geotextile bags still touts their success even though they were shown to be ineffective. The sand-filled bags installed at Manasota Key as back-shore sills settled, buckled, rotated, dislocated, and had no positive effect on the beach according to a state report. One of the problems with the so-called alternative technologies is that the structures become clutter and obstacles on the beach.

Another anecdote illustrates the difficulty of determining the success of shoreline stabilization devices. The Cape Hatteras Lighthouse in North Carolina had been threatened by shoreline retreat for many years. Groins, emergency revetments, and beach nourishment failed to hold the shoreline in place. A group of concerned citizens proposed installing Seascape, a form of artificial seaweed consisting of plastic fronds anchored to stay on the bottom and intended to slow down wave and current activity and cause sand accumulation. Studies indicating that Seascape did not work were ignored, and the seaweed was emplaced. Within weeks a small storm swept the coast and the beach widened! The group immediately claimed success; the widened beach was evidence that all could see. But the same storm also widened the beach along much of the 50-mile reach to the north of the lighthouse! The wind direction had caused onshore sand movement and temporarily widened the beaches. In the following weeks and months, the beach again narrowed and storm waves ripped out the artificial seaweed, washing much of it ashore to clutter the beach. Seascape and other coastal engineering devices could not decrease the lighthouse's vulnerability to future storm damage or destruction, so the structure was relocated 2,900 feet to the southwest of its original location. Its new position places the light 1,600 feet from the Atlantic Ocean's edge, just about the same distance as when it was first built in 1870.

In summary, consider the following before purchasing nontraditional engineering devices:

1. No device creates new sand. The sand comes from somewhere and is going somewhere.
2. Any structure that traps sand will cause a downdrift shortage.
3. One size does not fit all; no device works on every shoreline.
4. Treat claims of success elsewhere with great skepticism. Success should mean 5–10 years of property protection with no beach loss on adjacent properties.
5. To measure success, a project must be monitored for 5–10 years. Very few such projects are monitored for even 1–2 years.
6. There is no proven low-cost shore protection. If it sounds too good to be true, it is.

Beach Nourishment

Beach nourishment consists of pumping or trucking sand onto the beach (fig. 4.11). The goals of most communities that employ it are to improve their recreational beach, to halt shoreline erosion, and to afford storm protection for beachfront buildings. In order to obtain federal funding for beach nourishment, storm protection is a required justification. A summary of the beach nourishment experience nationwide can be found in *The Corps and the Shore*, by Orrin Pilkey and Katherine Dixon (appendix C, ref. 41). Table 4.1 summarizes beach nourishment for the Alabama-Florida Gulf coast. Many famous beaches in developed areas are now artificial.

Remember that the beach or zone of active sand movement actually extends out to a water depth of 30 or 40 feet. With nourishment, only the

4.11 Beach replenishment has gained favor as a shoreline management alternative, but it is very expensive, and nourished beaches almost always erode faster than the natural beach. Here an offshore dredge is pumping sand onto the beach at Indian Shores. Photo by Richard A. Davis Jr.

upper beach is covered with new sand, so a steeper beach is created. This new steepened profile often actually increases the rate of erosion; in fact, replenished beaches almost always disappear at a faster rate than their natural predecessors. West Florida may be an exception to this general rule because of the lower wave energy or the nature of beach sand (i.e., its size and composition).

Sand for beach nourishment is available from sounds and embayments, nearby inlets and associated tidal deltas, the adjacent continental shelf, and mainland sources. On barrier islands, sand from the sound is rarely used anymore because of the potential for ecological damage in that very delicately balanced ecosystem. Taking sand from the tidal delta may increase the rate of shoreline retreat on adjacent beaches. In general, marine sand should be taken from locations as far from the beach as possible in order to reduce the impact of seafloor changes on wave patterns. In a number of locations (e.g., Grand Isle, Louisiana) the hole dug on the continental shelf to obtain the nourishment sand actually led to the early demise of the nourished beach. Because modification of the nearshore bottom can cause wave refraction resulting in unintended erosion of the beach, the Dutch require that nourishment sand be obtained from more than 15 miles offshore!

Ignorance of the shelf geology and sediment can be costly. A late-1990s nourishment project at Naples Beach drew on sand from offshore sinkholes, but large quantities of rock were dredged up as well, degrading the quality of one of the state's most important tourist beaches. At least 25,000

Table 4.1. Alabama and West Florida Beach Nourishment, 1923–1997

Beach Location	No. of Episodes	Span of Years	Type of Project*	Total Volume (cubic yds)	Total Adjusted Cost (in 1996 $)
Alabama					
Perdido Pass	1	1986	FN	660,000	1,815,000
Dauphin Island	1	1996	FN	20,000	55,000
Alabama Total	2			680,000	1,870,000
West Florida					
Perdido Key	2	1985–90	FN	7,795,597	21,437,892
Pensacola Harbor	1	1986	FN	35,000	96,250
Santa Rosa Island	1	1961	SL	75,300	357,675
Destin	3	1986–88	SL	433,000	2,056,750
Port St. Joe Harbor	1	1986	SL	500,000	2,375,000
Apalachicola	1	1986	FN	138,000	379,500
Panama City Beach	7	1976–98	E/FN	8,443,990	37,666,973
Mexico Beach	2	1965–75	SL	201,250	631,210
St. Joseph spit	2	1980–86	FN	832,000	1,016,200
Honeymoon Island	2	1969–89	SL	1,670,000	7,932,500
Clearwater Beach	4	1949–84	SL/FN	610,000	2,537,500
Sand Key, north end	4	1973–84	SL/FN	1,152,000	4,848,000
Belleair Beach	1	1992–93	SL	82,300	390,925
Sand Key Phase IV	1	1997	FE	2,079,000	5,300,000
Indian Shores, Sand Key Phase III	1	1992	FE	480,000	16,016,000
Indian Shores, Sand Key Phase II	1	1990	FE	1,300,000	16,697,000
North Redington Beach	2	1981–86	FE	1,780,000	693,150
Sand Key Phase I	1	1988	FE	529,150	3,439,475
Madeira Beach	1	1961	SL	30,000	1,848,000
Treasure Island	12	1964–97	E/FE/FN	2,618,500	13,433,714
Upham Beach	6	1968–96	FE/SL	1,012,000	6,952,620
St. Petersburg Beach	1	1971–75	SL	25,000	1,584,560
Mullet Key	3	1964–77	FE/SL	645,000	2,988,480
Anna Maria Key	4	1963–93	FN/SL	2,526,000	14,954,500
Longboat Key	3	1977–93	FE/FN	3,331,480	20,899,070
Lido Key	8	1964–91	FE/FN/SL	1,589,000	7,789,460
Venice Beach	5	1963–96	E/FE/FN/SL	902,254	20,140,000
Port Charlotte Beach	1	1980	FN	49,700	136,675
Gasparilla Island	2	1981–93	FN	264,000	8,577,000
Captiva Island	7	1961–89	FE	1,595,000	10,367,500

Beach Location	No. of Episodes	Span of Years	Type of Project*	Total Volume (cubic yds)	Total Adjusted Cost (in 1996 $)
South Seas Plantation	3	1981–95	E/LP	658,800	5,562,975
Sanibel	1	1995	SL	N/A	N/A
Fort Myers Beach	2	1961–86	FN	886,000	2,436,500
Bonita Beach	2	1976–95	SL	198,000	1,133,000
Naples–Gordon Pass	1	1986	FU	119,000	714,000
Barefoot Beach	1	1991	FN	N/A	N/A
Wiggins State Park	2	1993–95	FN	35,000	96,250
Vanderbilt Beach	2	1983–95	FN/LP	90,000	355,500
Vanderbilt/Park Shore/ Naples	1	1996	FE	1,132,000	10,000,000
Keewaydin Island	6	1963–85	FN	1,037,800	2,853,950
Marco Island	2	1989–95	SL	1,202,400	6,356,822
West Florida Total	113			48,083,521	225,385,603

* E = Emergency, FE = Federal Storm and Erosion, FN = Federal Navigation, FU = Federal Unknown, LP = Local/Private, SL = State/Local.
Source: Duke University Program for the Study of Developed Shorelines.

cubic yards of rock had to be hauled away, and a lot of buried rock material is still coming out of the nourished beach. The various contracting parties traded the blame and a lawsuit resulted, adding to the ongoing cost of the project. Meanwhile, tourists seeking the perfect beach moved elsewhere.

The Florida-Alabama beach nourishment experience is given at the web site www.geo.duke.edu/psds.htm, and table 4.1 summarizes the extent, frequency, and cost of beach nourishment in west Florida. At the time of this writing, the most frequently replenished beaches are Treasure Island (11 times since 1968), Captiva Island (7 times since 1965), and Lido Key (8 times since 1964). Studies conducted by the Duke University Program for the Study of Developed Shorelines found it difficult to obtain exact total costs for the nourishment; however, documented expenditures through 1996 for west Florida totaled more than $225 million. The total cost of nourishment for the much shorter Alabama shoreline was probably less than $2 million (two beaches) by 1996. The number of beaches being nourished is increasing, and communities opting for beach nourishment are finding that federal, state, and local governments (the taxpayers) are less inclined than before to pick up even a share of the costs.

Beach replenishment along the west coast of Florida generally uses less than 250,000 cubic yards of sand per mile of shoreline, in contrast to the east coast, where more than 1 million cubic yards of sand per mile is the norm. Miami Beach was given 5 million cubic yards of sand between 1979 and 1981. The two largest Florida Gulf projects are Panama City, where approximately 3 million cubic yards of sand per mile was used, and Perdido Key, where 2.5 million cubic yards of sand was emplaced. Although little hard data is available, Gulf coast nourished beaches probably last longer than those on the east coast in spite of using less sand.

Figure 4.12 illustrates what happens when a beach is nourished. Immediately after replenishment, a protective berm exists as well as a wider dry beach (the recreational beach at high tide). The profile also is steepened somewhat, and wave energy begins to redistribute the sand out onto the subaqueous portion of the beach. The sand is moved out beyond the surf zone and no longer offers much resistance to storm waves, especially if storm surge occurs, which it often does. The protective storm berm is diminished and the high-tide dry beach is very narrow or absent. And underwater sand is useless for beach volleyball unless the players can hold their breath for long periods.

Most beach communities will consider nourishment at some point in their response to shoreline retreat. For a Gulf community considering the nourishment option, the following generalizations should be kept in mind.

1. Beach nourishment is costly. See table 4.1.

2. Beach nourishment is not a one-time solution, and it requires a long-term financial commitment by the community. The beach must be nourished again and again and again (e.g., Treasure Island, Captiva Island, Lido Key).

3. The environmental impact of replenished beaches is poorly understood. Beaches such as Naples and Captiva probably have created serious problems for the local fauna and flora. Nourishment sand containing rocks degrades turtle nesting grounds and may prevent the turtles from nesting at all. Dredging and pumping may leave behind hard ground for organisms or may cause fish kills where turbidity is increased. Such impacts need to be studied and evaluated before new replenishments are undertaken.

4. If the project is to be done with federal funding by the U.S. Army Corps of Engineers, it will take 8–15 years to come to fruition because a clash between the state and federal agencies involved is almost inevitable. The state insists that nourishment projects be small on southern Gulf beaches in order to reduce the amount of damage to offshore organisms on hard grounds. The Corps of Engineers is generally not interested in small projects, and the communities are thus forced to pay for their own beach, as in Naples.

5. A favorable cost-benefit ratio is required for federal participation.

Recreational benefits usually do not count. The principal justification in most cases must be storm protection.

6. The Corps of Engineers is required to predict long-term (usually 50-year) costs and required sand volumes. These predictions will be highly optimistic; that is, costs and sand volumes are likely to be too low.

7. Much of the design process may not be useful. Each nourishment project is different, but in most cases the community or state will pay the lion's share of the beach design costs, which can be millions of dollars. Sophisticated studies that gather wave data and use mathematical models rarely accurately predict the cost and durability of a nourished beach. No one knows when the next big storm — the major determinant of the beach's longevity — will occur.

8. The best estimate of the durability, cost, and sand volumes for a beach project can be obtained by reviewing the experience of neighboring beaches or of previous nourishments on the same beach. This approach is not precise, but it often proves to be much more reliable than a coastal engineering estimate based on oversimplified or unrealistic models.

9. There is little or no difference between a nourished beach and a dredge-spoil-disposal beach, and dredge spoil is free! Nourishment sand taken from navigation projects often works very well, even though the replenishment was not "designed." The Corps of Engineers considers such beaches to be dredge-spoil disposal, and thus no design effort is required. In theory, such navigation projects can be done only if beach disposal is the cheapest way to get rid of dredge spoil. In practice, this is a highly politicized process. Be warned that the quality of dredge spoil may not be appropriate in all cases (e.g., muddy sand rather than clean sand).

10. Nourished beaches often erode at higher rates than do the original natural beaches. As noted, nourishment may increase the state of disequilibrium by steepening the profile or introducing materials that differ from the natural beach in terms of grain size and composition.

11. Replenished beaches do not recover as well from storms as natural beaches do. According to past experience nationwide, perhaps 10–20 percent of nourished beaches come back, but the more general case is little or no storm recovery whatsoever.

12. A lesson based on the experience of Virginia Beach, Virginia, suggests that frequent small nourishments may be more effective than less frequent large nourishment projects in maintaining the beach's width and longevity.

13. The sources and cost of nourishment sand are highly variable.

14. Sand can be a rare commodity on the continental shelf off west Florida, which is not covered with a blanket of beach-quality sand. Sand deposits are localized and a search for sand must be carried out using seis-

mic surveys and coring. This aspect of the design process is essential and cannot be avoided. Even when deposits are located, the quality of the deposit may not be uniform, as in the case of the rocky sediment deposited at Naples.

15. Consider the possibility of using trucked sand, especially to respond to erosion "hot spots," both before and after nourishment. Every nourished beach has such rapidly eroding areas of nourished beach. Sometimes relatively small amounts of sand — for example, a few hundred truckloads — can repair the hot spot until the next nourishment project.

16. It is to a community's advantage to have its own source of sand. Hire a geologist to find a long-term sand supply.

17. Once a nourished beach is in place, it is essential to monitor its progress. This can be done simply by taking repetitive photos from the same spot, making sure a sunbather or surfer is in the photo for scale. Alternatively, cross-beach profiles can be taken using elementary leveling techniques to provide a more quantitative view of the loss or gain rate (a good community project for high school students).

18. Offshore sand, below the low-tide line, is useless for either recreation or community storm protection. When a replenished beach disappears more quickly than expected (the usual case), the consultants or the Corps of Engineers often assert that the sand is just offshore providing protection. This is not the case. The portion of the nourished beach that is most effective for storm protection is the artificial dune (sometimes called a *berm* in engineering parlance) at the back or landward side of the beach, as well as exposed beach width (fig. 4.12).

19. Where dunes are part of the natural system, dune building and maintenance should be part of beach nourishment projects. Dunes are sand reservoirs, and sand entrapment can be encouraged through stabilization with vegetation and sand fences.

20. Keep in mind that the usual impetus behind beach nourishment is the fact that the first row of buildings is threatened with destruction. No beachfront buildings: no erosion problem. That being the case, who should pay for the beach?

Beach scraping (bulldozing) should not be confused with beach nourishment. Beach scraping involves beach sand being moved from the low-tide beach to the upper back beach (independent of building artificial dunes) as an erosion-mitigation technique. A relatively thin layer of sand (1 foot or less) is removed from over the entire lower beach using some sort of heavy machinery (dragline, grader, bulldozer, front-end loader) and spread over the upper beach. The objectives are to build a wider, higher high-tide

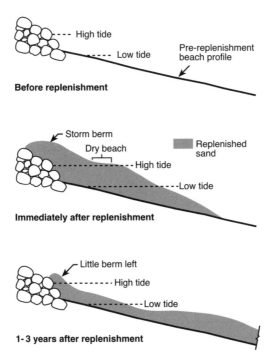

4.12 Replenished beach before sand emplacement (top), immediately after emplacement (middle), and 1–3 years after emplacement (bottom). Often the sand from the storm berm is removed offshore, where it plays no role in storm protection.

dry beach; to fill in any troughlike lows that drain across the beach; and to encourage additional sand to accrete to the lower beach.

The newly accreted sand can, in turn, be scraped, leading to a net gain of sand on the manicured beach. Beach scraping may enhance the recreational beach for the short term, but the drawback is that no new sand is added to the system. Ideally, scraping is intended to encourage onshore transport of sand, but most of the sand "trapped" on the lower beach is brought in by the longshore transport. Removal of this lower-beach sand deprives downdrift beaches of their natural nourishment, steepens the beach profile, and destroys beach organisms. So beach scraping may accelerate beach erosion.

Dune building is often an important part of beach nourishment design; it can also be carried out independent of beach nourishment. Coastal dunes, a common back-beach landform, are part of the dynamic equilibrium of barrier beach systems. Although extensive literature exists about dunes, their protective role often is unknown or misunderstood by laymen.

Frontal dunes are the last line of defense against ocean storm wave attack and flooding from overwash, and interior dunes provide high ground and protection against penetration of overwash and against the damaging effects of storm-surge ebb scour.

Wide dune fields (both natural and bulldozed) can be a main line of frontal defense against property damage during hurricanes, as demonstrated by Frederic in Alabama and Opal in Florida. In each case, wide, high dunes were more effective protection to property than any shore-hardening structure. Nature's price, however, was to take the dunes. Post-hurricane recovery and routine hazard mitigation include artificial dune building and encouraging new dune growth through the use of sand fencing and/or dune grass plantings. Numerous projects followed Hurricane Opal to reestablish lines of dune protection against future storms.

Plugging dune gaps should be a part of nourishment and sand conservation projects. Because dunes are critical geomorphic features with respect to property damage mitigation, they are now protected, right down to the plants that are critical to dune growth. Prior to strict coastal-zone management regulations, however, frontal dunes were often excavated for ocean views or building sites, or notched at road termini for beach access. Waves, storm surge, and storm surge ebb flows exploit these artificially created gaps. Wherever dune removal for development has occurred, the likelihood of complete overwash and possible inlet formation has increased. The combined threats of storm flooding, inlet formation, and the burial of roads by overwash sand make areas where dunes have been removed prime zones for evacuation in case of a hurricane warning. Dune gaps can be refilled (plugged), of course, many with just a few truckloads of new sand. Maintaining dunes in the interior of islands is an equally important means of reducing property damage.

Proper use of sand fencing is crucial in dune-building projects. Dune gaps and dune lines can be augmented and repaired by encouraging or enhancing natural processes. Typically, such augmentation includes placing sand fences and planting dune grasses to trap windblown sand. Sand fencing also serves as a barrier to foot traffic over dunes, allowing vegetation to gain a foothold and flourish. Effective use of fencing to build dunes should follow these guidelines:

1. Do not place fence on the beach because landward transport of sand may be reduced, the small dunes that build up are out of equilibrium, and fencing is likely to wash out in the first storm.
2. Fencing on the face of the dune may encourage seaward dune toe growth.

3. Do not use double rows of dune fencing, which act as impenetrable rather than permeable barriers (block inland sand flow).
4. Do not attach new fence to old fencing as the dune grows upward.
5. Remove fencing periodically.
6. Vegetate the newly formed dunes with native species.
7. Vegetation is just as effective as sand fences in building dunes over the long term.
8. Trapping sand on the landward side of the dune is as important as trapping sand on the front and top of the dune.

The last guideline is especially important because dune width affords protection as well as dune height. The principle is often violated when property owners notch the back side of the dune for house construction, driveways, patios, play areas, etc. Poststorm reconstruction is a time when the landward sides of dunes suffer loss of sand and reduction of width. Instead of placing overwash sand from roads, driveways, and parking lots back onto the dune, the sediment sometimes is removed from the area. Remember:

Both dune width and height are important.
Keep all the sand in the system, and add new sand if possible.
Allow the dune to migrate (maintain equilibrium).
Vegetate with native species.

Sand fencing and artificially planted dune grass are most effective at building (or rebuilding) dunes when structures are set back far enough to provide an adequate space for dunes to build and stabilize in a natural equilibrium profile and location. A healthy sand supply also is needed. Shorelines with low sand supplies defy efforts to build dunes artificially.

Dune management must be guided by the principles of dynamic equilibrium. A fundamental rule is that the dune zone may have to migrate if it is to retain its protective characteristics. Unfortunately, some people view dunes as if these natural sand accumulations can be designed, engineered, and constructed in the same fashion as groins and seawalls. If dunes are to function in their natural protective role, a "preserve, augment, and restore" approach must mimic the equilibrium setting. A dune bulldozed or built into a nonequilibrium location will not be stable. In fact, dunes artificially "cemented" in place are like seawalls, blocking sediment derivation and migration, and thus creating new problems in other parts of the beach-dune system or island interior on barrier islands. Dunes are not static, rigid, permanent structures, and the dune line must migrate inland as the shoreline retreats.

Similarly, the natural vegetation that stabilizes dunes is in equilibrium with the sediment and biota. The roots of sea oats are colonized by vesicular-arbuscular mycorrhizal (VAM) fungi, which improve the sea oats' ability to take in nutrients and water. Artificial plantings of dune grasses do not fare well in pumped-in nourishment sands or in areas where these sands have been used to construct artificial dunes, because the VAM fungus is missing. Plant root systems can be inoculated with the VAM fungus in the nursery to improve colonization of the artificial plantings, but the point is that nature is far more complex than a simple engineering design. Even the differences in grain size and sorting between bulldozed sediment and natural windblown sand may influence dune stability and plant growth.

Retreat through Relocation

Moving buildings back or letting them fall into the sea has a long tradition along American shores. Retreating from the shoreline is the best way to ensure preservation of beaches for future generations. Although politically difficult, of course, this course of action is chosen by states that prohibit seawalls. On a shoreline lined with high-rise buildings, such as Pinellas County, Florida, or Gulf Shores, Alabama, retreat would be very difficult, but not impossible. It would be less difficult on Dauphin Island, Alabama, or St. George Island, Florida, where there are fewer and smaller buildings.

Gulf coast residents must make a choice. In the long run (decades), in a time of rising sea level, decreasing sand supplies, and decreasing funding, they can have beaches, or they can have shorefront buildings on beachless armored shores or shorter-lived artificial beaches. Having both buildings and beaches will be difficult and very costly. If we opt in favor of buildings, the beaches will be lost — as, ultimately, will be the buildings.

Relocation can be encouraged or implemented in many ways. Federal and state governments can end expenditures in support of beachfront development. Undeveloped beach areas can be acquired, an approach the state of Florida is currently using. Poststorm reconstruction of destroyed buildings and buildings that have exceeded their design lives can be prohibited. New developments can be required to purchase and set aside retreat areas. Strong incentives can be provided to encourage development in low-risk areas and to move development already in existence into low-risk areas. The Federal Emergency Management Agency (FEMA) encourages relocation through partial support for buying residences that have suffered repeated flooding (e.g., Baldwin County, Alabama, 1997). Relocation is the ultimate mitigation; however, support for it is very limited. Continued public education, especially for property purchasers, regarding risks from coastal hazards and the long-term costs of coastal development is essential to change public policy. For more information about implementing the relocation option, visit www.geo.duke.edu/psds.htm.

Are Variances Eroding Beach Protection Efforts?

The problem of shoreline engineering leading to beach narrowing and degradation is not exclusive to Florida and New Jersey, or to any one part of the continent. On Oahu, Hawaii, 30 percent of the island's sandy beaches have disappeared as a result of seawalls. The beaches of California are disappearing as well, although here the starvation of the beaches is partly because of dam construction and harbor protection, factors that are also contributing to the erosion of the Puerto Rico coastline. All in all, however, the Atlantic, Pacific, and Gulf stories are identical, only the names are different. Shore-hardening structures of various kinds either directly or indirectly cause loss of beaches wherever they are.

All around the country, the individual coastal states are finally beginning to view beaches as the national treasures they truly are. There is no question that the time will come when our remaining beaches will be like national parks, protected forever for the benefit of the public at large. Unlike Yellowstone Park, however, where one can be sure that Old Faithful will be in the same location 50 years from now, beach management policy will have to take into account that the sea level is rising and that the beaches are moving. Thus the beaches of the future may become mobile national parks! The National Park Service already has declared that beach movement will be allowed to occur on national seashores at whatever rate and style nature chooses.

The stated general policy of the Florida Department of Environmental Protection's Bureau of Beaches and Coastal Systems is to use armoring only as a last resort where no alternative is available to protect habitable and major public structures. Unfortunately, variances abound because all developed areas have habitable and major public structures, and relocation is not taken seriously as an alternative of less impact. So, agencies charged with protecting natural resources yield to political and economic pressure and opt to protect buildings.

Beaches and dunes are the Gulf coast's most valuable natural resources, arguably more valuable than private condos or cottages. These shores need help — the help of the public and of far-sighted planners and developers — if they are to be available for today and tomorrow.

Truths of the Shoreline

Studies of long-developed shorelines have generated a set of principles, or "universal truths," that are fundamental to low-risk, aesthetically pleasing development. These truths are evident to scientists who have studied the shoreline and to old-timers who have lived there all of their lives.

1. *Beach erosion is not a natural disaster.* Shoreline retreat is an integral and expected part of beach response to rising sea level, increased wave energy, or diminished sediment supply. Landward migration of beaches is particularly important to barrier island evolution.

2. *Erosion is not a problem until someone builds a stationary structure on a dynamic shoreline.* No buildings: no problem. Visit one of the state parks to verify this principle. The once-great beaches of the urbanized barriers no longer match the beauty of the near-natural park beaches.

3. *Shoreline erosion creates no problem for the beach.* What we call shoreline erosion is actually shoreline retreat. The beach simply changes its position in space. The beach does not disappear. Surfers, swimmers, fishers, and strolling lovers can't tell the difference.

4. *Human activities increase the rate of shoreline retreat.* Most shoreline modifications made by humans, including shoreline engineering, dune destruction, building construction, channel dredging, and jetty construction, reduce the sand supply to beaches.

5. *Shoreline engineering protects the interests of a very few, often at a very high cost to taxpayers.* On a typical Gulf coast reach, especially on barrier islands, the shorefront property that is responsible for the erosion problem (see truth no. 2) is owned by a few hundred people. Engineering structures protect the interests of those property owners rather than the interests of the thousands or hundreds of thousands of people who use the beaches.

6. *Shoreline stabilization, especially beach nourishment, can lead to intensified development.* The presence of a wide, new nourished beach replacing a narrow, eroded beach with waves rolling under buildings is a temptation developers cannot resist.

7. *Once you begin shoreline engineering, you can't stop it!* Shoreline hardening is rarely removed. Instead it usually grows larger and longer. And once a beach is nourished, it must be nourished again and again.

8. *You can have buildings or you can have beaches; but in the long run you cannot have both.* The ultimate truth is that we should avoid

the hazards, but if we choose to locate on the coast, then prudence dictates that we evaluate the level of risk. Structures and nourished beaches will not prevent hurricanes or stop the sea-level rise.

The final truth is that it is better to work with nature than to attempt to out-engineer nature. Learning to live by the rules of the sea will save time, money, and lives.

Simply stated, low-lying coasts and barrier islands are not safe for development! Given the right conditions, hurricanes, floods, winds, wave erosion, and inlet formation and migration can attack any coastal reach. The low-lying marshy coastal reaches are particularly susceptible to coastal flooding from storm surge. Furthermore, human activity such as dune or mangrove removal, and particularly construction, reduces the relative stability of the natural environment and raises the vulnerability to damage from natural hazards. When static (immobile) human-built structures are placed in a dynamic (mobile) system, they disrupt the balance of that system (fig. 5.1). Interference with the sand supply, disruption of vegetative cover, topographic alteration, and similar effects of structures actually create conditions favorable to the damage or loss of those structures. The wise coastal dweller will look for site safety clues that indicate the lowest possible risk before making a purchase, and afterward will utilize natural features (e.g., dune integrity, vegetation cover, elevation) to reduce the risk of property damage. The approach to assessing site safety presented here is modified from *Living by the Rules of the Sea* (appendix C, ref. 48).

The idea is to place your home in the least dynamic zone where it is most likely to survive a storm. For example, a condominium built in the pine forest on the back side of Perdido Island, Florida, should prove to be in a much safer site than the same condominium built on one of the low and narrow stretches of Gasparilla Island. Identify the rates and intensities of storm activity for a given segment of shoreline and use this knowledge as a basis for safe site selection.

Most individuals who buy property on or near Gulf beaches know very little about the environment they have moved there to enjoy. Often the

5.1 Storms are part of the process moving barrier islands upward and landward during a rising sea level. Buildings get in the way of that process. Here, Hurricane Opal damaged and destroyed many buildings near Destin, Florida. Notice the overwash into the interior of the island and along the roadway in the upper right. Photo by Rob Young.

only advice they receive with regard to site safety comes from realtors and developers, who are not known for their objectivity in this regard. Sometimes home or condo purchasers take the attitude that "since thousands of people live on this island, it can't be all that unsafe." To make that assumption when choosing a Gulf coast homesite is a serious and fundamental error (figs. 5.1 and 5.2).

The following sections might well be entitled "What you've wanted to know about near-the-beach site selection but couldn't figure out whom to ask."

Coastal Stability: Terra Infirma

Among the lessons taught by Hurricanes Andrew, Opal, Danny, Georges, Frederic, Camille, and associates is that coastlands, especially spits and barrier islands, respond to storms and other coastal processes as a single system. To design a structure able to live with the flexible nature of a mainland shore or barrier island, you must first evaluate the entire system in terms of physical processes and nature's response to human activities. The second step is to focus on the characteristics of the neighborhood, and then the individual building site. Keep in mind that neither a barrier island nor a low mainland coast is safe from hurricane winds, storm surge flooding, wave erosion, overwash, or, for barriers, inlet formation and migration. However, a low, bare, potentially migrating St. Joseph Peninsula or Santa Rosa Island, Florida, or Dauphin Island, Alabama, is more likely to suffer from these hazards than the inner-island forested beach ridges of St. Vincent Island or Sanibel Island. The latter will be subjected to coastal hazards, but with less frequency and probably less intensity than the former, at least over the short term. An island's or mainland coast's elevation and forest cover offer immediate clues to its stability. In general, you must consider how the coastal area has responded to previous storms.

Another important aspect for evaluating overall stability is to check the area's response to past human activity, particularly construction. For example, an island is not necessarily at low risk merely because it has been developed or because there are stabilization structures in place. More likely, the opposite is true. The shoreline of the central-southern section of Anna Maria Key, Florida, has been retreating since the 1920s at rates of between 1 and 3 feet per year. Photos from the 1950s and 1960s show a mix of coastal structures with no significant beach other than minor pockets. Since the 1950s, seawalls and groins have masked natural shoreline varia-

5.2 No recreational beach at high tide and condos crowded on the shore are the end result of building too close to the water, as illustrated at the northern end of Sand Key. Photo by Richard A. Davis Jr.

tions, and buildings and roads, initially built too close to the shore, suffer the consequences: frequent storm damage, continuous structural repairs, and no recreational beach.

As chapter 4 indicated, shore-hardening structures create conditions favorable both to beach loss and to their own destruction. The presence of groins, seawalls, or revetments on the beach tells you that the shoreline is subject to erosion, now compounded by the engineering structures (fig. 5.2). Such a shoreline certainly is to be avoided, even on a mainland coast.

Removal of vegetation, for purposes of construction or to get a better view of the sea, increases the potential for storm damage and creates a blowing sand nuisance. Roads to the beach built through the dune line act as overwash passes. Removal of dunes invites storm disasters because the elevation is lowered and the protective buffer action of the dune is lost. Hurricanes Fran (1996, North Carolina), Opal (1995, Florida and Alabama) and Hugo (1989, South Carolina) proved the effectiveness of high, wide dunes in preventing or reducing property damage. In contrast, coastal armoring failed to provide equivalent protection in all three cases; the walls were overtopped, breached, and became part of the damage statistics.

The political infrastructure of your prospective island or coastal community also has a strong bearing on overall safety. Unchecked growth or unenforced building and sand-dune protection codes are examples of social conditions that may create threats to health or safety. Overloaded sewage treatment systems, inadequate or unsafe escape routes, loss of natural storm protection, buildings lacking structural integrity, and vulnerable utilities are but a few examples of politically derived development problems. Developers and real estate interests often take a "head in the sand" attitude and are reluctant to face the reality that the beaches are retreating, that development disrupts the natural dynamics, or that the density of development often exceeds carrying capacity with respect to natural resources and processes.

Potential buyers aren't encouraged by words like *hazard, risk, mitigation,* and *cost.* And these terms apply community-wide, not just to individual properties. Eroding beaches, removed dunes, disappearing forest cover, beach nourishment projects, and failing seawalls are examples of community problems that all individual property owners pay for, whether or not their property is directly involved.

Once you are satisfied with an area's natural stability, its response to past storms and property development activities, and the political setting, the next important step is selecting the general location and specific site. The following site selection guide applies to your specific property; however, property lines are an artificial grid put down over dynamic environments.

Look at your site in the context of the developed or developable neighboring properties.

Selecting Your Site: Sunny Playground or Watery Tempest?

Human nature is such that we are willing to gamble if the potential reward is worth the risk. In the case of coastal living, the rewards are the amenities of the seashore and other coastal environments. Sunny-day decisions may overlook the realities of risk for losing your property and even your life. Like smart gamblers who know the odds and try to reduce the house advantage, beach-house buyers can and should identify the natural odds of coastal hazards and act accordingly. And you don't have to brave a storm to do this!

Structures placed in the least dynamic zones (stable areas subject to less sediment movement or change) are less likely to be damaged by coastal storms. If you can identify areas, rates, and intensities of natural physical activity, you have a basis for choosing a specific homesite. Consider, for example, an inland river and the flat areas (called the *floodplain*) next to it. Even casual observation reveals that rivers flood occasionally. Long-term observations show that the time and size of the floods follow a pattern of sorts. Perhaps the area adjacent to the river is flooded every spring, but the lower floodplain is flooded only every 5–10 years on average. Once or twice in a person's lifetime the flood will be devastating, covering an area greater than the adjacent floodplain, although that once or twice may be closely spaced in time. On this basis, you can predict the frequency and size of floods expected in a given area. Individual floods are described on the basis of the frequency of a given flood level. For instance, if water has reached a certain level only twice during a 100-year period of record, a flood rising to that level is called a 1-in-50-year flood. Unfortunately, this terminology leaves the impression that one need not worry about such a flood level for another 50 years after its occurrence. Not so! Such flood levels are spaced in time randomly, and can occur in successive years or even the same year! A better way of thinking about such floods is in terms of probability. Property in a 100-year-flood zone has a 1 percent probability of flooding in any given year. You could have two such floods in successive years, and it would not preclude the 1 percent probability of having another the third year. Like flipping pennies, you don't expect to see three heads in a row when you start with the first flip, but after two in a row, the chance that the third flip will be a head is the same as on the first flip — 50:50. And while not worrying about the next 100-year flood, you may experience the 70-year flood, or the 1,000-year flood of which we know nothing because we have no weather records of sufficient length to even make a prediction! Such big events have occurred and will happen again. Tens of thousands did not expect the great flood of 1997 in Minnesota and the Dakotas, but its occurrence does not preclude a repeat event very soon.

The same is true for the coastal zone and barrier islands. Floodwaters on the mainland coast may come from rivers, but more likely the flood is storm surge, the rising of the sea level during a storm, plus winds, waves, and sediments, mixed in the cauldron of a hurricane or southwester.

Of course, to build a house in a place that is flooded once every year, or even once every 10 years, would be foolish. Far better to locate where the likelihood of flooding is 1 percent in any given year (the likelihood of flooding being nearly 100 percent in the lifetime of the building), or, preferably, a much lower probability. Whether you choose to locate in a flood-prone area at all should be determined by how important it is to choose that site, the level of economic loss you are willing to sustain, and, most of all, the level of risk to which you are willing to expose family and friends occupying the site.

The frequency and elevation of storm surge flooding in coastal areas is somewhat predictable. Potential storm surges for hurricanes of all strengths are calculated using a mathematical model called SLOSH (for *s*ea, *l*ake, and *o*verland *s*urges from *h*urricanes). The flooding levels are displayed in a series of maps showing what areas would be flooded in each category of hurricane. The main use of SLOSH maps is for selecting evacuation routes and shelters. SLOSH models are usually run under a cooperative program between the U.S. Army Corps of Engineers, the Federal Emergency Management Agency, the National Hurricane Center, and the local state emergency management agency. You should be able to access the SLOSH data from your local community government office or from the agencies just mentioned. SLOSH maps for the Alabama and west Florida coastal counties show that potential storm surges for category 1 storms range from around 2–3 feet in Escambia and Okaloosa Counties, Florida, to 8 feet or more in Dauphin Island, Alabama, and Wakulla and Dixie Counties, Florida. For a category 3 or greater storm, surges will be at least in the 10-foot range, and around 15 feet in Wakulla County. The storm surge potential is greater where the offshore profile is gentler, and also increases where the shoreline is concave to funnel the surge water.

Although no one can predict exactly when a storm that causes flooding to a certain level will occur, the SLOSH maps can be used as a basis in planning coastal structures. If the 1-in-100-year storm surge flood level is the basis for planning and is 25 feet for a particular stretch of coast, the elevation of the house should be greater than 25 feet. Because storm waves will further increase that height requirement, you should seek even higher elevations in addition to using a construction technique that raises the house several feet off the ground (see chapter 8).

The 100-year flood level is a standard used in both inland and coastal regions as the basis for building codes and zoning ordinances adopted by communities that participate in the National Flood Insurance Program (see chapter 9). Flood level data and calculated wave heights are available from the Federal Emergency Management Agency or can be obtained from community planning and insurance offices (Flood Insurance Rate Maps show these elevations; see appendix B). By comparison, the Dutch use 1-in-500-year and even 1-in-1,000-year event probabilities for planning and regulating purposes!

Stability Indicators:
Can You Read Nature's Record?

Coastal processes often leave a record of past events or reflect the natural dynamic history of an area. The natural attributes of a site can guide prospective buyers and builders in evaluating the site's vulnerability to potentially hazardous processes and events. The primary natural indicators include terrain (landform types), elevation, and vegetation type and cover, but numerous parameters should be considered (table 5.1).

Terrain and Elevation

Terrain and elevation are good measures of an area's safety from various adverse natural processes. Low, flat areas are subject to destructive wave attack, overwash, storm surge flooding, and blowing sand (fig. 5.3). The flooding of low areas is often from the landward side. Figure 3.7 shows expected storm surge levels for different parts of the west Florida and Alabama coasts.

Vegetation

Vegetation often indicates relative environmental stability, age, and elevation. For example, the pine forests along stretches of the Bay County and Walton County shorelines are inundated relatively rarely. However, the marshy or mangrove shorelines of Dixie and Levy Counties in the Big Bend area and Collier and Monroe Counties in the Ten Thousand Islands area are subject to frequent flooding. Pine forests do not survive frequent salt-

Table 5.1. Parameters for Evaluating Site-Specific Risks from Coastal Hazards (designed specifically for shorelines developed in unconsolidated, potentially erodible materials, such as bluffed shorelines or sandy systems [e.g., barrier islands, barrier beaches])

| Parameter | Risk Level | | |
	High	Moderate	Low
Site Elevation	<3 meters	3–6 meters	>6 meters
Beach Width, Slope, and Thickness	Narrow and flat, thin with mud, peat, or stumps exposed	Wide and flat, or narrow and steep	Wide with well-developed berm
Overwash	Overwash apron or terrace (frequent overwash)	Overwash fans (occasional overwash)	No overwash
Site Position Relative to Inlet or River Mouth	Very near	Within sight	Distant
Dune Configuration	No dunes (see Overwash)	Low, or discontinuous dunes	High, continuous, unbreached ridge, dune field
Coastal Shape	Concave or embayed	Straight	Convex
Vegetation on Site	Little, toppled, or immature vegetation	Well-established shrubs and grasses, none toppled	Mature vegetation, forested, no evidence of erosion
Drainage	Poor	Moderate	Good
Area Landward of Site	Lagoon, marsh, or river	Floodplain or low-elevation terrace	Upland
Natural Offshore Protection	None, open water	Frequent bars offshore	Submerged reef, limited fetch
Offshore Shelf	Wide and shallow	Moderate	Steep and narrow

Source: From table 6.2 in *The North Carolina Shore and Its Barrier Islands*, by Orrin H. Pilkey et al. (appendix C, ref. 48).

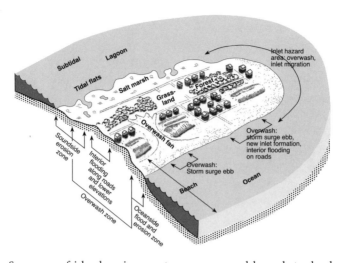

5.3 Summary of island environments, processes, and hazards to development. The development grid enhances these hazards by removing protective shrub and forest cover, providing avenues for overwash, and siting buildings at low elevations too close to the shoreline.

water intrusions. Mangroves and salt marsh vegetation, on the other hand, require frequent intrusion.

In general, the taller and thicker the vegetative growth, the more stable the site and the lower the risk for development (see fig. 1.10). Maritime forests grow only at elevations high enough to preclude frequent overwash. The fact that a mature maritime forest takes at least 100 years to develop is further assurance that forest areas are generally the most stable and offer the lowest-risk homesites (fig. 5.4). Another advantage of construction in a maritime forest is the sheltering effect of the trees from hurricane-force winds. The problem is that building in these low-to-moderate-risk sites disturbs the vegetation, destroying the very aspect that helps reduce risk. Major clearance of such vegetation for large structures or extensive development not only increases the new buildings' vulnerability but also increases risk to adjacent properties.

The exception to the low-risk-forest-site rule is where rapidly eroding shorelines have advanced into the maritime forest, and where inlets are cutting into forested beach ridges.

Along the southern Florida coast, mangroves fill the ecological niche that marsh grasses fill farther north. Mangroves perform the same ecological function — that is, as sediment stabilizers, flood control, and habitat — as marsh grass and are sensitive to the same negative impacts of development and pollution.

5.4 Maritime forests offer low-risk homesites and indicate a more stable environment than the shorefront, as shown by this walkway through the forest at Vanderbilt Beach. The trees offer protection from storms. The thicker the vegetation, the more protection. Photo by Jason Smith.

Mangroves once lined the quiet-water shorelines of much of west Florida. The most famous and extensive mangroves in Florida are those lining the Ten Thousand Islands. But mangroves, like dunes, have fallen victim to the bulldozer and are no longer a common sight on developed Florida shorelines. Where they remain they should be protected. They are excellent erosion buffers, and in fact their intertwining roots capture and stabilize sediment, causing the shoreline to build outward.

Salt marshes, ecosystems that also flourish in quiet waters, often line the bay sides of islands and the mainland margins of bays, especially in the Big Bend area. The true salt marsh is a unique botanical environment because it consists of a single plant, *Spartina*. Marshes are important breeding grounds for many marine species and offer considerable protection from wave attack as well. Many west Florida salt marshes were filled in for development, but that practice is now illegal. Areas around finger canals often have been built up with material dredged from the marsh to form the canal. Nature usually takes revenge on those who occupy such sites. Buried marsh offers poor support for building foundations and does not provide a quality groundwater reservoir. Thus, such sites typically have an inadequate supply of fresh water and septic systems that do not function properly, and their effluent waste has often closed adjacent marshes to shell-fishing. Furthermore, as low-elevation areas they are susceptible to flooding from even minor storms. New marsh can be created on bay shorelines, and such replanting should be considered as an erosion buffer alternative to bulkheads and seawalls.

If you are building in a vegetated area, preserve as much vegetation as possible, including undergrowth. Trees are excellent protection from flying debris during hurricanes. Remove large, dead trees from the construction site, but conserve the surrounding forest, including the undergrowth, to protect your home. Stabilize bare construction areas as soon as possible with new plantings. Destabilized dunes or the presence of an active, migrating dune field on the margin of a forest may threaten the stability of a forest site.

Maritime forests and thickets are characterized by a diverse flora (for more information, check with the Florida Department of Environmental Protection, Division of Recreation and Parks). Honeymoon Island has one of the few remaining virgin slash pine stands in south Florida, along with mangrove swamps, seagrass beds, salt marshes, tidal flats, and sand dunes. Caladesi Island, Florida, has auburn hairgrass near the Gulf shore, mangrove forests on the eastern shore, and grass flats. The dunes have sea oats, beach morning glory, and sea purslane, while the more stable environment behind the dunes has palmetto, hercules club, and sea grape. Farther into the island is maritime hammock, more stable because of the higher elevation, with a relatively closed canopy of live oak, red bay, sabal palm, and southern red cedar. The high ground of Caladesi has slash pines in an open-canopy forest with an understory of wax myrtle and palmetto. In contrast, highly developed islands do not have a diverse biota. The seaward edge of the natural forest on such islands has a lower forest canopy and may be "pruned" by the salt spray.

Australian pines (*Casuarina*) flourish on the beaches of west Florida, but they are now considered to be unwelcome intruders. They have shallow root systems and are easily blown over or knocked over by storm waters to cause damage or become obstructions to evacuation and recovery. They do not stabilize dunes or help them to grow, and they generate large amounts of debris to be cleaned up after beach storms. Their toxic needles do not support undergrowth or encourage a diverse biota. These pines are attractive, but it is better to remove them and plant dune vegetation. They illustrate the principle that it is better to use native species when attempting to stabilize a site through artificial plantings.

Seashells

Even seashells can provide clues regarding stability because they are moved about by both humans and natural processes. A mixture of brown-stained and natural-colored shells often washes onshore from the ocean side during storms. When they are found inland of the beach, such shells indicate overwash zones. Don't build where overwash occurs. If you must do so, elevate the building enough so as not to interfere with the process.

Mixed black and white shells without brown or natural-colored shells are almost certainly a sign that material has been dredged and pumped from nearby waterways. Such material is used to fill low areas on islands, to fill inlets that break through islands during storms, or to nourish eroding beaches. Thus, such a shell mixture may indicate an unstable area where development should be avoided.

Soil Profiles

A soil profile takes a long time to develop, so a mature soil suggests building-site stability. White-bleached sand overlying yellow sand to a depth of 2–3 feet (often found in forest areas) suggests such stability. Note the soil profile by looking in a road cut, finger canal, or a pit that you have dug. Keep in mind that even formerly stable areas can be eroded by a migrating shoreline, so you may find a "stable" soil profile in an unstable position, such as in the wave-cut scarp at the back of a beach. Such is the case along the shoreline from Apalachicola Bay westward, where beautifully developed soil profiles are exposed on actively eroding sand bluffs. Avoid areas where profiles show layers of peat or other organic materials. Such layers have a high water content and lack the strength to support an overlying structure. The weight of a house can compress the layers, causing the house to sink. Furthermore, such soil conditions cause septic tank problems.

Coastal Environments: How Does Your Site Fit the Bigger Picture?

Inland developments typically occupy a single environment such as a pine forest or former pastureland. In contrast, the coastal zone is characterized by small areas of very different environments (see figs. 1.9 and 1.10), and typical developments overlap environmental boundaries without regard to the consequences. By knowing which environment(s) a building site and adjacent properties occupy, you can identify prevailing conditions that may or may not be conducive to development. Typical barrier island and sandy coast environments in southern Florida include primary dunes, dune fields, overwash fans, grasslands, inlets, maritime forests and thickets, marshes, and mangroves. On the Big Bend and southwestern coasts of Florida even the slightest variation in elevation or substrate will change the environment.

Primary Dunes

The next best thing to being at a high elevation is to have some rows of dunes between you and the forces of the sea (fig. 5.5). Dunes are formed by wind blowing sand in from the beach. Primary dunes, the most important, are usually defined as the row of dunes closest to the ocean, although a distinct line or row may be absent. They serve as a sand reservoir that feeds the beach, island interior, and back island, and they provide elevation and width as a temporary line of defense against wind and waves. Primary dunes should be protected at all costs. An example of a well-developed, essentially undisturbed primary dune system presently can be seen on St. Joseph spit in Gulf County. Although primary dunes are the natural main line of defense against erosion and storm damage to man-made structures, this line of defense is a leaky one because of the overwash passes between the dunes. Storm surge will find its way through, across, and around these passes to help destroy the dunes, as history will attest. Alabama lost much of its dune line in Hurricane Frederic (1979), and Opal (1995) removed dunes in the Florida Panhandle. However, buildings in locations with good dunes before the storm suffered less damage from Hurricane Opal than did

5.5 Which houses are safer? The houses to the left, built back behind the frontal dunes, have a lower potential for damage during storms. The houses closer to the beach, at the front right, are at higher risk for property damage. Simple rules such as prudent siting of structures on lots can prevent damage later on. Photo by Rob Young.

adjacent properties without dunes, even though the dunes themselves were destroyed (appendix C, ref. 17).

Unfortunately, many, if not most, primary dunes have been removed for beach views or beach access in places of heavy development. When development interferes with the dune system, both the natural and the developed environments suffer. Many existing houses were constructed by notching the landward side of the frontal dune, creating built-in destabilization. We must recognize the mobility of dune systems, even those stabilized by vegetation. Off-road vehicles, foot traffic, drought, and fire destroy vegetation and destabilize dunes. The construction of wooden dune walkovers should be encouraged to eliminate interference with dune processes. By prohibiting vehicles on the dunes and by building boardwalks and footbridges over rather than through them, we may preserve the dunes that remain.

Remedial steps can be taken to restore or stabilize dunes artificially in cases where dunes (oceanfront or interior dunes) were destroyed or are being threatened. Planting dune grasses and sea oats in bare areas stabilizes existing dunes and encourages additional dune growth. Sand fencing also is commonly used to trap sand and promote dune growth (see chapter 4 for more details).

The high elevation of a dune does not in itself render a site safe. An area adjacent to the shore with a high erosion rate is likely to lose its dune protection during the average lifetime of a house. Even setback ordinances, which require that structures be placed a minimum distance behind the dune, do not ensure long-term protection. Setbacks sometimes are based on historical erosion rates, and nothing guarantees that future erosion rates will be the same. If your home is located on a primary dune, you should expect to lose it during the next major storm.

Dune Fields

Dune fields are open, bare-to-grassy dune areas found between the primary dunes and the maritime forest (if present), or on the back side of the island. Stable dune fields offer sites that are at relatively low risk from the hazards of wave erosion, overwash, and storm surge flooding, if the elevation is sufficiently high. However, digging up the dunes for construction may cause blowing sand, destabilize vegetation, and increase sand movement. Do not build where dunes show bare, unvegetated surfaces; such dunes are active. When blowing sand does accumulate on roads, drives, and such, the sand should be returned to the area from which it came rather than hauling it away, as is often done.

Overwash Fans

Overwash fans develop when water thrown up by waves and storm surge flows between and around dunes, or across developments. Such waters carry sand that is deposited in flat, fan-shaped masses (see fig. 2.9). Stained, bleached, and natural-colored shells are also transported to the inner island in this manner. Overwash fans provide sand to form and maintain dunes and to build up the island's elevation. Where primary dunes are high and continuous, overwash is relatively unimportant and is restricted to the back beach and nearshore areas. Where dunes are absent, low, or discontinuous, overwash fans may extend across the entire island.

During severe hurricanes, only the highest elevations (generally above 15–20 ft) are safe from overwash. Hurricane Opal left extensive overwash deposits more than 3 feet thick along much of the coast from Gulf Shores, Alabama, to Fort Walton Beach, Florida. Santa Rosa Island, Florida, was completely overwashed in places by Opal (appendix C, ref. 36).

The overwash fans created when low-elevation islands are struck by major hurricanes are sometimes so extensive that they coalesce into sheets called overwash terraces. Overwash sand may damage or bury roads (see figs. 2.7 and 5.1) and block escape routes. Level roads that are cut straight to the beach often become overwash passes during storms, especially where they notch dunes. Roads built to increase development may contribute to the destruction. Such roads should end landward of the dune and curve or cross an island obliquely rather than perpendicular to the shore. Only emergency vehicle accesses should go over the dunes.

Try to avoid building on overwash fans, especially if they are fresh and unvegetated. Such areas may be difficult to recognize, however, if the fans have been destroyed by bulldozing or sand removal. If no alternative site is available, elevate the building and keep the area under the building open to allow overwash to continue and to build up sand. Use overwash deposits removed from roads and driveways to rebuild adjacent dunes, or return the sediment to the beach; do not remove the sand from the area. Planting dune grass and other natural vegetation on overwash deposits may help stabilize the deposit and trap additional sand.

Grasslands

Grasslands are typically located either behind dune fields or on the back side of islands just inside the salt marsh. Such areas may be relatively flat, built up as a terrace of coalescent overwash fans, and generally are subject to future flooding and overwash. Natural grasslands may be difficult to distinguish from areas flattened for development by bulldozers, but the former are characterized by a diversity of plants (e.g., saltmeadow cordgrass, yucca, cactus, and thistle).

Inlets

Inlets are the rivers or channels that separate islands. As a hurricane approaches a barrier island, strong onshore winds drive storm surge waters and waves against the island and up the estuaries. As the storm passes, the wind either stops blowing or shifts to blow seaward, causing surge waters to return seaward. If existing inlets do not allow the water to escape fast enough, the returning water cuts a new inlet from the marsh side. Such a situation occurred near East Pass following Hurricane Opal.

Low, narrow island areas that lack extensive salt marsh and are near the mouths of rivers or estuaries are likely spots for inlet development. Spits, common on the ends of barrier islands, are particularly vulnerable (e.g., the northern end of St. Joseph Peninsula). Residents are wise not to develop on this bit of expanding sand as the inlet will eventually, and perhaps suddenly, change the location of its channel. Islands, particularly the low areas in inlet zones, are often breached by small channels during storms, either by the storm surge flood or, more often, by strong storm surge ebb currents. These channels are not inlets in a strict sense, but rather develop and persist to accommodate internal island drainage. Temporary swashes off small creek mouths are similar. While these features are temporary and often fill with sediment naturally, the likelihood of reactivation make them extreme-risk zones with respect to development. The Army Corps of Engineers or the state Department of Transportation is often prompt in filling in such channels after storms, and the future property owner may not realize that the site is in the throat of a former channel, or that the access route (escape) to and from the property will be cut during a storm.

Once formed, some inlets tend to migrate laterally along the barrier island, although there is wide variation in individual inlet behavior through time. In western Florida, however, many inlets are stabilized with jetties to prevent their natural migration. A migrating inlet will destroy any structures and property in its path. Sediment carried seaward through the inlet builds an underwater ebb-tidal delta. In time the delta may fill the inlet, closing it naturally.

You may recall from chapter 2 that tidal delta formation is an important means of island widening. The tidal deltas in back of old inlets may make the sites of old inlets relatively safe areas on which to build. The width promotes dune and vegetation growth, and provides ample room to build far back from the beach. Also, the likelihood of a new inlet forming at the site of an old, naturally closed one is relatively low. Artificially filled inlets, on the other hand, are unstable areas for development.

Water Resources, Services, and Utilities

In addition to assessing risks from natural hazards in your site analysis, you should consider water resources, pollution potential, infrastructure, density of present and future development, and similar human-development aspects of the site. Some of these topics are covered in chapter 7. If you are relying on groundwater, will the supply be adequate and unpolluted? Is the soil suitable for a septic system, and is the septic system compatible with maintaining groundwater quality? If you are relying on service lines (e.g., water, waste disposal, electric, telephone), will they survive a storm? Or are the utility poles lining your escape route potential obstructions when blown down? The more construction in the area, the greater the amount of debris that will be moved about in a storm.

Finger Canals

A common island alteration of the 1960s and 1970s that still causes coastal problems is the finger canal (fig. 5.6). *Finger canal* is the term applied to channels dug into an island for the purpose of providing additional waterfront lots. Finger canals can be found in many developed coastal communities in Florida and Alabama.

When finger canals are dug, they cut into the natural underground water system and can cause a host of problems (fig. 5.7). There are six major problems associated with finger canals:

1. They lower the groundwater table.
2. Salt or brackish canal water seeps into the groundwater table and pollutes the groundwater.
3. Septic seepage into the canal pollutes the canal water.
4. Stagnation resulting from lack of tidal flushing or poor circulation with sound waters pollutes the canal water.
5. Higher canal water temperatures cause fish kills.
6. Nutrient overloading and deoxygenation of the water cause fish kills.

A further problem is that finger canals sometimes begin to fill with sediment. This leads to requests for dredging, which is expensive and may not be permitted for the above reasons.

5.6 Before the ecological importance and environmental sensitivity of marsh-lands were understood, such areas were considered wasteland. Finger canals were dredged to create "waterfront property," as in this example from Marco Island. The Marco Island Yacht Club is located on the bank of the Marco River at right rear. Courtesy of Herb Savage.

Bad odors, flotsam of dead fish and algal scum, and contamination of adjacent shellfishing grounds are symptomatic of polluted canal water. Thus, finger canals often become health hazards or simply places too un-pleasant to live near. Residents along some older finger canals have built walls to separate their homes from the canals.

If you consider buying a lot on a canal, remember that canals are usually not harmful until houses are built along them. Short canals, a few tens of yards long, are generally much safer than long ones. Also, while most ca-nals are initially deep enough for small-craft traffic, sand movement on the back side of barrier islands results in the filling of the canals, which can lead to navigation problems.

Finally, on narrow islands, finger canals dug almost to the ocean side offer a path of least resistance to storm waters and are therefore potential locations for new inlets. Hurricane Frederic in 1979 exploited finger canals as easy sites to cut into islands (fig. 5.8). Property owners along finger ca-nals on Dauphin Island, Alabama, found themselves owning tiny islands or open water after Frederic.

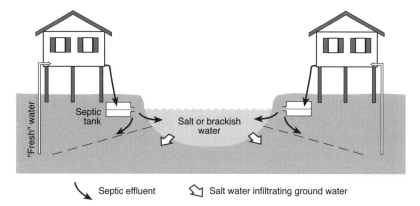

| Septic effluent | Salt water infiltrating ground water |

5.7 The finger canal saga. Saltwater intrusion ruins the freshwater supply. Intrusion of septic tank effluent pollutes the canal.

5.8 Post–Hurricane Frederic (1979) view of finger canals on Dauphin Island, Alabama. As the sea washed over the island, the canals became channels that focused erosion, leading to their breaching and the isolation of intercanal property (islands). In other cases, overwash sand filled in canals. Photograph provided by the Topographic Bureau of the Florida Department of Transportation.

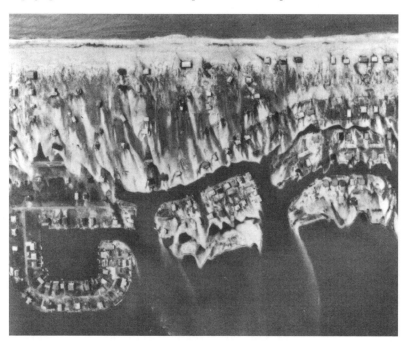

Site Risk: Do You Know the Rules for Survival?

In order to determine a site's vulnerability or risk potential, it is necessary to evaluate all of the prevalent dynamic processes. Information on storm surge, overwash, erosion rates, inlet migration, longshore drift, and other processes may be obtained from maps, aerial photographs, scientific literature, or personal observations. Appendix C provides an annotated list of scientific sources, many available at little or no cost. You are encouraged to obtain those pertinent to your situation. Although developers and planners usually have the resources and the expertise to use them in making decisions, they sometimes ignore critical information. In the past, the individual buyer was not likely to seek the information needed to determine the suitability of a given site. Today's buyer should be better informed.

Buyers, builders, or planners can assess the level of risk they are willing to take with respect to coastal hazards. The listing of specific dangers and cautions below provides a basis for taking appropriate precautions in site selection, construction, and evacuation plans. Our recommendation is to avoid extreme- and high-risk zones. Keep in mind, however, that small maps of large areas are generalized and that every site must be evaluated individually. Low-risk sites may exist in high-risk zones, whereas very dangerous sites may exist in moderate-to-low-risk zones.

The following list summarizes characteristics essential to site safety:

1. The site's elevation is above the anticipated storm surge level (see fig. 3.7).
2. The site is behind a natural protective barrier such as a line of sand dunes that are preferably 30 or more feet in height and 100 feet in basal width.
3. The site is well away from a migrating inlet.
4. The site is in an area of shoreline growth (accretion) or low shoreline erosion. Evidence of an eroding shoreline includes:
   a. sand bluff or dune scarp at back of beach;
   b. stumps or peat exposed on beach;
   c. slumped features such as trees, dunes, or man-made structures; and
   d. protective devices such as seawalls, groins, or replenished sand.

   You can also contact the Florida Department of Environmental Protection, Bureau of Beaches and Coastal Systems, or the Alabama Department of Environmental Control (see appendix B for addresses and phone numbers) for more information on erosion rates.
5. The site is located on a portion of the island backed by healthy salt marsh.

6. The site is away from low-elevation, narrow portions of the island.
7. The site is in an area of no or infrequent historic overwash.
8. The site is in a vegetated area that suggests stability.
9. The site drains water readily.
10. The fresh groundwater supply is adequate and uncontaminated. There is proper spacing between water wells and septic systems.
11. Soil and elevation are suitable for efficient septic tank operation.
12. No compactible layers such as peat are present in the soil. (The site is not on a buried salt marsh.)
13. Adjacent structures are adequately spaced and of sound construction.
14. Structure design preserves natural protection.

Escape Routes: Do You Have an Emergency Plan?

The 1995 multiple hurricane experience in the Panhandle illustrates the evacuation problem faced by most coastal residents. According to newspaper reports, emergency operations officials noted after Hurricane Erin that the region could not handle massive evacuation. Shortly thereafter, Hurricane Opal sent thousands "onto clogged roadways which prevented many from escaping the storm's fierce winds. . . . People were trapped . . . on all roads leading out of the two-county area, including Interstate 10 and U.S. 29. Those heading west, ran into Alabama residents fleeing Baldwin County and the Mobile area" (*Pensacola News Journal*, October 5, 1995). Traffic was backed up for 10–30 miles, in part because of bottlenecks created by road construction projects (bad timing) and the usual individual auto breakdowns. By noon, just 5 hours before Opal's eye wall made landfall, 20–40 accidents had occurred and hundreds of cars were abandoned in the medians and roadsides of the major arteries. Loss of a bridge caused more re-routing — all in pouring rain and wind. Local shelters, some not built to shelter standards, were overcrowded. Crowded local motels ran out of food and were without electricity.

Some believe this experience is a strong argument for more and larger roads, but more roads will simply bring more people into the hazard zone. Once you are stuck in four lanes of traffic gridlock — or six lanes — you have nowhere to go. In the case of Opal, officials finally had to tell the remaining residents *not* to evacuate out of the area, but instead to go to the nearest shelter. Clearly, the emphasis should be on strengthening, enlarging, and increasing the number of shelters, along with road improvement. But the real issue is how many people can the system handle?

If the Panhandle's Opal experience sounds frightening, consider that in 1992, southwest Florida was ranked first in the "Worst Case Top Ten Problem Areas" for evacuation clearance times; southeast Florida was ranked fourth; and the Florida Keys ranked fifth (appendix C, ref. 50). The Panhandle didn't even make the top ten! The point is, you need to be informed, and you need to have an emergency plan.

The threat of hurricanes makes it essential to have a route that will permit escape from an island to a safe location inland within a reasonable length of time. The presence of a ready escape route near a building site is essential to site safety, especially in high-rise and high-density housing areas where the number of people to be evacuated, transported, and housed elsewhere is large.

Although the allure of a vacation is "getting away from it all" and being out of touch, coastal vacationers should make one exception. Always keep an eye and ear out for the weather.

Remember: STAY INFORMED. DON'T WAIT. LEAVE EARLY.

Select an Escape Route ahead of Time

Check to see if any part of a potential escape route is at a low elevation, and thus subject to blockage by overwash or flooding; if so, seek an alternate route. Several exit routes from islands are flood-prone. Note whether there are bridges along the route. Remember that some residents will be evacuating pleasure boats and that fishing boats will be seeking safer waters; thus, drawbridges will be accommodating both boats and automobiles. Periodically reevaluate the escape route you have chosen — especially if the area in which you live has grown. With more people using the route, it may not be as satisfactory as you once thought.

Use the Escape Route Early

Be aware that several coastal areas and islands have only one route for escape to and/or via the mainland, and in some cases the mainland route is through a very extensive flood zone. In the event of a hurricane warning, leave the hazard area immediately; if you wait, the route may be blocked or flooded. Anyone who has experienced the evacuation of a community knows about the chaos at such bottlenecks. Depend on it: excited drivers will cause wrecks, cars will run out of gas and have flat tires, and cars with frightened occupants will be lined up for miles behind them. Be sure to have plans for where you will go. Keep alternative destinations in mind in case you find the original refuge filled or in danger. Finally, find a place of last refuge where you can go rather than being stuck in your car should the situation arise. Often, parking garages *above* the first floor and the lee-side rooms of high-rise condominiums and hotels are good bets. Remember to plan and then follow your plan. Nothing less than your lives are at stake.

Armed with knowledge of historical and active coastal processes, hazards, vulnerability, and risks of coastal areas, you can evaluate your favorite coast, island, community, neighborhood, existing house, or building site. Observations of Gulf shores and their communities, particularly barrier islands, after several hurricanes and winter storms suggest that property damage can be lessened significantly by prudent site selection and proper location and construction of structures.

The coastal hazard summaries and maps in this chapter assess the risks of hurricane and winter storm damage based on the geologic setting and natural processes of the various coastal reaches. This technique, known as *coastal risk mapping,* uses physical processes and coastal landform characteristics to rate the overall risk of storm damage to coastal property as "extreme," "high," "moderate," or "low." Coastal and island characteristics considered in making the risk maps (RMS) include elevation and forest cover; island width; frontal and island interior sand dune height, width, and distribution; potential for inlet formation; modern inlet dynamics; erosion or accretion rates; historical storm response; engineering structures and projects; and other human modifications of the natural environment (see appendix C, ref. 48, for more information on risk mapping). The risk maps are available for viewing in more detail at the following web site: http://www.geo.duke.edu/Research/psds/psds_hazmaps.htm. The maps are based on published data, aerial photographs, maps, and personal communications and observations. They present risk zones (extreme, high, moderate, or low) relative to the potential property damage from the passage of a low category 3 hurricane, such as Opal (1995).

Risk maps can guide community planning and individual site selection, and can help determine viable property damage mitigation alternatives for individual sites. Ultimately, the mitigation measures you take beforehand will help reduce storm-loss expenditures, result in more affordable insurance, and ease the burden on government disaster response and recovery programs. The risk categories used in the assessments and on the maps are defined below.

Areas or sites classified as *extreme risk* are at low elevation, within the 100-year flood level, and exposed to open ocean, an inlet, or a wide lagoon, so that waves greater than 3 feet are likely (FIRM V zones; see chapter 9). These areas are highly susceptible to wave attack, overwash, storm surge scour, and flooding from heavy rains, and often are affected by erosional shoreline retreat. Vegetation consists only of sparse beach or dune grasses, and protective dunes are nonexistent. The potential for inlet formation or migration and perilous evacuation routes add to the hazards. An *extreme risk* designation makes a site or reach unsuitable for development.

High risk indicates that at least three real dangers are present from among the following: flood potential, wave impact, erosion, overwash, inlet migration or formation, poor escape routes, and lack of natural protection from dunes, elevation, or vegetation. These areas are at low elevation and within the 100-year flood zone (FIRM A zones), making them very susceptible to wave attack and flooding by storm surge and heavy rains. High-risk zones are unsafe for development.

Moderate risk implies that two of the high-risk processes listed above put the property at risk. The area or site is above the 100-year flood zone (FIRM X zone) but lacks maritime forest or dense shrub thicket, resulting in high vulnerability to wind attack. Moderate-risk zones may or may not be subject to flooding and are unlikely to suffer direct wave attack, but the probability of damage to or loss of property is high over the lifetime of the property. Short-term or high-rainfall flooding cannot be ruled out.

Low-risk areas or sites are above the 100-year flood zone (FIRM X zone), away from wave attack, and well forested. A low-risk zone is an area where no more than one of the high-risk hazards is likely. Keep in mind, however, that one of these processes is all it takes for damage or destruction, so "low risk" is not risk free!

Some Gulf communities and individuals have attempted for decades to protect their tourist economies and beachfront properties from natural coastal processes by building walls and other engineered structures. These hardened shores are likely to be high- or extreme-risk areas and should be avoided for building sites.

Virtually all coastal areas are at high to extreme risk from a category 4 or

5 hurricane. Differentiation into risk zones is useless for such storms! The relative risk zones presented here are based on the risk afforded to property by a low category 3 hurricane hitting at or near the site in question. A low category 3 hurricane will have winds of 111–120 mph. The typical storm surge will range from 5 to 12 feet, depending on coastal configuration and offshore bathymetry.

Note that this assessment emphasizes the risk of property damage but does not assess risks to inhabitants. In general, areas with high potential for property damage are also areas of high risk for humans, but low-risk sites are not always safe for their inhabitants either. Difficulty of evacuation is an example of a human risk that may be entirely independent of building site safety (e.g., the only escape route from your moderate-risk site is through a high-risk zone). So, regardless of site location, always evacuate if ordered to do so, and know your evacuation route ahead of time.

This risk assessment focuses mainly on the developed and developable Gulf coast and offers risk maps for more than 450 miles of coastline. Most of the undeveloped islands are either military installations or within national seashores or state parks and were not mapped because they will not be developed in the foreseeable future. The same is true for wetland coasts of the mainland.

The coastal descriptions are organized geographically into four sections, presented clockwise from Alabama to the Florida Panhandle, around the Big Bend, and down the western Florida peninsula: (1) the Northwest Barrier Island Chain, (2) the Big Bend Marsh Coast, (3) the West-Central Florida Barrier Island Chain, and (4) the Ten Thousand Islands Mangrove Coast (see fig. 1.7).

The Northwest Barrier Island Chain

Alabama

The Alabama open-Gulf coast includes Dauphin Island and a few nearby smaller islands in Mobile County west of Mobile Bay and the Baldwin County barrier shoreline east of Mobile Bay (see fig. 1.2). Along approximately 55 miles of open-water shoreline about half of the beaches are receding, typically by 2–5 feet per year in recent decades. On both sides of Mobile Pass, beaches are receding — up to as much as 50 feet per year on the eastern end of Dauphin Island. Inlet jetties and dredging have caused marked shoreline changes. At Perdido Pass, sand is trapped west of the jetty, widening that section of the beach. On the other hand, the coastal construction control line (CCCL) on the eastern end of Dauphin Island was

6.1 Hurricane Georges (1998) caused flooding along the interior roadways of places such as Dauphin Island in Mobile County, Alabama, by a combination of storm surge and rain. Photo by Tracy Monegan Rice.

overtaken by shoreline recession. Beach fluctuations are common throughout the area from Dauphin Island to Perdido Key.

Mobile County (RM 1)

Mobile County shorelines include Dauphin Island, several small islands, the Mobile urban shoreline, and other waterfront properties along the northern shore of Mississippi Sound and western Mobile Bay. Much of this area is highly vulnerable to flooding from storms such as Hurricane Georges (fig. 6.1). Storm surge from Hurricane Georges in September 1998 ranged from 5 to 12 feet, with the peak high estimated at 11.9 feet at Fort Morgan and more than 9 feet in West Mobile Bay. These shores are considered high-to-extreme-risk areas.

Dauphin Island (RMS 1, 2)

Dauphin Island has the distinction of being the only barrier island along the coast of Alabama, since Petit Bois Island migrated out of the state and into Mississippi during the nineteenth century (fig. 6.2). Dauphin Island is a low, narrow strip of sand, except for the wider eastern end. Approximately 15 miles long, it protects Mississippi Sound and the mainland shore of Mobile County from the direct onslaught of hurricanes. Regular dredging of the Mobile Ship Channel affects Dauphin Island, depending on whether the dredged sand is placed offshore or onto the Sand Island shoal system, which provides sheltering from waves. Over the years, as much as

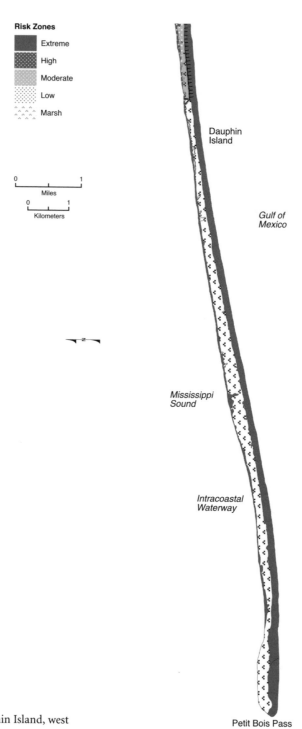

Risk Zones

- Extreme
- High
- Moderate
- Low
- Marsh

0   1
Miles

0   1
Kilometers

N

Dauphin
Island

Gulf of
Mexico

Mississippi
Sound

Intracoastal
Waterway

Petit Bois Pass

RM 1   Dauphin Island, west

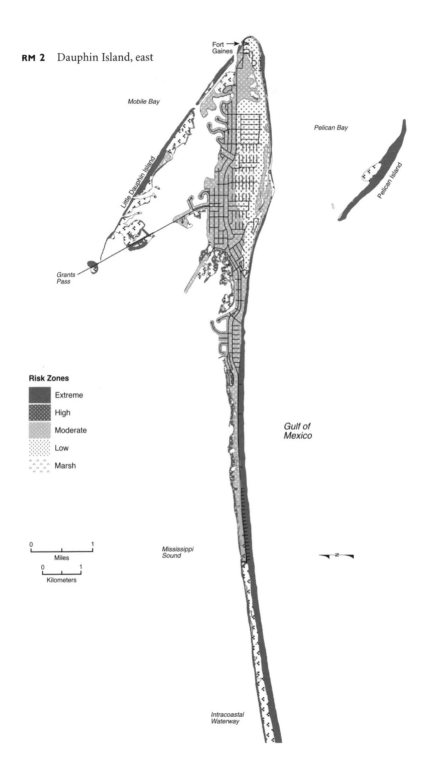

RM 2 Dauphin Island, east

Fort Gaines

Mobile Bay

Pelican Bay

Little Dauphin Island

Pelican Island

Grants Pass

Risk Zones

Extreme

High

Moderate

Low

Marsh

Gulf of Mexico

0   1
Miles

0   1
Kilometers

Mississippi Sound

N

Intracoastal Waterway

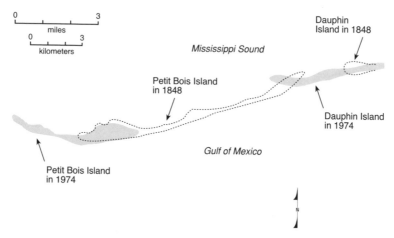

6.2 Westward migration of Petis Bois Island and western Dauphin Island, Alabama, in the direction of longshore sand transport.

50 million cubic yards of dredged sand may have been disposed of in deeper water, influencing both the Sand Island shoals and Dauphin Island. Scott Douglass, of the Department of Civil Engineering, University of South Alabama, Mobile, has studied and written extensively about the coast of Alabama.

Shoreline armoring on Dauphin Island is minimal, consisting primarily of revetments at Pelican Point and groins from Pelican Point to the front of the island that have caused downdrift beach loss to the west. The groin field is a classic example of how groins fail due to detachment (see fig. 4.8). This eastern area is the home of the Audubon Bird Sanctuary and the Fort Gaines Historic Site, which guards the entrance to Mobile Bay along with Fort Morgan on the east side of the pass.

Dauphin Island did not form offshore and then migrate into its present position like some other barrier islands. The eastern high part of the island was once a hill on the mainland coastal plain when the sea level was lower. As the sea level rose, the mainland flooded, leaving the top of the hill exposed to form Dauphin Island. Winds, waves, and longshore drift worked their magic, and eventually Gulf-side beaches formed, with a dune field behind. Sand was carried westward to create a spit, lengthening the island. Trees and other vegetation grew to create a protective cover, resulting in a moderate-risk zone. Now, however, both ends of the island are receding (except for the small accreting section near the golf course), and the low, narrow, sparsely vegetated western section of the island is an extreme-risk zone. Between 1917 and 1974 the erosion rate was above 10 feet per year, but this rate varies. This shoreline segment is one of the most dangerous on the Alabama coast and cannot be developed safely. Island access is by bridge on Highway 193 to and from Mobile, and can be closed when a hurricane passes.

Numerous hurricanes have attacked this area. An early twentieth-century hurricane breached Dauphin Island, forming a 5-mile-wide shallow inlet that had closed by 1942. The September 4, 1948, hurricane breached the island about 4,000 feet west of Oro Point, leaving extensive overwash sands across the island. The eye of Hurricane Frederic passed directly over Dauphin Island in 1979, with winds of 145 mph sending storm surge waters across the island and overwash sand into the sound. The 100-year-storm still-water surge level for this island is 11.5 feet above mean sea level, but during Frederic the flood level exceeded 13 feet in the Bienville Beach area, where houses were heavily damaged or destroyed. The only access road to the island, the Dauphin Island Parkway Bridge, was destroyed. Finger canal properties became miniature islands when storm surge currents, focused by the canals, breached the land connections. Overwash sands clogged other canals. Cleanup was an expensive operation, but many property owners rushed to rebuild after the storm regardless of the increased danger. In July 1997, the eye of Danny, a small hurricane, passed over the mouth of Mobile Bay, near Fort Morgan, producing 80 mph winds. The eye wall and western edge of the eye crossed Dauphin Island, causing sustained hurricane-force winds with gusts above 100 mph and flooding from torrential rains. Seaward-flowing floodwaters from the 43 inches of rain cut channels and breached low dunes. Hurricane Georges (September 1998) left behind extensive flood and wind damage (fig. 6.1).

Along with the typical hazards of storms, such as shoreline erosion and potential for inlet formation, the low elevation and the lack of protective dunes and stabilizing vegetation increase the risk for most of the island. The interior of the eastern portion of the island is forested behind frontal dunes and is a moderate-risk area. The island is wider here, extending to 1.5 miles, and the dunes have good elevation, providing a protective barrier for some properties. The dunes, however, are migrating north in places and could become a nuisance, if not a hazard. Hazard zones to be avoided here include the oceanfront area between the beach and the high dune line, and the back side of the island on Mississippi Sound and Dauphin Island Bay. Plan to evacuate early from Dauphin Island in the face of a storm, as the single evacuation route may be destroyed or blocked.

Little Dauphin Island, Sand Island, and Pelican Island
Islands such as these are totally unsuitable for development. Fortunately, these areas are protected.

Baldwin County (RMs 3, 4, 5)

The Baldwin County coast consists of more than 30 miles of open-Gulf shoreline, plus many times that length of shoreline within Mobile Bay, Bon Secour Bay, Wolf Bay, Perdido Bay, Bayou St. John, Old River, and numerous other smaller bays and bayous. Adjoining land areas are all highly vulnerable to flooding from hurricane or storm runoff.

Fort Morgan to Gulf Highlands (RM 3)
This shoreline segment includes Fort Morgan on the east side of Mobile Pass, portions of Bon Secour National Wildlife Refuge, and the developed areas of Surfside Shores and Gulf Highlands. The entire segment, including Pine Beach, is classified as a high-to-extreme-risk area with the exception of the urbanized areas, which are considered at moderate risk. Inlet formation during hurricanes is a real possibility in narrow reaches along the western half of the peninsula. Storm surge flooding, wave attack, erosion, and overwash from Hurricane Frederic in 1979 effectively destroyed both natural and man-made structures in this area. Frederic's floodwaters penetrated up to 1,000 feet inland, destroying or extensively damaging houses. Flood levels up to 13.6 feet above mean low water leveled or severely eroded dunes, leaving any future developments at even higher risk from Mother Nature's fury. During Hurricane Danny in July 1997, the maximum storm surge measured over 6.5 feet along Highway 182w between Fort Morgan and Gulf Shores, causing flood damage. Hurricane Georges brought more destruction to the area in September 1998. As multifamily dwellings are added to the development mix, the number of inhabitants to be evacuated increases. In case of a hurricane warning, evacuate early, as low places along Highway 180 will flood, blocking your escape.

West Beach to Gulf Shores (RM 4)
This stretch is mostly at extreme to high risk with a wide variety of hazards. The history of high storm surge, low elevations, lack of natural protection, and inlet-forming potential (e.g., Little Lagoon, Shelby Lakes) characterizes an area to be avoided. Yet, although this area is completely unsuitable for development, there are cottages here. Many were destroyed during Hurricane Frederic and then rebuilt with no apparent thought to future storms or their real danger.

Gulf Shores, with its growing population, faces the Gulf at the eastern end of Little Lagoon. Highway 59 leads directly into the community from the north, with Highway 182 providing east–west access along the shore. In the early 1940s, development here consisted of a single row of cottages.

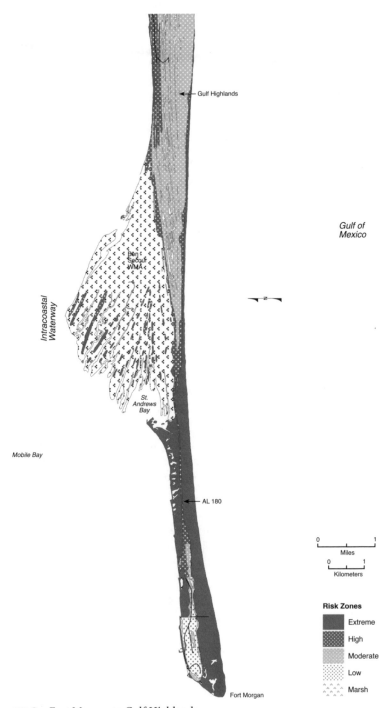

Gulf of
Mexico

Intracoastal
Waterway

Gulf Highlands

Ben
Secour
WMA

St.
Andrews
Bay

Mobile Bay

AL 180

Fort Morgan

0 — 1
Miles
0 — 1
Kilometers

Risk Zones

Extreme

High

Moderate

Low

Marsh

RM 3 Fort Morgan to Gulf Highlands

When development began to boom in the 1950s, the demand for beach-front real estate led to the adjoining marsh being filled with dredge spoil from finger canals in order to create more waterfront property. The entire area is very low in elevation, with no or low dunes. This is an extreme-risk zone that is unsafe for development.

The 100-year storm surge level for Gulf Shores is 11.4 feet above mean sea level. Hurricane Camille in 1969 generated flood levels 6–9 feet above mean low water, but Hurricane Frederic, 10 years later, totally devastated Gulf Shores with its flood level reaching 11–12 feet, both along the beach-front and in the back marsh area. Although Gulf Shores normally has a low potential for new inlet formation, an inlet was cut just east of town during Frederic. Waves battered the structures, and the entire community was flooded, leaving nearly every cottage and building either heavily damaged or destroyed; sand dunes were flattened. Highway 182 was washed out in several places or buried by overwashed sand, making escape impossible. The overwash moved across the island into Little Lagoon and Shelby Lakes.

Extensive storm surge damage also occurred at southeastern Mobile Bay and Gulf Shores when Hurricane Opal struck in October 1995, even though landfall was near Pensacola Beach, Florida. Hurricane Georges in September 1998 clogged the roadway with debris and caused flood damage and beach erosion (fig. 6.3). These events clearly demonstrate the folly of building in such high-risk areas. Future storms will find these areas more vulnerable because the protective dunes are gone, the sand reservoir is depleted, and more and bigger buildings have been constructed. The addition of more people to this congested, dangerous space means that evacuation will be more difficult. Access to the main road (Highway 59) nearby will ease evacuation pressures in the face of a large storm, but heed storm warnings and evacuation orders immediately if you are in this extreme-risk zone.

Romar Beach to Perdido Key (Alabama-Florida Line) (RMS 5, 6)

This stretch of mainland beaches from Shelby Lakes to Perdido Pass is characterized by extreme-to-moderate-risk zones. The east end, adjacent to Perdido Pass, historically is an area of rapid shoreline erosion (greater than 10 feet per year). The inlet was stabilized in the 1960s by the construction of a seawall/breakwater. Fill placed behind the breakwater and accretion to the west of the jetty widened the area but did not lower the risk of adjacent property damage. Much of the area inland from the beach is part of Gulf State Park and is very low in elevation or consists of marsh. About 2.3 miles west from the junction of Highways 161 and 182, dunes provide some natural protection. Sites at higher elevations and behind protective dunes are considered to be at moderate risk, even though floodwaters may reach these elevations.

In 1979, Hurricane Frederic's flood level was in excess of 15 feet above mean low water in places along this stretch. Farther east, Frederic pushed waters nearly 17 feet deep onto the land, causing flooding and overwash in the low areas north of the highway. Frederic's storm surge, coupled with wave run-up, brought water to elevations of nearly 24 feet above mean low water level, eroding away protective dunes and leaving properties highly vulnerable to future storm processes. Even the small category 1 hurricane Danny (1997) produced a 2–5-foot storm surge from Dauphin Island to the Florida border, causing erosion and flood damage. Hurricane Georges (1998) attacked this shore too, proving once again that dangerous shore-front property should be avoided as a building site.

To the east of Perdido Pass, Perdido Key extends into Escambia County, Florida (RM 6). Alabama's short section of Perdido has high storm surge and inlet-forming potential in addition to possible inlet migration at Perdido Pass. This low-elevation barrier coast is totally unsuitable for development. Sand dunes are poorly developed and sparsely vegetated, overwash has been extensive, and the evacuation route is easily blocked.

Florida

The northwestern barrier coast of Florida, the Panhandle, stretches approximately 220 miles from the Alabama-Florida state line eastward to include Escambia, Santa Rosa, Okaloosa, Walton, Bay, Gulf, and Franklin Counties (see fig. 1.2). Over this great reach, the beaches behave in strikingly different ways, from accreting at rates of more than 65 feet per year to eroding at rates of 23 feet per year, both occurring historically in Gulf County. More typical erosion rates are in the 3–6-feet-per-year range.

Based on shoreline shape and orientation, the Florida Panhandle can be divided into western and eastern segments, with the boundary at the entrance to St. Andrews Bay in Bay County. The shoreline along the western segment is concave and is characterized by two barrier islands to the west (Perdido Key and Santa Rosa Island) with mainland beaches to the east. The absence of barrier islands for some distance east of Santa Rosa Island is related to the steep slope of the inner shelf. Beaches along the western segment are wide, backed by dunes with an average elevation of about 16 feet, and are made up of medium-sized, clean quartz sands. The eastern segment is characterized by prominent changes in shoreline orientation and morphology, which can be observed in the north–south orientation of St. Joseph Peninsula in Gulf County and the southwest–northeast orienta-

6.3   Structural debris blocks the street in Gulf Shores, Baldwin County, following Hurricane Georges in September 1998. These pieces of lumber could have acted as battering rams, destroying other buildings and increasing damage from the storm. Photo by Tracy Rice.

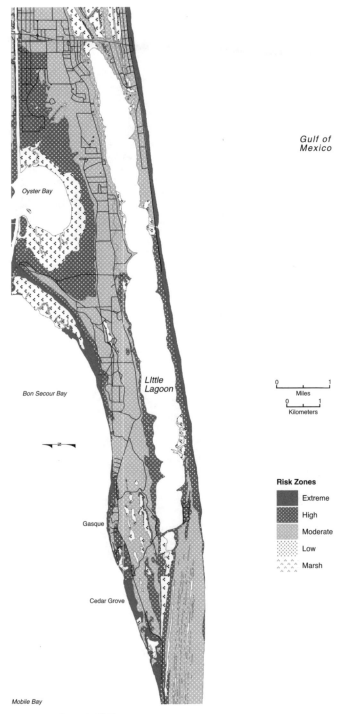

Gulf of
Mexico

Oyster Bay

Bon Secour Bay

Little
Lagoon

Gasque

Cedar Grove

Mobile Bay

0 _____ 1
Miles
0 _____ 1
Kilometers

Risk Zones

- Extreme
- High
- Moderate
- Low
- Marsh

RM 4 West Beach to Gulf Shores

tion of the barrier islands in Franklin County. The Panhandle beaches generally experience waves with low to moderate energy, but they have the highest rates of net longshore sediment transport along the Gulf coast. Notably, sediment transport along this coastal segment is not hindered by groins and jetties, except for a few such structures in Okaloosa, Bay, and Gulf Counties affecting about 2,600 feet of coastline. The Florida Panhandle has 56 miles of urban developed coastline, of which 15 miles (about one-fourth) is "protected" by engineering structures.

Escambia and Santa Rosa Counties (RMs 5, 6, 7, 8, 9, 10, 11)

Escambia County's shoreline consists of two barrier islands, both shared with other counties: Perdido Key with Baldwin County, Alabama (RM 5), and Santa Rosa Island with both Santa Rosa and Okaloosa Counties. Escambia County has about 40 miles of shoreline on the Gulf of Mexico, and an additional 40 miles on Pensacola, Perdido, and Escambia Bays (appendix C, ref. 51). Perdido Key includes the eastern portion of the Gulf Islands National Seashore and Florida's westernmost beaches (RM 6). Bridges provide access to both the Florida and Alabama portions of the island. With the exception of a 1.5-mile stretch centered on the fixed-span bridge, where the island is about 3,000 feet wide and at moderate risk, Perdido Key is low and narrow. Beaches on the Gulf side vary in width from about 50 to 75 feet, and dunes are usually less than 10 feet high with sparse vegetation. The entire shoreline is an extreme-risk area, but the landward areas are rated primarily as moderate risk.

Santa Rosa Island (RMS 8, 9, 10, 11)

Santa Rosa Island lies in three counties across most of the entrance to Pensacola Bay and includes Fort Pickens State Park, Pensacola Beach, and a portion of Gulf Islands National Seashore in Escambia County; Navarre Beach in Santa Rosa County; and Eglin Air Force Base and Fort Walton Beach in Okaloosa County. Santa Rosa Island is narrow over much of its length, and two areas along Pensacola Beach, along with much of Navarre Beach in Santa Rosa County, were designated as critical erosion areas by the Florida Department of Environmental Protection (FDEP) in 1998. You can find out more about designation of critical erosion areas in Florida from the FDEP (see appendix B for address). About half of the eastern segment of Santa Rosa Island is relatively wide with moderate-risk areas behind the more vulnerable beachfront. Dune heights range from 6 to 7 feet on the ends of the island to between 8 and 12 feet in the central area. Overwash occurs during storms, and inland areas are not well protected due to the low elevation of these islands.

Although the shorelines of Santa Rosa Island and Perdido Key have a history of erosion, with most beaches having widths between 10 and 50 feet, some beaches on Santa Rosa Island are up to 125 feet wide. Portions of both Santa Rosa Island and Perdido Key have been nourished in the past, leaving the replenished beaches generally more than 50 feet wide.

Unlike Perdido Key, a large part of Santa Rosa Island is developed. Both islands have a minimal number of seawalls, thus maintaining the advertised "sugar white" ribbons of sand largely in their natural or renourished state. Overall, Escambia County has about 9 miles of developed shoreline, with 1.5 miles of seawalls. Santa Rosa County has nearly 3 miles of development and about 0.3 mile of seawalls, where beaches are generally narrower.

Aside from alongshore development, the Gulf beaches on Santa Rosa Island and Perdido Key are largely undisturbed, except for the navigational jetties at East Pass (in Okaloosa County) and the artificially deepened (35 feet) 500-foot-wide Pensacola Bay channel. Navigational channels have compounded and increased the natural beach retreat rates west of the passes. However, the properties west of these passes are owned by the federal government and managed as natural areas, so the problems of erosion are not as serious as they would be if these sections were privately developed. Erosion problems are considered more serious along Escambia Bay, Big Lagoon, and Santa Rosa Sound, behind the barrier islands, where the rising sea level is drowning the bay shoreline. These areas, as well as the coastal reaches, are threatened when storms arrive.

More than a dozen major hurricanes struck this coast during the twentieth century, most notably in 1901, 1906, 1911, 1916, 1917, 1926, 1932, 1947, 1950, 1969, 1975, 1979, 1985, and 1995. During the 1906 hurricane, the water levels on Santa Rosa Island reached 11.6 feet above mean sea level at Fort Pickens, breached Santa Rosa Island just east of the Coast Guard life-saving station, and claimed 151 lives in Florida and Alabama. The total damage exceeded $3.2 million, quite a sum at that time. The storm of 1926 caused a 10.5-foot storm surge at Fort Pickens and more than $4.7 million in total damages. During Hurricane Frederic, which made landfall just west of Mobile in 1979, storm surges of 14 feet and 12 feet above mean sea level were recorded at Perdido Key and Pensacola Beach, respectively. More than 90 percent of Santa Rosa Island and Perdido Key was underwater! Eastern Santa Rosa Island suffered dune erosion and extensive washover. The total dollar damage from Hurricane Frederic exceeded $62 million in Escambia County and $9.4 million in Santa Rosa County. A direct hit would have caused much greater damage, but landfall was about 50 miles west of Pensacola. Hurricane Juan made landfall near Pensacola in October 1985. A decade later, Hurricane Erin (1995) made its second landfall (after hitting Vero

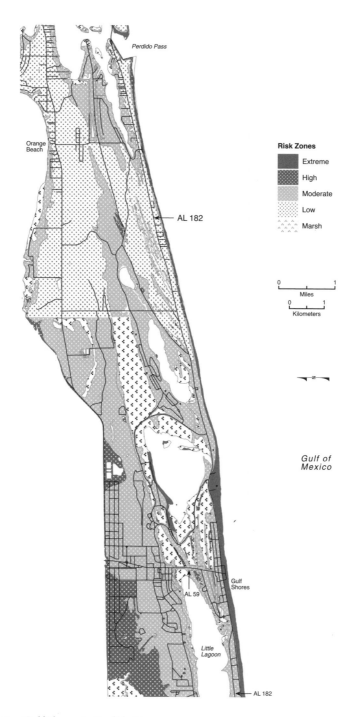

Risk Zones

Extreme
High
Moderate
Low
Marsh

Perdido Pass

Orange
Beach

AL 182

Gulf of
Mexico

Gulf
Shores

AL 59

Little
Lagoon

AL 182

0   1
Miles

0   1
Kilometers

RM 5   Gulf Shores to Perdido Pass

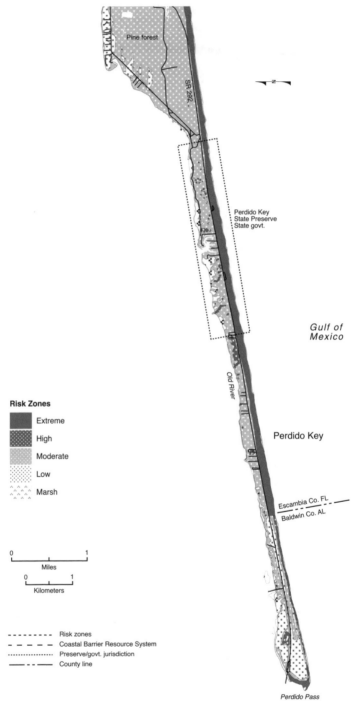

Risk Zones

Extreme

High

Moderate

Low

Marsh

```
0                    1
      Miles
  0              1
    Kilometers
```

- - - - - - - - Risk zones
- - - - - - - - Coastal Barrier Resource System
. . . . Preserve/govt. jurisdiction
— - — - — County line

Pine forest

SR 292

Perdido Key
State Preserve
State govt.

Gulf of
Mexico

Old River

Perdido Key

Escambia Co. FL
Baldwin Co. AL

Perdido Pass

RM 6 Perdido Key, west, including Alabama-Florida state line

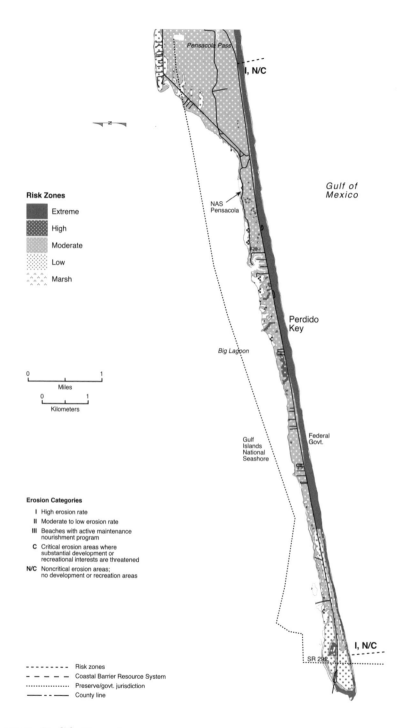

Risk Zones

Extreme

High

Moderate

Low

Marsh

Erosion Categories

I High erosion rate

II Moderate to low erosion rate

III Beaches with active maintenance
nourishment program

C Critical erosion areas where
substantial development or
recreational interests are threatened

N/C Noncritical erosion areas;
no development or recreation areas

- - - - - - - - - -   Risk zones
- - - - - -   Coastal Barrier Resource System
· · · · · · · · · · · ·   Preserve/govt. jurisdiction
——— - · ———   County line

Pensacola Pass

I, N/C

Gulf of
Mexico

NAS
Pensacola

Perdido
Key

Big Lagoon

Federal
Govt.

Gulf
Islands
National
Seashore

I, N/C

SR 292

0 ———— 1
Miles
0 ———— 1
Kilometers

RM 7 Perdido Key, east

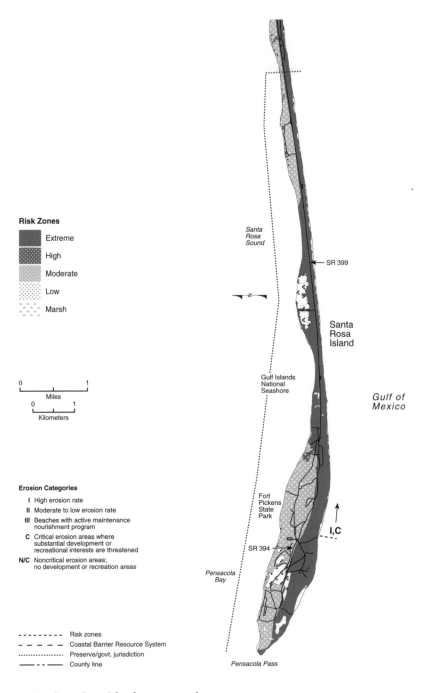

Risk Zones

- Extreme
- High
- Moderate
- Low
- Marsh

0   1
Miles

0   1
Kilometers

Erosion Categories

  I   High erosion rate
  II   Moderate to low erosion rate
  III   Beaches with active maintenance
      nourishment program
  C   Critical erosion areas where
      substantial development or
      recreational interests are threatened
N/C   Noncritical erosion areas;
      no development or recreation areas

-------- Risk zones
- - - - Coastal Barrier Resource System
.... Preserve/govt. jurisdiction
——-··—— County line

Santa Rosa Sound

SR 399

Santa Rosa Island

Gulf Islands National Seashore

Gulf of Mexico

Fort Pickens State Park

I,C

SR 394

Pensacola Bay

Pensacola Pass

RM 8   Santa Rosa Island, western end

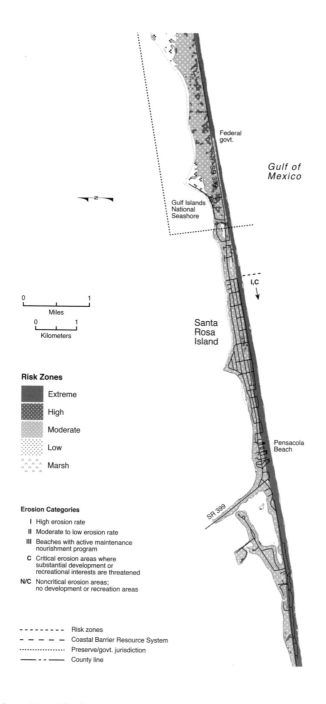

Gulf of
Mexico

Federal
govt.

SR 399

Gulf Islands
National
Seashore

I,C

Santa
Rosa
Island

Pensacola
Beach

SR 399

N

0 _____ 1
Miles

0 _____ 1
Kilometers

Risk Zones

▮ Extreme

▓ High

░ Moderate

⠄ Low

⋀⋀⋀ Marsh

Erosion Categories

I High erosion rate

II Moderate to low erosion rate

III Beaches with active maintenance
nourishment program

C Critical erosion areas where
substantial development or
recreational interests are threatened

N/C Noncritical erosion areas;
no development or recreation areas

- - - - - - - - Risk zones

– – – – – Coastal Barrier Resource System

.... Preserve/govt. jurisdiction

——– - –—— County line

RM 9 Santa Rosa Island, Pensacola Beach

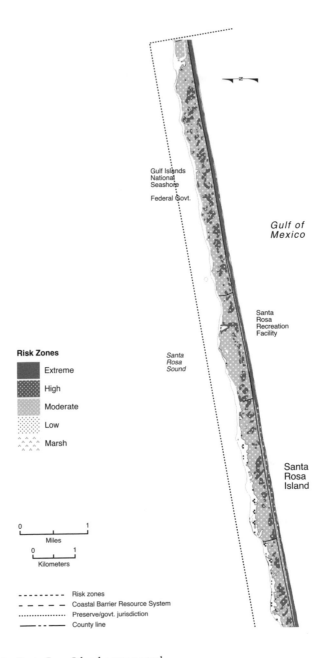

Risk Zones

- Extreme
- High
- Moderate
- Low
- Marsh

Gulf Islands
National
Seashore

Federal Govt.

Gulf of
Mexico

Santa
Rosa
Recreation
Facility

Santa
Rosa
Sound

Santa
Rosa
Island

0 ——————— 1
Miles

0 ——————— 1
Kilometers

- - - - - - - - - Risk zones
- - - - - Coastal Barrier Resource System
.... Preserve/govt. jurisdiction
——— - - ——— County line

RM 10   Santa Rosa Island, west central

Beach on Florida's east coast) near Pensacola, generating a 6–7-foot storm surge just west of Navarre Beach and leaving major structural damage in its wake. Hurricane Georges, in September 1998, brought a 5–10-foot storm surge to the three counties after damaging more than 1,500 homes and completely destroying nearly 200 homes in the Florida Keys.

Perdido Key and Santa Rosa Island were hit hard by Hurricane Opal in 1995. The center of the eye passed over Pensacola Beach (appendix C, ref. 15). Many miles of dunes were eroded, but they protected the houses behind them. Where dunes were low or absent before Hurricane Opal, damage to buildings was more severe. Throughout the Panhandle, more coastal structures were damaged or destroyed by Opal than by all the coastal storms in Florida since 1975 combined (appendix C, ref. 12). Severe structural damage occurred primarily to homes constructed prior to the establishment of the coastal construction control line in 1975 (appendix C, ref. 60) and to those not built to CCCL standards. The majority of such damage occurred about 200–300 feet from the shoreline (appendix C, ref. 16). In Escambia and Santa Rosa Counties, 249 single-family residences and 47 multifamily dwellings were 50 percent or more destroyed during Opal. Elevated houses fared better than those built at or near ground level, but some elevated homes were damaged by nonelevated houses that floated off their foundations and into the elevated buildings (appendix C, ref. 17). Houses built after the establishment of the CCCL program have been subject to the more rigorous construction standards needed for survival in this extreme-to-high-risk coastal zone.

In addition to damaging numerous man-made structures, Hurricane Opal caused major beach erosion, storm surge flooding, and overwash from Gulf Shores, Alabama, to Mexico Beach, Florida. These processes were most severe on Santa Rosa Island from Pensacola Beach to Fort Walton Beach in Okaloosa County (see fig. 1.3). After Hurricane Opal, 5.7 miles of Pensacola Beach (up from 4.9 miles in 1993) and 3 miles of Fort Walton Beach were categorized by the Florida Department of Environmental Protection as critical erosion areas where substantial development or recreational interests are threatened. Navarre Beach (RM 11) was one of the hardest-hit areas, with 3.6 miles of critically eroded shoreline. However, a portion of the shoreline in eastern Escambia County had accreted about 100 feet by November 1995 at the site of an exposed nineteenth-century shipwreck (appendix C, ref. 15). Generally, shoreline retreat has been about 2 feet per year.

Hurricane Opal also caused damage in areas defined as being outside the coastal flood areas with velocity hazards, otherwise known as coastal high-hazard zones. In some places, evidence of wave impact and sand deposition was found in structures up to 18 feet above mean sea level (appendix C, ref. 12)! Flood effects of the magnitude of Hurricane Opal have approximately a 1 percent chance of occurring in any given year along the Florida Panhandle coast. Hundred-year flood levels are estimated at 10.5–11.5 feet along this coast. Hurricane Opal, with a 5–14-foot storm surge, lowered and recessed both the beaches and dunes, creating a flat poststorm beach and leaving all structures at higher risk of damage by future storms. After Hurricane Opal, flattened dunes were rebuilt by beach scraping and retrieving overwash sand to again provide some protection.

Historically, some of the worst floods in this area have resulted from high-intensity rainfall during hurricanes, sometimes as much as 24 inches over a storm's duration (appendix C, ref. 51). Extreme storm surge associated with hurricanes also may raise the water levels 12–16 feet above normal along the open coast. The annual probability of a tropical storm or hurricane striking Escambia and Santa Rosa Counties is 21 percent and 13 percent, respectively. Some 15–20 frontal systems strike the coast every winter. Because of the long east–west fetch of Santa Rosa Island and Perdido Key, storms produce moderately high waves that refract into the shore. The El Niño winter of 1997–98 saw severe storms batter this area, leaving the most severe erosion on Perdido Key along a 3–4-mile stretch west of the Naval Air Station.

The shorefronts of Escambia and Santa Rosa Counties will continue to be subject to future storms, leaving homes at low elevations that are unprotected by either vegetation or dunes extremely vulnerable to damage.

Okaloosa County (RMs 11, 12, 13, 14)

The Gulf of Mexico shoreline of Okaloosa County has nearly 25 miles of beaches: about 18 miles of barrier beach on Santa Rosa Island west of the East Pass navigational channel, 2 miles of barrier spit east of the East Pass channel, and about 5 miles of beaches on the Moreno Point Peninsula. This portion of Santa Rosa Island, which is completely developed and one-third armored with seawalls, is the Okaloosa County community of Fort Walton Beach. Eglin Air Force Base also occupies a portion of Santa Rosa Island. Okaloosa County contains part of the Gulf Islands National Seashore and the city of Destin, where more than half of the developed shoreline is fronted by seawalls. Near Destin, East Pass into Choctawhatchee Bay is bounded by jetties, which affect erosion rates on Santa Rosa Island to the west.

The Gulf beaches are generally wide (greater than 45 feet) and flat,

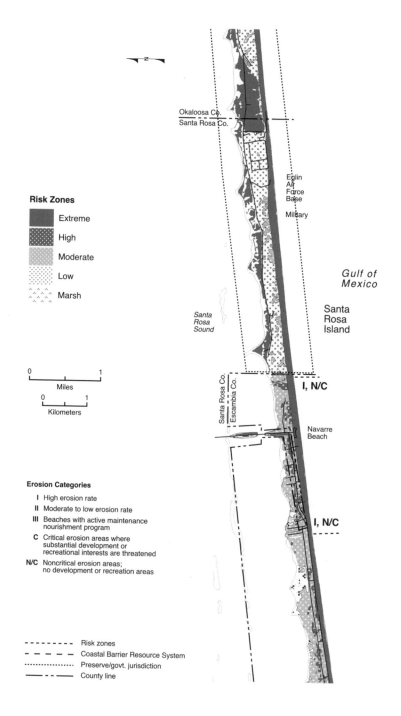

Risk Zones

- Extreme
- High
- Moderate
- Low
- Marsh

0 —————— 1
Miles

0 —————— 1
Kilometers

Erosion Categories

I High erosion rate

II Moderate to low erosion rate

III Beaches with active maintenance nourishment program

C Critical erosion areas where substantial development or recreational interests are threatened

N/C Noncritical erosion areas; no development or recreation areas

- - - - - - - - - Risk zones
- - - - - Coastal Barrier Resource System
.... Preserve/govt. jurisdiction
—— - - —— County line

Okaloosa Co.
Santa Rosa Co.

Eglin
Air
Force
Base

Military

Gulf of Mexico

Santa
Rosa
Island

*Santa
Rosa
Sound*

Santa Rosa Co.
Escambia Co.

I, N/C

Navarre
Beach

I, N/C

RM 11 Santa Rosa Island, Navarre Beach area

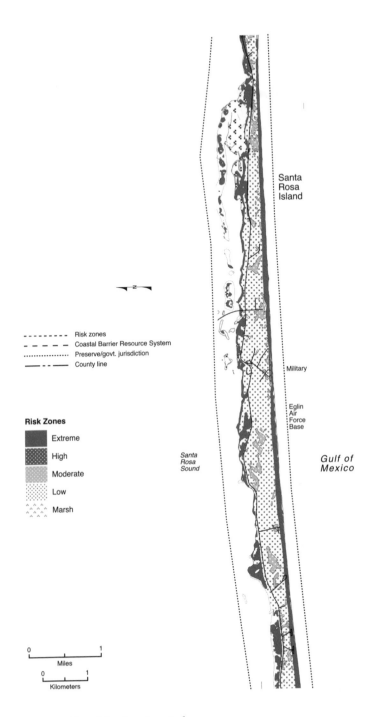

Santa
Rosa
Island

Military

Eglin
Air
Force
Base

Santa
Rosa
Sound

Gulf of
Mexico

- - - - - - - Risk zones
- - - - - Coastal Barrier Resource System
· · · · · · · · · Preserve/govt. jurisdiction
——— · · ——— County line

Risk Zones

▓ Extreme

▓ High

▓ Moderate

Low

⌃⌃⌃ Marsh

0   1
Miles

0   1
Kilometers

RM 12   Santa Rosa Island, east central

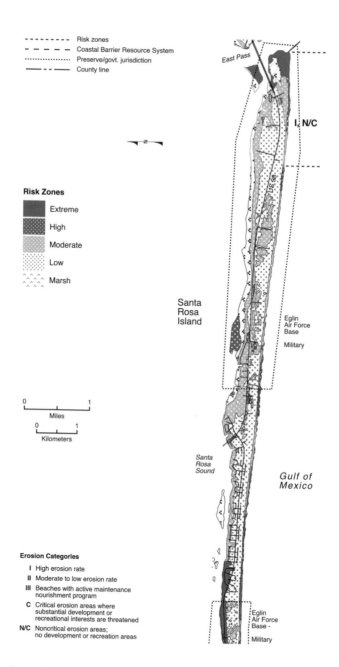

Risk zones
Coastal Barrier Resource System
Preserve/govt. jurisdiction
County line

East Pass

I, N/C

US 98

Risk Zones

Extreme

High

Moderate

Low

Marsh

Santa
Rosa
Island

Eglin
Air Force
Base

Military

0   1
Miles

0   1
Kilometers

Santa
Rosa
Sound

Gulf of
Mexico

Erosion Categories

I   High erosion rate
II Moderate to low erosion rate
III Beaches with active maintenance
    nourishment program
C   Critical erosion areas where
    substantial development or
    recreational interests are threatened
N/C Noncritical erosion areas;
    no development or recreation areas

Eglin
Air Force
Base -

Military

RM 13   Santa Rosa Island, eastern end, Fort Walton Beach backed by foredunes 6–12 feet high with even higher primary dunes, but for a distance of about 2 miles on either side of the East Pass channel the beaches lack foredunes or primary dunes and are considered to be extreme-risk areas. Hurricane Opal leveled or lowered many dunes in its path, leaving structures even more vulnerable to future storms. Portions of the Okaloosa County shoreline from Destin east to the county line were nourished in 1986, 1987, and 1988, leaving beaches in this erosional area adequate for the time being. Sites with good elevation fronted by dune protection may be at moderate to low risk; however, this does not mean risk free!

The chance of a hurricane striking this county is about 14 percent in any given year. Major hurricanes occurred in 1887, 1889, 1896, 1906, 1926, 1936, 1948, 1953, 1956, 1975, and 1995. Severe winds and storm surge occurred in September 1926 and September 1975 (Eloise), causing extensive property damage. During both of these hurricanes the storm surge ranged from 10 to 12 feet along the Destin coast. Although the 1926 storm caused more loss of life than any other, Hurricane Eloise was by far the most physically destructive storm prior to Hurricane Opal, due to the tremendous amount of development close to the coastline. The Fort Walton Beach region has experienced flooding from several hurricanes since 1870. High-water marks 8.4 feet above mean sea level at Fort Walton Beach and 7–8 feet at Destin were recorded during the hurricane of 1936 (appendix C, ref. 51). During Hurricane Eloise in 1975, the barrier beaches experienced storm surge of 9.5–14.4 feet above mean sea level along the Gulf and about 6–7 feet in Choctawhatchee Bay and Santa Rosa Sound. The coastal areas of Destin are subject to flooding and damage from storm surges associated with hurricanes and tropical storms and have been affected on an average of once every 6.5 years since 1886 (appendix C, ref. 51). The 100-year flood levels are estimated at 9–10 feet above mean sea level.

When Hurricane Opal made landfall between Pensacola and Fort Walton Beach, more than 150 miles of coastline was affected, with major beach and dune erosion occurring on the beaches of Okaloosa County. The estimated cost of repairing Opal's damage throughout the county was more than $1 million, including the costs of debris removal, sand fencing, revegetation, dune restoration, and rebuilding dune walkovers (appendix C, ref. 12; fig. 6.4).

Okaloosa County experienced the highest winds of Hurricane Opal (84 mph with gusts to 145 mph at Hurlbert Field), and storm surge and wave activity ranging from 10 to 21 feet leveled dunes, particularly along the 20 miles of eastern Santa Rosa Island (appendix C, ref. 12). After Opal, a 3-mile stretch of the coastline at Fort Walton Beach, 2.9 miles at Destin, and 2.1 miles along eastern Okaloosa County were designated as critical ero-

6.4 Okaloosa County officials installed signs on the beaches to warn people of the possible danger remaining. Removal of debris after storms is a huge undertaking, and the likelihood of finding every piece of glass or every nail is slim. Heed such signs for your own protection. Photo by Norma Longo.

sion area with substantial development or recreational interests threatened (appendix C, ref. 15). The Fort Walton Beach area lost up to 200 feet of vegetated dune width, and severe dune erosion caused large breaches in the dune field on the east end of Santa Rosa Island. A temporary inlet formed and a segment of U.S. Highway 98 was destroyed (appendix C, ref. 12). Although a wide prestorm beach and high dunes helped to reduce damage here, most of the area was overwashed, leaving sand deposits more than 3 feet thick inland, and overwash fans moved into the lagoon behind the island. Near Destin, channelized overwash resulted in intense storm surge flood scour, leaving areas prone to future flooding. More than 100 homes and about 3,450 feet of armoring along the Okaloosa County coast were damaged by Hurricane Opal. Artificial dunes were constructed for protection because the storm leveled the natural dunes, and sea oats were planted to help retain sand (fig. 6.5). Buildings without dune protection or surviving prestorm seawalls have few—if any—remaining mitigation options other than relocation.

Coastal construction setback lines were established for Okaloosa County on March 5, 1979 (appendix C, ref. 60). Of the 134 dwellings in this county that are seaward of the control line, 74 sustained damage during Hurricane Opal. Following the passage of the more stringent rules, some newer homes

6.5 Sprouts of dune grasses cover this beach in Okaloosa County. The sign tells the story. Sea oats will help to retain blowing sand and rebuild dunes in the area. Photo by Norma Longo.

have been built with a first-floor elevation above the Base Flood Elevation for flood protection. For Okaloosa County, FEMA proposed new FIRMS with new Base Flood Elevations and flood risk zones that were adopted.

The shoreline along the Gulf as well as in the bays has been retreating. East Pass was formerly about 2 miles east of its present location, and Santa Rosa Island's eastern tip once extended to a position in front of Destin. Between 1871 and 1929, the seaward end of the pass migrated about 2,500 feet westward, and the original pass shoaled and closed sometime between 1935 and 1938. The present East Pass formed in 1928 when a severe storm surge breached the narrow, low portion of Santa Rosa Island.

During the last few decades, development on the county's beaches has intensified. Many buildings were placed in areas of past overwash and flooding, or in old inlet positions. Dense developments include the Fort Walton Beach area, Destin, and east of Henderson Beach along Old U.S. 98. These areas had critical erosion problems in the past, and variable levels of property damage will occur in the future.

Walton County (RMs 14, 15, 16, 17)

The change in the Panhandle coast orientation from east–west to south-east–northwest occurs in Walton County, which has about 25 miles of shoreline along the Gulf, plus 11 miles of marsh shoreline on Choctawhatchee Bay. Some 18 mainland beaches make up the beaches of South Walton; these communities, unincorporated towns, and neighborhoods lie along Old Scenic Highway 98, Highway 98, and Scenic Highway 30-A (Dune Allen Beach, Blue Mountain Beach, Grayton Beach, Seaside, Seagrove Beach, Seacrest Beach, Inlet Beach, and Carillon Beach). This stretch of coast is lined with vacation resorts, single-family beach houses, seaside cottages, townhouses, and the like, with new housing developments and communities springing up nearby. Rapid population growth and development along the Panhandle in the 1990s has put a strain on both the infrastructure and the community leaders struggling to maintain the quality of life.

Fourteen miles of Walton County coastline is developed, and many individual buildings are fronted by low, short walls. Most of the beaches are more than 50 feet wide; however, sections totaling 2 miles in front of and adjacent to several walls are narrower, typically between 10 and 50 feet wide. Dunes in this area range between 12 and 30 feet in height.

North of the beaches lie marsh and swamplands punctuated by numerous small and medium-sized freshwater lakes, some of which are connected by outlets to the Gulf. Blue Mountain Beach has some high elevations and perhaps some of the lowest-risk coastal sites in the county (fig. 6.6). Grayton Beach State Recreation Area, between Grayton Beach and Seaside, is advertised as the "Best Beach in the Continental U.S." in a Florida travel guide.

During Hurricane Eloise in 1975, Grayton Beach State Recreation Area's beaches and dunes suffered severe scouring and erosion by 16-foot waves. Several bridge approaches over the coastal creeks and streams emptying into the Gulf were washed away by floodwaters. During Hurricane Frederic in 1979, the entire Walton County Gulf beachfront experienced loss of foredunes and erosion of primary dune lines by about 10 feet horizontally and 3 feet vertically. There were several washovers at the discharge outlets of coastal lakes and lagoons.

In 1993, Walton County had no erosion problem areas identified anywhere along its coastline, but Hurricane Opal caused major beach and dune erosion along the entire county shoreline in 1995. Following Hurricane Opal, reaches totaling 25.6 miles of Walton County were designated as erosion problem areas, with 13.9 miles categorized as critical, where substantial development or recreational interests are threatened (appendix C, ref. 15). Sixty-nine single-family and 20 multifamily structures with 75 units were 50 percent or more destroyed by Hurricane Opal (appendix C, ref. 16). Risk designations change quickly along this coast, and sites on the shoreline or adjacent to inlets are at high to extreme risk. Remember, these

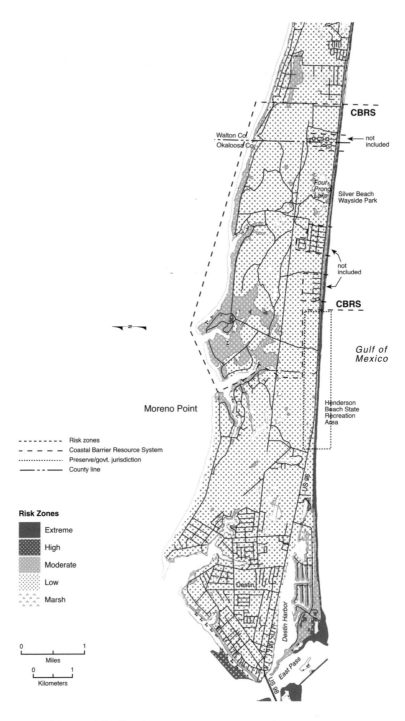

CBRS

← not included

Walton Co
Okaloosa Co

Four
Prong
Lake

Silver Beach
Wayside Park

← not included

CBRS

*Gulf of
Mexico*

Henderson
Beach State
Recreation
Area

Moreno Point

- - - - - - - - - - Risk zones
- - - - - Coastal Barrier Resource System
.... Preserve/govt. jurisdiction
—— - - —— County line

Risk Zones

	Extreme
	High
	Moderate
	Low
^ ^ ^	Marsh

Destin

Destin Harbor

US 98

East Pass

US 98

0 ————————— 1
Miles

0 ————————— 1
Kilometers

RM 14   Moreno Point, Destin area

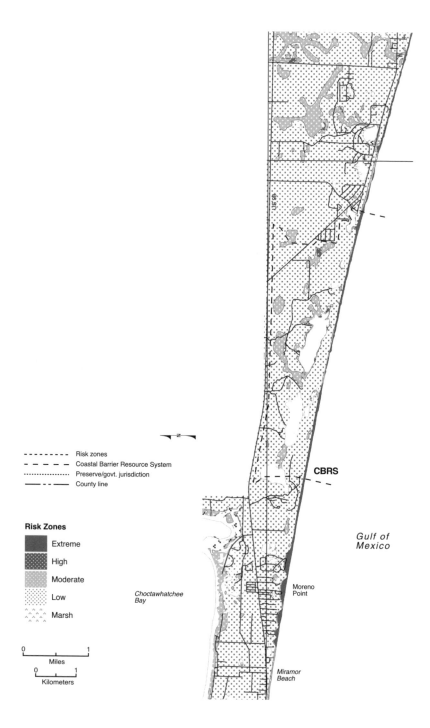

Risk zones

- - - - - - - - - Risk zones
- - - - - Coastal Barrier Resource System
· · · · · · · · · · · · Preserve/govt. jurisdiction
—— - - —— County line

CBRS

Risk Zones

- Extreme
- High
- Moderate
- Low
- Marsh

0 ————————— 1
Miles

0 ————————— 1
Kilometers

Choctawhatchee Bay

Gulf of Mexico

Moreno Point

Miramor Beach

RM 15 Moreno Point, Miramar Beach area

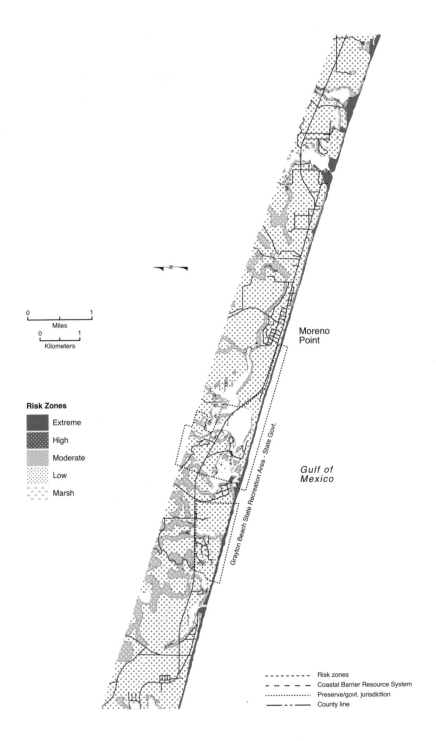

Risk Zones

Extreme

High

Moderate

Low

Marsh

Moreno
Point

*Gulf of
Mexico*

Grayton Beach State Recreation Area - State Govt.

- - - - - - - - - Risk zones
- - - - - Coastal Barrier Resource System
· · · · · · · · · · · · Preserve/govt. jurisdiction
— · — · — County line

0   1
Miles
0   1
Kilometers

RM 16   Moreno Point, Grayton Beach State Recreation Area

6.6 Homes at Blue Mountain Beach in Walton County sit atop or slightly behind dunes about 15 feet high. The good elevation will afford protection from storm surge, but winds will certainly affect those structures that are not sheltered by the dunes. Photo by Norma Longo.

are mainland beaches rather than barrier islands, so safer sites that still have good beach access may be found inland.

As urban development proceeds on this coast, the losses to structures and property will increase, even with good setbacks, because the shoreline is naturally retreating. From 1872 to 1935, Walton County's shoreline retreated 100–299 feet. In recent years the shoreline has experienced average erosion of 1–2 feet per year. Erosion around Choctawhatchee Bay, which has more development than the beach, is mainly due to the erosive shore and the drowning of the bay shoreline by the rising sea level. Bay erosion is considered most serious in the communities of Villa Tasso and Choctaw Beach. Serious shoreline recession had been experienced in the areas around Inlet Beach, Seagrove Beach, Grayton Beach State Recreation Area, Dune Allen Beach, and Miramar Beach even before the devastating effects of the hurricanes (fig. 6.7). In 1999, dunes were being restored and Walton County beaches were recovering from the devastation wrought by Hurricane Opal, but in the storm cycle yet to come the recovery hinges on whether the shore will be allowed to retreat.

The probability of a hurricane striking the Walton County coast is 7 percent in any given year, and the 100-year flood level is estimated at 8.5 feet above mean sea level. However, during Hurricane Eloise in 1975, a storm surge of 11–18 feet caused extensive scouring and erosion of dunes and

6.7 Erosion and storm damage are evident in this photo of dunes and storm drains taken in Walton County following Hurricane Earl, September 1998. Note the crumpled sand fences along the side of the dune and the uncovered cement pipe in the foreground. Photo by Norma Longo.

beaches. The total damage to coastal property and structures was a relatively low $3 million, primarily because of scanty development at the time and builders' observance of the CCCL which was established in Walton County on June 4, 1975 (appendix C, ref. 60).

Bay County (RMs 17, 18, 19, 20)

Bay County's Gulf shoreline of almost 44 miles is the second longest in the Panhandle, after Franklin County. Well-known beaches here include Hollywood Beach, Panama City Beach (RM 18), and Mexico Beach, all composed primarily of fine quartz sand and shell fragments in varying proportions. Most of the mainland and island beaches are backed by dunes that range in height from 5 to 25 feet. Crooked Island, most of which has emerged since 1779, is composed of low beach ridges, 5–7 feet high, at the accreting northwestern end and at old inlet sites, whereas high dunes (12–25 feet) predominate along the retreating narrow southeastern section (less than 550 feet wide). Several high dune areas now mark the positions of old filled inlets. Most of the natural beaches are 100–200 feet wide. Shell Island (RM 19) includes St. Andrews State Recreation Area and Tyndall Air Force Base, which occupies the eastern end of Shell Island and the whole of

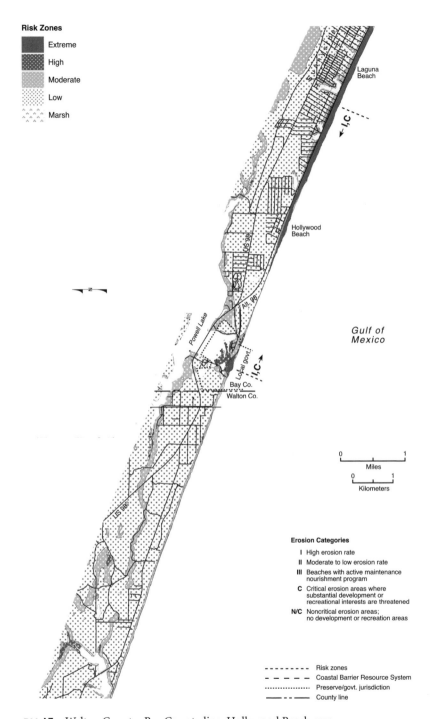

Risk Zones

- Extreme
- High
- Moderate
- Low
- Marsh

Laguna Beach

I,C

Hollywood Beach

US 98

Alt. 98

I,C

Powell Lake

Local govt.

Bay Co.
Walton Co.

US 98

Gulf of
Mexico

0   1
Miles

0   1
Kilometers

Erosion Categories

- **I**   High erosion rate
- **II**   Moderate to low erosion rate
- **III**   Beaches with active maintenance nourishment program
- **C**   Critical erosion areas where substantial development or recreational interests are threatened
- **N/C**   Noncritical erosion areas; no development or recreation areas

- - - - - - - - Risk zones
- - - - - Coastal Barrier Resource System
· · · · · · · · · · Preserve/govt. jurisdiction
——— - - County line

RM 17   Walton County–Bay County line, Hollywood Beach area

6.8 Panama City Beach in Bay County is highly developed and armored with seawalls. The beach in front of the wall shown here will be gone at high tide, leaving tourists to walk in the water. The slope of the shoreface along these beaches is shallow, making it possible for storms to send floodwaters far back into the island's interior. Photo by Norma Longo.

Crooked Island. Both of these islands have extreme-risk classifications and are unsuitable for any other type of development.

Jetties constructed near the middle of Shell Island for navigation purposes have contributed to some erosion problems west of the channel that was dug in 1934. The Army Corps of Engineers estimated that since the jetties were opened, retreat of more than 11.4 feet per year occurred for 26 miles west of the jetties, including the beaches of St. Andrews State Recreation Area and Panama City Beach. Between 1934 and 1945, the rate immediately west of the jetty was 19 feet per year. Since then, the erosion rate has slowed somewhat due to the placement west of the jetties of material dredged during channel maintenance. However, the average erosion rate was still 7 feet per year for the period from 1935 to 1971. Gradual retreat has been common for the entire 18.4 miles of Bay County beaches west of the jetties.

The major changes in the area's barrier beaches take place during severe hurricanes and storms, but slow and continuing changes occur as a result of wind-generated waves, longshore currents, rise in sea level, and emplacement of man-made structures for erosion control and navigational purposes. Bay County has more than 8 miles of armoring structures, primarily low seawalls, making it the most heavily armored section of the Panhandle coastline (fig. 6.8). Most of the beaches are highly developed, including Gulf Lagoon Beach, Laguna Beach, Mexico Beach, and Panama

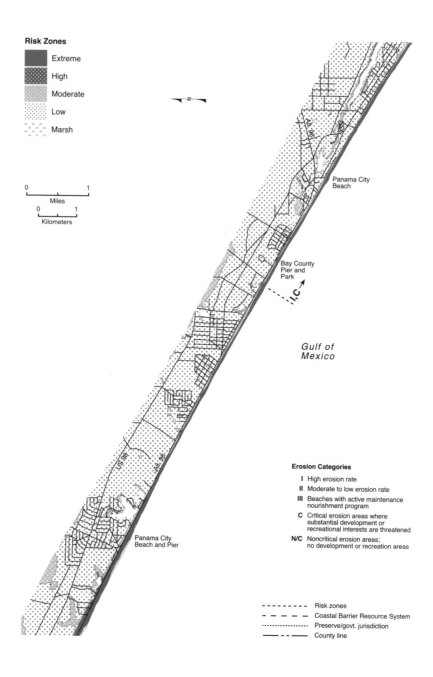

Risk Zones

- Extreme
- High
- Moderate
- Low
- Marsh

0 Miles 1

0 Kilometers 1

Panama City Beach

Bay County Pier and Park

Gulf of Mexico

Panama City Beach and Pier

Erosion Categories

I High erosion rate

II Moderate to low erosion rate

III Beaches with active maintenance nourishment program

C Critical erosion areas where substantial development or recreational interests are threatened

N/C Noncritical erosion areas; no development or recreation areas

- - - - - - - - - Risk zones
- - - - - Coastal Barrier Resource System
.... Preserve/govt. jurisdiction
——— - - ——— County line

RM 18   Panama City Beach

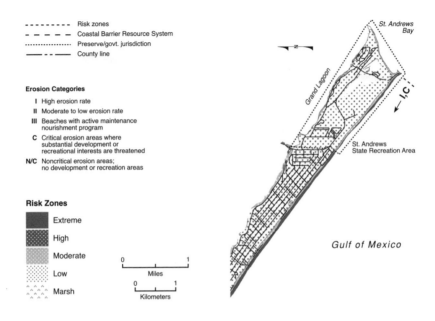

RM 19 St. Andrew Bay area

City Beach. The Panama City Beach area has the highest percentage of seawalls in the county and has been nourished numerous times since 1976 in order to maintain an intermediate-width beach. This segment of shoreline is an extreme-risk zone, backed by low-to-moderate-risk areas along the bay shores behind adjoining marshes. By the late 1990s, Mexico Beach was listed as a critical erosion area by the Florida Department of Environmental Protection, not having been nourished for more than 20 years. At the time of this writing, the Laguna Beach area has no beach at all fronting more than two-thirds of its armored shoreline and is highly vulnerable to storm effects. Generally, the dry beaches in front of seawalls are between 10 and 50 feet wide, but many stretches of beach are less than 10 feet in width. Nearly 26 miles of coastline in Bay County were designated as erosion problem areas in 1993, including 6.8 miles from Panama City Beach to St. Andrews Inlet (appendix C, ref. 53). Although daily wind, wave, and current action affect sand movement on and off shore, severe storms have the greatest effect on beach erosion.

Extreme storm surge associated with hurricanes may raise the water levels on this shoreline 10–20 feet above mean sea level. From 1899 to 1921, 21 major hurricanes and more than 82 tropical storms and smaller hurricanes hit the Panama City Beach area, an average of about one every 4 years for big hurricanes and one every 1.5 years for tropical storms and small hurricanes. One major storm occurred on August 30, 1856, with recorded storm surge of 10 feet above mean sea level. A storm on September 27, 1906, produced storm surge of 6–10 feet in Panama City, causing property damage. Other hurricanes hit this coastline in 1924, 1926, 1929, 1936, 1950, 1953 (Florence), 1956 (Flossy), and 1972 (Agnes), and there have been more recent storms as well. Weather conditions October 5–11, 1970, caused severe erosion of beaches throughout the entire county.

Hurricane Eloise (September 12, 1975), one of the most severe in northwest Florida's history, made landfall about 40 miles west of Panama City. The strongest wind gusts near Panama City exceeded 155 mph, with sustained winds of 130 mph. The storm surge ranged from 12–16 feet from just east of Fort Walton Beach (Okaloosa County) to Mexico Beach, east of Crooked Island. Waves intensified by winds and high tides reached a maximum of 20.2 feet above mean sea level. Storm surge and waves undercut the dunes and scoured the beaches from Phillips Inlet to Mexico Beach, undermining the foundations of many buildings. In Bay County, losses exceeded $88 million.

In 1979, Hurricane Frederic caused dune retreat of about 10–15 feet at Mexico Beach, while Panama City beaches lost an immense amount of

6.9 Although Hurricane Earl did most of its damage farther east, Bay County beaches and infrastructure needed repair work, as shown in this photo. The dune here has good height, but damage occurred to the dune and the large drainpipe running through it toward the beach. Photo by Norma Longo.

sand with maximum erosion of 50 feet horizontally and 7 feet vertically. All of this happened with Frederic making landfall 160 miles west of Panama City Beach! Although Hurricane Opal's landfall was near Pensacola Beach (1995), the devastating effects were felt throughout Bay County as well. At the point of impact, Opal's winds were 125 mph and its barometric pressure was 940 millibars. Hurricane-force winds (75 mph) occurred over approximately 125 miles of the coast, from Navarre Beach (Santa Rosa County) to Cape San Blas (Gulf County), causing higher-than-normal waves and storm surge flooding, all of which led to severe coastal damage (appendix C, ref. 7). Dunes were either overtopped or destroyed, and buildings were damaged by the high-velocity floodwaters and wave action. During Hurricane Opal, the peak storm surge at Panama City Beach was 8.3 feet several hundred feet offshore, and high-water marks indicated a 12–14-foot peak surge onshore. Opal's flood level recurrence interval is 60 years, or a 1.7 percent annual chance.

Flood and erosion damage to the beach dune systems and structures during Hurricanes Opal and Eloise were greater in Bay County than in either Walton County or Okaloosa County to the west (fig. 6.9). The latter two counties were able to recover much more quickly, with minimal structural losses from floodwaters, due to less development and a better adherence to the coastal construction control line, which had protected primary and secondary dunes from being leveled for development (fig. 6.10). After Hurricane Opal, 17.5 miles of Panama City beaches and 2.8 miles of Mexico Beach were designated as critical erosion areas by the state. According to the Army Corps of Engineers, if a Panama City beach restoration project planned prior to Hurricane Opal had been in place, an estimated 70 percent of the damage resulting from Opal might have been prevented (appendix C, ref. 52). Post-Opal studies also showed that Bay County sustained the greatest damage overall because of its high density of development and the large number of inadequately designed buildings (appendix C, ref. 16). A total of 538 single-family dwellings and 1,783 multifamily units sustained 50 percent or more damage. All but one of the single-family houses damaged were constructed seaward of the CCCL, which now has been reestablished 100 feet farther landward of the original setback line recorded on September 17, 1974 (appendix C, ref. 60). The original line chopped the dune crests in half and in many cases permitted leveling of the dunes to build bulkheads close to the water. Following Hurricane Opal, the FDEP adopted a preventive measure for the entire Panhandle coast that requires the underside elevation for the first floor of houses to be greater than 17 feet (appendix C, ref. 16). Damaged houses that were landward of the original line now fall under the improved design and siting standards (appendix

6.10 Notice where the high-water mark on the sand is, and you can't help but wonder where someone can build a home on this extremely narrow, flat beach in Bay County! This sign was standing within a few feet of the road and only another few feet from the water. Photo by Norma Longo.

C, ref. 16), which may help reduce future storm damage along this moderate-to-extreme-risk shoreline.

Gulf County (RMs 20, 21, 22, 23)

The Gulf County shoreline is characterized by nearly 30 miles of mainland beaches and barrier spits. St. Joseph Peninsula, oriented north–south with an east–west dogleg at the southern end, and Indian Peninsula, aligned east–west, protrude off either side of the southern headland. Cape San Blas, the southernmost point of these unstable strips of sand, lies at the "elbow" in St. Joseph Peninsula. Most of St. Joseph Peninsula is about 0.5 mile wide, with the narrowest section being about 800 feet wide at Eagle Harbor, near the midpoint. St. Joseph Peninsula State Park and Eglin Air Force Base occupy parts of the peninsula, and St. Vincent National Wildlife Refuge lies adjacent, within St. Joseph Bay east of the peninsula. The state and federal lands are undeveloped, but much of the remainder of the peninsula is developed with both single-family and multifamily dwellings. The northern part of the peninsula has large dunes, generally 20–30 feet high but in excess of 50 feet in one area, and the southern 3 miles of the peninsula is backed by 10–15-foot dunes.

Erosion has been a long-term problem throughout the entire peninsula, with the exception of a 2.2-mile stretch at the northern tip where the shore is accreting or stable (appendix C, ref. 12; fig. 2.1). The beaches on the mainland to the north of the peninsula advanced about 200–300 feet between 1855 and 1935. Nearly 17 miles of Gulf County's Gulf-front beaches on both St. Joseph and Indian Peninsulas have erosion problems. Some sections of St. Joseph Peninsula have been nourished in the past, but the southern part, just north of Cape San Blas, has been eroding at rates up to 15 feet per year. The southernmost 3-mile portion of the cape is the most rapidly eroding shoreline in Florida, averaging 25 feet per year for the 150-year period of record (appendix C, ref. 53). The Cape San Blas lighthouse has been relocated six times! St. Joseph Peninsula is characterized by extreme-to-high-risk zones (RMS 21, 22).

Historically, the shoreline of Indian Peninsula retreated 100 feet from

RM 20   Mexico Beach, St. Joseph Bay, north

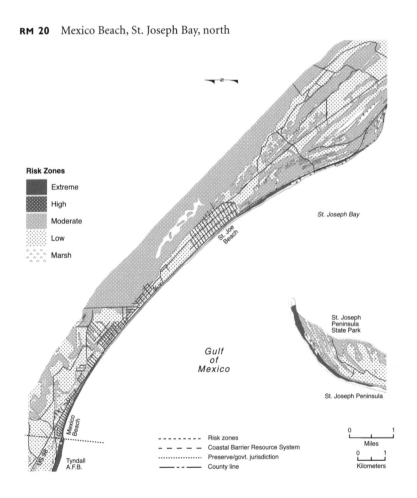

Risk Zones

- Extreme
- High
- Moderate
- Low
- Marsh

St. Joseph Bay

St. Joseph Peninsula State Park

Gulf of Mexico

St. Joseph Peninsula

Mexico Beach

Tyndall A.F.B.

- - - - - - - - Risk zones
- - - - - Coastal Barrier Resource System
· · · · · · · · · · Preserve/govt. jurisdiction
——— · · ——— County line

0 ___ 1 Miles

0 ___ 1 Kilometers

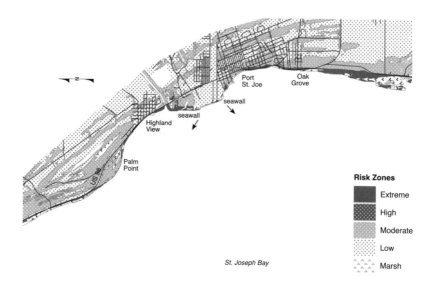

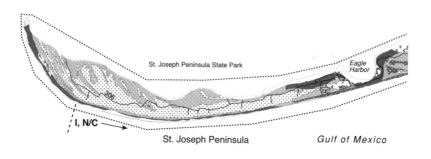

Risk Zones

■ Extreme

▒ High

▒ Moderate

⋮ Low

∧ Marsh

St. Joseph Bay

St. Joseph Peninsula State Park

Eagle Harbor

I, N/C

St. Joseph Peninsula

Gulf of Mexico

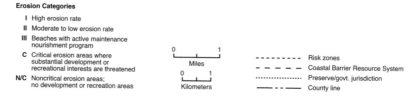

Erosion Categories

I   High erosion rate

II Moderate to low erosion rate

III Beaches with active maintenance
    nourishment program

C   Critical erosion areas where
    substantial development or
    recreational interests are threatened

N/C Noncritical erosion areas;
    no development or recreation areas

0 ___ 1
Miles

0 ___ 1
Kilometers

------- Risk zones

— — — Coastal Barrier Resource System

········· Preserve/govt. jurisdiction

—··— County line

RM 21   St. Joseph spit, north

1855 to 1945. Generally, the western 3 miles from the headland to the cape
have eroded, but there has also been intermittent localized buildup. At the
east end of the county, the beach width on 2.2-mile Indian Peninsula has
fluctuated over the years but appears to be widening (moderate-risk zone).

Hurricanes and tropical storms have struck Gulf County more than a

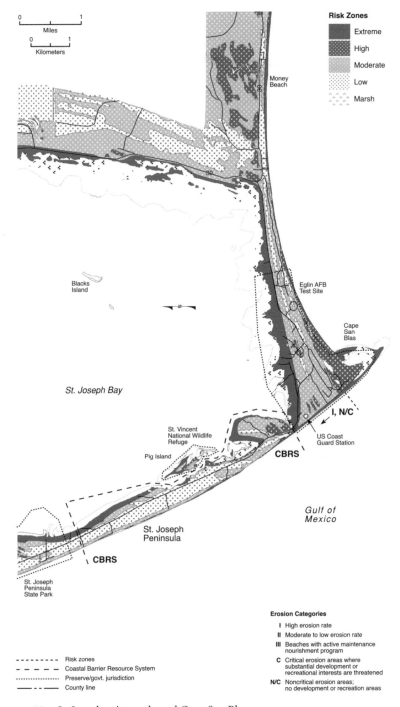

Risk Zones

- Extreme
- High
- Moderate
- Low
- Marsh

Money Beach

Blacks Island

Eglin AFB Test Site

Cape San Blas

St. Joseph Bay

I, N/C

St. Vincent National Wildlife Refuge

US Coast Guard Station

Pig Island

CBRS

Gulf of Mexico

St. Joseph Peninsula

CBRS

St. Joseph Peninsula State Park

Erosion Categories

I   High erosion rate

II   Moderate to low erosion rate

III   Beaches with active maintenance nourishment program

C   Critical erosion areas where substantial development or recreational interests are threatened

N/C   Noncritical erosion areas; no development or recreation areas

- - - - - - - -   Risk zones
- - - - -   Coastal Barrier Resource System
···············   Preserve/govt. jurisdiction
— ·· — ·· —   County line

RM 22   St. Joseph spit, south, and Cape San Blas

dozen times in the past century. A hurricane in 1844 breached the St. Joseph spit and destroyed the original town of Port St. Joe. A hurricane in 1915 made landfall near Port St. Joe on St. Joseph Bay, as did another in 1924; the latter storm caused damage estimated at $275,000. Interestingly, Hurricane Frederic in 1979 did not produce hurricane-force winds in this area and raised water levels only between 3 and 4 feet in St. Joseph Bay, but the bay rose about 6 feet above its normal level during Hurricane Eloise in September 1975. Normally, homes along St. Joseph Bay and Indian Lagoon are protected from waves by the St. Joseph and Indian Peninsulas, but houses on the Gulf coast are extremely vulnerable to storm damage. The 100-year flood levels for Gulf County are 9.5–12.5 feet above mean sea level.

Gulf County's mainland beaches just north of and bordering St. Joseph Bay and the Indian Pass shoreline experienced only minor erosion from Hurricane Opal (October 1995). Beaches and dunes on St. Joseph Peninsula, however, were extensively damaged, leaving a total length of 7,300 feet of shoreline in need of dune restoration (estimated cost, $147,376). Stump Hole, just north of Cape San Blas, was severely overwashed and eroded. Also, the county access road, C-30-A, was destroyed by storm surge from Hurricane Opal (fig. 6.11). About 14 miles of the southern peninsula was already eroded prior to Opal, leaving structures along this stretch highly susceptible to storm impact. Many houses are located seaward of the coastal construction setback line, recorded for this county on March 21, 1975 (appendix C, ref. 60), and Hurricane Opal damaged 14 percent of those buildings. Several other houses and townhouses remain threatened by erosion.

Hurricane Earl caused severe erosion and damage along the central and southern peninsula when it passed through in September 1998. At Cape San Blas, sustained winds from Earl were measured at 55 mph, and Stump Hole was again overwashed (see fig. 2.6).

In all, Gulf County has about 7.5 miles of developed shoreline, with only a few seawalls affecting some 770 feet of the developed coast. Development along St. Joseph Peninsula will continue to be extremely vulnerable to the high natural erosion rate as well as to future storm surge and wave attack. Moderately developed Indian Peninsula is currently accreting and therefore not as threatened. The entire county coastline ranks from moderate to extreme risk.

Franklin County (RMs 23, 24, 25, 26, 27, 28, 29)

The barrier-beach-and-inlet pattern is maintained in Franklin County, including, from west to east, Indian Pass, St. Vincent Island, West Pass, Little

6.11 A stretch of Highway c-30-a at Stump Hole near Cape San Blas (Gulf County) has been overwashed during several storms, compelling the state to fortify the area with a huge mound of rocks. A rock mound once fronted the road south of the lighthouse after Hurricane Kate in 1985, but it was destroyed by severe erosion and Opal (1995). The new mound was emplaced in 1998. Photo by Norma Longo.

St. George Island, Bob Sikes Cut, St. George Island, East Pass, and Dog Island, followed by the Alligator Point–Lighthouse Point–Bald Point peninsula complex.

St. Vincent Island (rms 23, 24) is an example of dune-and-swale topography resulting from thousands of years of swash action moving sediment shoreward. Since about 1965, erosion has occurred along the southern edge (appendix C, ref. 27). Both the curved eastern section of the island and the southern shore have wide, sandy beaches with a history of landward retreat. Although the beaches are 80–100 feet wide, very low dunes along these reaches allow flooding during storms. The western part of the island, near Indian Pass, is advancing seaward, and East Pass appears to be narrowing. St. Vincent Island is a national wildlife refuge, and private development is not anticipated here.

Little St. George Island (rm 24), sometimes referred to as Cape St. George Island, was formed from the western segment of St. George Island when Bob Sikes Cut was dredged across St. George Island in 1954 by local interests. Although the artificial cut generated controversy regarding its impact on the salinity in the bay and the associated fishery, the Corps of

Engineers constructed two jetties and redredged the channel in 1956. The channel was dredged annually between 1958 and 1975 (appendix C, ref. 24). Earlier, in 1855, a breach occurred in the middle of the northwesterly extension of Little St. George Island, north of Cape St. George, but the resulting inlet was closed by 1902 due to alongshore drift. The beach west of Sikes Cut receded approximately 300 feet between 1856 and 1934, and now is a high-to-extreme-risk zone. Much of this island is backed by marsh and is at extreme risk. The beaches at the St. George Island Lighthouse are severely eroded, leaving the lighthouse in a precarious position. Hurricane Opal tilted the lighthouse to 17 degrees, and Earl knocked it off its foundation, leaving it standing directly on the beach (see fig. 3.5).

St. George Island's (RMS 25, 26) shoreline has a long history of fluctuation. The eastern end built outward more than 1 mile, and a section from Sugar Hill to about 1.5 miles east of Sikes Cut advanced toward the Gulf on the average of about 100 feet from 1855 to 1935. At the same time, the beach from the eastern tip to near Sugar Hill retreated landward by 300–400 feet. The section of St. George Island between Sikes Cut and the state park on the island's eastern end is developed with multifamily and single-family homes, most of which are set back well away from the beach (fig. 6.12). The western portion of the St. George Island Plantation development has low dunes and a high erosion rate of about 5 feet per year. The ends of St. George Island and the low points near the old inlet sites, as well as the section between East Slough and Shell Point, are flooded by 10-year storm surge. Given the retreating shoreline and extreme-risk nature of this island, building here is a poor decision. The only evacuation route is a causeway. Evacuate early from this hazardous locality.

Except for its accreting ends, Dog Island (RMS 26, 27) has undergone constant shoreline recession. Between 1855 and 1935 the west end actually advanced about 1 mile. The beaches on this island are narrow, and the offshore Gulf profile is moderately steep. Dog Island is another example of curving dune-and-swale topography, with well-developed late Holocene beach ridges in a relatively natural state (appendix C, ref. 27). Three-quarters of the island is protected by dunes averaging 8–23 feet in height, with the highest more than 35 feet tall. The low, narrow western end of the island has been subject to frequent overwash during even minor storms. About half of the island is developed, primarily with single-family homes, and those at the east end of the island are threatened by erosion. All beachfront development here is vulnerable to storm loss, and most of Dog Island is rated as an extreme-risk zone. The only access is by water, so hurricane evacuation is tenuous at best.

Much of the Alligator Harbor Peninsula (RM 29), in eastern Franklin

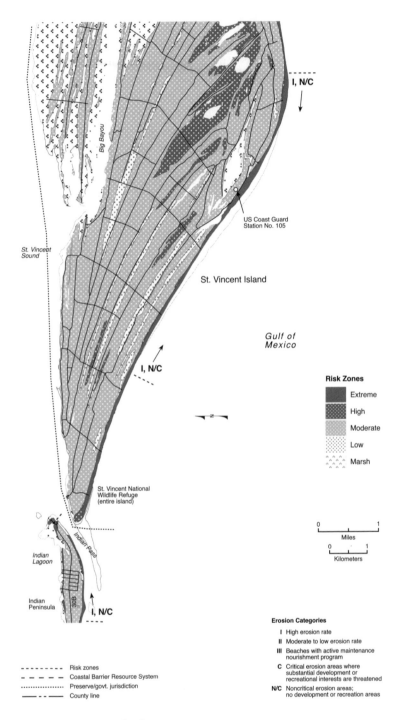

I, N/C

Big Bayou

US Coast Guard
Station No. 105

St. Vincent
Sound

St. Vincent Island

Gulf of
Mexico

I, N/C

Risk Zones

- Extreme
- High
- Moderate
- Low
- Marsh

St. Vincent National
Wildlife Refuge
(entire island)

Indian
Lagoon

Indian Pass

Indian
Peninsula

30B

I, N/C

0		1
Miles		

0		1
Kilometers		

Erosion Categories

I   High erosion rate

II Moderate to low erosion rate

III Beaches with active maintenance
nourishment program

C   Critical erosion areas where
substantial development or
recreational interests are threatened

N/C Noncritical erosion areas;
no development or recreation areas

- - - - - - - -   Risk zones
- - - - - -   Coastal Barrier Resource System
·················   Preserve/govt. jurisdiction
——— - - ———   County line

RM 23   St. Vincent Island area

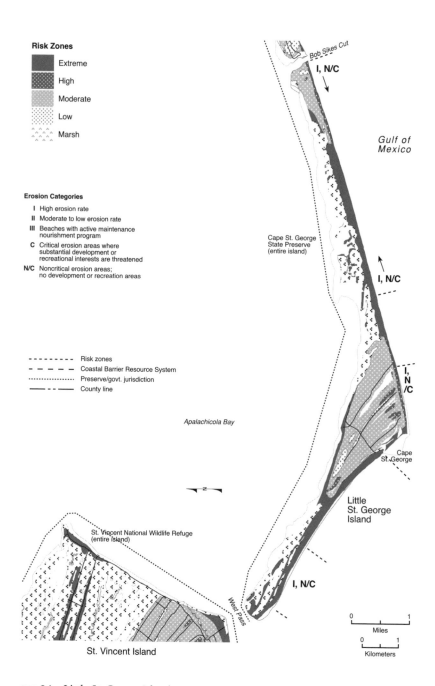

Risk Zones

Extreme

High

Moderate

Low

Marsh

Erosion Categories

I High erosion rate

II Moderate to low erosion rate

III Beaches with active maintenance
   nourishment program

C Critical erosion areas where
   substantial development or
   recreational interests are threatened

N/C Noncritical erosion areas;
   no development or recreation areas

- - - - - - - - - Risk zones
- - - - - Coastal Barrier Resource System
················· Preserve/govt. jurisdiction
—— - - —— County line

Bob Sikes Cut

I, N/C

Gulf of
Mexico

Cape St. George
State Preserve
(entire island)

I, N/C

I,
N
/C

Apalachicola Bay

Cape
St. George

Little
St. George
Island

St. Vincent National Wildlife Refuge
(entire island)

West Pass

I, N/C

St. Vincent Island

0 _____ 1
Miles

0 _____ 1
Kilometers

RM 24   Little St. George Island area

6.12 St. George Island, Franklin County, following Hurricane Earl; winds from Hurricane Georges were just around the corner. Piles of seaweed decorate the wide, flat beach. Houses here are set back from the water, but dune protection is minimal and flooding can still be a problem. Photo by Norma Longo.

County, has been fronted with 8–10-foot dunes. Beaches in this area have been relatively stable in the past and averaged about 50 feet wide. The northern half of the eastern shore, from Bald Point southward, has built out eastward, while the southern half toward Lighthouse Point has retreated westward, producing a mildly curved shoreline. Advance and retreat in this area have varied from 200 to 300 feet between 1856 and 1943. The shoreline north from Lighthouse Point to Bald Point is at extreme risk and is moderately developed. The rest of the barrier spit has retreated landward and extended westward. Several low-lying areas here are subject to overwash during storms, and man-made canals and land clearing in the past have produced three or four potential inlet sites for hurricanes to exploit.

More than a dozen hurricanes and dozens of lesser tropical storms have battered Franklin County's coast since the mid-1800s, flooding and overwashing the islands with storm surges of 9–15 feet. Hundred-year flood levels are estimated at 12–14 feet along this open coast. St. Vincent Island, Little St. George Island, and St. George Island lend some protection to the mainland city of Apalachicola, but their relatively low elevations allow overwash during severe storm surges.

Fifteen hurricanes passed within 50 miles of Sikes Cut between 1837 and 1977, approximately 1 every 10 years. During a severe hurricane in 1842 (September 30–October 6), water was said to have been 20 feet above the

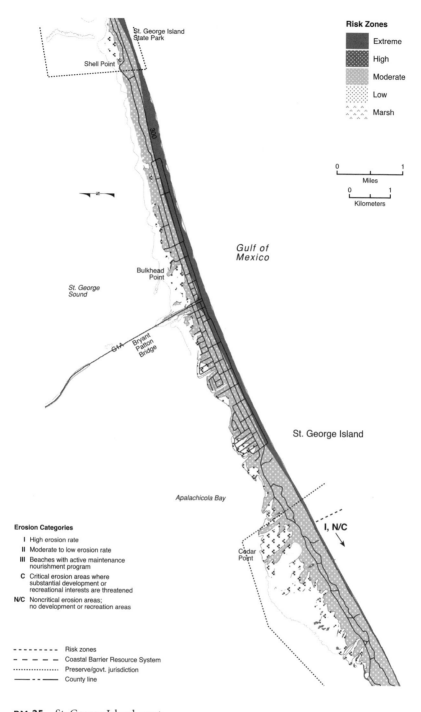

Risk Zones

- Extreme
- High
- Moderate
- Low
- Marsh

St. George Island
State Park

Shell Point

300

*Gulf of
Mexico*

Bulkhead
Point

*St. George
Sound*

G1A

Bryant
Patton
Bridge

St. George Island

Apalachicola Bay

I, N/C

Cedar
Point

0   1
Miles

0   1
Kilometers

Erosion Categories

I   High erosion rate

II   Moderate to low erosion rate

III   Beaches with active maintenance
nourishment program

C   Critical erosion areas where
substantial development or
recreational interests are threatened

N/C   Noncritical erosion areas;
no development or recreation areas

- - - - - - - - -   Risk zones
- - - - -   Coastal Barrier Resource System
....   Preserve/govt. jurisdiction
——— - - ———   County line

RM 25   St. George Island, west

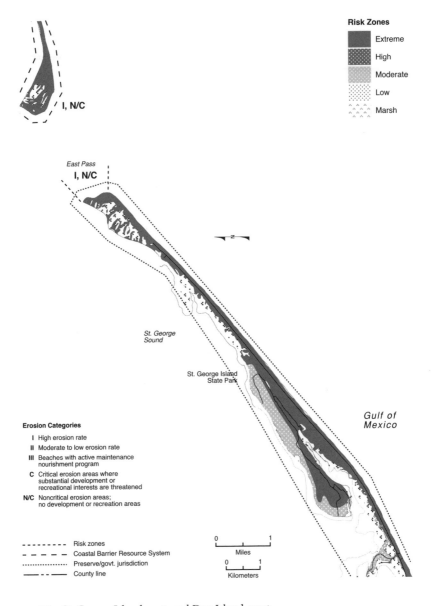

Risk Zones

- Extreme
- High
- Moderate
- Low
- Marsh

I, N/C

East Pass
I, N/C

St. George
Sound

St. George Island
State Park

Gulf of
Mexico

Erosion Categories

I   High erosion rate
II Moderate to low erosion rate
III Beaches with active maintenance
    nourishment program
C   Critical erosion areas where
    substantial development or
    recreational interests are threatened
N/C Noncritical erosion areas;
    no development or recreation areas

- - - - - - - - - Risk zones
- - - - - - Coastal Barrier Resource System
· · · · · · · · · · Preserve/govt. jurisdiction
— · · — County line

0 _____ 1
Miles

0 _____ 1
Kilometers

RM 26   St. George Island, east, and Dog Island, west

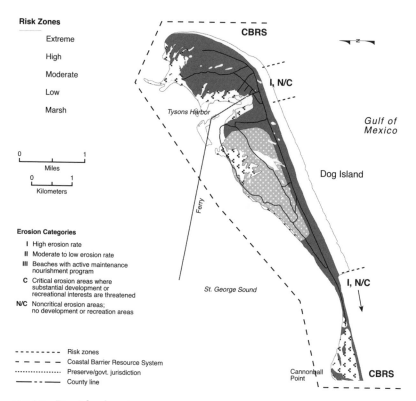

Risk Zones

Extreme

High

Moderate

Low

Marsh

0   1
Miles
0   1
Kilometers

Erosion Categories

I High erosion rate
II Moderate to low erosion rate
III Beaches with active maintenance
     nourishment program
C Critical erosion areas where
   substantial development or
   recreational interests are threatened
N/C Noncritical erosion areas;
     no development or recreation areas

- - - - - - - -   Risk zones
- - - - -   Coastal Barrier Resource System
· · · · · · · · ·   Preserve/govt. jurisdiction
——— · · ———   County line

CBRS

I, N/C

Gulf of
Mexico

Dog Island

Tysons Harbor

Ferry

St. George Sound

I, N/C

Cannonball
Point

CBRS

RM 27   Dog Island, east

low-water mark near Apalachicola (appendix C, ref. 24). An August 1851 hurricane, the "Apalachicola Storm," flooded Apalachicola and destroyed the nearby town of St. Teresa. The October 9, 1852, hurricane caused a breach across St. George Island, 2 miles east of West Pass, that closed by 1917. Several other hurricanes (1915, 1924, 1941) brought high winds and storm surge up to 7 feet above mean sea level to the area. The "Western Florida Hurricane" of 1837 generated a 10–15-foot storm surge at St. George Island and opened New Inlet, 10 feet wide and 21 feet deep. Engineer Ralph Clark of the FDEP notes that Pilot Cove is the deep-channel remainder of this inlet. The state park has been severely eroded by several storms, including Hurricanes Agnes (1972), Elena and Kate (1985), and Opal (1995). Storm surge from Agnes was 7–8 feet on St. George Island where 8 miles of road was destroyed. During Opal, both the state park and Dog Island were severely overwashed and required dune restoration measures. The cost estimate for post-Opal recovery in the park alone was more than $1 million (appendix C, ref. 12).

Hurricane Opal also eroded the Southwest Cape and Lighthouse Point

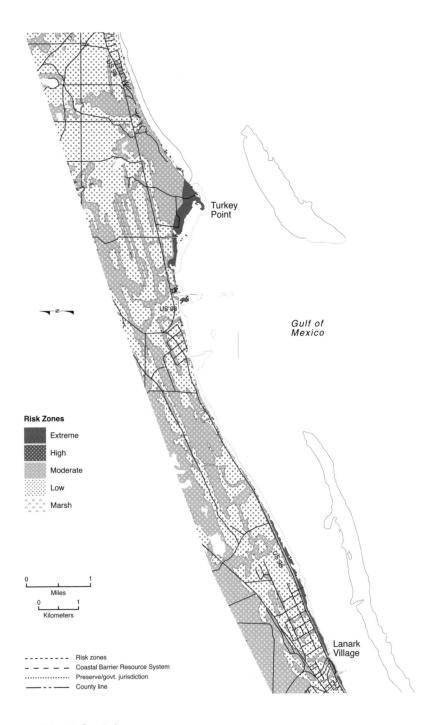

Risk Zones

■	Extreme
▨	High
▨	Moderate
⠿	Low
⌃⌃⌃	Marsh

Turkey Point

Gulf of Mexico

Lanark Village

0 _____ 1
Miles

0 _____ 1
Kilometers

--------- Risk zones
— — — — Coastal Barrier Resource System
················· Preserve/govt. jurisdiction
——— · — · County line

RM 28 Turkey Point area

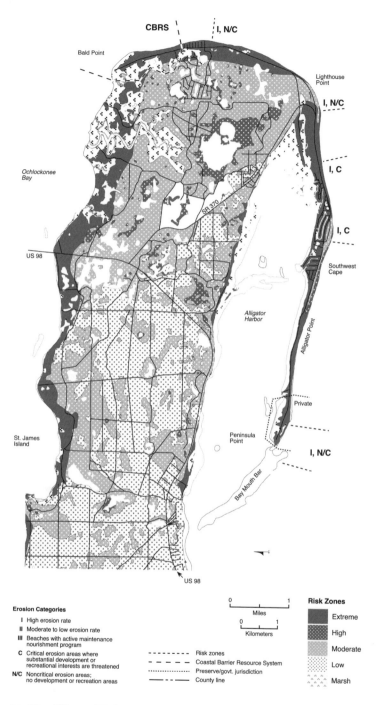

CBRS

I, N/C

Bald Point

Lighthouse
Point

I, N/C

Ochlockonee
Bay

I, C

SR 370

I, C

US 98

Southwest
Cape

Alligator
Harbor

Alligator Point

St. James
Island

Private

Peninsula
Point

I, N/C

Bay Mouth Bar

US 98

Erosion Categories

I   High erosion rate

II   Moderate to low erosion rate

III Beaches with active maintenance
     nourishment program

C   Critical erosion areas where
     substantial development or
     recreational interests are threatened

N/C Noncritical erosion areas;
     no development or recreation areas

0 ————————— 1
Miles

0 ————————— 1
Kilometers

- - - - - - - Risk zones

- - - - - -   Coastal Barrier Resource System

· · · · · · · · · Preserve/govt. jurisdiction

———— · ———— County line

Risk Zones

■ Extreme

▨ High

▩ Moderate

▫ Low

△ Marsh

RM 29 Alligator Harbor area

areas and severely damaged most of the beaches. Of the 377 major buildings built seaward of the coastal construction setback line, which was established September 17, 1974, 181 were permitted buildings, and none of these was damaged. Nine of the unpermitted buildings were damaged by Opal (appendix C, refs. 16, 60).

The nearly 8-foot storm surge during Hurricane Earl (September 1998) caused further damage, with Alligator Point losing roadway, a wooden seawall, and upland sand. Waves and rain pounded the area again during Hurricane Georges a few weeks later, increasing the erosion and structural damage (fig. 6.13). The most vulnerable developments at present are on Dog Island and along the Southwest Cape and Lighthouse Point areas of Alligator Point, where development is dense. Loss of the only access road adds to the danger of shorefront living in these areas.

The Big Bend Marsh Coast

Florida's expanse of barrier island chains is interrupted between Franklin County in the eastern Panhandle and southern Pasco County north of Tampa Bay. The Big Bend shoreline is characterized by extensive coastal

6.13 Structural damage to homes on Alligator Point from Hurricane Earl was worsened by the hit from Georges two weeks later. Septic tanks and drain fields were exposed to the open water, presenting a health hazard. These houses must be moved landward or they will fall into the ocean. Photo by Norma Longo.

marshes and swamps, including mangroves. Small islands, some with limestone outcroppings, are set apart by a complex of small bays and tidal creeks (see fig. 2.2). A number of small rivers empty into the Gulf along this coast, and small beaches are found here and there throughout the region. The irregularity of the shoreline, extensive wetlands, karst topography, and paucity of sandy beaches are all in complete contrast to the barrier island segments of the Gulf shore. Eight counties (Wakulla, Jefferson, Taylor, Dixie, Levy, Citrus, Hernando, and Pasco) border this great coastal curve at the northeast edge of the Gulf of Mexico (see fig. 1.2).

A significant portion of this area is underlain by limestone and is fed by rivers draining limestone terrain that do not supply sand for beaches. As a result, barrier islands are absent and sandy beaches and dunes are rare. Although the area has a sand supply offshore, the wave energy here is too weak to transport sand toward land in amounts sufficient to form barrier islands. Breaker-zone energy levels are very low, with average breaker heights measured only in inches. This low-energy regime is attributable to several factors, including a predominantly seaward wind direction, the concave coastline, a wide offshore shelf of shallow profile, and resulting low wave activity. The domination by rivers and creeks and the almost horizontal slope of the land have resulted in the marsh-swamp-delta plain that often extends inland for miles.

The geography of this portion of the Gulf coast illustrates that even a slight rise in sea level will result in thousands of feet of shoreline retreat (see fig. 2.5). In this case, flooding by the rising sea level over the last few hundreds to thousands of years has produced a vast, watery transition zone between land and sea. As a result, this coastal segment, more than 200 miles in length, has remained relatively untouched by humans, and rightly so, because it is unsuitable for development.

Wakulla and Jefferson Counties

The St. Marks National Wildlife Refuge lies along almost the entire marshland-swamp coast of Wakulla and Jefferson Counties. The boundary between sea and land is not always distinct as coastal marshes give way to swamps going inland. Thought to be Ponce de León's first hope for a "fountain of youth," Wakulla Springs, inland on Florida Highways 61 and 267, discharges roughly 575 million gallons of water daily. The Sopchoppy and St. Marks Rivers, plus numerous creeks, account for the marsh-swamp-delta plain that lies at sea level and rises inland only a few feet over several miles. The primary flood hazard in these low-lying areas is from storm surge. Figure 6.14 shows the coastal high-hazard flood area for Wakulla

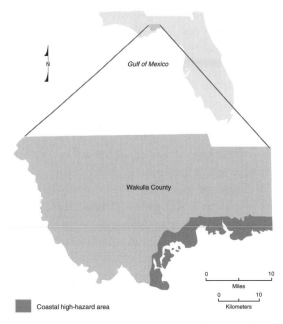

6.14 Location of Wakulla County, Florida, showing the coastal high-hazard area in black. Adapted from the Wakulla County Comprehensive Plan, 1994.

County as an example. Other coastal counties in the Big Bend area will have similar hazard zones. It is best to check with your local town hall for detailed information on high-hazard areas.

Base Flood Elevations range from 12 to 23 feet, and the area was flooded to considerable depths by several hurricanes (e.g., 1837, 1843, 1966; fig. 6.15). In 1972, Hurricane Agnes caused a peak storm surge of nearly 8 feet above sea level at St. Marks in Wakulla County (appendix C, ref. 51). Hurricane Allison, in June 1995, produced a storm surge of 6–8 feet, and Hurricane Opal caused erosion along this shoreline in 1995. The storm surge from Hurricane Earl (September 1998) was nearly 8 feet here and in Taylor County. Generally, southwest winds generate waves that cause significant erosion of the marsh edge, although this section of the Florida coast has not been the subject of detailed study. The numerous marsh islands — for example, Mashes, Porter, Piney, Palmetto, Smith, Big Pass, and Sprague Islands — are particularly susceptible to erosion.

The refuge designation takes this extremely hazardous area out of the development market. However, several older communities, such as Panacea Park and Panacea, are present some distance away from the coast at moderate elevations of 10–15 feet. During Hurricane Agnes in 1972, Panacea's high-water mark was 8 feet. People in these communities should be

6.15 In the coastal area of Wakulla County, the 100-year flood elevation is in excess of 30 feet, which explains why this building is on such high stilts. The explanation for the unusually high elevation of the 100-year flood level lies in the great width and shallow slope of the adjacent continental shelf. A very flat continental shelf forces storm surge waters to pile up to high elevations. Photo by David Bush.

aware of the likelihood that low spots along U.S. Highway 98 and Florida Highways 30 and 61 flood well in advance of an approaching hurricane, and early evacuation should be the rule.

With elevations around 5 feet, Shell Point, near Oyster Bay, is one of the few locations along this stretch of coast with a sand beach. Development faces the open water, and finger canals may create water problems. Highway 367, the escape route, traverses a wide expanse of marsh and swamp that is likely to flood in advance of an approaching storm. The same problems exist at Spring Creek at the head of Oyster Bay. Live Oak Island also is in a hazardous position at the end of Highway 367A.

These areas are not likely targets for extensive development because they are remote and lack the amenities that many coastal dwellers seek, namely, beaches and dunes near urban support centers. Fishers and nature lovers enjoy this area because of its wilderness appeal. Two of the developed areas are considered by the FDEP to be critically eroding: 0.7 mile of shoreline at Mashes Sands, near the mouth of Ochlockonee Bay, and 1 mile at Shell Point. Any future development in Wakulla County likely will occur in the northern and southwestern regions of the county (appendix C, ref. 51). As a flood protection measure, present flood regulations require structures to be elevated up to 30 feet in some areas. A coastal construction control line has not been established for counties in the Big Bend region.

The 5-mile Jefferson County coast is marsh, accessible only by boat, and lies entirely within the St. Marks National Wildlife Refuge. Apalachee Bay and the Aucilla River form the boundaries, so both the river and the Gulf are sources of flooding.

Taylor County

This vast coastal marsh owes its origins and natural wildlife productivity to its flooded state and to the fact that it is repeatedly flooded by storms. Erosion is severe due to the southeastern orientation of the coast — an alignment that allows larger waves to approach during storms. Many creeks and small rivers, such as the Ecofina and Fenholloway Rivers, indent the shoreline. Along its southeast section are numerous marsh islands and oyster bars. Sinkhole ponds and lakes, within both wetlands and uplands, are typical of this karst coastline.

A few fishing camps are accessible off Highway 361, as are a few small coastal settlements, such as Dekle Beach, Jug Island, and Keaton Beach, at the end of Highway 361. These older developments are situated in relatively high hazard zones, sited at low elevations and facing the Gulf with no natural protection. At Dekle Beach, 0.2 miles of the coastline has a critical erosion problem (appendix C, ref. 53). In October 1996, Tropical Storm Josephine made landfall in eastern Apalachee Bay between Dekle Beach and St. Marks, with 69 mph winds contributing to flooding and erosion in the area. Similar storm conditions can be expected along this high-risk shoreline in the future.

Steinhatchee lies about 1.5 miles up the Steinhatchee River on the southeast border of the county. The town's location away from the shore and on a ridge with elevations in excess of 20 feet affords some safety. Low elevations along Highway 51 will flood in advance of approaching storms. Inhabitants should evacuate early to a safer inland location in the event of a storm warning.

Dixie County

Extensive marsh-swamp lowlands extend far inland here and are pocked with sinkhole ponds. Only three roads traverse these wetlands to provide access to the few minor coastal developments. Florida Highway 351 leads to Horseshoe Beach, about a quarter of a mile inland from the Gulf, with elevations greater than 10 feet. Some developed sites are at low elevations.

6.16 Shired Island, Dixie County, has been severely eroded by storms in the past. Photo by Ralph Clark.

At Horseshoe Point, houses line an extreme-risk shore that is eroded by waves out of the south and southwest. The small communities of Suwannee and Barbree Island lie at the end of Florida Highway 349, north of the famous Suwannee River. The surrounding marsh affords protection from erosive wave attack, but the area is in the 100-year flood zone and considered at high risk.

A county road runs through California Swamp to the small development of Shired Island, a narrow ridge that rises to 15 feet and is surrounded by protective marsh. Cottages located on the edge of the mouth of Shired Creek are in the most perilous position here. The north end of the sandy beach shoreline at Shired Island has been severely eroded by several storms, including Hurricane Elena in 1985, the "Storm of the Century" in 1993, and Tropical Storm Josephine in 1996 (fig. 6.16).

This region is subject to significant storm surge flooding and erosion, such as that which occurred with the passage of Tropical Storm Josephine in October 1996 and Hurricanes Earl and Georges in September 1998. Storm surge from Earl rose to approximately 6–7 feet (see the report by Max Mayfield at the National Hurricane Center's web site: http://www.nhc.noaa.gov/1998earl.html). Evacuation requires a long drive across the flood zone to reach safety.

Levy County

The marsh coast along Suwannee Sound has numerous tidal creeks extending into a wide expanse of swamp. A few isolated topographic highs, without access, exist within the swamp, and similar offshore high areas have produced small islands (Clark, Deer, Long, Cabbage, Hog, Seabreeze, Richards) north of Cedar Key. Some of these islands have elevations of 15 feet, but they are not suitable for development.

Florida Highway 24 leads to Cedar Key, a small community of about 700 people just inland from the shore on the only high ground for many miles. The elevation rises to about 25 feet, and building sites above 15 feet are in the moderate-risk category. Houses on sites below 10 feet will be flooded even in a moderate storm. An 1898 hurricane destroyed Cedar Key, and in more recent times Hurricanes Alma (1966) and Agnes (1972) caused storm surges of nearly 10 feet at Cedar Key.

Tropical Storm Josephine (1996) produced storm surge up to 9 feet in Levy County. As far south as Lee County, storm surge from both Josephine and Earl was about 3 feet. Along this entire coastline, the high tides brought widespread flooding of homes, roads, and businesses (see the report by R. J. Pasch at the National Hurricane Center's web site: http://www.nhc.noaa.gov/1997danny.html). Highway 24 is adjacent to and crosses marsh and swamp, and low spots along the highway flood in the advance of approaching storms. Although large numbers of people would not be evacuating along this route, prudence dictates early evacuation.

Cedar Key is the gateway to Cedar Keys National Wildlife Refuge, a complex of very small islands, some rising strikingly above sea level. Mangrove swamps fringe some of the islets and are important protection against shoreline erosion. Seahorse Key has 1.2 miles of eroding shoreline (appendix C, ref. 53), and Atsena Otie Key has experienced severe erosion along approximately 1,000 feet of its shoreline (fig. 6.17). Fortunately, these islands are uninhabited and should remain so.

6.17 Atsena Otie Key, Levy County, shows severe erosion. Fortunately, no homes are located here and should never be! Photo by Ralph Clark.

East of Cedar Key, the shore turns east along the north side of Wacca-sassa Bay within another complex of creeks, ponds, marsh, and swamp. The swamp area is known as Gulf Hammock and is cut by the Waccasassa River. Only a few scattered hunting and fishing camps are located here, at elevations of less than 5 feet — an extremely high-risk area.

Yankeetown lies on the southern boundary of Levy County about 2 miles inland on the banks of the Withlacoochee River. Most of the buildings in town are on sites with elevations of less than 10 feet and are in the high-risk zone. Highways 40 and 40A are the access routes to Yankeetown and Pumpkin Island, and, like other coastal routes, they have low areas that will flood. Be ready to leave early when storms approach.

Citrus County

From the Withlacoochee River to the Crystal River the marsh-swamp zone narrows, but the shoreline continues as marsh fringe cut by numerous tidal creeks. South of Crystal River is the highly dissected marsh coast, a maze of mangrove keys and marsh islands, some of which lie in the Chassahowitzka National Wildlife Refuge on Homosassa Bay and extend into Hernando County.

More than 30 percent of the county's population lives in the coastal zone (appendix C, ref. 51). The small communities that lie along rivers or at the heads of estuaries some distance inland are often still within the 100-year flood zone. Flooding occurred as a result of Hurricane Dora, which passed to the north of Citrus County in 1964, and Elena (1985) blew down trees along the marsh coast. Storm surge produced by Tropical Storm Josephine (1996) ranged between 4 and 9 feet, and the 1998 hurricanes (Earl and Georges) brought more damage to the area. The entire lowland area is at high risk from storm flooding and sea-level rise.

Hernando County (RM 30)

South of the Chassahowitzka River is the swamp of the same name. Highway 50, from Weeki Wachee Spring, provides access to small developments, including tiny Pine Island, Cooglers Beach, and Bayport. One-half mile of Pine Island's shore is at low elevation and erosive. Bayport, on the other hand, rises to a higher elevation of about 20 feet, which, along with the protective marsh fringe, provides a few lower-risk sites. Even so, the area really cannot support safe development. The same is true for other developments served by Highway 595 and those near the coast in Indian Bay, where a few houses along tidal creeks are in a moderate-hazard zone.

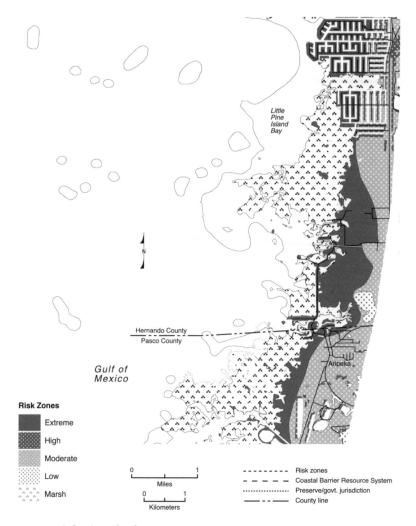

Little
Pine
Island
Bay

Hernando County
Pasco County

Gulf of
Mexico

Aripeka

Risk Zones

- Extreme
- High
- Moderate
- Low
- Marsh

0   1
Miles

0   1
Kilometers

- - - - - - - -   Risk zones
- - - - - -   Coastal Barrier Resource System
....   Preserve/govt. jurisdiction
—— - ·· ——   County line

RM 30 Little Pine Island Bay area

Hernando Beach, between Weeki Wachee Swamp and the Gulf of Mexico, is a low-lying community of fewer than 2,000 people. Many homes here are fronted by seawalls that may not withstand hurricane forces. Storm surge flooding is the main threat in these areas of high to extreme risk.

Pasco County (RMs 30, 31, 32, 33)

Just inside the northern line of Pasco County, on Highway 595, is the small community of Aripeka, some distance inland from the coast but only about 5 feet in elevation and in the flood zone. Early evacuation is encouraged in the event of a hurricane warning. The same is true for residents along Old Dixie Highway and in Hudson. Many homesites are at low elevations; nearly all are below 10 feet. Hudson Beach, with its coastal development, has a serious erosion problem over a 0.2-mile stretch (appendix C, ref. 53).

Pasco County's shoreline is essentially unsuitable for development because it is a continuation of the marshy coast. Locally, there are fringes of reef and mangrove. The marsh zone is about a mile wide, rising over a mile or two through intermittent swamp into a sinkhole-pocked upland about 30 feet in elevation. People seeking to locate in this area should look for

RM 31 Yellow Point area

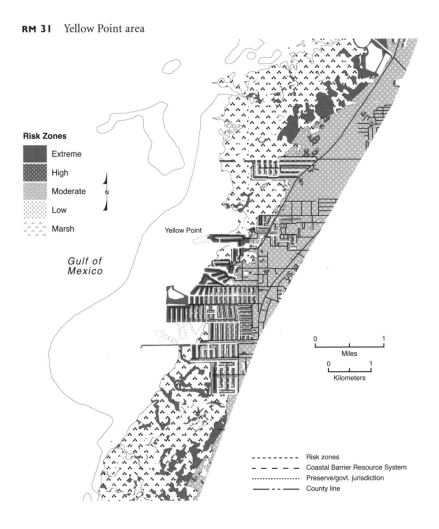

Risk Zones
- Extreme
- High
- Moderate
- Low
- Marsh

N

Yellow Point

Gulf of
Mexico

0   1
Miles
0   1
Kilometers

- - - - - - - - Risk zones
- - - - - Coastal Barrier Resource System
.... Preserve/govt. jurisdiction
— - - — County line

inland, upland sites, away from sinkholes, and at maximum elevations.

The highly developed communities of Port Richey, New Port Richey, and Gulf Harbors are the first significant developments south of the somewhat protected communities of Jasmine and Jasmine Estates. These communities hint of the urbanization that lies in the densely populated and developed counties farther south. The city of Port Richey lies on the Gulf shore joining New Port Richey within the Pithlachascotee River flood zone (RM 32). While elevations here range from sea level to about 20 feet, many cottage sites near the river are less than 10 feet in elevation, and others are less than 5 feet.

Flooding in these extreme-risk zones results primarily from storm

RM 32 Port Richey area

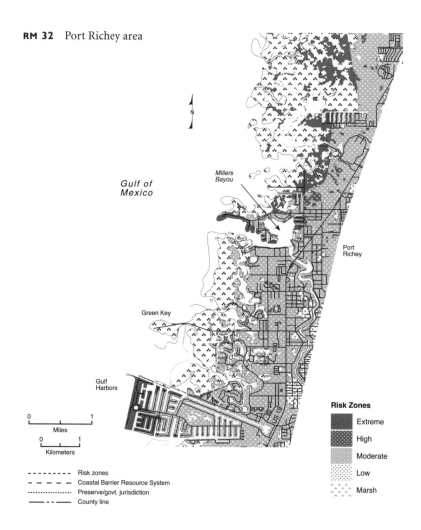

Gulf of
Mexico

Millers
Bayou

Port
Richey

Green Key

Gulf
Harbors

0   1
Miles

0   1
Kilometers

- - - - - - - - Risk zones
- - - - - Coastal Barrier Resource System
············· Preserve/govt. jurisdiction
—— ·· —— County line

Risk Zones

Extreme

High

Moderate

Low

Marsh

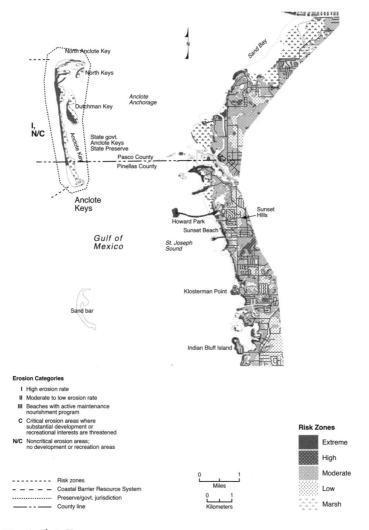

RM 33   Anclote Key area

surges caused by hurricanes and tropical storms (appendix C, ref. 51). Several hurricanes have struck the Port Richey area, the most severe being the storms of October 1921, August–September 1935, September 1950 (Hurricane Easy), Hurricane Alma in June 1966, and Hurricane Agnes in June 1972. The area experienced storm surge ranging up to 10 feet during some of these storms. Gulf Harbors (RM 32) lies in an even more untenable position, jutting into the open-Gulf waters. The 100-year storm surge at the Port Richey shoreline ranges from 9.5 feet to 19 feet (appendix C, ref. 51). Suggested flood-proofing measures include elevating houses, mangrove conservation, and possibly seawall construction. Although seawalls are detrimental to beach quality, sandy beaches are not common in this area. The seawalls and bulkheads that have been constructed here might remain intact during a 100-year storm surge but are too low to be effective against flooding from storm waves. The Pasco County coastline is essentially all at high to extreme risk for storm damage.

A significant natural change occurs along the southern shoreline of Pasco County (RM 33): the return of moderate wave energy and barrier islands. Anclote Key lies at the northern end of an extensive barrier island chain bounding the west-central Florida peninsula. The southern portion of Anclote Key extends into Pinellas County. The island suffers from the same hazards that are listed again and again in these pages: high to extreme rates of shoreline erosion, storm surge flooding with wave impact and overwash, the potential for new inlets to form or old inlets to migrate, and other coastal processes faced by barrier islands. Anclote Key State Preserve protects people and property by preventing development on this barrier island. The islands to the south are another story.

The West-Central Barrier Island Chain

The west-central Florida coastline consists of a chain of small barrier islands separated by numerous inlets, with major mainland beaches — Venice Beach and Naples Beach — in Sarasota and Collier Counties, respectively. Prevailing winds along this coast are from the northeast and north during the winter and from the east and south during the remainder of the year. Anclote Key is the beginning of the west coast peninsular barrier island chain, whose sand comes primarily from erosion of prominent local headlands. The continental shelf is broad and gently sloping along the peninsula. This coastal segment extends approximately 185 miles from Anclote Key in the north to Cape Romano in the south and includes six counties: Pinellas, Manatee, Sarasota, Charlotte, Lee, and Collier.

Because more than 100 miles of this shoreline is densely developed, the task of protecting both beaches and beachfront properties is regarded as important to maintain a way of life in which tourism is a top priority. The estimated late-1990s tourist population in Pinellas County alone was approximately 4.6 million per year (appendix C, ref. 53). Beaches along the other coastal counties are also popular, which in turn influences shorefront development and protection measures. A law enacted in 1941 by the state of Florida (House Bill No. 1746) authorized counties to attempt to control beach erosion by doing whatever was deemed necessary to prevent it, including to "construct, establish and erect all bulkheads, seawalls and other

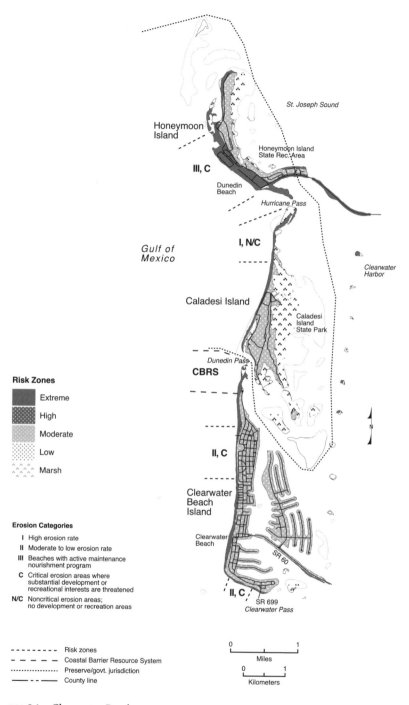

St. Joseph Sound

Honeymoon
Island

Honeymoon Island
State Rec. Area

III, C

Dunedin
Beach

Hurricane Pass

*Gulf of
Mexico*

I, N/C

Clearwater
Harbor

Caladesi Island

Caladesi
Island
State Park

Dunedin Pass

CBRS

Risk Zones

▓	Extreme
▓	High
░	Moderate
⋮	Low
∧∧∧	Marsh

II, C

Clearwater
Beach
Island

Erosion Categories

I   High erosion rate

II   Moderate to low erosion rate

III   Beaches with active maintenance
nourishment program

C   Critical erosion areas where
substantial development or
recreational interests are threatened

N/C   Noncritical erosion areas;
no development or recreation areas

Clearwater
Beach

SR 60

II, C

SR 699
Clearwater Pass

- - - - - - - -   Risk zones
— — — —   Coastal Barrier Resource System
· · · · · · · · · · · ·   Preserve/govt. jurisdiction
——— · ——   County line

0		1

Miles

0		1

Kilometers

RM 34   Clearwater Beach area

structures" (appendix C, ref. 60). Now, 56 miles (more than 50 percent) of the developed west-central peninsula shoreline is armored with seawalls, revetments, groins, and jetties. One-half of the armoring is built parallel to the shore; nearly 10 percent consists of jetties, groins, or sand tubes extending into the surf; and more than 40 percent of the armoring is a combination of the two types. Beach nourishment is a viable alternative to shore armoring as a shore protection measure and for erosion mitigation and has been used widely along this highly developed coastline. Although many segments of this shoreline are considered stable, numerous beaches have been nourished in an effort to protect buildings and control beach retreat. Erosion problem areas have been identified in the vicinity of some inlets where a variety of coastal processes, such as obstruction of littoral drift by jetties, contribute to downdrift beach erosion.

Most of the barrier beaches along the west-central peninsula trend northwest–southeast, which may contribute to their erosion potential and to the demand for nourishment or armoring. Natural protection is accomplished by mangroves farther south along the peninsula, in what appears to be a relict of a barrier chain that continues south of Naples as the Ten Thousand Islands (appendix C, ref. 3). All of the islands and barrier beaches along this coast are vulnerable to damage from wave action and storm surge resulting from the passage of tropical storms or hurricanes.

Although hurricanes along the west-central peninsula are relatively infrequent, several hurricanes and tropical storms have passed over or near this coast, notably in 1921, 1950 (Easy), 1960 (Donna), 1972 (Agnes), 1985 (Elena), 1995 (Opal and Erin), and 1998 (Mitch). Hurricane Elena was the first hurricane to have a major impact on Pinellas County since significant development has taken place (appendix C, ref. 13). Winds from Elena increased wave energy and produced a storm surge that caused extensive damage to the barrier islands, resulting in Pinellas, Hillsborough, and Manatee Counties being declared federal disaster areas (appendix C, refs. 13 and 45). Hurricane Opal caused flooding and moderate erosion along beaches in Pinellas, Manatee, and Sarasota Counties, and minor erosion all the way south to Key West. Beach nourishment projects constructed in the late 1980s and early 1990s probably reduced damage from Opal, particularly in Sarasota, Manatee, and Pinellas Counties (appendix C, ref. 16).

Pinellas County (RMs 33, 34, 35, 36, 37)

In 1993, Pinellas County was the most densely populated county in Florida with 2,890 residents per square mile. Tourism is the mainstay of the county's economy. The completion of the first causeways between the mainland

and the barrier islands in the 1920s led to early growth and development on the barriers. This was followed by rapid unregulated growth and urbanization in the 1940s and 1950s in response to the postwar demand for housing (appendix C, ref. 13). As the demand for waterfront property increased after World War II, extensive dredging projects were undertaken (see fig. 5.6). From Indian Rocks Beach (RM 35) to Pass-a-Grille (RM 36), the growth was phenomenal. It continued with the later addition of high-rises on the shore (appendix C, ref. 53). Pinellas County has about 37 miles of Gulf shoreline, almost 25 miles of urban shorefront development, just under 23 miles of eroded and critically eroded beaches, and approximately 20 miles of armoring. Nine of its beaches are 100 percent developed, and 7 are 100 percent armored with seawalls, revetments, or a combination of the two: Clearwater Beach Island, Sand Key north, Belleair Beach and Shores, Indian Rocks Beach, Indian Shores, Redington Shores, and North Redington/ Redington Beach. The shoreline of Pinellas County has been noted to accrete or recede up to 66 feet or more per year over the short term (approximately 10-year intervals), but historically the changes range from about 23 feet of recession to 13 feet of accretion per year. Although bulkhead lines were established here in 1958, coastal construction control (setback) lines were not established for Pinellas County until January 16, 1979 (appendix C, ref. 60). Many structures are too close to the beach to allow normal beach width fluctuations. The problem is amplified by the miles of beachfront armoring.

Anclote Key to Caladesi Island (RMs 33, 34)
The Anclote Keys (RM 33), which are shared by Pasco and Pinellas Counties and have no direct connection to the mainland, are largely undeveloped and unarmored. The southernmost one-half mile of Anclote Key State Recreation Area lies within the northern border of Pinellas County. This key is low and narrow, only a few hundred feet wide. About half of the area is intertidal mangrove. During even moderate storms with associated storm surge, the island will be awash; it should remain undeveloped.

Formation of islands in this area is thought to be controlled by a topographic ridge in the underlying limestone. In 1969, a new island, Three Rooker Bar (RM 33), emerged between Anclote Key and Honeymoon Island, near a saddle-shaped depression on the bedrock beneath shallow water where a series of sand shoals were separated by deeper-water channels (appendix C, ref. 26). Three Rooker Bar, with its convex shore facing the Gulf, is believed to have formed by in-place, upward shoaling of the linear sandbars. The newly emerged island is low, approximately 6 miles long and nearly 60 feet wide, with a stable, vegetated back beach and dune complex.

The island has migrated landward since 1969 and has grown northward by attachment of nearshore bars and overwash deposits. Since its emergence, Three Rooker Bar has been breached by storm activity several times: 1983, 1985 (Hurricane Elena), and during the winter of 1991. Three Rooker Bar should be left in its natural state, given its changing morphology, low elevation, and areas of breaching.

South of Three Rooker Bar lies Honeymoon Island (RM 34), which was used in the sixteenth and seventeenth centuries by Indians, pirates, traders, and fishermen. Honeymoon Island was known as Sand Island in the 1830s, and as Hog Island by 1880, evidently because a hog farm survived when the island was flooded by 5 feet of water during the hurricane of 1848. The 1921 hurricane split the island in two, forming Caladesi Island to the south of the newly formed inlet, Hurricane Pass. Honeymoon Island was promoted as a glamorous spot for newlyweds in the early 1940s, hence its present name. Subsequent development and a causeway from the mainland in the 1960s changed the island, and in 1974 a state park with close to 3 miles of Gulf shoreline was created. The southeastern end, Dunedin Beach, became part of the 600-acre Honeymoon Island State Recreation Area in 1982. The developed portion of the beach (less than 4 percent) is armored with rubble and sand tubes (or concrete-filled-bag groins) placed in 1960, and has been nourished twice, in 1969 and 1989 (fig. 6.18). Additional information about Honeymoon Island and Caladesi Island is available from the FDEP and the Pinellas County Beach Restoration Management Plan of 1988. The entire open-Gulf coast of the narrow island is an extreme-risk zone.

Caladesi Island (RM 34), the widest in the Pinellas County barrier chain, is undeveloped except for camping facilities associated with the state park that encompasses Caladesi and the five small adjacent islands: North Island, Lone Oak Island, Moonshine Island, Malone Island, and Core Island. The 653-acre state recreation area opened to the public in 1972 and is connected to Honeymoon Island and the mainland by ferry. Both Honeymoon Island and Caladesi Island are fronted with dunes and support mangroves, sea grasses, salt marshes, and tidal flats. Caladesi Island is low and flat, with about 2 miles of extreme-risk shoreline, and it should not be subjected to further development.

Clearwater Beach Island to Madeira Beach on Sand Key (RMS 34, 35, 36, 37)
South of Caladesi Island and Dunedin Pass lie miles of beach communities with extreme-risk zones facing the Gulf and moderate-risk areas on the back sides of the islands. From Clearwater Beach Island (RM 34) south are Clearwater Pass, Sand Key (RMS 34, 35), John's Pass, Treasure Island (RM 36),

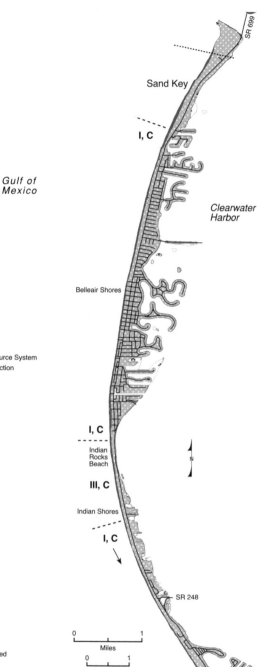

Gulf of
Mexico

Sand Key

Clearwater
Harbor

SR 699

I, C

Belleair Shores

I, C

Indian
Rocks
Beach

III, C

Indian Shores

I, C

SR 248

SR 699

N

Risk zones
Coastal Barrier Resource System
Preserve/govt. jurisdiction
County line

Risk Zones

Extreme

High

Moderate

Low

Marsh

Erosion Categories

I High erosion rate

II Moderate to low erosion rate

III Beaches with active maintenance
nourishment program

C Critical erosion areas where
substantial development or
recreational interests are threatened

N/C Noncritical erosion areas;
no development or recreation areas

0   1
Miles

0   1
Kilometers

RM 35 Indian Rocks Beach area

6.18 These sand tubes (concrete-filled-bag groins) on Honeymoon Island have taken large amounts of sand out of the alongshore system, creating a wide beach updrift and a greatly offset beach downdrift. Beach nourishment has added additional sediments to the shoreline of this island. This beach is in the state recreation area, and no houses are at risk from erosion. Photo by Norma Longo.

Blind Pass, and Long Key (RMS 36, 37). With the exception of the northern end of Sand Key, Pinellas County's barrier islands are densely developed with single-family dwellings, hotels, motels, and high-rise condominiums. The back sides have been extended into Clearwater Harbor and Boca Ciega Bay by dredge fill and finger canal construction. These islands and fill areas are low — most are less than 5 feet — and are subject to severe erosion. Except for the northernmost Pinellas barriers, all are categorized as critical erosion areas by the FDEP because of the threat to development or recreational interests.

Clearwater Beach Island is densely developed as a resort and residential area, with armoring along all of the developed stretches. This island is about 3 miles long, with natural elevations generally less than 10 feet above mean low water. The island has a history of retreat and advance, notably from 1873 to 1950, when the shoreline receded an average of 121 feet, but then accreted about 175 feet between 1950 and 1979, for a net advance of 54 feet. Few natural low dunes remain, as most have been destroyed. Portions of this area have been nourished four times since 1949, and Clearwater Beach itself has been nourished twice, in 1977 and 1981. Other extensive engineering projects have included groin, seawall, and jetty construction.

The shorelines of Clearwater Beach Island, Madeira Beach on Sand Key, and St. Petersburg Beach on Long Key have been altered by the effects of

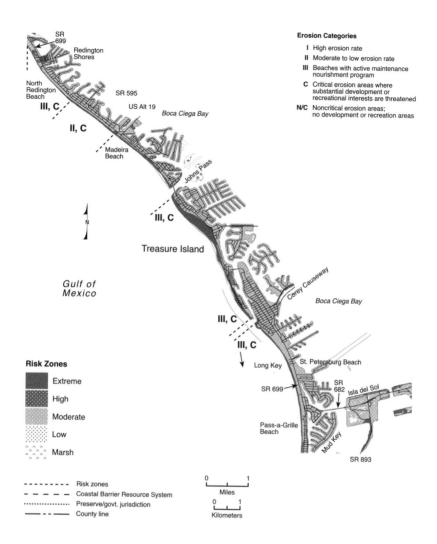

Erosion Categories

I   High erosion rate

II Moderate to low erosion rate

III Beaches with active maintenance nourishment program

C   Critical erosion areas where substantial development or recreational interests are threatened

N/C Noncritical erosion areas; no development or recreation areas

Risk Zones

- Extreme
- High
- Moderate
- Low
- Marsh

- - - - - - - - Risk zones
- - - - - Coastal Barrier Resource System
· · · · · · · · · · · Preserve/govt. jurisdiction
———— - · - County line

0 _____ 1
Miles

0 _____ 1
Kilometers

RM 36   Redington Shores–Treasure Island area

rock jetties constructed at Clearwater Pass, Blind Pass, and John's Pass, respectively (fig. 6.19). Blind Pass, with a 555-foot-long jetty on the north and a 261-foot-long jetty on the south, must be dredged periodically to keep it open. John's Pass also has been dredged and is federally maintained. At Clearwater Pass, a 4,200-foot-long jetty was built at the southern shore in 1975, and a 550-foot-long jetty was placed at the northern shore in 1981. Clearwater Pass was dredged throughout the 1980s, and the dredged sand was placed on the north end of Sand Key for nourishment. Approximately 14 miles long, Sand Key (RMS 35, 36), with its nine resort towns from Belleair Beach south to Madeira Beach, is a narrow, low, arc-shaped island presenting its convex face to the setting sun. The north end of Sand Key, a public park, has been nourished many times in the past, but at least a mile of shoreline has no beach in front of the seawalls. In 1996, beginning about three-quarters of a mile south of the jetty on the north end of Sand Key, a fairly wide beach (between 10 and 50 feet) existed for a distance of less than

6.19 The rock jetty at the south end of Clearwater Beach Island creates a dangerous zone for beach-goers while it captures sand to widen the beach. The concave curvature of the beach to the north of the jetty is a direct result of the presence of the jetty because the structure changes the shape of the shoreface and the direction of currents in the area. Photo by Norma Longo.

6.20 This small beach created by a sand tube enclosure protrudes into the surf zone along Sand Key in Pinellas County. Without the enclosure, no beach would be present along this entire shorefront, as evidenced by the seawalls fronting highrises at the edge of the water. Photo by Norma Longo.

half a mile. The shore then narrowed to the point of having no dry beach at high tide as far south as the sand tube enclosure (placed in 1993) that created a small beach fronting the Ultimar condos (fig. 6.20). Ultimately, Sand Key will require additional nourishment projects to maintain its tourist appeal. Not particularly tourist friendly, some beaches are advertised as private (Belleair Shores, Redington Beach) while others are public but with private access (Belleair Beach; fig. 6.21). The island is already completely developed with high-rises and other structures, so new construction on this armored shoreline would be a dubious undertaking.

Numerous seawalls and bulkheads were built on Sand Key between the 1950s and late 1970s, and the shoreline receded an average of 83 feet from south of the northern end to Belleair Shores (fig. 6.22). Both Belleair Beach and Belleair Shores (RM 35), which are completely developed and armored, have no recreational or dry beach at high tide, even though a nourishment project was carried out here in 1992–93. South of Belleair Shores, Indian Rocks Beach (RM 35) is a headland in the center of the Pinellas County island chain. Wave energy tends to concentrate on headlands to produce severe erosion. Erosion of the Indian Rocks headland historically provided sand for the longshore system, naturally nourishing the islands to the

6.21 Not particularly tourist friendly, some beaches along Sand Key are advertised as private while others are public with private access. The problem here is that no beach is present! The waves are breaking right on the seawalls. In order to walk along this stretch of shoreline, one must trespass on "private property." Photo by Norma Longo.

6.22 The variety of hard structures armoring this beach make it nearly impossible — not to mention dangerous — to get to the water. Without the armoring, the buildings would all be standing in the surf. Here the choice was to save buildings rather than the beach. Photo by Norma Longo.

north and south (fig. 6.23). Unfortunately, shoreline armoring has altered the natural processes. Indian Rocks Beach itself is 100 percent armored with walls, and is about 50 feet wide, having been nourished in 1990. To the south, at Redington Shores (RM 36), a 350-foot detached breakwater was constructed in front of an existing wall between December 1985 and January 1986 to control beach erosion and reduce beach nourishment requirements (see fig. 4.10; appendix C, ref. 45). Fill was added at the time of construction, and the beach also has been nourished since that time. The breakwater appears to have stabilized the eroding beach, but it has also created dangerous conditions in the water, and swimming is not allowed around this section of the beach (fig. 6.24).

Madeira Beach (RM 36) is completely developed but not totally armored. Just over 80 percent of the developed reaches are armored with wooden groins, some in combination with shore-parallel structures (fig. 6.25). This beach has been nourished only once, in 1961. Madeira Beach is joined to the mainland near St. Petersburg by a causeway. Early evacuation is extremely important.

These stretches of Gulf shoreline, with their massive development and armoring, are at extreme risk to storm destruction and to roadway congestion in the event of an evacuation.

Treasure Island to St. Petersburg Beach on Long Key (RMs 36, 37)
Treasure Island and Long Key, including Upham and St. Petersburg Beaches, are long, narrow, low islands with elevations of 10 feet or less. Bridges pro-

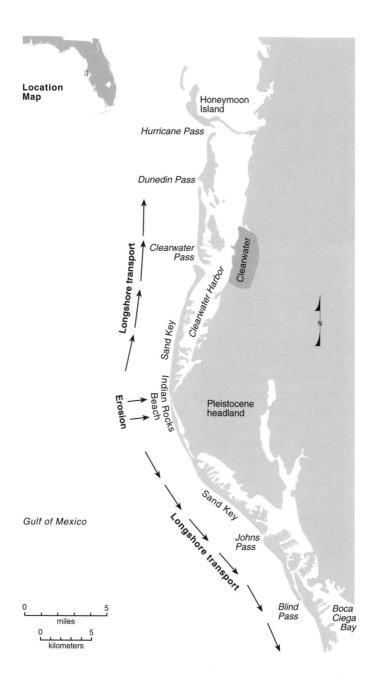

6.23 The convex shoreline at Indian Rocks Beach is a natural headland that normally would provide sand to beaches both north and south of it. With the addition of armoring to protect the headland beaches from eroding, sand supply in both directions is diminished, causing erosion.

6.24 This wide beach, created by nourishment sand and the detached break-water, is fenced off from the ocean to keep swimmers away from the breakwater. Several deaths have occurred here in the past because of the breakwater. Photo by Norma Longo.

vide access to both. The shoreline of Treasure Island has a long history of movement: retreat between 1873 and 1950, and advance from 1950 to 1979. Long Key also advanced from 1950 to 1979, about 4 feet per year. The shorelines of Treasure Island (RM 36), Upham Beach (north end of St. Petersburg Beach; RM 36), and St. Petersburg Beach (RM 37) are all totally developed. The south end of St. Petersburg Beach is classified by the FDEP as a critically eroding area. Even though these beaches have been nourished numerous times, particularly Upham Beach (6 times between 1968 and 1996) and Treasure Island (11 times between 1964 and 1997), they remain at extremely high risk to damage from wind and wave action and storm surge.

The National Oceanic and Atmospheric Administration (NOAA) has calculated the 100-year storm surge height along Pinellas County beaches to be 13.9 feet above mean sea level. A great hurricane (e.g., Camille in 1969 or the Florida Keys hurricane of 1935) could bring a storm surge as high as 26 feet above mean sea level. A fierce storm that hit the area in 1848 generated storm surge of about 14 feet and opened Johns Pass; a similar storm struck in 1921. Hurricane Gladys (October 1968) caused severe damage to the Pinellas County beaches, particularly Treasure Island (RM 36). Treasure Island was replenished in 1969 from 104th Avenue, near the middle of the island, to 600 feet south of 77th Avenue, at the south end, with about 790,000 cubic yards of fill. In 1971, this project was extended north to 108th Avenue, adding another 75,000 cubic yards. Additional nourishment projects and groins were constructed in the 1970s and 1980s, and future nourishment projects are expected.

Access to the mainland from the Pinellas barriers is by seven wide causeways that are low and subject to early closing in time of flooding. Also, many of the finger canals in the bay are separated from the main sections of the islands by additional low causeways that potentially will be underwater early in periods of flooding. Tens of thousands of people live and vacation on these vulnerable strips of sand, and roads will be congested when evacuations become necessary in the face of a hurricane or storm. Early evacuation from all of these communities is extremely important!

Long Key to Mullet Key (RM 37)
Pass-a-Grille Channel and a series of low, mangrove-covered islands separate Long Key from Mullet Key, a V-shaped island at the entrance to Tampa Bay (RM 37). The Fort DeSoto National Memorial park has kept development on Mullet Key to a minimum. Even so, the Gulf side of Mullet Key has been nourished. A 1973 beach erosion control project added a 60-foot-wide beach along a 6,750-foot reach, along with a 420-foot-long groin and a 1,150-foot-long revetment that is meant to protect the Fort DeSoto lookout tower at the southwest point of the key.

Egmont Key National Wildlife Refuge lies in the mouth of Tampa Bay in Hillsborough County, separated from Mullet Key by Egmont Channel, the main shipping channel into Tampa Bay. This protected island is undeveloped, not connected to the mainland, and was not mapped in terms of risk for property damage. A hurricane in 1921 almost completely covered Egmont Key with water. Currently, the Gulf shore of Egmont Key is critically eroded and vulnerable to further storm damage.

6.25 Madeira Beach groin field in 1997. The captured sands are starting to cover the structures and the beach is flat and fairly wide. The large buildings are still subject to flooding and wind damage. Photo by Norma Longo.

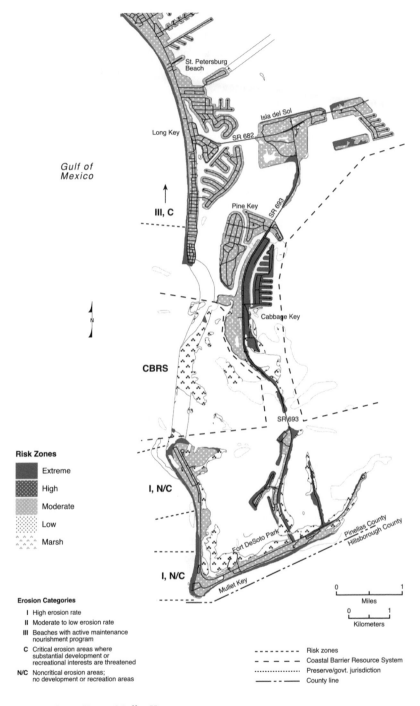

Gulf of
Mexico

III, C

CBRS

I, N/C

I, N/C

St. Petersburg
Beach

Isla del Sol

Long Key

SR 682

Pine Key

SR 693

Cabbage Key

SR 693

Pinellas County
Hillsborough County

Fort DeSoto Park

Mullet Key

Risk Zones

Extreme

High

Moderate

Low

Marsh

Erosion Categories

I   High erosion rate
II Moderate to low erosion rate
III Beaches with active maintenance
    nourishment program
C   Critical erosion areas where
    substantial development or
    recreational interests are threatened
N/C Noncritical erosion areas;
    no development or recreation areas

0   1
Miles

0   1
Kilometers

- - - - - - - -   Risk zones
- - - - - - -   Coastal Barrier Resource System
. . . .   Preserve/govt. jurisdiction
— - - — - -   County line

RM 37   Long Key to Mullet Key

Between 1921 and the 1980s, Pinellas County received no major damage from hurricanes. During this apparent lull, development in the area was increasing, and many people were not familiar with hurricane forces. Historically, hurricanes have passed within 50 miles of Pinellas beaches once every 6 or 7 years. Storms much farther away also can cause severe beach retreat and substantial damage. Hurricane Elena and Tropical Storm Juan in 1985, although some distance to the west, caused erosion of hundreds of thousands of cubic yards of sand from nourished beaches, particularly on Clearwater Beach Island and Sand Key, along with damage to several buildings and armoring structures. Other hard-hit areas during Elena and Juan were Indian Shores, St. Petersburg Beach, North Redington Beach, the southern two-thirds of Long Key, and Treasure Island. The damage assessment for beach erosion was $1,240,000 (appendix C, ref. 13). Coastal flooding and moderate erosion resulted from Opal and Erin in 1995, and from Earl in 1998. The "No Name Storm" of June 1982 may have been the most devastating storm so far for Pinellas County, with its storm surge of 10 feet. However, even a small hurricane can cause considerable damage and lead to the evacuation of hundreds of thousands of people, overcrowding the causeways. Early evacuation is imperative.

Manatee County (RMs 38, 39)

Passage Key to Longboat Key (RM 38)

The generally narrow and steep beaches of the Manatee County shoreline are composed of fine sand and shell fragments probably derived from the island itself and the offshore and nearshore bottom of the Gulf. Manatee County has a short Gulf shoreline of some 12 miles, made up of Passage Key, a national wildlife refuge, and two low-lying barrier islands: 7.5-mile-long Anna Maria Island and the 4.5-mile northern section of Longboat Key, which are separated by Longboat Pass but connected by Highway 789. Anna Maria Island varies in width from 1.25 miles near the north end to 400 feet near the southern end. The width of Longboat Key varies from 300 feet in the middle section of the Manatee County portion to 800 feet at the south end. Elevations of these two islands are generally less than 10 feet.

Holmes Beach on central Anna Maria Island and Bradenton Beach at the southern end are extensively developed. Anna Maria Island has advanced and retreated over time, particularly the northern end, which flooded during a hurricane in 1921; about a half-mile reach was eroded as of 1993. This area is particularly vulnerable to storm surge through the entrance to Tampa Bay. Currently, both ends of the island are critically eroded. More than half of the shoreline of this island is armored for protec-

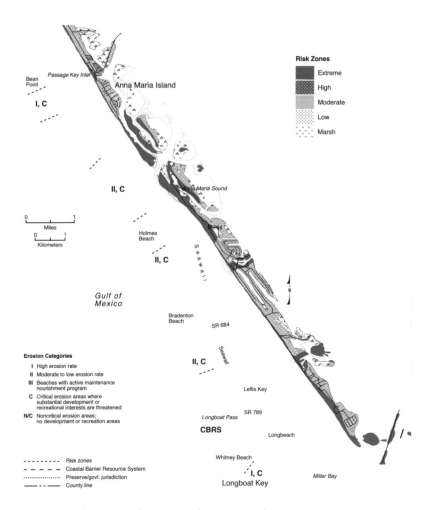

Risk Zones

- Extreme
- High
- Moderate
- Low
- Marsh

Bean Point

Passage Key Inlet

Anna Maria Island

I, C

II, C

Anna Maria Sound

0 — 1
Miles

0 — 1
Kilometers

Holmes Beach

II, C

Gulf of
Mexico

Seawall

Bradenton Beach

SR 684

Erosion Categories

I   High erosion rate
II Moderate to low erosion rate
III Beaches with active maintenance
    nourishment program
C   Critical erosion areas where
    substantial development or
    recreational interests are threatened
N/C Noncritical erosion areas;
    no development or recreation areas

II, C

Seawall

Leflis Key

Longboat Pass

SR 789

CBRS

Longbeach

-------- Risk zones
- - - - Coastal Barrier Resource System
.... Preserve/govt. jurisdiction
——··—— County line

Whitney Beach

I, C

Longboat Key

Miller Bay

RM 38   Bradenton Beach area, Longboat Key, north

tion of properties, and some sections of the beach have been nourished about every 10 years since 1963. A headland at Holmes Beach causes along-shore sand transport away from the area to both the north and south, with the headland itself susceptible to wave erosion. An evaluation of Holmes Beach by the city's Public Works Department specified two areas of active erosion on the beach: at 52nd Street near 75th Street, and at the end of 31st Street, where post-Josephine nourishment is gone in front of the revet-ment. All of Holmes Beach is designated a critical erosion problem area by the FDEP. The shoreline of the entire island is an extreme-to-moderate-risk area, as is Longboat Key to the south.

Longboat Key (RMS 38, 39) is made up of beach ridges and overwash ter-

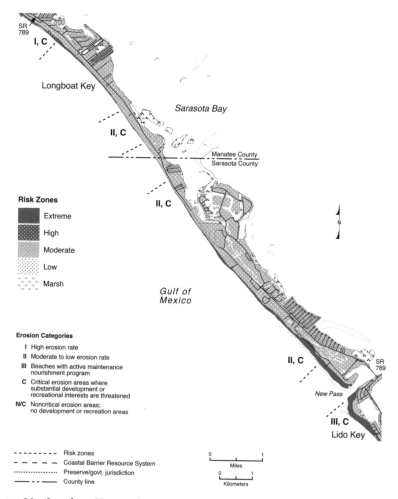

Risk Zones

- ▓ Extreme
- ▓ High
- ░ Moderate
- ⋯ Low
- ^^^ Marsh

Erosion Categories

I High erosion rate

II Moderate to low erosion rate

III Beaches with active maintenance
nourishment program

C Critical erosion areas where
substantial development or
recreational interests are threatened

N/C Noncritical erosion areas;
no development or recreation areas

- - - - - - - Risk zones
- - - - - Coastal Barrier Resource System
⋯⋯⋯ Preserve/govt. jurisdiction
— - - County line

0   1
Miles

0   1
Kilometers

RM 39 Longboat Key, south

races with few dunes. Prior to 1883, Longboat Key was two islands separated by an inlet. At some point the inlet closed, leaving a long, narrow
island with a northwest–southeast-trending shoreline. The north end of
Longboat Key next to Longboat Pass has a history of migration and changing morphology due to tides and channel changes within the pass. Near
Passage Key Inlet, north of Anna Maria Island, and Longboat Pass, both of
which are federally maintained inlets, the beaches are characterized by
rapid erosion and buildup. Erosion rates around the Manatee-Sarasota
County line have been about 0–1 foot per year, but toward the south approximately 2–3 feet per year (appendix C, ref. 25). More than 9 miles of the
county's shores is classified as critically eroded or eroded, including 4.6

miles along Holmes Beach and Bradenton Beach and 3.9 miles of Longboat Key. Nevertheless, many people have built on these shores.

The Manatee County portion of Longboat Key's shoreline is 100 percent developed and, like Anna Maria Island, is fronted by armoring structures that are ineffective in reducing the long-term beach erosion that is evident here. In some places where seawalls and rock revetments have been constructed there is no natural beach. On northern Longboat Key, the percentage of developed-armored shoreline with no dry or recreational beach is nearly three times that of Anna Maria Island. Some beaches, like Holmes Beach, have been nourished over the top of groins and rock revetments and appear natural. Groins were a preferred method of beach erosion mitigation in Florida in the 1930s.

Construction of seawalls, revetments, and groin fields along Anna Maria Island started in the 1950s when major development began along the coast. A groin field and a terminal groin were placed at the southern end of the island around that time. Along Longboat Key, groins and seawalls have been constructed since the 1960s as the rapidly developing shorefront was threatened by erosion. To more effectively protect upland structures, coastal construction control lines for the islands in Manatee County were established on October 28, 1977.

Storms in this vicinity have produced severe tidal flooding and damage. NOAA estimates that 10- and 25-year storm surge levels at Anna Maria will be 5.6 feet and 8.9 feet above mean sea level, respectively, flooding most of the barrier islands. The eastern portion of the Holmes Beach community, along Sarasota Pass, is susceptible to flooding. Both Holmes Beach and Bradenton Beach are subject to flooding by a 100-year storm.

Over the last 100 years, more than 30 known hurricanes and tropical disturbances have passed within 50 miles of the Manatee County shoreline, at a frequency of about one per 2.5 years. Some of the more remarkable hurricanes and storms that have affected Manatee County include the hurricane of October 1910 and the hurricane of October 1921, which caused storm surge flooding of around 7 feet, covering the northern end of Anna Maria with 5 feet of water. The hurricane of September 1926 flooded the barrier islands and caused $1 million in flood damage in the Bradenton Beach area. A severe tropical storm in 1935 undermined and damaged the entire reach of Manatee County beaches. The October 1946 hurricane passed almost directly across the Manatee County shoreline, flooding all low-lying beaches and causing significant property damage. The September 1950 hurricane (Easy), with 6–8-foot storm surge, cut through the beach road at several locations and almost completely flooded Anna Maria Key, causing 15–20 feet of beach retreat. During Hurricane Donna in September 1960, the storm surge was from 1 to 3 feet north of Bradenton. Hurricane Gladys (October 1968) caused 40 feet of beach retreat on the north end and 20 feet of erosion along central Anna Maria Island. Hurricanes Donna and Brenda in 1960 caused substantial property and seawall damage on Longboat Key. Seawalls, revetments, roads, and homes were damaged again by storm surge of 3–6 feet with the passage of Hurricane Agnes in June 1972 (appendix C, ref. 51). The "No Name Storm" in June 1982 caused severe beach retreat on Longboat Key and damaged the newly nourished beach. In 1985, Elena and Juan generated flooding and major damage or destruction to homes, condos, motels, and armoring structures; and Tropical Storm Keith damaged several structures in November 1988. Erosion and coastal flooding also occurred with the passage of Erin and Opal in 1995. In September 1998, Earl raised the water level an extra 2–3 feet along this coast while battering the eastern Panhandle and Big Bend areas.

The 100-year storm surge in Manatee County is estimated at 13.5 feet above mean sea level, excluding wave height. Manatee County barrier beaches are at extreme to moderate risk due to low elevation, erosion potential, and difficulty of evacuation in the face of a hurricane.

Sarasota County (RMs 39, 40, 41, 42)

Southern Longboat Key to Casey Key (RMS 39, 40, 41)

Sarasota County's 35-mile stretch of barrier island beaches includes southern Longboat Key, Lido Key, Siesta Key, Casey Key, and most of Manasota Key. The mainland beaches of the Venice area lie between Casey Key and Manasota Key. The Venice beaches are formed along a headland with limestone outcrops and sand and peat layers. The sand here consists of quartz, shells, other minerals, and fossils, such as sharks' teeth (appendix C, ref. 25), for which Venice is well known. Barrier beaches are formed as pocket beaches and are generally narrow and steep, with the exception of the public beaches at Lido Key, Siesta Key, and Casey Key, where beach nourishment or jetty construction has provided wider beaches. To date, neither Siesta Key nor Casey Key has been nourished, but Lido Key was nourished eight times at 2–6-year intervals between 1964 and 1991, and further restoration was being planned in 1999.

Each of the islands in this part of the chain has advanced and retreated during the twentieth century, and the trend continues. The state has classified 20 miles of Sarasota County's beaches as critically eroded, with about 400 structures threatened by a 25-year storm. Problems with erosion led to artificial shoreline stabilization in the past. Property owners built numerous seawalls, revetments, and groin fields as protective measures for their luxury condominiums, homes, and resorts. Half of the county's 25 miles of developed shoreline is armored with combinations of these hardened structures, and public beach access is limited. The beach is gone at high tide along about 2 miles of shoreline. This shoreline is subject to severe erosion during storms, with passes between the islands contributing to the erosion problems on the islands.

Longboat Key is a relatively low island, mostly below 10 feet, and densely developed on the Gulf side (91.5 percent), with extensive finger canal development on the southern end facing Sarasota Bay. More than half of southern Longboat Key is fronted by armoring structures, and parts of the beach were nourished in 1982 and 1993. As an alternative shore protection method, about 650 feet of artificial seaweed (Seagrid system) was placed at Longboat Key in 1984, but it lasted less than one year.

Southern Longboat Key (RM 39) is separated from Lido Key by New Pass, which was created in September 1848 by a hurricane that breached Longboat Key. New Pass is a federally maintained navigation channel that historically has been dredged at 3–5-year intervals. Highway 789 connects these two extreme-risk islands and is the only exit to the mainland from Lido Key, across the Ringling Causeway to Sarasota.

The shoreline of Lido Key (RM 40) is said to be entirely man-made, having been constructed in the 1920s by filling in between a set of small islands (appendix C, ref. 25). The shorefront developed rapidly during the 1970s and 1980s, but the coastal construction setback line for Sarasota County was not recorded until September 5, 1978 (appendix C, ref. 60). Lido Key is more than three-quarters developed along the Gulf, with additional dense development on the bay side and on St. Armands Key at the end of the long causeway to Sarasota. Armoring on this island is even more prevalent than on southern Longboat Key to the north. Most of this narrow island is now classified as a critical erosion problem area, making Lido Key an extreme-risk zone for storm damage to shorefront property (fig. 6.26). Evacuation can be problematic, particularly if the lone causeway becomes clogged with motorists. Leave early from this risky barrier.

Big Sarasota Pass separates Lido Key from Siesta Key; its stabilized south shore is classified as a critical inlet shoreline. Siesta Key (RM 40) is nearly 5 miles long with beaches that vary between 10 and 50 feet in width, although north of the Point of Rocks headland the beach is wider. This large pocket beach lies between the armored north end of the island and Point of Rocks and historically has accreted. The beach just south of Point of Rocks, however, eroded between 1995 and 1996. In 1995, the dunes were healthy with a cover of vegetation, but in 1996, little vegetation was present

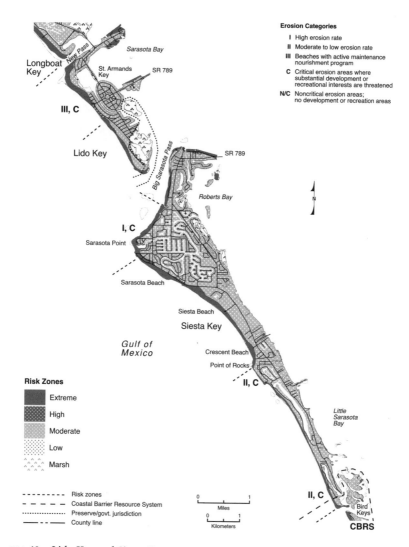

Erosion Categories

I   High erosion rate
II   Moderate to low erosion rate
III Beaches with active maintenance
     nourishment program
C   Critical erosion areas where
     substantial development or
     recreational interests are threatened
N/C Noncritical erosion areas;
     no development or recreation areas

Risk Zones

Extreme
High
Moderate
Low
Marsh

- - - - - - - -   Risk zones
- - - - - - -   Coastal Barrier Resource System
....   Preserve/govt. jurisdiction
——— - - ———   County line

RM 40   Lido Key and Siesta Key area

and the dunes appeared to have been bulldozed. As of 1999, no beach nourishment had been placed on Siesta Key, and the recreational beach was absent in front of nearly half of the seawalls and other armoring structures (fig. 6.27). Although the entire Gulf shoreline of Siesta Key is lined with buildings, less than half of its shore is armored. Notably, Siesta Key has developed with canals, fill, and beach engineering projects. Significant erosion problem areas exist along north Siesta Key and from Point of Rocks south to Midnight Pass, which has been closed since 1983. Storm surge from a moderate category 3 hurricane can be expected to reach up to

6.26 This building on south Lido Key surely wasn't built out into the water this way! Beach erosion on this island has been severe. This property is in extreme danger of damage from storms and the everyday surf. Photo by Jason Smith.

7 feet, which will cause flooding over much of the area. The entire shoreline of Siesta Key is subject to extreme destruction from storms and waves.

South of Midnight Pass lies Casey Key, a low, narrow, highly developed barrier island (RM 41). Public beaches here include Nokomis Beach and North Jetty Park, both toward the southern end of the island. Casey Key is a major headland associated with a topographic high in the underlying limestone. This area is subject to severe erosion during major storms. Significantly, the road has been washed out repeatedly since the 1930s (appendix C, ref. 25). Two routes, near either end of the island, lead to the mainland for escape in the event of a hurricane, assuming you can get to them. Nearly 3 miles of the Casey Key shoreline is classified as an erosion problem area, and almost half of the island is armored for the purpose of protecting upland property from tides and wave action. In most places, Casey Key is only a few hundred feet wide and less than 15 feet high. Casey Key development is at high to extreme risk.

Venice Inlet to South Sarasota County Line
on Manasota Peninsula (RMS 41, 42)
Beaches along this portion of Sarasota County are composed of fine quartz sand and shell fragments. The northern and middle segments of Manasota Peninsula are highly developed and armored, but Caspersen Beach and South Venice Beach remain undeveloped. Venice Inlet, between Casey Key and Venice, is maintained by the Corps of Engineers as part of the Intracoastal Waterway. The placement of dredged materials from the

inlet and Intracoastal Waterway maintenance program has provided some occasional temporary relief to the beaches south of Venice Inlet, but shoreline retreat continues. Jetties at Venice Inlet, constructed in the late 1930s, prevent sand from moving downdrift, although the southern end of Casey Key has accreted. No beaches remain where seawalls and groins or revetments have been placed (fig. 6.28). Emplacement of seawalls, revetments, and groins to stop natural island migration has not stopped erosion, and in many instances the problem has been accentuated by steepening offshore depth profiles. This problem is particularly critical between the Venice jetty and Venice public beach to the south. Most of the area is currently designated a critical erosion area by the FDEP and presents extreme-risk potential.

The Venice headland, a mainland beach from the south end of Tarpon Center Drive to Red Lake, also has a significant erosion problem. Erosion rates in this area range between 1 and 3 feet per year, with more than 5 miles of coastline between Venice and Caspersen Beach considered a critical erosion problem area (appendix C, ref. 53). Venice Beach itself has been nourished five times since 1963. Interestingly, beaches in Sarasota County are considered stable because they occur in association with the mainland and longer islands, and have fewer active inlets.

The beaches south of Venice Inlet are narrow and backed by low berms

6.27   A long rock revetment fronts these condos on Turtle Beach, Siesta Key. The beach is narrow to nonexistent at high tide and likely will require nourishment in the future. Beach sands appear behind the revetment as well. What if the buildings could be moved and the rocks removed? An improved beach would result. Photo by Jason Smith.

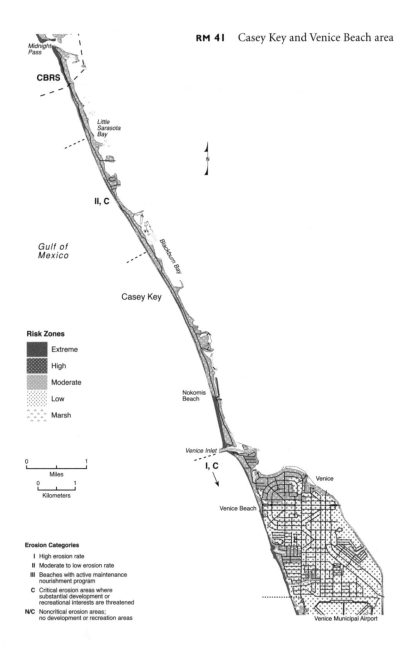

Midnight
Pass

CBRS

Little
Sarasota
Bay

II, C

Gulf of
Mexico

Blackburn Bay

Casey Key

N

Risk Zones

■ Extreme

■ High

□ Moderate

□ Low

△ Marsh

0 — 1
Miles

0 — 1
Kilometers

Nokomis
Beach

Venice Inlet

I, C

Venice

Venice Beach

Erosion Categories

 I   High erosion rate
 II Moderate to low erosion rate
 III Beaches with active maintenance
     nourishment program
 C   Critical erosion areas where
     substantial development or
     recreational interests are threatened
 N/C Noncritical erosion areas;
     no development or recreation areas

Venice Municipal Airport

and a few dunes south of Caspersen Beach. Manasota Key has some of the highest elevations on the southwest Florida coast, averaging 10–12 feet and in a few places exceeding 16 feet. However, this peninsula is also one of the narrowest, ranging in width from less than 100 feet to no more than 1,500 feet. Beaches along the middle section of Manasota Key range between 10 and 50 feet in width, except in front of and adjacent to walls and the groin field, where beaches are generally less than 10 feet wide. Storms understandably play a large part in shaping the beaches.

In this century, more than 32 hurricanes and tropical storms have passed within 50 miles of Sarasota County, with a frequency of one storm every 3 years and one hurricane every 6.5 years. Historically, hurricanes or storms of note occurred in 1921, 1944, 1950, 1960, 1972, and 1982. The October 1944 hurricane entered the west coast of Florida near Sarasota and caused extremely high water levels to the south of Tampa. Sarasota County was also affected by the "No Name Storm" of June 1982, which caused severe beach erosion and flooding on the islands. Hurricane Opal (1995) brought coastal flooding and moderate erosion. Storm surge from a category 4 or 5 hurricane could be expected to raise water levels to between 17 and 20 feet as far inland as the Myakka River and I-75. The 100-year storm surge on the Gulf is estimated at between 11.5 feet and 12.5 feet above mean sea level, excluding wave heights. Implications for flood damage are obvious for the coast because it is mostly below 10 feet in elevation. Coastal property in Sarasota County is at high to extreme risk.

Charlotte County (RMs 42, 43, 44)

Southern Manasota Key to Gasparilla Island (RMs 42, 43, 44)

Charlotte County's barrier islands include the southern 4 miles of Manasota Key, with Punta Gorda Beach, Englewood Beach, and Port Charlotte Beach State Recreation Area (RM 43); the Knight-Bocilla–Don Pedro–Little Gasparilla Island complex (RM 43); and the northern 2.5 miles of Gasparilla Island (RM 44). The Don Pedro complex is made up of 6 miles of connected barrier islands that were separated at different times over this century by at least five different inlets, including Bocilla Pass, Blind Pass, and Little Gasparilla Pass, all now closed. The 115-acre Don Pedro Island State Recreation Area, accessible only by boat, occupies part of Don Pedro Island. Gasparilla Island contains a 144-acre state recreation area on County Road 775. Publicly held land helps minimize development on these islands.

Prior to 1883, Old Blind Pass inlet was located just south of the Manasota Key headland, near Englewood. A 1944 storm opened a new 400-foot-wide inlet 3,500 feet north of present Stump Pass, which separates Manasota Key from the Don Pedro complex. Stump Pass has migrated more than 1.3 miles south. Because of extensive erosion, the south shore of Stump Pass is now designated a critical inlet shoreline by the FDEP. Generally, beaches within about a mile of inlets are the most dynamic areas on barrier islands and must be considered extreme-risk zones for structures.

6.28　A beach scene in Venice Beach, Florida, showing the shoreline cut back from the seawall protecting the high-rise building. Clearly this is a community with an erosion problem, and efforts to halt the erosion are having a negative effect on the beach. Photo by Amy Reesman.

The northern 2 miles of Charlotte County's beaches, characterized by both localized buildup and erosion, have withdrawn up to 100 feet during the twentieth century. The southern mile of Manasota Key has been extremely unstable, as evidenced by 50–170 feet of recession during the period from 1953 to 1975. About 1 mile of Port Charlotte Beach north of Stump Pass (RM 43) was nourished in 1980, and another nourishment project was completed in this area in 1993.

These islands range in width from 80 to 2,000 feet and have elevations ranging from 5 to 9 feet, with the average being slightly above 5 feet. North of Englewood Beach, the beach is about 30 feet wide. Opposite the Manasota Bridge and south to the Manasota Beach Club, the beach is more than 50 feet wide. The low and narrow sections are subject to periodic overwash, flooding, and erosion, which has led to armoring along some reaches.

The islands of Charlotte County have approximately 12 miles of Gulf shorefront, of which about 8 miles is developed. The shoreline is completely developed along Knight Island, Little Gasparilla Island, and the northern segment of Gasparilla Island, although many homes are set well back from the beach. The other shorelines are about half developed. More than a mile of the developed reaches, all on south Manasota Key, is protected with armoring structures, primarily rock revetments. More than half of the armored stretches have no dry beach at high tide, making beach play a challenge. On Manasota Key, about 3,730 feet of the developed-armored shoreline had no recreational beach at high tide as of 1996. Also,

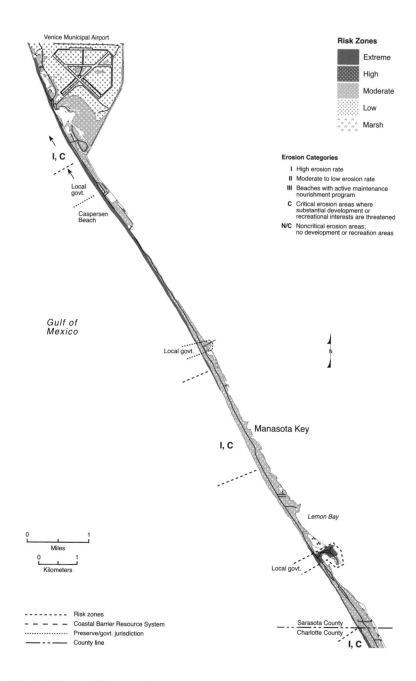

RM 42 Manasota Key, north

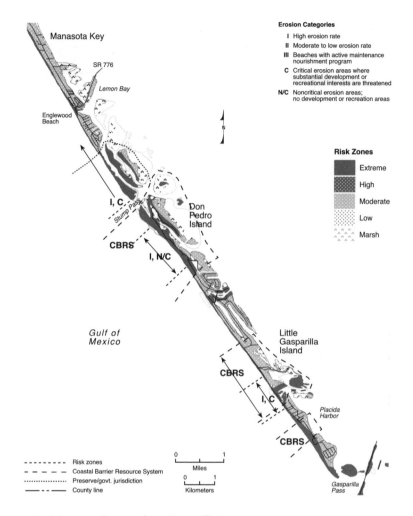

Manasota Key

SR 776

Lemon Bay

Englewood
Beach

Risk Zones

■ Extreme

▨ High

▦ Moderate

⋮ Low

⌃⌃⌃ Marsh

I, C

Stump Pass

Don
Pedro
Island

CBRS

I, N/C

Gulf of
Mexico

Little
Gasparilla
Island

CBRS

I, C

Placida
Harbor

CBRS

Gasparilla
Pass

- - - - - - - - - Risk zones
- - - - - Coastal Barrier Resource System
· · · · · · · · · · · · Preserve/govt. jurisdiction
——— - · - County line

0   1
Miles

0   1
Kilometers

RM 43   Manasota Key, south, to Gasparilla Pass

6,600 feet of developed shorefront on the Don Pedro island complex with no armoring structures lacks a beach buffer zone to absorb wave or storm energy. Several homes on Little Gasparilla Island were standing in the surf along a 1,150-foot section. These homes may be forward of the coastal construction setback line, which was established and recorded here in 1978 (fig. 6.29). Nearly 6 miles of Charlotte County's beaches are classified as erosion problem areas, some critically eroded. Much of the Don Pedro complex has recently been added to the FDEP's critical list. Nourishment sands were placed on Gasparilla Island in 1981 and 1993 in an attempt to restore adequate protective beach widths. Englewood Beach installed a beach dewatering system in 1993 along a 600-foot reach as an alternative method of shore protection, but with little effect. Even though Charlotte County is the least armored county along the west-central Florida coast, the lack of wide protective beaches contributes to the possibility of potential storm damage. Beach width can vary significantly with the movement of sand on a daily basis or due to storm activity, particularly during the June–October hurricane season.

Since 1900, more than 30 hurricanes and tropical disturbances have passed within 50 miles of the county's shoreline. Memorable hurricanes that affected coastal property here include the October 1921 hurricane that produced 7–11-foot flood levels along the coast and 8-foot flood levels at Punta Gorda, a community of about 10,700 people on the northeast side of Charlotte Harbor. The September 1926 hurricane, one of the most destructive in Florida's history, produced 11–12-foot storm surge and opened Redfish Pass on Captiva Island in Lee County to the south. The hurricane of September 1935 produced wave heights estimated at 16 feet, flooding the barrier islands with several feet of water. The hurricane of October 1944 spawned 100 mph winds, and its 7-foot storm surge overtopped Gasparilla Island, eroding 50–60 feet of beach. Hurricane Donna (September 1960), one of the great storms of the century, caused severe erosion damage and flooding. Storm surge of 4–6 feet topped the barrier islands in several places, cutting through the narrow beaches to Lemon Bay. The total damage in Florida caused by Donna exceeded $87 million (1960 dollars), with more than $26 million of the damage in Charlotte County. Hurricanes Frederic and David in 1979 caused storm surge flooding, overwash, and erosion in the state park area and in the Don Pedro island complex. When

6.29 Erosion on Little Gasparilla Island. Houses are set well back in the vegetation, but the island is quite flat and can flood. Photo by Jason Smith.

Hurricane Opal struck the Panhandle in October 1995, coastal flooding and erosion damage also occurred in Charlotte County. Hurricane Earl (1998) produced storm surge along this coast up to 3 feet. Based on historic data, the maximum storm surge is estimated to be about 11.5 feet above the still-water mean sea level for Charlotte County. During storms, wave heights are added to this level to produce tremendous flooding and erosion potential. Surges during category 3, 4, or 5 storms may cause water to rise to between 12 and 20 feet or more. The entire length of Charlotte County coastline is at moderate to extreme risk for storm damage. The two roadways connecting these islands to the mainland will undoubtedly be overcrowded during storm evacuations. Exit from Little Gasparilla will have to be by boat, so plan accordingly.

Lee County (RMs 44, 45, 46, 47, 48, 49)

Lee County's 47-mile barrier coastline is one of the longest on the Gulf. The low islands here generally follow a northwest–southeast trend. From north to south, Lee County beaches and passes include southern Gasparilla Island (the town of Boca Grande) (RM 44), Boca Grande Pass, Cayo Costa (RM 45), Captiva Pass, North Captiva Island, Redfish Pass, Captiva Island (RM 46), Wulfert Channel inlet, Sanibel Island (RM 47), San Carlos Bay inlet, Bunch Beach, Matanzas Pass, Fort Myers Beach on northern Estero Island, Estero Island, Big Carlos Pass (RM 48), Lovers Key, Little Carlos Pass, Big Hickory Island, Big Hickory Pass, and Bonita Beach (RM 49). The northern islands range from 4 to 7 miles in length, with widths between 200 feet and more than a mile. Most of the islands are less than 8 feet high and lack prominent dunes. Somewhat L-shaped Sanibel Island (RM 47) is the largest at approximately 12 miles long, with widths ranging between about 0.5 mile and almost 2.5 miles. Since the growth of tourism in the 1950s, many of Sanibel's bow-shaped dunes have been leveled to make way for houses and resorts.

Twenty-seven miles of Lee County's shoreline is developed; roughly 8 miles of that is armored with seawalls, revetments, groins, jetties, and combinations of these; and approximately 1.5 miles has totally lost its beach in front of the armoring structures. The northern side of Boca Grande Pass leading into Charlotte Harbor is held in place by a cement wall and rocks. The Army Corps of Engineers keeps the pass open with periodic dredging. Two other passes are also armored: Redfish Pass and Wulfert Channel inlet. The remaining passes are not stabilized. Erosion is prevalent and affects 25 miles of shoreline. About 15 miles along southern Gasparilla Island, the southern end of North Captiva, Captiva, the northern end of Sanibel,

Estero Island, and Bonita Beach is designated as critically eroding beach by the FDEP. By the late 1990s, however, the northern end of North Captiva had stopped eroding and was accreting. To improve the mid-county beaches, nourishment projects were completed on Captiva and a western segment of Sanibel in 1996.

Gasparilla Island to Captiva Island (RMs 44, 45, 46)

Narrow Gasparilla Island (RM 44) is about 7 miles long and mostly between 5 and 7 feet above mean sea level. About 145 acres of the island is protected as a state recreation area. The southern 5 miles of Gasparilla Island lies in Lee County and is extensively developed at Boca Grande. Almost 4 of the 5 miles is designated as critically eroding beach. Armoring here consists of approximately 2 miles of revetments, cement walls, and groins; most have no

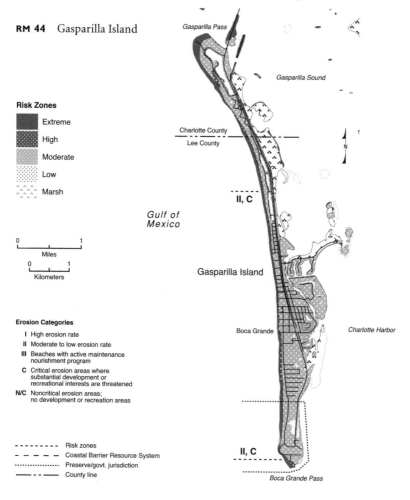

RM 44   Gasparilla Island

Gasparilla Pass

Gasparilla Sound

Risk Zones

- Extreme
- High
- Moderate
- Low
- Marsh

Charlotte County
Lee County

Gulf of
Mexico

II, C

0   1
Miles

0   1
Kilometers

Gasparilla Island

Erosion Categories

I   High erosion rate
II Moderate to low erosion rate
III Beaches with active maintenance nourishment program
C   Critical erosion areas where substantial development or recreational interests are threatened
N/C Noncritical erosion areas; no development or recreation areas

Boca Grande

Charlotte Harbor

- - - - - - - - Risk zones
- - - - - Coastal Barrier Resource System
.... Preserve/govt. jurisdiction
——— · · — County line

II, C

Boca Grande Pass

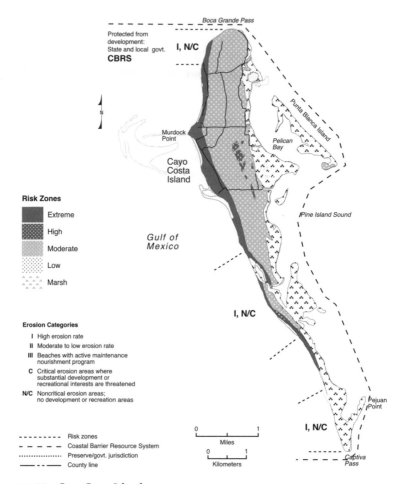

Boca Grande Pass

Punta Blanca Island

Murdock
Point

Pelican
Bay

Cayo
Costa
Island

Pine Island Sound

Risk Zones

Extreme

High

Moderate

Low

Marsh

Gulf of
Mexico

I, N/C

Erosion Categories

I   High erosion rate
II Moderate to low erosion rate
III Beaches with active maintenance
    nourishment program
C   Critical erosion areas where
    substantial development or
    recreational interests are threatened
N/C Noncritical erosion areas;
    no development or recreation areas

Pejuan
Point

- - - - - - - -   Risk zones
- - - -   Coastal Barrier Resource System
. . . .   Preserve/govt. jurisdiction
———— - ——   County line

0   1
   Miles

0   1
   Kilometers

I, N/C

Captiva
Pass

RM 45   Cayo Costa Island

dry beach at high tide. The hodgepodge of armoring includes two sheet-metal groins, five timber groins, 13 permeable concrete groins, 22 stone groins, and 9,600 feet of seawall. About 70 feet of seawall on the southern end, part of a 700-foot section constructed by the county to protect the road, failed during Hurricane Gladys in October 1968 and was rebuilt in the same location. A 200-foot terminal groin was built at Boca Grande Historic Lighthouse Beach in 1970. In a 1981 emergency, sandbags were used to protect the lighthouse and a bigger, "better" terminal groin was proposed. Large amounts of replenishment sand have been placed on this beach in recent decades, but the beach-lighthouse area continues to erode. Old charts suggest that the island built out to the north about 750 feet in the last 100 years while the central section of the island retreated about 150 feet landward and the southern end lost about 500 feet. The one exit to the mainland, at the northern end of the island in Charlotte County, could become blocked and prevent timely evacuation during a hurricane.

Cayo Costa (RM 45) and North Captiva Island (RM 46) are approximately 7 and 4 miles long, respectively, with elevations of only 5–6 feet above mean sea level. The width of Cayo Costa varies from about 300 feet at the narrows near the south end to roughly 6,400 feet at its widest point just north of the middle of the island. The northern end of Cayo Costa near Boca Grande Pass and the southern end near Captiva Pass show steep scarps, indicating erosion. The southern end of the island is separated from the wider midsection by an old pass that is closed off. Cayo Costa is home to a 2,506-acre state recreation area that is accessible by boat from Boca Grande, so few structures are present on this shorefront and no armoring is in place.

North Captiva varies in width from about 200 feet near the south end to about 3,200 feet near the middle. Redfish Pass was formed in 1926 by a hurricane that destroyed much of the new development on the Florida peninsula at that time. North Captiva is about one-fourth developed, with 780 feet of rock revetment fronting several homes. Both Cayo Costa and North Captiva are in a relatively natural state compared with their neighbors, and study of old charts shows that they are undergoing normal migration. Someday they may attach to the mainland. Currently neither island is connected to the mainland by road, and evacuation by boat may be a dangerous proposition when hurricanes come calling.

Captiva Island (RM 46) is about 6 miles long and varies in width from less than 200 feet wide at the southern end to about 2,000 feet wide near the center. The narrow southern strip of sand represents the recent natural closure of Blind Pass, which used to separate Captiva Island from Sanibel Island. Blind Pass has a long history of migration, openings, and closings: it was closed in 1962, reopened in 1972 by Hurricane Agnes, and then closed again. Wulfert Channel cut about a 100-foot swath through this section and separated the two islands as of 1996, but the moving sands may close the channel at any time. On Captiva, many elegant homes are tucked among trees that lend good protection from storms. Presently, more than three-fourths of the Gulf side of Captiva is developed as residential and resort areas. South Seas Plantation is a privately owned resort with a history of beach nourishment projects (1981, 1985, and 1995). Other parts of the island's beaches have been nourished several times since the 1960s but have continued to experience serious ongoing erosion nevertheless. In 1993, more than 5 miles of Captiva's shorefront was classified a critical erosion area by the FDEP. Armoring fronts nearly half of the developed shoreline on this island.

Along with groins, revetments, seawalls, and bulkheads, two alternative shore protection projects have been tried on Captiva: 450 feet of "submerged breakwaters" (large sandbags) in 1979, and an unknown number of "perpendicular stabilizers" (sandbag groins) in 1986. Each of these alternatives lasted less than one year, and neither could be considered an effective method of shore protection.

Captiva Island is not connected directly to the mainland, but instead has

RM 46   North Captiva Island and Captiva Island

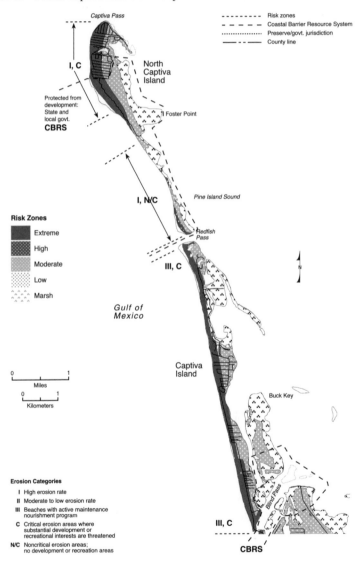

Risk zones
Coastal Barrier Resource System
Preserve/govt. jurisdiction
County line

Captiva Pass

I, C

North
Captiva
Island

Protected from
development:
State and
local govt.
CBRS

Foster Point

Pine Island Sound

I, N/C

Risk Zones

Extreme
High
Moderate
Low
Marsh

Redfish
Pass

III, C

Gulf of
Mexico

0 _____ 1
Miles

0 _____ 1
Kilometers

Captiva
Island

Buck Key

Erosion Categories

I   High erosion rate
II Moderate to low erosion rate
III Beaches with active maintenance
    nourishment program
C   Critical erosion areas where
    substantial development or
    recreational interests are threatened
N/C Noncritical erosion areas;
    no development or recreation areas

III, C

Blind Pass

CBRS

indirect access through Sanibel Island. Hurricane Gladys (1968) and a number of tropical storms have repeatedly damaged the coastal roadway, which the district and Lee County have tried to protect by beach-fill projects and rock revetments. The lone road and bridge between Captiva and Sanibel is subject to flooding during storms. This effectively maroons residents of Captiva, leaving them to weather the storm. Evacuation from Captiva should begin immediately in the face of a hurricane, and even so may not be easy. Should you reach Sanibel, the 3-mile-long causeway to the mainland will also be overcrowded.

Sanibel Island (RM 47)

Sanibel Island, with its interesting shape, is among the largest of the barrier islands on the Gulf coast. Although the island is more than 2 miles wide at its widest point, elevations are generally below 6 feet. The highest point remaining on Sanibel is only about 8 feet above mean sea level. The 100-year storm surge level for Sanibel Island is 10.2 feet above mean sea level, which means that most of the island would be covered by 3 or more feet of water in the event of such a storm. The island has an area of approximately 11,000 acres, more than half of which is wetland. More than 6,000 acres make up the J. N. "Ding" Darling National Wildlife Refuge, established in 1945.

The northwest–southeast-trending section of the Sanibel shoreline has been extremely dynamic due to the influence of the now-closed Blind Pass. From 1858 to 1943, the northern half of Sanibel grew seaward about 320 feet. Since then, the stability of the island's shoreline along the Gulf, as well as on the back bays, has been inconsistent.

Regardless of its changing morphology, people have lived on Sanibel for centuries. The Calusa Indians, residents of the island in the 1500s, are thought to have elevated their structures on piles of shells or on pilings for protection against high storm water, an example worth following. Today, elevating shorefront houses is routine for high-risk coastal living conditions. Although settlers attempted to live here in the 1830s, most evidently did not stay. Early tourists arrived in the 1880s along with more homesteaders, and the island has been a favorite vacation spot since, regardless of the threat of hurricanes.

Severe hurricanes struck the area in 1873, 1894, 1910, 1921, 1926, and 1947, with storm surges ranging from 9 to 13 feet. The 1926 storm flooded the entire island. Subsequently, little growth or development took place until 1944, and the addition of the causeway access in 1963 brought an influx of people that continues to mushroom. The number of causeway crossings increased from about 750,000 in 1975 to more than 3 million in 1997 (check out www.islandwater.com)! A significant number of these crossings may have been made by tourists coming to develop their "Sanibel slump" from collecting seashells. The approximately 5,500 year-round residents and additional part-time tourist populations are made up mainly of retired people. The Gulf front is almost completely developed with individual homes and hotels. About 1.5 miles of revetments and seawalls front the buildings and threaten the beaches.

As of 1993, the state had classified nearly 2 miles of Sanibel's Gulf-front shoreline as critical erosion areas. The erosion problem appears to be more acute on the bay side of the island, and extensive seawalls and bulkheads have been built from the lighthouse to Woodrings Point. Sections of the causeway at the southeastern tip of the island are so low that they can flood before hurricane evacuation begins, leaving the escape route from both Captiva and Sanibel blocked. Homes on this beautiful island are situated in moderate-to-extreme-risk zones.

Bunch Beach to Bonita Beach (RMs 48, 49)
Bunch Beach (RM 48) is a sheltered barrier beach welded to the mainland behind San Carlos Bay, east of Sanibel's Point Ybel. The area consists primarily of red and black mangrove swamp with narrow (50–150 feet) beach berms. From Sanibel Causeway to Pelican Bay the beach is about 4 miles long, bordered on the mainland side by freshwater Grassy Pond Slough. There is little development on this beach.

Fort Myers Beach (RM 48) lies on the northern end of Estero Island, south of the Bunch Beach area. The Gulf shoreline of Estero Island is about 7 miles long, and the island width varies from about 400 to 3,800 feet, with elevations generally below 7 feet. In several locations along the island, artificial canals have been dug from the bay side toward the beach, making the island vulnerable to breaching during hurricanes and tropical storms. The entire Gulf front has been intensively urbanized for commercial, resort, and residential uses. Just over one-fourth of the shorefront here is armored with groins, seawalls, and rock revetments. Additional seawalls, bulkheads, and revetments have been placed on the back bays of the island coastline. The southern end of Estero Island has retreated about 400 feet over the past 100 years, and the north end receded 80–150 feet between 1957 and 1969 (fig. 6.30). During the Matanzas Pass channel maintenance dredging in 1980, about 130,000 cubic yards of sand was placed along the northern mile of Estero Island beach. Currently, the north end of the island is designated a critical erosion area. One road links Estero Island and the mainland, and the southeast end is connected by a road to Black Island, a small island in the Lovers Key group. Again, this is part of the expected south

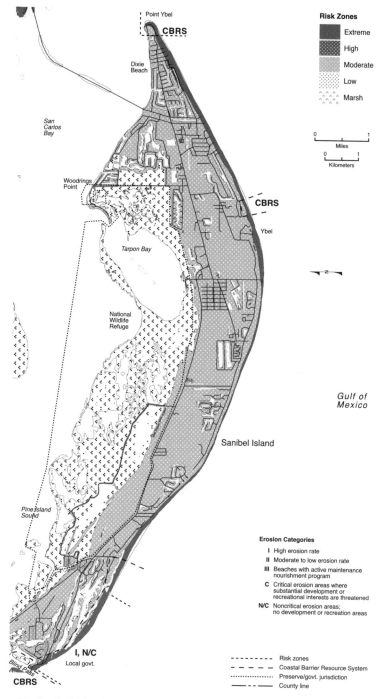

Risk Zones

- Extreme
- High
- Moderate
- Low
- Marsh

Point Ybel

CBRS

Dixie Beach

San Carlos Bay

Woodrings Point

CBRS

Ybel

Tarpon Bay

National Wildlife Refuge

Gulf of Mexico

Sanibel Island

Pine Island Sound

0   1
Miles

0   1
Kilometers

Erosion Categories

I High erosion rate

II Moderate to low erosion rate

III Beaches with active maintenance nourishment program

C Critical erosion areas where substantial development or recreational interests are threatened

N/C Noncritical erosion areas; no development or recreation areas

- - - - - - - - - Risk zones
- - - - - Coastal Barrier Resource System
. . . . Preserve/govt. jurisdiction
— - — - County line

I, N/C
Local govt.

Blind Pass

CBRS

RM 47 Sanibel Island

Florida evacuation congestion in the event of a hurricane.

The Lovers Key group of barrier islands — Black Island, Inner Key, and Lovers Key — have a combined beach length of 2.7 miles and a total area of about 300 acres of upland and wetlands. The width of Lovers Key on the Gulf varies from 30 feet to about 900 feet. Inner Key, which used to be on the Gulf before the formation in 1952 of the present-day Lovers Key, is about 600 feet at the widest point, including the mangroves. Elevations are generally below 5 feet on Black Island, 3 feet on Inner Key, and 2–4 feet on Lovers Key. These islands have no erosion control structures along the beach, except for 500 feet of rock revetment on the northwestern tip of Black Island. No urban development exists on these islands at this time, with the exception of Florida Highway 865 and county park facilities, and they should remain undeveloped.

Big Hickory Island's shoreline receded 50 feet at the northern end and advanced 20 feet at the southern end between 1995 and 1996. The shorelines here and on Little Hickory Island are characterized by major fluctuations.

The Lee-Collier County line cuts Little Hickory Island in half. The northern half, also called Bonita Beach Island, is about 6 miles long and varies in width from 300 feet to roughly 3,200 feet. The natural berm is about 5 feet high. Bonita Beach (RM 49), on the northern end of the island, is completely developed along the Gulf shoreline but had only about a half mile of armoring in place as of 1996. The beach was nourished in 1995 with 217,000 cubic yards of sand, and two terminal groins were added to the north on Big Hickory Pass.

Low elevations combined with lack of dunes and nearly 8 miles of developed-armored beaches make Lee County's barrier island chain especially susceptible to storm damage. NOAA estimates the 10-year still-water flood conditions on Lee County's barriers at 13.6 feet, more than 5.5 feet above the maximum 8-foot elevation of most of the islands. Remember that storm surge will increase the flood levels.

Since 1900, more than 30 hurricanes and tropical storms have passed within 50 miles of this coastline. Records suggest that the frequency of hurricanes is one per 4–6 years, and the frequency for all tropical storms is one in 2–3 years. In October 1873, a storm destroyed Punta Rassa, north of Bunch Beach, and produced a storm surge of 14 feet. An October 1910 hurricane produced 90 mph winds, with storm surge of 14.3 feet at Punta Rassa, and caused $258,000 in damage in Lee County. In September 1926, a hurricane with winds up to 140 mph, one of the most destructive in Florida's history, produced storm surge of 12 feet at Sanibel, Captiva, and Punta Rassa, with 11-foot storm surge near Fort Myers. This storm opened

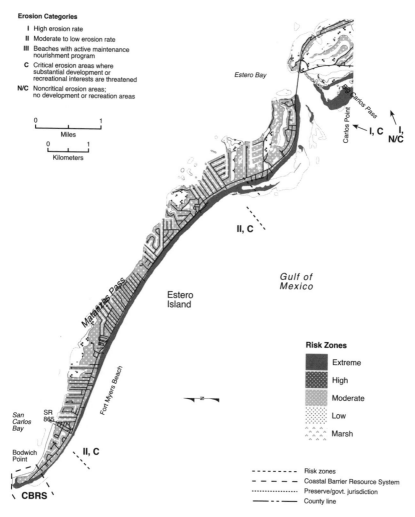

Erosion Categories

I   High erosion rate

II Moderate to low erosion rate

III Beaches with active maintenance
     nourishment program

C Critical erosion areas where
     substantial development or
     recreational interests are threatened

N/C Noncritical erosion areas;
     no development or recreation areas

Estero Bay

Carlos Point

Carlos Pass

I, C I,
       N/C

0 — 1 Miles

0 — 1 Kilometers

II, C

Gulf of
Mexico

Estero
Island

Matanzas Pass

Fort Myers Beach

San
Carlos
Bay

SR
865

Bodwich
Point

II, C

CBRS

Risk Zones

Extreme

High

Moderate

Low

Marsh

- - - - - - - - - Risk zones
- - - - - Coastal Barrier Resource System
· · · · · · · · · · · · Preserve/govt. jurisdiction
— - - — County line

RM 48   Estero Island

Redfish Pass on Captiva Island and caused about $3 million in damage from flooding. In October 1944, a hurricane with winds of 115 mph produced 8–11-foot storm surge in Lee County. A September 1947 storm with sustained winds of 100 mph produced heavy rains, causing $2 million in flood damage in the Fort Myers area. Hurricane Donna (September 1960) was the most severe of the storms on record, with 100 mph winds and 11-foot storm surge. All of the barrier islands were overtopped, and the property damage in Lee County alone was $16.5 million. Hurricane Alma (June 1966) produced storm surge of 5 feet at Fort Myers and caused erosion and flooding along the islands. Opal (1995) caused minor erosion and coastal

6.30 The southern end of Estero Island is severely eroded, leaving chunks of rocks exposed on the beach. Trees and other vegetation grow right up to the beach now, but they are potential victims of the erosion. Photo by Jason Smith.

flooding all the way to Key West. Even Earl (1998) raised water levels up to 3 feet above normal.

Historically, storm surge up to 12–15 feet has been reported in the Sanibel Island and Fort Myers areas. Major storms in this area are capable of producing extreme storm surge because of the very broad and shallow continental shelf. Storm surge from a category 3, 4, or 5 hurricane can be expected to rise from 14.5 to 20.5 feet at Point Ybel, and even higher at other points. The implications for future losses during hurricanes are enormous because of low elevations, exposed beaches, and the intensive development for resort and residential use. Most of Lee County's coastline is in the extreme-risk category.

Collier County (RMs 49, 50, 51, 52, 53, 54)

Collier County has roughly 50 miles of Gulf shoreline, including about 34 miles of beaches that are composed of fine quartz sand and shell fragments. The beaches of Sea Gate, at the northern boundary, are south of Bonita Beach on Little Hickory Island. South of Little Hickory Island lies Barefoot Beach State Preserve, Del-nor-Wiggins Pass, the Del-nor-Wiggins State Recreation Area, Clam Pass, Vanderbilt Beach, Doctors Pass, and the mainland beaches of Naples, bounded on the south by Gordon Pass. South of Gordon Pass lie numerous other barrier islands and passes: Keewaydin Island, Little Marco Pass, the Little Marco Island group, Hurricane Pass, Sea Oat Island, Capri Pass, Coconut Island, Big Marco Pass, Marco Island,

Caxambas Pass, Kice Island, Blind Pass (presently closed), Morgan Island, Morgan Pass, and Cape Romano Island. The Ten Thousand Islands lie south of Cape Romano and extend into Monroe County as mangrove coast. Collier County's beaches and islands are between 5 and 8 feet in elevation, with the exception of small areas on Naples City Beach and Marco Island at above 10 feet. There are no pronounced dunes. Where undeveloped, most islands are vegetated and have abundant mangrove cover. With the exception of Sea Gate, sections of the developed beaches have been nourished.

The barrier beaches of Collier County are the least densely developed of any county barrier shoreline on the western peninsula. More than 20 miles of eroding beaches are recognized by the FDEP; of these, more than half are designated critical. Approximately 15 miles of shoreline is developed, primarily with homes, condominiums, and resorts. Some owners have constructed seawalls and other structures, to the detriment of the beaches, and more than half of the county's developed shoreline (9 miles) is armored, particularly around the Naples area. Naples is virtually completely developed and has amassed 100 percent armoring. On the other hand, the Gulf front in the Sea Gate area was only about 30 percent developed as of 1996. Vanderbilt Beach, from Del-nor-Wiggins Park to Vanderbilt Drive in north Naples, is almost 75 percent developed, with about 50 percent of the developed stretches fronted by both shore-parallel and shore-perpendicular armoring structures. A beach restoration project completed in 1996 was still generating controversy in 1999 because of rock rubble it introduced to the beach. Large parts of the Vanderbilt and Naples beaches are designated as critical erosion areas by the FDEP. Keewaydin Island has a limited amount of construction along 2,020 feet of its shoreline fronted by rock revetments (fig. 6.31).

Of the six major passes affecting Collier County, three are stabilized: Doctors Pass, between Vanderbilt Beach and Naples, and Gordon Pass, between Naples and Keewaydin Island, have stone jetties on both sides; Caxambas Pass, to the south of Marco Island, had a large cement wall extending into the surf as of 1996. The breakwater project here was completed in September 1996 following some controversy. The stabilized Doctors Pass varies in depth from 4 to 10 feet and is 150 feet wide. Wiggins Pass is an unstabilized inlet with a channel depth of about 6 feet, kept open in the 1990s by maintenance dredging.

Del-nor-Wiggins Pass to Gordon Pass (RMS 50, 51)
The barrier island shoreline from Del-nor-Wiggins Pass to Clam Pass is about 4.7 miles long, including 1 mile within the state recreation area. Ap-

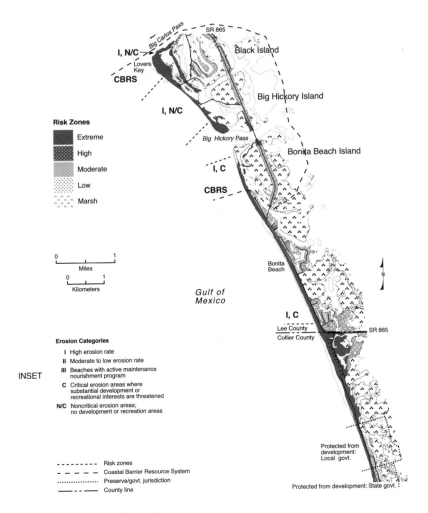

Risk Zones

- ◼ Extreme
- ▦ High
- ▨ Moderate
- ⸭ Low
- ⋏ Marsh

0   1
Miles

0   1
Kilometers

Erosion Categories

I   High erosion rate

II   Moderate to low erosion rate

III   Beaches with active maintenance nourishment program

C   Critical erosion areas where substantial development or recreational interests are threatened

N/C   Noncritical erosion areas; no development or recreation areas

INSET

- - - - - - - -   Risk zones
- — — — —   Coastal Barrier Resource System
- ··············   Preserve/govt. jurisdiction
- —— - - ——   County line

RM 49   Bonita Beach Island area

proximately 844 acres of this island is wetland. The island is 300–2,500 feet wide with elevations dipping from a high of 5 feet along the beach to the back-bay wetlands. Clam Pass is a natural, unimproved, shallow pass, about 3–4 feet deep.

The barrier island between Clam Pass and Doctors Pass is about 3 miles long and varies in width from 250 feet in the north to about 1,800 feet in some parts in the middle, and has an approximate area of 245 acres, of which about half is wetlands. The island has a 5-foot berm along much of its length, except near the southern end.

South of Doctors Pass is Naples City Beach, a 5.6-mile-long mainland beach bounded on the south by Gordon Pass, which has been stabilized with timber-and-stone terminal jetties to provide a navigation channel 12 feet deep and 150 feet wide. The Gulf beach here is generally low and only 20–50 feet wide. Extensive dredge-and-fill finger canals on the south end adjoining Naples Bay increase vulnerability to storm breaching. Islands behind the Gulf beach are made up of dredge spoil, material removed from navigational channels, and behave as barrier islands. These areas are subject to flooding during storms. Naples Beach illustrates one of several problems associated with beach nourishment. Unscrupulous suppliers and poorly understood borrow sand supplies resulted in rocks being pumped onto the beach, diminishing its recreational value. The political fallout from such engineering projects continues.

Keewaydin Island to Romano Island (RMS 52, 53, 54)

The Keewaydin Island group is about 9.3 miles long and 2,980 acres in area and comprises roughly 2,230 acres of wetlands and 750 acres of upland. Elevations are generally 3–6 feet along the beach and dip toward the back bay. The width varies from about 4,000 feet in the north to 200 feet in the south, with narrow, steep beaches. Keewaydin Island has been nourished at least five times since the 1960s, but most other Collier County beaches did not receive nourishment until the 1980s. In 1983, more than 450 feet of artificial seaweed (Beachbuilder system) was installed on Keewaydin Island as an alternative shore protection measure, but it lasted less than one year. Keewaydin Island presently is eroding in the north and accreting southward.

6.31 On Keewaydin Island in the shadow of the jetty on the south side of Gordon Pass, a construction site for about 20 houses was developed where the former Keewaydin Club stood. Photo by Dan Wagner/*Naples Daily News*, Naples, Florida.

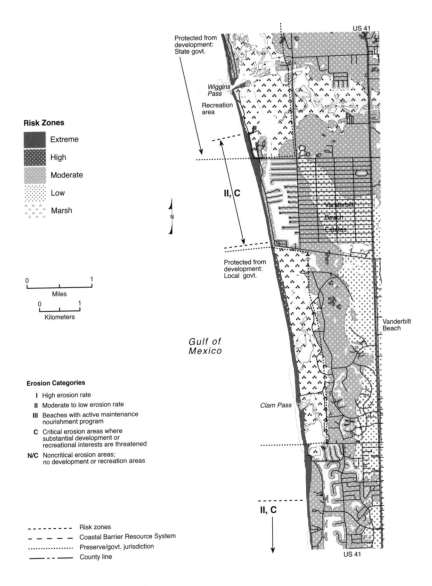

Risk Zones

- Extreme
- High
- Moderate
- Low
- Marsh

Erosion Categories

- **I** High erosion rate
- **II** Moderate to low erosion rate
- **III** Beaches with active maintenance nourishment program
- **C** Critical erosion areas where substantial development or recreational interests are threatened
- **N/C** Noncritical erosion areas; no development or recreation areas

- - - - - - - - Risk zones
- - - - - Coastal Barrier Resource System
.... Preserve/govt. jurisdiction
——— - - County line

0 _____ 1
Miles

0 _____ 1
Kilometers

Protected from development: State govt.

Wiggins Pass

Recreation area

II, C

Vanderbilt Beach Estates

Protected from development: Local govt.

Vanderbilt Beach

Gulf of Mexico

Clam Pass

II, C

US 41

RM 50 Vanderbilt Beach area

Little Marco Island, about 1.5 miles long, is bounded by Hurricane Pass and Little Marco Pass. Much of the island is below 5 feet and less than 1,500 feet wide. This island once faced the Gulf, but the southerly buildup of Keewaydin Island now protects it. Sea Oat Island, Capri Pass, and Coconut Island lie south of Keewaydin. All of these areas are in the extreme-risk category.

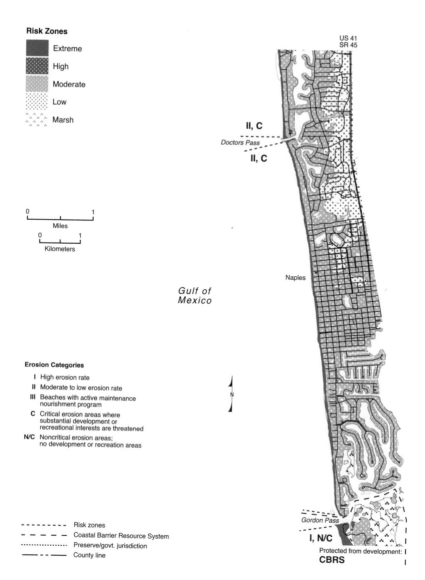

Risk Zones

- Extreme
- High
- Moderate
- Low
- Marsh

0 ——————— 1
Miles

0 ——————— 1
Kilometers

Gulf of
Mexico

US 41
SR 45

II, C
Doctors Pass
II, C

Naples

Erosion Categories

I   High erosion rate
II Moderate to low erosion rate
III Beaches with active maintenance
    nourishment program
C   Critical erosion areas where
    substantial development or
    recreational interests are threatened
N/C Noncritical erosion areas;
    no development or recreation areas

- - - - - - - - - Risk zones
- - - - - Coastal Barrier Resource System
·················· Preserve/govt. jurisdiction
———— - · — County line

Gordon Pass
I, N/C
Protected from development: I
CBRS

RM 51   Naples area

Marco Island: An End Point in Coastal Development (RM 53)
Although many coastal communities could be taken as historic examples
of rapid coastal development in high-risk zones spurred on by access to
the coast and our desire for waterfront property, Marco Island is symbolic
because it is the last developed barrier island on Florida's southwest coast.
The island is geologically young, the end product of accreted beach ridges

A

6.32 Marco Island.
(A) During development.
Photo courtesy of Herb
Savage and the *Marco Island
Eagle*. (B) Marco Island as it
is today, after development.
Photo by Jason Smith.

B

and a healthy beach system. Wetlands, shoals, backwaters, and beaches were once pristine, offering a sanctuary for birds, nesting sea turtles, shellfish, and marine life. Although about 4.6 miles long and 5,100 acres in area, most of the island is well below 10 feet in elevation, and much of it was originally wetlands. But late twentieth-century affluence and engineering brought a swift change in the character of the island (fig. 6.32).

Marco Island remained almost in its natural state until the mid-1960s. In 1964 the island was subdivided, an airport was constructed to bring in prospective buyers, and an extensive system of finger canals was dredged to provide more waterfront lots, destroying salt marsh, mangroves, and wilderness habitat. Even after extensive dredging and filling, about 785 acres of wetlands remained in the 1970s. The first access bridge was constructed in 1970, opening the door to accelerated development, and a second bridge was added in 1978. By 1980 there were 1,000 houses and 2,500 condominiums supporting a population of between 7,000 and 10,000 people. By 1990 those numbers had doubled and were still growing.

The developers were either ignorant of or chose to ignore the risk fac-

RM 52 Halloway Island area

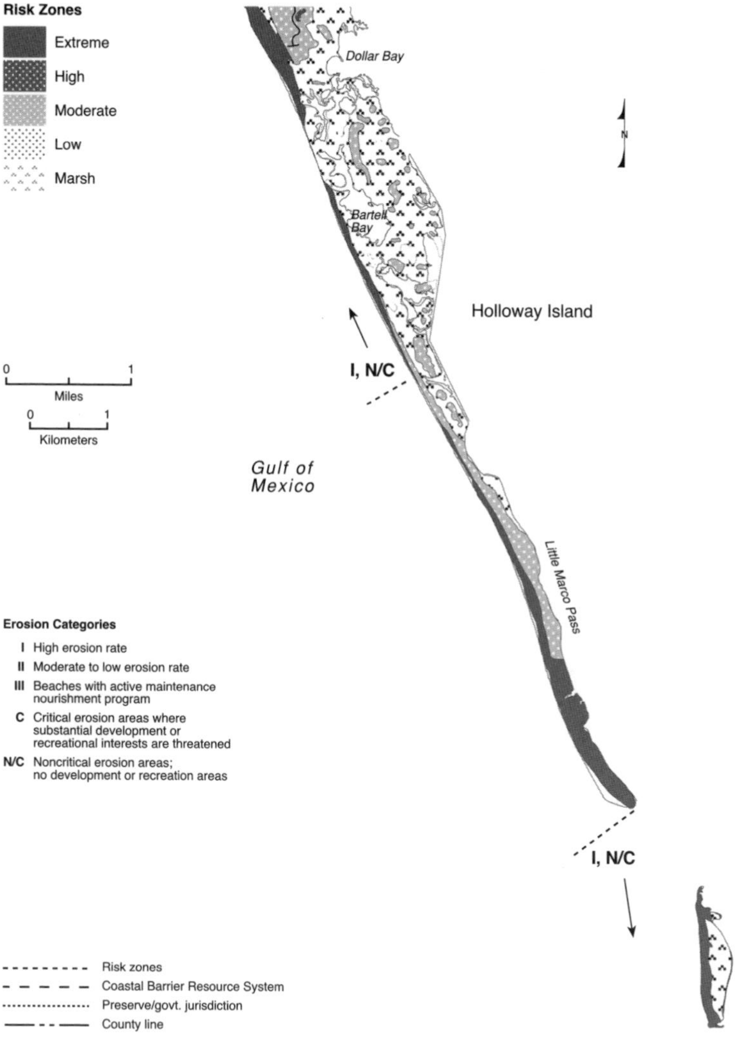

Risk Zones

- Extreme
- High
- Moderate
- Low
- Marsh

Dollar Bay

Bartell Bay

Holloway Island

I, N/C

0 _____ 1
Miles

0 _____ 1
Kilometers

Gulf of Mexico

Little Marco Pass

Erosion Categories

I High erosion rate

II Moderate to low erosion rate

III Beaches with active maintenance nourishment program

C Critical erosion areas where substantial development or recreational interests are threatened

N/C Noncritical erosion areas; no development or recreation areas

I, N/C

- - - - - - - - Risk zones
- - - - - Coastal Barrier Resource System
.... Preserve/govt. jurisdiction
——— - - ——— County line

tors, particularly the island's history of hurricane response. Remember, most of the island is less than 10 feet in elevation. The storm of October 18, 1910, raised floodwaters 8–10 feet above sea level in this area, and in 1947 the flood level reached 7.4 feet. Then, in 1960, Hurricane Donna drowned the island in a 10.2-foot flood. The potential flood levels were known, and ground examination would have revealed other aspects of the hurricane risk such as overwash deposits. Although nothing of value was threatened by erosion in predevelopment times, a study of aerial photos would have suggested that potential shoreline retreat warranted deep setbacks for buildings. Instead, buildings were placed right at the back of the beach.

Marco Island now has dense beachfront development. Passive armoring probably contributed to the narrowing of the beach. Over the years, private developers have placed undetermined amounts of sand on Marco Island's shore, suggesting that erosion was a problem from the beginning. In 1979, two hurricanes, David and Frederick, struck the area, producing damage and erosion. By the late 1980s, beach maintenance was definitely needed, even though in predevelopment times part of the island had experienced accretion. Two beach replenishment projects were completed to mitigate erosion problems on the critically eroding southern end in 1991 and on Hideaway Beach near the northern end in 1995. Marco Island's beaches vary between 100 and 150 feet in width. In 1998, T-groins were installed at Hideaway Beach at a cost of $427,041 to the county. (See www. marcoeagle.com/1998 for more information.) By 1999 sand was collecting at the entrance to Collier Bay. Was it natural deposition or the result of the T-groins? Whatever the cause, sand was now a perceived problem rather than a blessing, and the city council adopted a resolution to ask the FDEP and the Army Corps of Engineers to allow dredging of the Collier Bay Inlet at the north end. Marco Island is learning as a community that once you opt for shoreline engineering, you can't do just one thing, and there is no turning back. The ultimate cost is going to be very high.

Since development, the island has dodged some close ones in terms of storms. Some residents probably think they've experienced a hurricane, but David and Frederic, despite all the damage they did, were misses. Thousands of feet of seawalls have been lost to storms. Andrew's winds blew here in 1992, the 1984 Thanksgiving storm blew through, and Opal generated some wind and waves in 1995. Georges was enough of a threat in 1998 to trigger an evacuation order, but did its damage elsewhere. But every year Mother Nature flips the coin again, and every time the odds are the same. Storms like those of 1910, 1947, and 1960 will return.

In addition to the development at extreme to high risk on the front side, the island's bay shore is extensively developed and armored. No protective

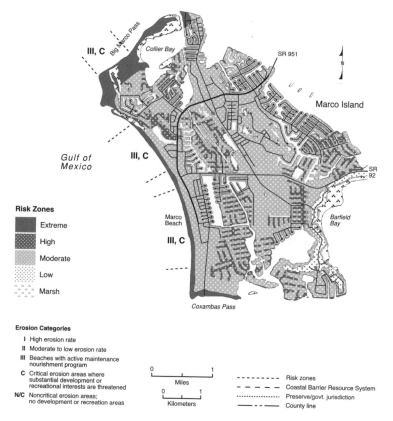

Risk Zones

- Extreme
- High
- Moderate
- Low
- Marsh

Erosion Categories

I   High erosion rate
II   Moderate to low erosion rate
III   Beaches with active maintenance nourishment program
C   Critical erosion areas where substantial development or recreational interests are threatened
N/C   Noncritical erosion areas; no development or recreation areas

0 — Miles — 1

0 — Kilometers — 1

- - - - - - - - - Risk zones
— — — — — Coastal Barrier Resource System
·················· Preserve/govt. jurisdiction
—— - - —— County line

RM 53   Marco Island area

beach fronts the walls at high tide, and the risk factors are nearly as high on the back side as on the front of the island.

Turtles still come to nest, though they may find the nourishment sand different from the natural beaches they've visited here over the last few millennia. Wetlands still exist, albeit reduced in area. The water quality is acceptable if we allow for an occasional exception. Sand Dollar Island, a sandbar off Tigertail Beach toward the north end of Marco Island, is preserved as a bird-nesting area — a window on the past life of the shore.

The birds on the sandbar might remind us that we too are clinging on the edge for survival. Marco Island is an extreme evacuation risk area in the event of a hurricane. The two roads leading off the island are likely to be flooded early in the low areas approaching the bridges. Traffic congestion will present problems as well. Jolley Bridge is two lanes. Highway 951 leading to U.S. 41 was widened to handle more traffic, but when you reach the mainland shore you have miles to go before you are at an elevation high enough to be out of the flood zone. Vertical evacuation may be necessary, but that is not a pleasant prospect or a proven survival response. And you're at the end of the development chain!

Kice and Cape Romano Islands (RM 54)

Kice Island, Morgan Beach, and Cape Romano appear to be a unified barrier island group not connected to the mainland. These islands have about 4.8 miles of sandy beach with a total area of about 2,650 acres, most of which is wetlands behind the narrow beach berm. This island complex is affected by three passes: the large Caxambas Pass to the north, the now-closed Blind Pass, and Morgan Pass on the south. Morgan Pass affects the morphology of the beaches on Morgan Island to the west and Cape Romano to the east. The Cape Romano Island group is the southern terminus of the West-Central Barrier Chain. The beaches along much of this island group are quite narrow, steep, unstable, low, and subject to frequent overwash and inlet formation. The entire island group is below 5 feet in elevation, and mostly below 2–3 feet. Approximately 958 acres of this island is owned by the state, and the entire area is unsafe for development. Indeed, the entire Collier coastline is vulnerable to storm surge and has experienced numerous storms.

The 10-year flood heights along Collier County are 12.5–14 feet above mean sea level. Winter storms, tropical storms, and hurricanes all threaten this southern shore. Since 1900, more than 25 hurricanes have passed within 50 miles of Naples, or an average of one every 2 years. Some of the notable hurricanes that severely affected Collier County were an 1873 storm that produced 14-foot storm surge at Punta Rassa in Lee County and 90 mph winds; a 1910 hurricane that generated 70–90 mph winds and 10.5-foot storm surge in the region when the eye passed over Naples; the 1921 hurricane that created storm surge up to 11 feet in Collier County; and the 1926 Labor Day hurricane that brought winds of 90–115 mph and storm surge of more than 6 feet to the area. The "Labor Day" hurricane in 1935 also generated high winds, and the October 1944 hurricane produced 7.4-foot storm surge in the south and 8–11-foot storm surge along Naples Beach. Flooding depths of 5 feet were reported at that time. During the 1944 storm, considerable beach erosion occurred along with destruction of more than 4 miles of wooden sheet-pile bulkhead and a 1,000-foot pier. The 1947 September hurricane produced storm surge of 5.5 feet, causing flooding in many low areas in Naples and to the south with water 2–3 feet deep. Hurricane Donna (September 1960) was the most severe storm prior to Andrew in 1992. Donna brought a storm surge of 9–11 feet (Naples) and flooding that extended up to 10 miles inland! Low areas in Naples were

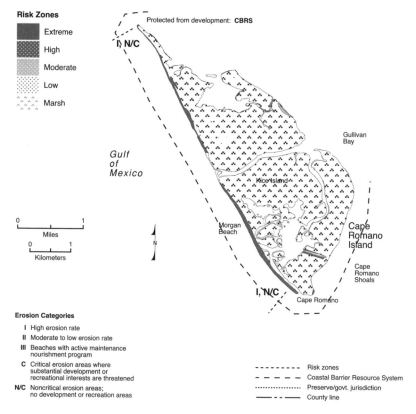

Risk Zones

- Extreme
- High
- Moderate
- Low
- Marsh

Protected from development: **CBRS**

I, N/C

Gulf
of
Mexico

Gullivan
Bay

Kice Island

Morgan
Beach

Cape
Romano
Island

Cape
Romano
Shoals

I, N/C

Cape Romano

0 — 1
Miles

0 — 1
Kilometers

N

Erosion Categories

I   High erosion rate
II Moderate to low erosion rate
III Beaches with active maintenance
    nourishment program
C   Critical erosion areas where
    substantial development or
    recreational interests are threatened
N/C Noncritical erosion areas;
    no development or recreation areas

- - - - - - - - Risk zones
— — — — — Coastal Barrier Resource System
· · · · · · · · · · · Preserve/govt. jurisdiction
—— - - —— County line

RM 54   Kice Island area and Cape Romano

flooded 3–4 feet deep. All the barrier beaches were overtopped and flooded. Storm surge and heavy wave action eroded beach berms and covered the beach roads with several feet of sand. Street ends were heavily eroded and undermined. Most homes on Vanderbilt Beach and other exposed beaches were severely damaged or destroyed, and nearly 300 homes and trailers in Collier County suffered heavy damage or were completely lost. Most of the seawalls, bulkheads, and groins suffered major damage, and the Naples city piers were destroyed. The total flood damage in Collier County exceeded $8.5 million (1960 dollars). Hurricane Betsy (September 1965) caused 5-foot storm surge and $166,000 in storm damage in Collier County. And all of these events occurred prior to the dense development on Marco Island! A storm in 1968 is said to have washed away the entire beach around the old missile-tracking station on Marco Island and created an inlet in Cannon Island, creating Capri Pass and Coconut Island (see www.marcoeagle.com).

Monroe County

The Gulf shoreline of Monroe County consists of the Ten Thousand Islands mangrove coast and Everglades National Park. This county extends down to Cape Sable and beyond, and includes a large part of the Florida Keys. Virtually all of its shore is protected, undevelopable, and at extreme risk.

Past Reflections: Future Expectations

In summary, locating at the shore calls for greater prudence than living in an inland environment. First, the coastal environment lacks uniformity and is never static. Topography, sediment, and vegetation change abruptly from beach to dune to overwash terrace to forest to marsh. These systems are unstable; they change or shift in response to storms, rising or falling sea level, shoreline migration, and placement of man-made structures. Look to the future when selecting a site. You will find that the future comes sooner at the shore.

Second, coastal hazards such as hurricane winds, storm surge flooding, wave attack, overwash, and persistent erosion are unlike anything you have experienced in the relative quiet and stability of an inland area. Choose your site with such forces in mind, and reinforce your construction to improve its strength to survive these forces. Expect maintenance to be more frequent and more expensive.

Third, coastal communities have their own set of social dynamics, both because they are resorts and because they must respond collectively to coastal hazards. Responses to erosion, flooding, overwash, and other hazards, as well as the kind and extent of development allowed, set a course that is more difficult to alter in coastal communities than in inland towns. Expect and support increasing regulation that protects the beaches of your shoreline. Remember that armoring ultimately destroys beaches, and loss of beaches will likely cause a decline in the economy of beach communities. Coastal areas require their own pattern of management and planning policies that are reflected in the extent and types of regulations. This pattern is suggested in chapter 9.

While our focus in this book is on coastal hazards and on evaluating the risk of property damage due to coastal processes and storms, other natural and human-induced hazards exist in the coastal zone as well. Unique aspects of Florida's climatic and geologic setting may contribute to some hazards that are unfamiliar to those visiting or moving into the state. Brief mention of these hazards is made here because when living at the shore we often look seaward when evaluating risk, and then are blind-sided by events that come from landward.

Sinkhole Collapse and Subsidence

Karst is a word that you should become familiar with if you live in Florida. Much of the state is underlain by limestone, a soluble rock in which subterranean solution channels and caves form. When a cavern roof collapses or the material overlying the zone of dissolution subsides, a *sinkhole* or *swale* is produced. Lowering of the water level in a cave may reduce internal support, and some collapses have been attributed to low water tables during periods of drought. In areas where sinkholes intersect the water table, circular lakes are abundant. If these depressions are above the water table, surface drainage may disappear down the sinkhole or reemerge as a stream rise. The surface characterized by this type of drainage and sinkhole topography, called karst terrain, is likely to be plagued by collapse sinks that undermine buildings or by unexpected changes in drainage or water quality in wells. Where limestone underlies the mainland coast, the shape of the shoreline is modified karst (e.g., the Woodville Karst Plain in Apalachee Bay and the drowned karst of the Big Bend coast). Even some of the barrier islands rest atop karst surfaces in the limestone bedrock.

Many shallow swales develop gradually due to subsidence, but the collapse of a new sinkhole may be sudden and unexpected. Rarely a year goes by without a news story of a Florida sinkhole swallowing a parcel of land, a building, or some other human trappings. Collapse may simply be a function of time, but loading the surface with buildings, vibrating the surface with traffic and construction, or modifying surface drainage can contribute to conditions that are already unstable. At Winter Park, not far from Orlando, a sinkhole formed in May 1981 that measured approximately 300 feet by 350 feet. It destroyed an entire house and shed, half of a municipal swimming pool, a few automobiles, and a section of street that went across the sinkhole.

Even though sinkholes are destructive, over time they may be beneficial to people in one way or another. As soon as they form, sinkholes begin to fill up with debris, organic material, silt, and clay from erosive processes. This material lines the surface of the hole and makes it able to retain water. Eventually the sinkhole becomes stabilized and may become a lake and be an asset to the community. A large part of Florida contains such lakes.

In addition to the threat of collapse and damage to surface property, other problems can result from karst conditions. When the system's drainage capacity is exceeded, surface flooding may result. Karst drainage systems also are very vulnerable to pollution because the open subsurface conduits of karst systems allow the rapid, free passage of water without filtering or attenuating particulate matter or dissolved ions. Karst has no natural ability to remove pollutants. The poorly known subsurface flow paths influence large areas of groundwater, Florida's primary source of domestic water supplies.

Figure 7.1 is a generalized map of sinkhole types, development, and distribution in west Florida adapted from the study by W. C. Sinclair and J. W. Stewart (appendix C, ref. 4). For more site-specific evaluation of property you should consult a standard U.S. Geological Survey (USGS) topographic map and look for karst features. Solution features are often developed along linear zones of weakness in the bedrock that allow passage of water (e.g., cracks in the rock). A site located in line with existing sinkholes is likely to be at higher risk for future sinkhole development than one that is not. If in doubt, contact a consulting engineering geologist.

Other Types of Subsidence

Other buried beds may also lack the strength to support building foundations or stilt (pole) houses. Buried peat, muck, mud, and old soils often compact and settle, causing nuisance or cosmetic damage to buildings. Fill over

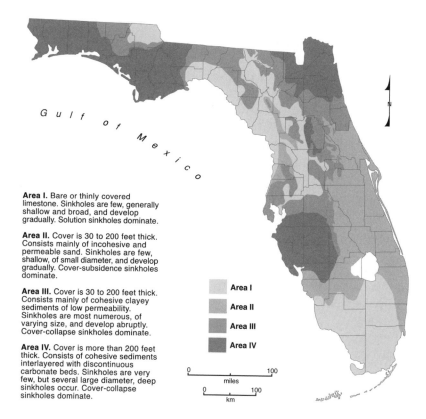

Area I. Bare or thinly covered limestone. Sinkholes are few, generally shallow and broad, and develop gradually. Solution sinkholes dominate.

Area II. Cover is 30 to 200 feet thick. Consists mainly of incohesive and permeable sand. Sinkholes are few, shallow, of small diameter, and develop gradually. Cover-subsidence sinkholes dominate.

Area III. Cover is 30 to 200 feet thick. Consists mainly of cohesive clayey sediments of low permeability. Sinkholes are most numerous, of varying size, and develop abruptly. Cover-collapse sinkholes dominate.

Area IV. Cover is more than 200 feet thick. Consists of cohesive sediments interlayered with discontinuous carbonate beds. Sinkholes are very few, but several large diameter, deep sinkholes occur. Cover-collapse sinkholes dominate.

Area I
Area II
Area III
Area IV

7.1 Sinkhole type, development, and distribution in Florida. The composition and thickness of limestone near the surface combines with the warm, humid climate of Florida to form different types of sinkholes. From *Sinkhole Type, Development, and Distribution in Florida,* by W. C. Sinclair and J. W. Stewart, 1985 (appendix C, ref. 4).

marsh beds, as in areas around finger canals, may be susceptible to settling. Withdrawal of groundwater also can cause subsidence.

River and Estuary Flooding

Flooding is the most pervasive threat to property in the Gulf coast counties. Although we associate coastal flooding with storm surge and wave run-up, particularly during hurricanes, property on river and estuary floodplains is also subject to flooding from surface runoff. High rainfall is common along the Gulf shore in association with both hurricanes and winter storms. Folks who winter in the Southeast after the hurricane season may have a false sense of security in regard to the weather, but southwesters can dump copious amounts of rainfall that result in flooding, including flash flooding.

One of these winter storms, the March 1993 "Storm of the Century," surprised many coastal and inland residents with flooding, especially in west Florida. Earlier, in 1988, west-central Florida experienced a 20-inch rainfall that required 1,000 homes to be evacuated. Records of claims filed by property owners for damage under their flood insurance policies show few years without significant flood losses. And it's a wise person who has flood insurance. Many property owners on floodplains are uninsured, either through ignorance or because they have the attitude that floods happen somewhere else, but "not to me." The fact that individual counties have emergency response plans for floods is a good indicator that such events are expected. If you are inland from the Gulf but near a waterway or wetland, especially at elevations below 10 feet, you should investigate the potential flood risk for your property. Consult the county or community FIRMs, flood-proof your building, obtain flood insurance, and have an evacuation plan.

Property in the vicinity of estuaries is exposed to a triple flood threat: onshore storm surge, flash flooding from heavy local rains, and downstream river flooding due to heavy inland rains. Because inland winds are also a threat associated with all storms, follow the construction guidelines outlined in chapter 8 and the same emergency procedures as for a hurricane (appendix A). Associated hazards such as tornadoes, lightning, and hail are likely. In these times of hurricanes, floods, El Niño, La Niña, drought, and wildfires, a change in the weather usually means a change in the hazard. Stay tuned for the weather!

At Least There Are No Earthquakes?

Well, not exactly. Seismic risk must be considered, although Florida is fortunate because the potential for destructive earthquakes is very low. Since 1727 there have been at least 25 earthquakes strong enough to be felt in Florida, and occasionally to do damage. A 1781 tremor shook ammunition racks from the barrack walls in Pensacola and is reported to have leveled houses. The 1886 Great Charleston Earthquake in South Carolina rang church bells in St. Augustine and was felt in Tampa. That great quake is the reason why a portion of north Florida is considered to be at some risk from future earthquakes. On Florida's west coast, quakes have been felt on Marco Island (1930), Fort Myers (1942), Captiva Island (1948), and in the Panhandle (1952).

Most of the earthquakes felt in Florida are seismic waves that originate outside the state, for example, from movement along faults such as those in the Charleston area. Although faults exist beneath the state, such as under the Apalachicola Embayment, and a few very minor quakes may be of local origin, the general indication is that Florida is seismically stable. Reactivation of these old faults does not seem likely, but Mother Earth is unpredictable. The seismic risk map produced by the U.S. Geological Survey indicates that the Apalachee Bay and northern Big Bend coast counties (eastern Franklin, Wakulla, Jefferson, Taylor, Dixie, Levy, and northern Citrus) are in a zone that is likely to experience at least minor damage from the largest expected distant earthquakes. The rest of the peninsula and Panhandle have a very low probability of damage from distant earthquakes.

One aspect of Florida's geology raises the potential for damage due to earthquakes. Poorly consolidated or unconsolidated sediments may amplify ground shaking. The extreme end result of prolonged shaking in unconsolidated sediments is soil liquefaction. Florida has not experienced a quake of the 1886 Charleston variety for well over a century, not since the advent of coastal growth and development. How will the dense housing developments of today respond to such an earthquake?

Buildings constructed to resist the forces of coastal storms incorporate construction principles that also are likely to reduce earthquake damage (see chapter 8). For additional information on earthquake-resistant construction and reducing the risks of nonstructural damage, see appendix C. In particular, water heaters should be securely fastened to the wall, and freestanding stoves to the floor.

Water Problems: Are You Ready for More Infrastructure?

One of the more significant hazards to barrier island living is contaminated water. Basically the problem involves three factors: water supply, waste disposal, and any form of island alteration that affects the first two factors (fig. 7.2). Dredge-and-fill operations (e.g., inlet cutting, digging channels in islands for canals and waterways, and the piling of dredge spoil) and other construction activities are factors that may alter the groundwater system.

Water Supply

Just as the quality and availability of water determine the plant and animal makeup of an island's ecosystem, water supply also determines, in part, the island's capacity to accommodate people. Water quality is measured by potability, freshness, clarity, odor, and the presence or absence of pathogens (disease-causing bacteria). Availability implies the presence of an adequate supply, which may be highly seasonal.

Unless an island is developed and has a municipal water system, the only fresh water directly available to a barrier island is from rainfall over the island. The rainwater seeps through the porous and permeable sands and builds up as a lens or wedge of fresh water beneath the island's surface. This lens overlies salt water, which seeps into the sediments from the adjacent ocean, inlet, or marsh. The higher the island's elevation above sea level and the greater the accumulation of fresh water, the greater the thickness of the freshwater lens. Where clean sands underlie the island, the thickness of the lens should be about 40 feet for every foot of average island elevation. This ideal is rarely the case because mud, peat, or bedrock may underlie the island. The top of the freshwater lens is known as the ground water table, and on many islands this shallow reservoir is the only source of domestic fresh water.

Too many wells drawing on the groundwater will lower the water table and potentially cause saltwater intrusion. Early occupants of a development should not be surprised if their shallow wells dry up as the development grows, ultimately requiring them to find another source of fresh water. Seeking alternative sources of water such as deep aquifers or building alternative sources such as municipal water systems (deep wells, pipe lines, filtration plants, desalinization plants) is expensive and is done only on densely developed islands. However, most developed barrier islands are moving in the direction of municipal systems and their necessary expansion, so property owners should expect to help pick up the costs. Water facilities and lines are vulnerable to storm impact, so long recovery periods without water should be expected, plus the added cost of paying to rebuild a system.

Saltwater intrusion will occur when individual wells remove water faster than it can recharge, or when too many wells depress the water table. When the water table goes down, the saltwater interface rises, and the freshwater lens may be breached. One of the intermediate-term effects of the current sea-level rise is that the saltwater interface below the shoreline is migrating landward, resulting in a loss of coastal freshwater resources. The Everglades illustrates this effect. The reduction of surface freshwater flow into the Everglades due to diversions and consumption (e.g., irrigation) allowed the salt-fresh groundwater interface to migrate inland well beyond the coastal shoreline of the Everglades.

Large developments sometimes draw their water supply from rock units beneath the younger surface sands and muds. These *aquifers* are rock formations that are exposed on the coastal plain (their recharge area) and dip seaward beneath the coast. The fresh water in such aquifers has been accumulating for thousands of years, but large developments withdraw it faster than it can be replaced (recharged). In effect, the water is being mined, and as it is pulled out, the space is filled with salt water, contaminating existing wells and destroying the adjacent aquifer as a freshwater source.

As condominiums and high-rises replace cottages, the demand on the water supply increases. Alternatives must be sought, and they will be expensive. Coastal property owners will bear the cost. Consult the proper authorities about water quantity and quality before you buy (see appendix B, *Water Supply and Pollution Control*)!

Waste Disposal

Wastewater disposal goes hand-in-glove with water supply. Remote properties and small communities often rely on home septic systems as the primary means of wastewater disposal. This type of system consists of a holding tank in which solids settle and sewage is biologically broken down and a drain field that allows water to percolate into the soil. Ideally the soil then filters and purifies the water, but the same natural system that is used to cleanse the water also may be the supply of potable water to residences (fig. 7.2).

Many communities are unaware of the potential water problems they face. Crowded development, improperly maintained systems, and systems installed in soils unsuitable for filtration have resulted in poorly treated or untreated sewage entering the surrounding environment. Polluted water is a primary source of hepatitis and other diseases. When such water enters

7.2 Barrier islands and spits are vulnerable to several types of environmental hazards. From *Coastal Zone Management Handbook,* by John R. Clark (appendix C, ref. 56).

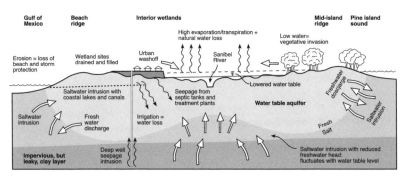

sounds and marshes, shellfish are contaminated and that resource is ultimately destroyed. Septic tanks have been blamed in the past for the pollution and subsequent closing of shellfishing areas. The sad irony is that we have the understanding and technology to make environmentally safe septic systems, but we sometimes fall short of the enforcement capability to ensure that they are always used. Of course, not all pollution of coastal waters comes from coastal development. Upstream effluents from agriculture, industry, and inland developments ultimately come to the coastal waters via streams. Oil spills may occur on a grand scale in the shipping lanes, or on a cumulative small scale from small boaters.

Public officials should require strict enforcement of existing codes and policing of existing systems, and should insist on proper site evaluation before issuing permits. In addition, homeowners should learn the mechanics of septic systems to prevent malfunctioning or to spot it early (see appendix B, *Health, Sanitation, and Water Quality*). Municipal waste-treatment plants may be one answer for larger communities, although such plants often become overloaded or inefficient.

Municipal sewer and water systems can create a less complicated life for island dwellers in terms of dependability of sewer and water service. But such systems almost inevitably result in intensified development, turning low-density, single-family-home communities into high-density communities. Some individual developments have so-called package plants, local sewer systems for a small number of houses. These can be satisfactory if well maintained and not overtaxed. In all cases, waste treatment systems tend to be damaged or destroyed during big storms, with the resulting escape of effluent into the surrounding waters. For example, after Hurricane Georges in 1998, sewage was pumped into Santa Rosa Sound. Even leakage from individual septic systems exhumed by a storm can contribute to the problem (see fig. 6.13).

Perhaps the most threatening waste-treatment approach is the use of offshore sewer outfalls. These pipes are designed to disperse treated or partially treated sewage offshore, but no one sits at the end of the outfall pipe to monitor compliance with regulations. Waste, treated or untreated, overloads the carrying capacity of the marine environment and changes the equilibrium of the ecosystem (see fig. 6.9). The quickest way to lose a beach crowd is for them to learn that they're swimming in "stuff."

El Niño: The Global Connection

El Niño, a warm-water event in the Pacific Ocean, sets off a chain reaction of weather changes worldwide, bringing drought to normally wet areas and flooding downpours to the driest of lands. It brought record amounts of rainfall and flooding to Florida during the winter of 1998, sparking one of the wettest winters on record. The copious rains produced a bumper crop of shrubs and brush that turned many of the state's forests into an impenetrable thicket of dense growth. When the wet winter was succeeded by a dry spring and a summer drought, that new growth subsequently became fuel for the fires sparked by the drought. The combination produced conditions for a flaming end to the state's vast tracts of pines, palmettos, and scrub oaks. From early spring to the first of July 1998, Florida residents lived in fear of wildfires that began to burn out of control. When the flames finally subsided in Brevard County, they had consumed some 71,000 acres of mostly uninhabited land and destroyed 32 homes and three businesses. Residents from the rural community of Scottsmoor and from portions of nearby Mims were evacuated, and residents all over Brevard and into Indian River County were trying to avoid smoke inhalation. Brush fires hit all of Florida's 67 counties. It is estimated that statewide, nearly 2,200 fires burned almost a half million acres, resulting in $393 million in damages. It was the worst outbreak of wildfires in Florida in 60 years.

The Final Hazard: Human Infrastructure

As coastal development continues to grow upward and expand laterally, it must be served by a growing infrastructure: roads, electrical services, water lines, storm drains, sewage lines, wastewater treatment plants, solid waste disposal, and all the other services associated with any development. In addition, shoreline armoring structures and other appendages (e.g., dune walkovers, stairways, decks, etc.) are likely to be present. This infrastructure is at the same risk from storms as individual property, and the impact of its destruction and failure is far greater at the shore than in an inland community. Sewer lines on barrier islands are going to rupture in hurricanes, putting both humans and the environment in jeopardy. Utility poles will come down and bridges wash out, blocking our escape routes. The debris from steps, decks, and failed buildings will become missiles and battering rams that destroy our well-built homes. The infrastructure that supports a population in excess of the natural carrying capacity becomes one of the hazards!

In spite of nature's lessons to the contrary, coastal development continues because some individuals are willing to gamble their lives and fortunes to be near the shore. You can reduce risk by following the principles of site selection, but even low-risk sites are no guarantee against property loss and damage in the coastal zone. Sound, storm-resistant construction is the last line of defense against wind, waves, and flood. Hurricane Andrew (1992) taught a hard lesson in regard to wind-resistant construction, and Hurricane Opal (1995) provided the complementary lesson of buildings' vulnerability to storm surge, waves, overwash, and flooding. When you choose your home, the rule is: Buyer beware.

Can We Learn from Past Experience?

Our memories of hurricanes fade quickly, but coastal property owners in Alabama and Florida would be foolish to ignore the problems that Andrew and Opal brought to light. Similarly, hurricanes in other areas (e.g., Fran, Hugo, Mitch, Gilbert, and Iniki) have taught lessons that must be heeded as well. Posthurricane damage inspections have been very revealing and have led to useful recommendations (see the references in appendix C under *Coastal Construction*).

Coastal Realty versus Coastal Reality

Buyer beware. Coastal property is not the same as inland property. The previous chapters illustrate that the Gulf shores of west Florida and Alabama are composed of variable environments that are subject to nature's most powerful and persistent forces. The reality of the coast is its dynamic character. Property lines are an artificial grid superimposed on this dynamism. If you choose to place yourself or others in this zone, prudence is in order.

A quick glance at the architecture of the structures on our coast provides convincing evidence that the sea view and aesthetics were the primary considerations in their construction, not the reality of coastal processes. Except for meeting minimal building code requirements, no further thought seems to have been given to the safety of many of these buildings. The failure to follow a few basic architectural guidelines may have disastrous results when structures are required to stand up to major storms.

The Structure: Concept of Balanced Risk

A certain chance of failure exists for any structure built within the constraints of economy and environment. The objective of the building design is to create a structure that is economically feasible and functionally reliable with a reasonable life expectancy. To obtain such a house, a balance must be achieved among financial, structural, environmental, and other special conditions. These conditions are intensified on the coast: property values are higher, the environment is more sensitive, the likelihood of storm hazards is increased, and greater pressure to develop exists as more and more people want to move into the coastal zone.

Anyone who builds or buys a house in an exposed coastal area should fully comprehend the risks involved and the chance of harm to home and family. The risks should then be weighed against the benefits. Similarly, the developer who is putting up a motel or apartment building should weigh the possibility of destruction and deaths during a hurricane against the advantages to be gained from such a building. Only with an understanding of the risks should construction proceed. For both the homeowner and the developer, proper construction and location reduce the risks.

The concept of balanced risk should take into account six fundamental considerations:

1. A coastal structure exposed to high winds, waves, or flooding should be stronger than a structure built inland.
2. A building with a planned long life, such as a year-round residence, should be stronger than a building with a planned short life, such as a mobile home.
3. A building with high occupancy, such as an apartment building, should be stronger than a building with a low occupancy, such as a single-family dwelling.

4. A building that houses elderly or sick people should be safer than a building housing able-bodied people.
5. Construction that incorporates a higher-than-usual margin of safety will be more expensive than an average home.
6. The risk of loss may make the project unfeasible.

If the principles of structural engineering are used, economical structures can be designed and built to resist all but the largest storms. These principles utilize an estimate of the forces to which the structure will be subjected and an understanding of the strength of building materials. The effectiveness of structural engineering design has been known for a long time and is reflected in the aftermath of each new hurricane: buildings not based on structural engineering principles suffer a much greater percentage of destruction and serious damage compared with structurally engineered buildings. The importance of building codes requiring standardized structural engineering for buildings in hurricane-prone areas is apparent.

Can We Rely on Building Codes?

The Florida Building Codes Act requires that each locality adopt one of the State Minimum Building Codes. These include codes such as the Standard Building Code and the South Florida Building Code in addition to the One and Two Family Dwelling Code for residential structures. Alabama also uses the Standard Building Code. Storms, particularly hurricanes, have demonstrated where earlier versions of these codes were inadequate, and changes are regularly introduced. Failures have taught us that pilings must be embedded deeper than called for in earlier codes; and to improve stability against wind, the revised code requires cross-bracing between pilings. In general, the minimum wind velocities for design have been raised. In other words, older structures are probably below present code standards, and the code is always only a minimum.

The Alabama Hazard Mitigation Plan calls for development of a new model building code that takes into account the lessons from damage and destruction of buildings in recent hurricanes.

Coastal Forces: Design Requirements

Hurricane Winds

Hurricane winds can be categorized in terms of the pressure they exert. The pressure varies with the square of the velocity of the wind. That is, doubling the velocity of the wind corresponds to increasing the pressure by a factor of four. A 50 mph (miles per hour) wind exerts a pressure of about 10 psf (pounds per square foot) on a flat surface. A 100 mph wind would exert a pressure of 40 psf, and a 200 mph wind would exert a pressure of 160 psf.

You can estimate the wind force that can be expected against a flat wall of a house by multiplying the expected force times the exposed area of the side of the house receiving that force. If the wall facing the hurricane is 40 feet long and 16 feet high, the area of the wall is 640 square feet. A 100 mph wind exerts a force of about 40 psf. Thus the total force on the wall will be 640 ft^2 × 40 lb/ft^2 = 25,600 lb, or about 13 tons of force. A 200 mph wind would exert a force of more than 50 tons on the wall! The amount of force the wind exerts on a building can be modified by several factors, which must be considered in building design. For instance, the pressure on a curved surface, such as a cylinder, is less than the pressure on a flat surface. Also, wind velocities increase with the height above the ground, so a tall structure is subject to greater pressure than a low structure. The pressures presented above were computed for a structure with a height of 33 feet. The Saffir/Simpson scale (see table 3.4) indicates the damage that can be expected from various wind velocities.

A house or building designed for inland areas is built primarily to resist vertical, and mostly downward, loads. Generally, builders assume that the foundation and framing must support the load of the walls, floor, and roof, and relatively insignificant horizontal wind forces. A well-built house in a hurricane-prone area, however, must be constructed to withstand a variety of strong wind and wave forces that may come from any direction. Although many people think wind damage is caused by uniform horizontal pressure, most of the damage is caused by uplift (vertical), suctional (pressure-differential), and torsional (twisting) forces. High horizontal pressure on the windward side is accompanied by suction on the leeward side. The roof is subject to downward pressure and, more important, to uplift (fig. 8.1). Often, roofs are sucked up by the uplift drag of the wind.

Usually, houses fail because the devices that tie their parts together fail. All structural members (beams, rafters, and columns) should be fastened together on the assumption that about 25 percent of the vertical load on each member may be a force coming from any direction (sideways or upward). Structural integrity is also important if it is likely that the building someday may be moved to avoid destruction by shoreline retreat. In a fanciful way, structural integrity means that you should be able to pick up a house (after removing its furniture, of course), turn it upside down, and shake it without it falling apart.

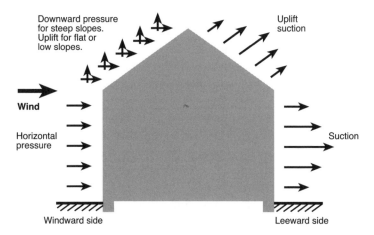

8.1 Wind-exerted pressures on a house.

Storm Surge

Storm surge is an abnormal rise in sea level caused by a storm. During hurricanes, the coastal zone is inundated by storm surge and the accompanying storm waves, and these forces cause much of the property damage and loss of life. Often the pressure of the wind backs water into streams or estuaries already swollen from the exceptional rainfall brought by the hurricane. The offshore storm piles water into the bays between islands and the mainland. In some cases islands are flooded from the bay side. This flooding is particularly dangerous when the wind pressure keeps the tide from running out of inlets, so that the next normal high tide pushes the accumulated waters back, and higher still.

Proper coastal development takes into account the expected level and frequency of storm surge for the area. In general, building standards require that the first habitable level of a dwelling be above the 100-year flood level, the level at which a building has a 1 percent probability of being flooded in any given year, plus the added height requirement due to expected waves.

Hurricane Waves

Hurricane waves can cause severe damage not only by forcing floodwaters onshore but also by throwing boats, barges, piers, houses, and other floating debris against standing structures, a process known as *ramrodding*. In addition, waves can cause coastal structures to collapse by scouring away the underlying sand. Buildings can be designed to survive crashing storm surf. Many lighthouses, for example, have survived hurricane waves, but in the balanced risk equation, it usually isn't economically feasible to build ordinary houses to withstand powerful wave forces. On the other hand, houses can be made considerably more stormworthy if the suggestions in this chapter are followed.

The force of a wave may be understood by considering that a cubic yard of water weighs more than three-fourths of a ton. A breaking wave moving shoreward at a speed of 30 or 40 mph can be one of the most destructive elements of a hurricane. A 10-foot wave can exert more than 1,000 pounds of pressure per square foot, and wave pressures higher than 10,000 psf have been recorded. Figure 8.2 illustrates some of the actions a homeowner can take to deal with the forces just described.

Lessons from Previous Storms

According to the South Florida Building Code, a structure should be able to withstand wind speeds of at least 120 mph at a height of 30 feet. During Hurricane Andrew, a peak 2-minute sustained wind speed of 141 mph was reported. The National Hurricane Center experienced peak wind gusts of more than 160 mph at an elevation of 150 feet. So, again, the first lesson is that building codes represent an acceptable minimum standard, not the maximum forces Nature can dish out.

Experience from previous storms indicates that damage to water, sewage, electrical, telephone, and cable TV utilities can often be avoided by proper installation. And recent storms have shown that appendages to houses such as porches or decks, whose support columns tend not to be deeply embedded, are particularly vulnerable to damage or destruction. Problems with breakaway walls (see below) include the following: breakaway wall panels installed seaward of cross-bracing can damage the cross-bracing when they break away; utilities such as air conditioners installed on or next to the breakaway panels can inhibit a clean breakaway, resulting in damage to the utilities; and sheathing installed such that the breakaway panels are connected to the foundation columns can retard a clean breakaway of the panels.

Many houses have a slab-on-grade as a floor for the breakaway area below the elevated structure. Slabs attached to the vertical foundation members can have the undesirable effect of transferring hurricane-related loading to the foundation. Also, a solidly constructed slab (with wire mesh or without sufficient contraction joints) can provide too much resistance to break into fragments small enough to avoid damaging the foundation system when waterborne.

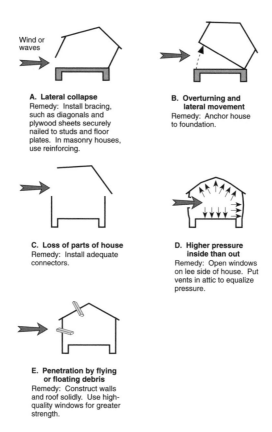

A. Lateral collapse
Remedy: Install bracing, such as diagonals and plywood sheets securely nailed to studs and floor plates. In masonry houses, use reinforcing.

B. Overturning and lateral movement
Remedy: Anchor house to foundation.

C. Loss of parts of house
Remedy: Install adequate connectors.

D. Higher pressure inside than out
Remedy: Open windows on lee side of house. Put vents in attic to equalize pressure.

E. Penetration by flying or floating debris
Remedy: Construct walls and roof solidly. Use high-quality windows for greater strength.

8.2 Modes of failure and how to deal with them.

Particularly vulnerable to storms are mobile homes, manufactured homes, and permanently installed RVs. The usual installation system of concrete-block foundations and metal tie-down straps with anchors to the ground perform poorly. Scour undermines the blocks, while the corrosion-weakened straps often fail. Also, the anchors are frequently pulled out.

The National Flood Insurance Program

The National Flood Insurance Program's (NFIP) Flood Insurance Rate Maps (FIRMS) for Florida communities led to a false sense of security prior to recent hurricanes. The buildings that suffered the greatest loss in Andrew, according to FEMA, conformed to the FIRM specifications, but the storm surge was a full 50 percent higher than the Base Flood Elevation (BFE) specified on the FIRM. Many buildings suffered significant damage to their first floor. In general, it is a good idea to investigate the FIRM to determine the vulnerability of your locality.

Construction Type

Building materials and construction methods have a profound effect on storm damage. Construction on the Gulf coast uses a number of building materials. Single-family homes are typically built of light wood, masonry, or a combination of wood and masonry. Newer structures are elevated on wooden pilings or cinder-block footings. Generally speaking, the older the structure, the less elevated it is likely to be.

When cinder-block houses failed during Opal, they broke into small pieces that were tossed about and caused damage to other structures through missiling and ramrodding. In addition, inadequately elevated wooden houses were knocked off their foundations and carried some distance from their original locations, in the process colliding with other houses, trees, utility poles, and automobiles.

House Selection

Some types of houses are better than others for the shore, and an awareness of the differences will help you make a better selection, whether you are building a new house or buying an existing one.

Worst of all are unreinforced masonry houses, whether they are brick, concrete block, hollow clay-tile, or brick veneer, because they cannot withstand the lateral forces of wind and waves and the settling of a foundation. Extraordinary reinforcing, such as concrete-block stucco reinforced with tie beams and columns, will alleviate some of the inherent weaknesses of unit masonry, if done properly. Reinforced masonry performed well in Hurricane Andrew. Reinforced concrete and steel frames are excellent, but are rarely used in the construction of small residential structures. Reinforced concrete construction typically is not considered aesthetically or economically appealing in the United States, although it is used in Florida, Hawaii, and Puerto Rico.

In Puerto Rico, where hurricanes are a way of life, residences are typically built of cast-in-place concrete or concrete masonry units with reinforced concrete columns and perimeter beams, and roof slabs approximately 4–5 inches thick. The design is governed by seismic codes, and this class of structure performed extremely well in Hurricane Hugo.

It is hard to beat a wood frame or concrete house that is constructed properly, with bracing and connections for the roof, wall, and floor components, as well as anchors for the foundation. A well-built wood house will hold together as a unit even after it is moved off its foundation, when other types of structures disintegrate.

Strengthening the Exterior Envelope

The term *building envelope* refers to the entire system by which the building resists wind penetration. A breach in the envelope occurs when an exterior enclosure fails, as when the garage door or a window is open. When this happens during a strong wind, pressure may build up inside the structure and roof uplift or wall suction may occur, leading to the failure of the entire system (fig. 8.3). The most susceptible parts of the house are the windows, garage doors, and double-wide doors.

Doors

All doors in a home should be certified by the seller as to their strength under a given design wind load, especially garage doors and double-wide doors. The strength must be adequate to prevent damage from projectiles or flying objects such as tree limbs. Existing doors can be upgraded by adding a deadbolt to the locking system for reinforcement. The deadbolt will act as an additional rigid connection to the house frame. If the house has a double entry door, one door should be fixed at the top and bottom with pins or bolts (fig. 8.4). In most cases, the original pins are not strong enough to resist strong wind forces. Homeowners should consider installing heavy-duty bolts (your local hardware store will be able to advise you as to the strength of the bolts or pins).

Garage doors also pose a risk to the building envelope. They often fail because of inadequate thickness, and they tend to bend when subjected to strong winds. Double-wide or two-car garage doors are especially suscep-

8.3 Building envelope breach due to failure of external doors or windows. From *Building Performance: Hurricane Andrew in Florida; Observations, Recommendations, and Technical Guidance,* 1992 (appendix C, ref. 71).

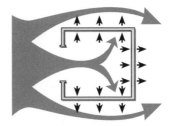

Wind pressure on roof.
Internal pressure adds to roof uplift.

Wind pressure on walls.
Internal pressure adds to wall suction.

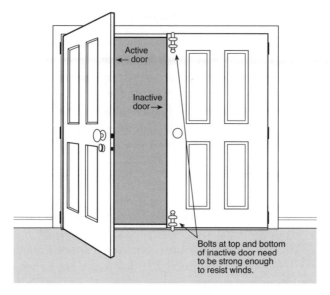

Active
← door

Inactive
door →

Bolts at top and bottom
of inactive door need
to be strong enough
to resist winds.

8.4 Double-wide entry doors. Adapted from *Against the Wind*, a wind-damage-protection brochure published by the American Red Cross (publication ARC-5023).

tible to high winds. When purchasing a new garage door, check the manufacturer's certification of its strength to verify the adequacy of the system. Retrofit existing garage doors by installing horizontal girts on each panel (fig. 8.5). A temporary strategy to reinforce a garage door during a windstorm is to back your car up against the inside of the door, providing extra support against bending. To prevent the garage door from falling off its tracks during high winds, strengthen the track supports and glider tracks. The rotation of the door along its edges can be reduced by chaining the door pin to the glider track connections.

Windows

All windows, including skylights, sliding glass doors, and French doors, must be protected from projectiles that could penetrate the building envelope. During a storm, missiles may be branches, roof pieces, lawn furniture, or anything else the wind can pick up. Protect windows by using storm shutters or precut plywood that is screwed to the outside of the windows (fig. 8.6). Strong windows are important in protecting the structure against high winds. Pay close attention to manufacturers' specifications of wind resistance for shutters and windows. On commercial or office buildings

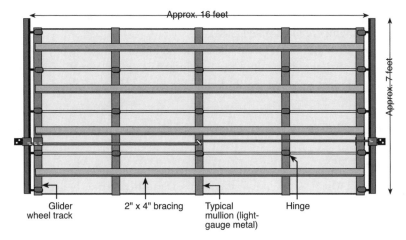

Approx. 16 feet

Approx. 7 feet

Glider wheel track 2" x 4" bracing Typical mullion (light-gauge metal) Hinge

8.5 Double-wide garage doors. Adapted from *Against the Wind*, a wind-damage protection brochure published by the American Red Cross (publication ARC-5023).

8.6 Typical installation of plywood over openings of wood-frame building. From *Building Performance: Hurricane Andrew in Florida; Observations, Recommendations, and Technical Guidance*, 1992 (appendix C, ref. 71), which also shows how to install plywood to masonry building).

Light wood-frame wall

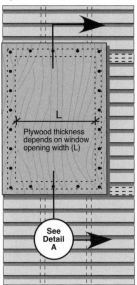

L

Plywood thickness depends on window opening width (L)

See Detail A

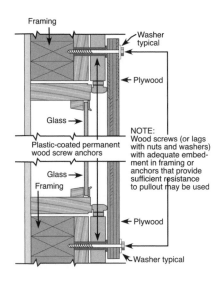

Framing

Washer typical

Plywood

Glass →

Plastic-coated permanent wood screw anchors

NOTE: Wood screws (or lags with nuts and washers) with adequate embedment in framing or anchors that provide sufficient resistance to pullout may be used

Glass →

Framing

Plywood

Washer typical

Detail A : Typical attachment of plywood openings protection to wood-frame building where shutters are impractical, windows can be reglazed (replacing normal glass with tempered laminated glass).

All windows and doors should be anchored to the wall frame to prevent them from being pulled out of the building. After missile impacts, this is the second most common mode of failure of the building envelope.

Structural Integrity

Building Shape

A hip roof, which slopes in four directions, resists high winds better than a gable roof, which slopes in two directions (fig. 8.7). The reason is twofold: the hip roof offers a smaller surface for the wind to blow against, and its structure provides better bracing in all directions.

The horizontal cross section of the house (the shape of the house as viewed from above) can affect the wind force exerted on the structure. The wind pressure exerted on a round or elliptical shape is about 60 percent of that exerted on a square or rectangular shape; the pressure exerted on a hexagonal or octagonal cross section is about 80 percent of that exerted on a square or rectangular cross section (fig. 8.7).

The design of a house or building in a coastal area should minimize structural discontinuities and irregularities. Minimize nooks and crannies and offsets on the exterior, as damage to a structure tends to concentrate at these points. Award-winning architecture will be a storm loser if the design has not incorporated the technology for maximizing structural integrity with respect to storm forces. When irregularities are absent, the house reacts to storm winds as a complete unit (fig. 8.7).

Roofs

When a roof fails, either by losing its shingles or by flying off the house, it spells disaster for the rest of the house and its contents. In high-wind areas, roofs fail for a number of reasons, including inadequate tie-downs of the roof framing and poor connections of the roof to the wall components. Poorly attached roof sheathing or poorly placed asphalt-on-roof shingles also cause roof failure.

To protect the contents of your home, judiciously select and adequately attach its roof covering. Check the manufacturer's rating of shingles and make sure they are recommended as satisfactory for high-wind areas. Asphalt shingles perform poorly because poor fastening techniques are often used. Metal is the least acceptable of all roof coverings. If your roof is cov-

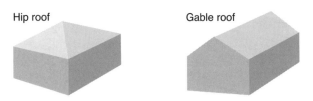

Hip roof is better than gable roof.

Wind has less effect on curved surfaces than on flat surfaces.

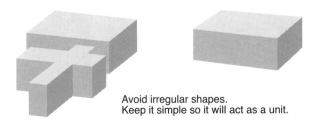

Avoid irregular shapes.
Keep it simple so it will act as a unit.

8.7 The influence of building and roof shape on wind resistance.

ered with metal or asphalt, it might be wise to change to wood shingles, which have a history of performing well in high-wind areas. Look around the neighborhood: what has worked in the past? Consult the building code.

Galvanized nails (two per shingle) should be used to connect wood shingles and shakes to wood sheathing, and they should be long enough to penetrate through the sheathing. Threaded nails should be used for plywood sheathing. For roof slopes that rise 1 foot for every 3 feet or more of horizontal distance, exposure of the shingle should be about one-fourth of its length (4 inches for a 16-inch shingle). If shakes (thicker and longer than shingles) are used, less than one-third of their length should be exposed.

If you choose to use asphalt shingles in hurricane-prone areas, they should be exposed somewhat less than usual. Use a mastic or seal-tab type, or an interlocking heavy-grade shingle, along with a roof underlay of asphalt-saturated felt and galvanized roofing nails or approved staples (six for each three-tab strip).

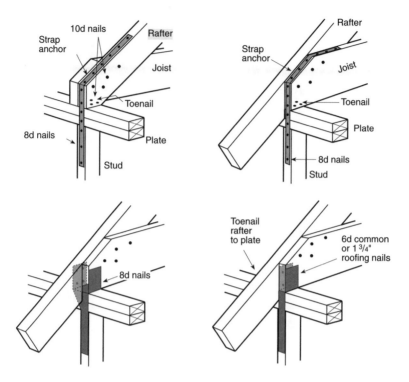

8.8 Roof-to-wall connectors. (Top) Metal strip connectors: (left) rafter to stud; (right) joist to stud. (Bottom left) Double-member metal plate connector, in this case with the joist to the right of the rafter; (bottom right) single-member metal plate connector.

As indicated in figure 8.7, the shape of the roof is an important considera-tion. Aerodynamic building shapes are advantageous. For example, when feasible, use a low-angled hip roof rather than a steep-angled gable-end or clerestory roof.

The roof trusses must be strong enough to withstand design wind loads. Structural rigidity can be obtained by using bracing and connectors (see fig. 8.8 in general and figs. 8.9 and 8.10 for hip roof framing). Secondary bracing within the truss system can help the roof resist lateral wind forces. An inherent method of bracing is accomplished by substituting hip roofs for gable roofs. Retrofitting gable roofs may be necessary to strengthen them. In addition to strengthening the trusses, the overhang must be con-sidered; minimal overhang prevents roof failure. Overhangs should extend only the distance required for proper drainage.

Finally, roof venting is necessary to relieve internal pressures. The venting must exclude the entry of any uncontrolled airflow, which could result in a buildup of internal air pressure.

Connectivity, High-Wind Straps, and Tie-Downs

A continuous load-transfer path is needed if a house is to remain structurally intact under extreme loads (fig. 8.11). Everything must be connected to the foundation. Use fasteners and connectors at all the joints. In high-wind areas, these connectors are commonly called hurricane straps if they hold the roof to the walls (fig. 8.12), and tie-downs or anchor bolts if they hold the house to the foundation (figs. 8.13 and 8.14). High winds cause uplift and lateral forces on the girders, trusses, and beams of the structure. Proper connectors can transfer the load away from these vulnerable areas, reducing the potential for structural damage and perhaps even saving the house. During windstorms, wood structures reinforced with metal connectors perform better than unreinforced structures.

A shear wall is an important addition to help a house resist lateral loads. Plywood is an excellent shear wall when nailed to the building frame accurately and completely. The larger the nails and the closer together they are, the better the plywood will perform as a shear wall. The use of nail guns

8.9 Recommended hip roof framing. From *Building Performance: Hurricane Andrew in Florida; Observations, Recommendations, and Technical Guidance*, 1992 (appendix C, ref. 71).

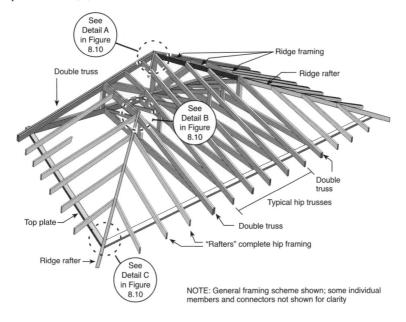

See Detail A in Figure 8.10

Ridge framing

Double truss

Ridge rafter

See Detail B in Figure 8.10

Double truss

Typical hip trusses

Top plate

Double truss

"Rafters" complete hip framing

Ridge rafter

See Detail C in Figure 8.10

NOTE: General framing scheme shown; some individual members and connectors not shown for clarity

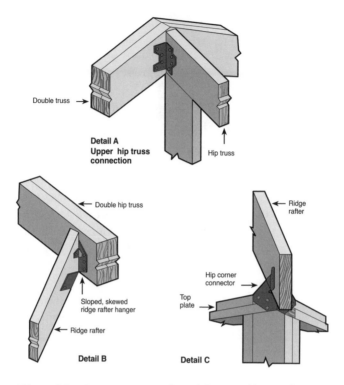

8.10 Hip roof framing connectors. Adapted from *Building Performance: Hurricane Iniki in Hawaii*, FEMA-FIA-23, 1993.

during construction, which do not allow the carpenter to sense whether or not nails are going into the framing, sometimes results in whole rows of nails that miss the framing. When inspecting, make sure the plywood is attached at all levels of the building.

A multistory house must have floor-to-floor connectors to transfer the load path correctly. The first floor should be connected to the second floor with either nailed ties or bolted hold-downs to transfer the uplift forces from the upper stud to the lower stud. In addition, all houses must have connectors in the rafters and trusses.

The load-transfer path must include a tie-down to the foundation of the building; generally this involves attaching a metal rod from the house frame into the concrete foundation. Have a professional check the foundation of an existing house for termite infestation and dry-rot damage and to make sure it is compatible with the planned tie-down system. Remember, if any component of the house is not connected, the whole house could fail.

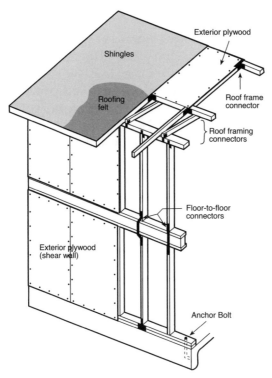

8.11 Recommended wood frame construction. Continuous load path. Adapted from figures in *Building Performance: Hurricane Andrew in Florida; Observations, Recommendations, and Technical Guidance*, 1992 (appendix C, ref. 71).

8.12 Typical hurricane strap-to-roof framing detail. Rafter or prefabricated roof truss. From *Building Performance: Hurricane Andrew in Florida; Observations, Recommendations, and Technical Guidance*, 1992 (appendix C, ref. 71).

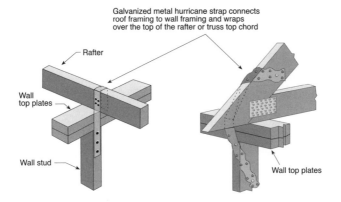

Keeping Dry: Pole or "Stilt" Houses

In coastal regions subject to flooding by waves or storm surge, the best and most common method of minimizing damage to houses is to raise the lowest floor above the expected highest water level. The first habitable floor of a house must be above a prescribed level to comply with regulations. Most modern structures built in flood zones are constructed on pilings that are well anchored in the subsoil. Elevating the structure by placing it on top of a mound is not a suitable strategy in the coastal zone because mounded soil is easily eroded. Construction on piles or columns is a required design criterion for pole-house construction under the National Flood Insurance Program. Pole-type construction with deeply embedded poles is best in areas where waves and storm surge will erode foundation material. The materials used in pole construction include piles, posts, and piers. We will call all three *poles*. Piles and posts are also often referred to as *piling*.

Pole construction can be of two types. First, the poles can be cut off at

8.13 Primary wood framing systems: walls, roof diaphragm, and floor diaphragm. From *Building Performance: Hurricane Andrew in Florida; Observations, Recommendations, and Technical Guidance*, 1992 (appendix C, ref. 71).

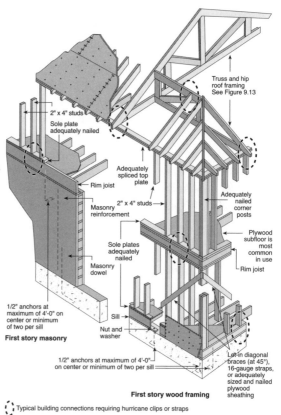

Truss and hip roof framing See Figure 9.13

2" x 4" studs
Sole plate adequately nailed

Adequately spliced top plate

Rim joist

Masonry reinforcement
2" x 4" studs

Adequately nailed corner posts

Plywood subfloor is most common in use

Sole plates adequately nailed

Rim joist

Masonry dowel

1/2" anchors at maximum of 4'-0" on center or minimum of two per sill

First story masonry

Sill

Nut and washer

1/2" anchors at maximum of 4'-0" on center or minimum of two per sill

Let-in diagonal braces (at 45°), 16-gauge straps, or adequately sized and nailed plywood sheathing

First story wood framing

Typical building connections requiring hurricane clips or straps

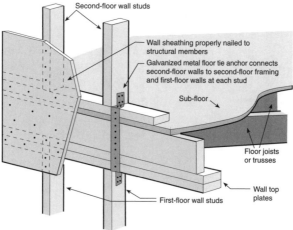

Note:
1. Horizontal sheathing joints should be minimized along second-floor line.
2. Straps should be sized appropriately for each building, i.e., maximum allowable uplift load resistance may
   vary from 300 lbs. to 950 lbs., for 20-gauge to 16-gauge thickness, respectively.

8.14 Upper-floor tie to lower floor for two-story buildings. From *Building Performance: Hurricane Andrew in Florida; Observations, Recommendations, and Technical Guidance,* 1992 (appendix C, ref. 71).

the first floor to support the platform that serves as the dwelling floor. In this case, piles, posts, or piers can be used. Second, the poles can be extended to the roof and rigidly tied into both the floor and the roof, thus becoming major framing members for the structure and providing better anchorage for the house as a whole (fig. 8.15). Sometimes both full-height and floor-height poles are used, with the shorter poles restricted to supporting the floor inside the house (fig. 8.15).

Piling Embedment

Erosion and scour can be devastating to coastal piling foundations. The loss of soil around a slender vertical member can have several deleterious effects. First, it increases the unsupported length of the member, which can result in more deflection or instability of that member. Second, there is less soil to oppose applied lateral piling loads, including the flow of the storm surge, wave forces, debris impact, and even the load of the building itself. Third, there is less friction surface to transfer loads between the piling and the ground, and hence less resistance to uplifting by the wind. The goal in coastal foundation design should be to withstand the 100-year flood and long-term erosion.

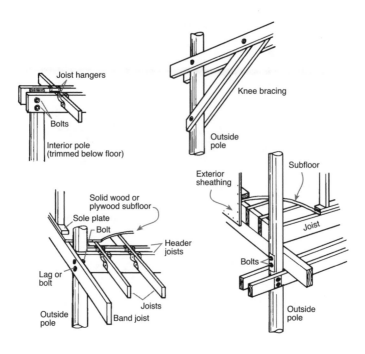

8.15 Tying floors to poles. Supplied by the Southern Pine Association.

Coastal buildings must be elevated so that water can pass underneath them. Buildings placed in coastal high-hazard areas — that is, the V zones on FIRMS — must be constructed so that the lowest floor is at or above the Base Flood Elevation. Also, there can be no obstructions below the buildings. Buildings with the lowest floor elevated above the BFE are eligible for lower flood insurance rates.

Cross-bracing below elevated buildings can be an obstruction that is counterproductive in terms of structural strength. Piling foundations should be designed to avoid cross-bracing by using thicker, longer pilings; placing pilings closer together; or utilizing an unroofed deck that increases the building footprint. If cross-bracing is necessary, design it to be adequate for possible wind and water loads, and use as little of it as possible, especially where it might be perpendicular to wave and debris forces.

Solid perimeter masonry foundation walls, which are supported on a continuous footing, are not acceptable in V zones. Away from the high-hazard areas, such walls should be viewed with caution and, as a minimum, be professionally designed. Walls are susceptible to scour on both seaward and landward faces.

Connection of Pilings to the Floor and Roof

The floor and roof should be securely connected to the poles with bolts or other fasteners. Connections are especially important if the floor rests on poles that do not extend to the roof. Metal straps are commonly used fasteners. Another method is to attach beams to piles with at least two bolts of adequate size. Unfortunately, builders sometimes simply attach the floor beams to a notched pole with one or two bolts. Hurricanes have proven this method to be unacceptable. During the next hurricane on the Florida coast, many houses will be destroyed because of inadequate attachments.

Local building codes may specify the size, quantity, and spacing of the piles, ties, and bracing, as well as the methods of fastening the structure to them. Building codes are often minimal requirements, however, and building inspectors are usually amenable to allowing designs that are equally or more effective.

Breakaway Walls below Elevated Buildings

The space under an elevated house, pole type or otherwise, must be kept free of obstructions in order to minimize the impact of waves and floating debris. If walls are constructed below elevated buildings they should be made of panels that break away when loaded by flood forces. That is, breakaway wall panels should be installed so that they can successfully withstand wind loads but will break away under flood loads. It is important that the exterior wall sheathing not extend over the foundation posts, that it not be placed immediately seaward of cross-bracing, and that it be weakly attached to the permanent structure.

Concrete Slabs below Elevated Buildings

Slabs below elevated buildings should be designed so as not to harm the building foundation when subjected to flood forces. These slabs should not be thicker than 4 inches, should be frangible so that they can break into relatively small pieces, and should not have reinforcing wire mesh extending through the joints so that the slab is permitted to break into pieces. The slab should not be connected to the vertical foundation members, especially if the soil is liable to be affected by erosion and scour.

Utility Systems

On-site utilities, such as air-conditioner/heat-pump compressors, electricity meters, and septic systems, must be installed carefully. The local or state health department will have regulations that control the installation of septic systems. Like the building they serve, compressors must be elevated on a platform that is at or above the level of the BFE. Make sure utilities do not interfere with breakaway panels and are not placed adjacent to vertical foundation members. Service connections, including sewer and water risers, should be located on the landward side of the most landward foundation posts.

Dry Flood-Proofing

NFIP regulations do not permit construction of walls that are impervious to the passage of floodwaters, referred to as "dry flood-proofing," in coastal high-hazard areas (V zones). However, regulations do allow dry flood-proofing of nonresidential buildings in the lower-risk A zones.

An Existing House: What to Look for, Where to Improve

If, instead of building a new house, you plan to select a house already built in an area subject to storm surge, waves, flooding, and high winds, consider the following factors: (1) where the house is located, (2) how well the house is built, and (3) how the house can be improved.

Location

Evaluate the site of an existing house using the same principles you would use to evaluate a building site. The elevation of the house, frequency of high water, escape route, and lot drainage should be emphasized, but you should go through the complete 14-point site-safety checklist given in chapter 5 (also see table 5.2).

You can modify the house after you have purchased it, but you can't prevent hurricanes or southwesters. First, stop and consider: do the pleasures and benefits of this location balance the risks and disadvantages? If not, look elsewhere for a home; if yes, then proceed to evaluate the house itself.

How Well Built Is the House?

In general, the principles used to evaluate an existing house are the same as those used in building a new one. Remember that many houses were built prior to the enactment of improved standards that have increased the hurricane-worthiness of newer buildings. Also, building codes are generally updated after devastating storms. Thus, a house built a couple of years after Opal will meet stricter hurricane standards than one built before. In the case of an older house, it is up to you, the buyer, to have someone check for deficiencies.

Before you thoroughly inspect the house in which you are interested, look closely at the adjacent homes. If poorly built, they may float against your house and damage it in a flood. You may even want to consider the type of people you will have as neighbors: will they "clear the decks" in preparation for a storm, or will they leave items in the yard to become windborne missiles? In Hurricane Andrew, accessory structures such as sheds, carports, porches, and pool enclosures contributed to the windborne debris. The house itself should be inspected for the following features.

The house should be well anchored to the ground, and the wall well anchored to the foundation. If the house is simply resting on blocks, rising water may cause it to float off its foundation and come to rest against a neighbor's house or out in the middle of the street. If the house is well built and well braced internally, it may be possible to move it back to its proper location, but chances are great that the house will be too damaged to be habitable.

If the house is on piles, posts, or poles, check to see if the floor beams are adequately bolted to them. If it rests on piers, crawl under the house (if space permits it) to see if the floor beams are securely connected to the foundation. If the floor system rests unanchored on piers, do not buy the house.

It is difficult to discern whether a house built on a concrete slab is properly bolted to the slab because the inside and outside walls hide the bolts. Try to locate the builder and ask if such bolting was done. Better yet, if you can get assurance that construction of the house complied with the provisions of a building code serving the needs of that particular region, you can be reasonably sure that all parts of the house are well anchored: the foundation to the ground, the floor to the foundation, the walls to the floor, and the roof to the walls.

The roof should be well anchored to the walls to prevent uplifting and separation from the walls. Visit the attic to see if such anchoring exists. Simple toenailing (nailing at an angle) is not adequate; metal fasteners are needed. Depending on the type of construction and the amount of insulation laid on the floor of the attic, these connections may or may not be easy to see. If roof trusses or braced rafters were used, it should be easy to see whether the various members, such as the diagonals, are well fastened together. A collar beam or gusset at the peak of the roof (fig. 8.16) provides some assurance of good construction.

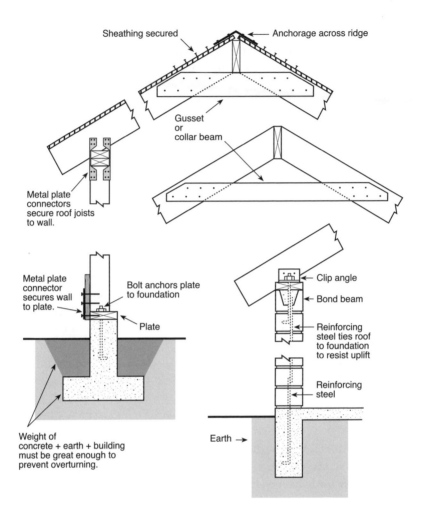

8.16 Where to strengthen a house.

Good-quality roofing material should be well anchored to the sheathing. A poor roof covering will be destroyed by hurricane-force winds, allowing rain to enter the house and damage the ceilings, walls, and contents.

With regard to framing, the fundamental rule to remember is that all the structural elements should be fastened together and anchored to the ground in such a manner as to resist all forces, regardless of the direction from which they come. This prevents overturning, floating off, racking, or disintegration.

Some architects and builders use a stacked bond (one block directly above another) rather than overlapped or staggered blocks because they believe it looks better. The stacked bond is definitely weaker than the overlapped or staggered blocks. Unless you have proof that the walls are adequately reinforced to overcome this lack of strength, you should avoid this type of construction. Some masonry-walled buildings have completely collapsed in hurricanes, resembling the flattened buildings associated with earthquakes.

In past hurricanes, the brick veneer of many houses separated from the wood frame, even when the house remained standing. Gypsum-board cladding (covered with insulation and stucco) has performed very poorly in past hurricanes, typically suffering wind damage and removal. Such cladding should not be used on any building along the coast of Florida that is more than 30 feet tall. Brick veneer and wallboard-cladding types of construction should also be avoided.

Windows and large glass areas should be protected, especially those that face the ocean. Many newer coastal houses have large areas of glazing. Windows and doors can fail when subjected to positive pressures and suction, and often are the weak link in the integrity of a structure. Objects thrown through a window during a storm cause dangerous flying glass as well as weakened structural resistance. Windblown sand can very quickly frost a window and thereby decrease its aesthetic value. Both of these problems can be avoided if the house has storm shutters. Check to see that they are present and functional.

Consult a good architect or structural engineer for advice if you are in doubt about any aspect of the house. A few dollars spent early for wise counsel may save you from later financial grief.

To summarize, a beach house should have the following:

1. Roof tied to wall, walls tied to foundation, and foundation anchored to the earth (the connections are potentially the weakest link in the structural system)
2. A shape that resists storm forces
3. Shutters for all windows, but especially those facing the ocean
4. Floors sufficiently elevated to be above most storm waters (usually the 100-year still-water flood level plus 3–8 feet to account for wave height)
5. Piles that are of sufficient depth or posts embedded in concrete to anchor the structure and withstand erosion
6. Well-braced piling

What Can Be Done to Improve an Existing House?

If you presently own a house or are contemplating buying one in a hurricane-prone area, you will want to improve its structural integrity. Suppose your house is resting on blocks but not fastened to them, and thus is not adequately anchored to the ground. Can anything be done? One solution is to treat the house like a mobile home and screw ground anchors into the ground and then fasten them to the underside of the floor systems. Figures 8.17 and 8.18 illustrate how ground anchors can be used. The number of ground anchors needed will be different for houses and mobile homes, because each is affected differently by the forces of wind and water. Note that recent practice is to put these commercial steel-rod anchors in at an angle in order to align them better with the direction of the pull. If a vertical anchor is used, the top 18 inches or so should be encased in a concrete cylinder about 12 inches in diameter. This prevents the top of the anchor rod from bending or slicing through the wet soil from the horizontal component of the pull.

Diagonal struts, either timber or pipe, may also be used to anchor a house that rests on blocks. The upper ends of the struts are fastened to the floor system, and the lower ends to individual concrete footings substantially below the surface of the ground. These struts must be able to take both tension and compression, and should be tied into the concrete footing with anchoring devices such as straps or spikes.

If the house has a porch with exposed columns or posts, you should be able to install tie-down anchors on their tops and bottoms. Steel straps should suffice in most cases.

When accessible, roof rafters and trusses should be anchored to the wall system. Usually, the roof trusses or braced rafters are sufficiently exposed to make it possible to strengthen joints (where two or more members meet) with collar beams or gussets, particularly at the peak of the roof (fig. 8.16).

A competent carpenter, architect, or structural engineer can review the house with you and help you decide what modifications are most practical and effective. The Standard Building Code (previously known as the Southern Standard Building Code and still frequently referred to by that name, available from the Southern Building Code Congress International, Inc., Birmingham, Alabama) says that "lateral support securely anchored to all walls provides the best and only sound structural stability against horizontal thrusts, such as winds of exceptional velocity." The cost of connecting all elements securely adds very little to the cost of the frame of the dwelling, usually less than 10 percent, and a very much smaller percentage to the total cost of the house.

If the house has an overhanging eave and there are no openings on its underside, it may be feasible to cut openings and screen them. These openings keep the attic cooler (a plus in the summer) and may help to equalize the pressure inside and outside the house during a storm with a low-pressure center.

Another way a house can be improved is to modify one room so that it can be used as an emergency refuge in case you are trapped in a major storm. Please note that this precaution is not an alternative to evacuation before a hurricane! Examine the house and select the best room to occupy during a storm. A small windowless room, such as a bathroom, utility room, den, or storage space is usually stronger than a room with windows. A sturdy inner room with more than one wall between it and the outside is safest. The fewer doors, the better; an adjoining wall or baffle wall shielding the door adds to the protection.

Consider bracing or strengthening the interior walls. This may require removing the surface covering and installing plywood sheathing or strap bracing. Where wall studs are exposed, bracing straps offer a simple way to achieve needed reinforcement against winds. These straps are commercially produced and are made of 16-gauge galvanized metal with prepunched holes for nailing. These should be secured to studs and wall plates as nail holes permit (figs. 8.8 and 8.11). Bear in mind that straps are good only for tension.

If, after reading this, you agree that something should be done to your house, do it now. Do not put off the work until the next hurricane or southwester is about to hit you!

Mobile Homes: Limiting Their Mobility

Because of their light weight and flat sides, mobile homes are exceptionally vulnerable to high winds, which can overturn unanchored mobile homes or smash them into neighboring homes and property. Nearly 5,000 mobile homes are damaged or destroyed by wind annually, and the number will rise unless protective measures are taken. Mobile homes suffered complete destruction during Hugo (1989) in areas where wind gusts exceeded 100 mph. An analysis of mobile homes after Hurricane Andrew (1992) showed that, in general, conventional residences suffered less damage than all types of manufactured homes, including mobile homes. Manufactured homes built using stricter construction standards fared better than those built before the standards were created.

Several lessons can be learned from past storms. First, mobile homes should be properly located. After Hurricane Camille (1969), observers noted that damage was minimized in mobile home parks surrounded by woods and where the units were close together; the damage was caused mainly by falling trees. In unprotected areas, however, many mobile homes were overturned and destroyed by the force of the wind. The protection afforded by trees outweighs the possible damage from falling limbs. Two or more

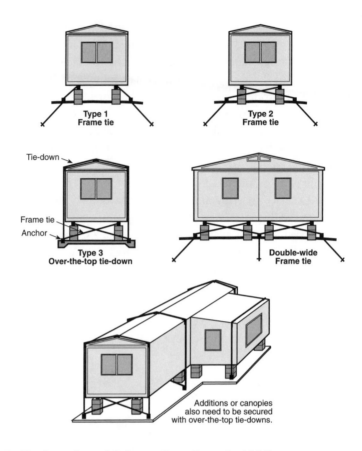

8.17 Tie-downs for mobile homes. From *Protecting Mobile Homes from High Winds*, 1974 (appendix C, ref. 95).

rows of trees are better than a single row, and trees 30 feet tall or taller give better protection than shorter ones. The exception may be Australian pines, which blow down easily and may create obstacles to evacuation and cause structural damage. If possible, position the mobile home so that a narrow side faces the prevailing wind direction.

Locating a mobile home in a hilltop park greatly increases its vulnerability to the wind. A lower site screened by trees is safer from the wind, but the elevation should be above storm-surge flood levels. Fewer low-risk locations exist for mobile homes than for stilt houses. (See *Manufactured Home Installation in Flood Hazard Areas*; appendix C, ref. 88.)

A second lesson taught by past experience is that the mobile home must be tied down or anchored to the ground so that it will not overturn in high winds (figs. 8.17, 8.18). Simple prudence dictates the use of tie-downs, and most community ordinances require it. Many insurance companies, moreover, will not insure mobile homes unless they are adequately anchored with tie-downs. The traditional single-wide mobile homes are now constructed with built-in tie-down straps. Figure 8.19 shows two types of anchoring systems.

A mobile home may be tied down with cable, rope, or built-in straps, or it may be rigidly attached to the ground by connecting it to a simple wood-post foundation system. Some mobile home parks provide permanent concrete anchors or piers to which hold-down ties can be fastened. A mobile home should be properly anchored with both ties to the frame and over-the-top straps; otherwise, it may be damaged by sliding, overturning, or tossing. The most common cause of major damage is the tearing away of most or all of the roof. When this happens, the walls are no longer adequately supported and are likely to collapse. Total destruction is more likely if the roof blows off, especially if the roof blows off first and then the home overturns. The necessity for anchoring cannot be overemphasized: mobile homes need both over-the-top tie-downs to resist overturning and frame ties to resist sliding off the pier foundations. A study of tie-down systems

8.18 Hardware for mobile home tie-downs. Modified from *Protecting Mobile Homes from High Winds*, 1974 (appendix C, ref. 95).

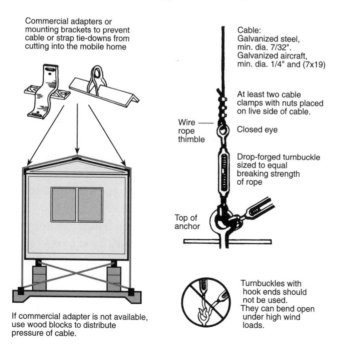

Commercial adapters or mounting brackets to prevent cable or strap tie-downs from cutting into the mobile home

Cable: Galvanized steel, min. dia. 7/32". Galvanized aircraft, min. dia. 1/4" and (7x19)

At least two cable clamps with nuts placed on live side of cable.

Wire rope thimble

Closed eye

Drop-forged turnbuckle sized to equal breaking strength of rope

Top of anchor

Turnbuckles with hook ends should not be used. They can bend open under high wind loads.

If commercial adapter is not available, use wood blocks to distribute pressure of cable.

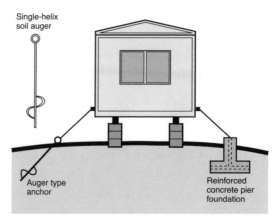

Single-helix
soil auger

Auger type
anchor

Reinforced
concrete pier
foundation

8.19 Possible anchoring systems.

after Hurricane Andrew reached the distressing conclusion that most anchoring systems are inadequate. In particular, anchors tended to pull out at force levels below values recommended by the standards.

A post–Hurricane Fran study conducted in North Carolina showed that most mobile homes, including permanently installed RVs, were tied down to foundations of dry-stacked masonry blocks. The anchoring systems used were metal straps anchored into the sand with embedded helical anchors, usually 2 feet long with 3-inch helical plates. Fran caused significant damage. Many mobile homes were moved laterally and flipped over by Fran's winds or a combination of wind and flood forces, usually from relatively shallow flood depths (less than 3 feet). The homes shifted because their foundation and tie-down systems failed; namely, localized scour undermined the dry-stack masonry-block piers, leading to collapse of the pier, failure of the strap, and anchor pullout. Corrosion-weakened straps were vulnerable to relatively small tensile loads. Straps can be weakened in a few (less than 6) years if they are exposed to salt spray and are not frequently cleansed by rainfall or hosing. Anchor pullout appeared to be related to the saturation of the sand during flooding; the saturated soil could not resist the pullout of the anchors fastened with small-diameter, shallowly embedded helical augers.

As a consequence of such hurricane experience, it is recommended that foundations exceed the anticipated scour depths by at least 1 foot. Also, if significant flow is possible in a region without highly dense sand, anchors should be at least 4 feet long and 0.75 inch in diameter, with helical plates at least 6 inches in diameter.

There remains a question as to the proper angle at which an anchor should be set. If anchors are set vertically or at angles not in the direction of the pull, there can be a tendency for the top of the anchor rod to bend or "slice" through the soil, especially when the soil is saturated with moisture. This kind of movement can have unfavorable consequences. To limit possible horizontal displacement, anchors can be placed at an angle more in line with the direction of pull. Anchors are sometimes set at angles not in the direction of the pull for cosmetic reasons, e.g., where the anchor is tucked behind the skirt that is placed around the base of the mobile home, or because the soil is such that the anchor cannot be properly set.

High-Rise and Medium-Rise Buildings: The Urban Shore

Any multistory building you see on the beach was probably designed by a qualified architect and a structural engineer aware of the requirements for buildings on the shoreline. Nevertheless, tenants should not assume that any building is invulnerable to storms.

Despite the assurances that come with an engineered structure, life in a high-rise has definite drawbacks that prospective tenants should take into consideration. They stem from high winds, high water, and potentially poor foundations. In addition, fire is particularly hazardous in high-rises.

Pressure from the wind is greater near the shore than it is inland, and it increases with height. If you are living inland in a two-story house and plan to move to the eleventh floor of a high-rise on the shore, you should expect five times more wind pressure than you are accustomed to. High wind pressure can actually cause the building to sway back and forth, sometimes enough to generate motion sickness. Before you buy, check with current residents of the high-rise to find out if it has undesirable motion characteristics. A more serious problem is that high winds can break windows and cause other damage that can result in injury. Tenants of severely damaged buildings must relocate until repairs are made; typically, these may take longer than single-family dwelling repairs.

If you own a condominium, you should encourage your homeowners' association to have the building inspected. The inspector should be a qualified engineer with experience in coastal construction codes and knowledge of water and wind loading. The inspector should be able to propose corrective retrofits to improve the safety of the building.

Modular Unit Construction: Prefabricating the Urban Shore

The method of building a house, duplex, or larger condominium structure by fabricating modular units in a shop and assembling them at the building site is common in shoreline developments. The largest prefabricated structures are commonly two to three stories tall and may contain a large number of living units.

If the manufacturer desires it, shop fabrication can permit a higher-quality product than one built on-site. Inspection and control of the whole construction process are much easier in the shop. For instance, there is less hesitation about rejecting a poor piece of lumber when a good supply is nearby than when there is only just the right amount of lumber available on the building site. On the other hand, because so much of the work is done out of the sight of the buyer, the manufacturer has the opportunity to take shortcuts if so inclined. Again, buyer beware, and carry out your own inspection.

Approach the acquisition of a modular unit with the same caution you use for other structures. If you are contemplating purchasing a modular dwelling unit, you would be well advised to take the following steps:

1. Check the reputation and integrity of the developer and manufacturer.
2. Check to see if the developer has a state contractor's license.
3. Check the state law to find out who is required to approve and to certify the building.
4. Check that building codes are enforced.
5. Check to make sure the state fire marshal's office has indicated that the dwelling units comply with all applicable codes. Also check to see if this office makes periodic inspections.
6. Check to see that smoke alarms have been installed, that windows are the type that can be opened, that the bathroom has an exhaust fan, and that the kitchen has a vent through the roof.

As with all other types of structures, also consider site safety and escape route(s) for the location.

What Should Be Done to Protect Property along the Gulf of Mexico Coast?

The public's growing desire for less "big government" and less regulation has left coastal property more and more vulnerable, not just to natural hazards, but also to weak or unenforced building codes; to construction cost reduction through the use of low-quality materials that at best meet minimum code requirements; and to rushed construction and use of un-supervised and inexperienced labor, which leads to poor-quality workmanship or, even worse, to shortcuts that render buildings unsafe. The adage "Buyer beware!" goes double for coastal property. Be ready to take on extra responsibility for your own safety, and expect more regulation even from "little government." As in the aftermath of every recent hurricane, the weeks that followed Hurricane Georges (1998) in Alabama were a time for reflecting on the storm's destruction and how it might have been avoided or reduced. Officials were reminding residents as they engaged in repairs that many simple improvements could reduce reported losses in the next storm. FEMA's suggestions for both coastal and inland houses included the following:

> Relocate or elevate water heaters, heating systems, and washers and dryers to a higher floor or at least 12 inches above the expected high-water level.
> Anchor fuel tanks to walls with noncorrosive metal straps and lag bolts, preferably elevated as above.
> Install septic backflow valves to prevent sewer backup into residences.
> Install a floating floor-drain plug at the lowest point of the lowest finished floor (again to prevent backup of sewage and floodwater).
> Elevate or relocate electric boxes to a higher floor or at least 12 inches above the high-water mark.

Coastal property owners and residents should insist that state and local governments follow the recommendations of postdisaster investigation teams. For example, the post-Andrew recommendations (appendix C, ref. 17) apply to all of Florida, particularly the following:

> The quality of workmanship needs to be improved. Both the construction industry and the building inspection and enforcement people need to be sure their personnel are properly trained.
> Building codes must be improved and better enforced.
> Guidance on correct methods of transferring loads must be provided to building contractors.
> Licensed design professionals should have more participation in the inspection of construction.
> Inspector supervision and accountability should be improved.

These activities should be ongoing and evaluated after each storm. Many of the recommendations made after Hurricane Andrew had been made — and ignored — after earlier hurricanes. When will we learn?

In 1998, FEMA launched Project Impact, a program to encourage community-based damage-reduction initiatives for all hazards. Baldwin County,

Mobile County with Dauphin Island, Alabama, and Deerfield Beach and Pensacola/Escambia County, Florida, were designated Project Impact communities, but the program is intended to set a pattern for all communities to follow. The toll in both lives and dollars lost to natural hazards is rising. To assess risks and vulnerability to hazards, to identify actions to reduce future impact, and to take those necessary actions are the responsibilities of individuals, neighbors, and communities. Given that such responsibilities are not always met and that poor choices continue to be made at the shore, regulations are necessary for our own protection.

The Gulf coast is both a vital natural resource and a recreational resource. Numerous regulatory laws are in place at the federal, state, and local levels so that these two often-opposing interests can coexist. Such laws are designed to protect the natural environment from development, and development from hazards. As noted in previous chapters, the Gulf coast is a dynamic system. Our philosophy on shoreline development is that if development must exist on our coasts, it must be in harmony with the natural processes and environments. This wisdom dictates that development should be prohibited in some areas.

Various segments of society view the coastal zone differently and, as a result, hold different philosophies of land use. The extremes range from untouched preservationism to total unplanned urbanization. Like other decisions affecting the public, decisions on land use are controlled in part by government. Special-interest groups create political pressures that often lead to legislation of compromise. In this manner, regulations have been and will continue to be established with the intention of ensuring reasonable multiple use of the coastal zone, and of protecting inhabitants as well as the natural environment.

Coastal management plans addressing flooding, beach erosion, inlet migration, and wind hazards are an effective way to mitigate these problems over the short to intermediate terms. Unfortunately, no unique solution exists as the best approach for all coastal segments, other than avoidance. Thus, a management program should provide general guidelines to deal with the consequences of natural hazards according to variable conditions, providing local communities with flexibility and latitude to adopt rules suited to their conditions. Important factors to be addressed in coastal management plans include defining setbacks for new development, establishing restrictions on the type of new construction on the shoreline, determining funding sources for coastal protection, establishing a statewide inventory of erosion and other hazard problem areas and setting priorities of protection, plus creating a shortcut through the bureaucratic path to obtain the permits for the implementation of individual projects. Current and prospective owners of coastal property should be aware of their responsibilities under current law with respect to development and land use, and of the likelihood of future regulation.

A partial list of current land-use regulations applicable to the Alabama and Florida coasts follows. Appendix B lists the agencies that will supply more specific information regarding these regulations and permit processes. Always remember to check local county and community codes, regulations, and laws before starting any project, as they may have changed or might be stricter than those of the state.

National Flood Insurance Program (NFIP)

The National Flood Insurance Program (NFIP) is one of the most significant legal pressures applied to encourage land-use planning and management in the coastal zone. Private insurance companies, realizing how hazardous the coastal environment is and the high risk of doing business in flood-prone areas, either do not provide flood insurance at all or charge extremely high premiums. In the past, the federal government had to step in and offer disaster relief after coastal storms and floods. In an effort to reduce the costs of flood disaster relief, Congress passed the National Flood Insurance Act of 1968 (P.L. 90-448), which established the NFIP. Amended by the Flood Disaster Protection Act of 1973 (P.L. 92-234), it requires that a homeowner meet certain conditions to be eligible to purchase flood insurance. Persons living in flood zones who do not purchase such insurance may not receive postflood federal financial assistance. Most banks will not provide a mortgage loan for a structure that does not have flood insurance. To encourage involvement in the program, flood insurance rates are kept at a level that everyone can afford.

Communities must adopt certain land-use and control measures in order to make flood insurance available at reasonable rates. Federal funds for shoreline engineering, waste disposal, or water treatment systems are available only when the individual and community involved comply with the requirements of the law. The Community Rating System was implemented so that communities that exceed the minimum standards set by the NFIP can receive reduced rates. The initiative for qualifying for the program rests

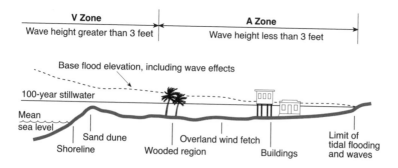

9.1 The V zone and A zone in a coastal flood zone, as defined by the Federal Emergency Management Agency. Modified from *Managing Coastal Erosion* (appendix C, ref. 57).

with the community, which must contact FEMA. Once the community adopts initial land-use measures and applies for eligibility, FEMA designates the community as eligible for subsidized insurance.

Insurance rates are determined by two main factors: the community's insurance rating, and the flood zone within which the building is located. Flood zones are represented on Flood Insurance Rate Maps (FIRMs) and are designated as V, A, or X zones (V, A, B, or C zones on older maps). These zones represent individual sites' susceptibility to floods with different floodwater heights (fig. 9.1). V and A zones are areas inundated by what is commonly referred to as the 100-year flood. As noted in chapter 5, the term *100-year flood* is misleading. A 100-year flood does not occur only once every 100 years; rather, it means that in any given year there is a 1 percent chance that a flood of that magnitude will occur. Thus, residents of the Florida Panhandle or Gulf Shores, Alabama, should not think they are safe for another 100 years after Opal.

The 100-year flood level (how high the floodwater will reach) is a theoretical still-water level. In reality, storm winds cause waves on top of the still-water level, and the true impact of high water plus waves is much greater than just still-water flooding. The areas that may have the highest waves are those most exposed to large, open bodies of water, either the Gulf of Mexico itself or large bays such as Mobile Bay or Tampa Bay. In order to designate that part of the A zone (the 100-year flood zone) that is also susceptible to high waves, FEMA also maps the V zone (velocity zone). V zones are areas where the exposure to wind in a 100-year flood event can theoretically cause waves greater than 3 feet on top of the flood level; A zones have waves smaller than 3 feet. X zones on the FIRMs are divided into

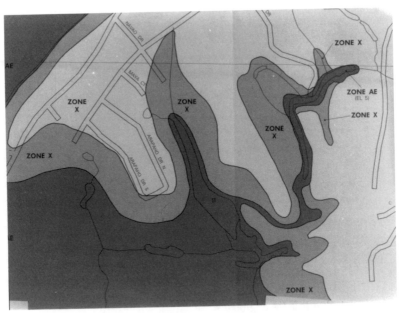

9.2 Portion of a Flood Insurance Rate Map (FIRM) from Dixie County, Florida. The FIRMS show flood zones as illustrated in figure 9.1 and are used in management and zoning decisions. Such maps are available for public examination in all town and city halls.

two categories, gray zones and white zones. Gray X zones are areas with elevations between the 100- and 500-year flood levels (B zones on older maps), and white X zones (C zones on older maps) are above the 500-year flood level. X zones are less hazardous places to build than V or A zones (fig. 9.2).

Most flood zones on FIRMS are divided into different subzones with a number given in parentheses below, such as A7 (EL14). The EL14 in this example refers to the minimum base elevation of the structure that FEMA requires, i.e., 14 feet above sea level. (For more information on how to interpret FIRMS, see appendix C, ref. 63.) Other FEMA building regulations include requirements for ground-floor breakaway walls, which help reduce overall damage by allowing storm surge waters to pass unobstructed under the building. (For further details, see chapter 8 and appendix C, refs. 86 and 91.)

The NFIP program undoubtedly has flaws. Some feel that requirements for insurance eligibility should be more stringent and suggest denying flood insurance and federal disaster assistance to current property owners located in coastal high-hazard areas whose houses and buildings do not meet the standards for new construction. Other problems include establishing actuarial rates, funding the necessary coastal studies to define high-hazard areas, and understanding the effects of long-term federal subsidies. Perhaps the greatest obstacle to the success of the program is the uninformed individual who stands to gain the most from it. One study that examined public response to flood insurance found that many people have little awareness of the threat of floods or the cost of insurance, and view insurance as an investment with the expectation of a return rather than a means of sharing the cost of natural disasters. Perhaps the greatest shortcoming of the NFIP is that the policy of "no federal assistance" to the uninsured is frequently circumvented under political pressure in the poststorm relief/reconstruction period, undercutting the intent of the law and increasing the cost of disaster relief.

Purists may debate the merits of taxpayer-subsidized federal programs, but the National Flood Insurance Program's objectives are worthwhile because pressure is applied to ensure wiser management of hazardous flood zones. Currently the percentage of communities and homeowners that participate in the NFIP is low. The same applies to inland and upstream residents and property owners. As taxpayers, we hope that in the long run this program will cost less than the growing expense of national disaster relief generated by flooding.

Upton-Jones Amendment (1987) and National Flood Insurance Reform Act (1994)

The Upton-Jones Amendment to the National Flood Insurance Program, passed in 1987, allowed homeowners of threatened buildings to use up to 40 percent of the NFIP-insured value of their homes for building relocation. The law recognized relocation as a more economical, more permanent, and more realistic way of dealing with long-term erosion problems. The federal government (i.e., taxpayers at large), that is, would pay a relatively small amount to assist with relocating a threatened house rather than paying a larger amount to help rebuild it, only to see the rebuilt house destroyed in a subsequent storm, and paying to rebuild again . . . and again. By 1995, North Carolina and Michigan (the home states of the law's sponsors) accounted for the majority of the claims under the program.

The National Flood Insurance Reform Act of 1994 terminated the Relocation Assistance Program as of September 23, 1995, and replaced the Upton-Jones program with the National Flood Mitigation Fund. Financed from penalty revenues collected for noncompliance with NFIP requirements, the new program provides state and local governments with grants for planning and mitigation assistance for activities that will reduce the risk of flood damage to structures covered under the NFIP. Demolition and relocation are eligible for grant assistance under the program, but they now compete with other mitigation approaches, including elevation and flood-proofing programs, acquisition of flood-zone properties for public use, beach nourishment activities, and technical assistance. Limits are placed on how much a state or community can receive in a 5-year period under the program (e.g., $10 million, state; $3.3 million, local community; $20 million collectively within any one state).

The Coastal Barrier Resources Act (COBRA)

The Coastal Barrier Resources Act (COBRA) (P.L. 97-348), passed in 1982, is administered by the Department of the Interior. COBRA denies federal subsidies to development-related projects on "undeveloped coastal barriers" on the U.S. Atlantic and Gulf of Mexico coasts. Coastal areas included become part of the Coastal Barrier Resources System (CBRS). The CBRS originally included 666 miles of the Atlantic and Gulf coasts. Its purpose is to minimize loss of life, stop wasteful expenditure of federal funds, and minimize damage to natural resources. COBRA does not prohibit development, but it shifts the financial responsibility from the federal government to the state, local, and private sectors. COBRA represents an effort to stop the federal subsidy of development in erosion and flood-prone areas. No federal funds are available within the CBRS for (including, but not limited to) infrastructure, roads, airports, boat docks/landings, bridges, causeways, shore hardening, or flood insurance.

Under COBRA an undeveloped coastal barrier is defined as a depositional geologic feature that consists of unconsolidated sedimentary materials subject to wave, tide, and wind. The program protects landward aquatic habitats as well as back-barrier environments (adjacent wetlands, estuaries, inlets, and nearshore waters). Undeveloped areas are defined as sites that contain few man-made structures, none of which "significantly impede geomorphic and ecologic processes."

Many COBRA zones in Florida and Alabama, as elsewhere, are undeveloped marshlands, state and federal parks, and military base property. However, future development will almost certainly occur in COBRA zones. Residents should be wary of neighbors who build in COBRA zones. How will those unprotected communities respond to disasters? Will they be able to rebuild? Do you want a poststorm ghost town located a few miles from your vacation home?

Table 9.1. Changes to the Coastal Barrier Resources System along the Alabama and West Florida (Gulf of Mexico) Coasts by the 1990 Coastal Barrier Improvement Act

	Alabama			West Florida		
	1982[a]	Change[b]	Total[c]	1982[a]	Change[b]	Total[c]
Number of Units	3	1	4	21	16	37
Total Acreage	10,678	703	11,381	41,374	124,067	165,441
Fastland[d] Acreage	2,940	105	3,045	14,274	5,601	19,875

[a] As included by the 1982 Coastal Barrier Resources Act.
[b] Net addition made by the 1990 Coastal Barrier Improvement Act.
[c] Total in CBRS after passage of the 1990 Coastal Barrier Improvement Act.
[d] Land above mean high tide.
Source: Barrier Islands Newsletter, December 1990.

The Coastal Barrier Improvement Act (CBIA or COBIA) of 1990 (P.L. 101-591) amended the Coastal Barrier Resources Act by expanding the Coastal Barrier Resources System. The CBIA, passed on November 16, 1990, broadened the definition of *coastal barrier* to include barriers composed of consolidated sediments. Areas in west Florida and Alabama were added to the CBRS by CBIA (table 9.1).

Flood insurance is not available in CBRS units. FEMA and the U.S. Geological Survey published special maps, effective August 3, 1992, to indicate such areas. CBRS units are indicated on the Coastal Risk Maps and are discussed in the coastal risk classification section in chapter 6.

Rivers and Harbors Act of 1889

The U.S. Army Corps of Engineers is the federal agency responsible for regulating dredging and filling, as administered through the Rivers and Harbors Act of 1889 (33 USC 403) and the Federal Water Pollution Control Act of 1972 (P.L. 92-500), as amended. If your project is within the Corps's jurisdiction, you must obtain one of these authorizations: (1) a nationwide permit — a general permit issued by the Chief of Engineers in 1982; (2) a regional permit — a general permit issued by the District Office of the Corps authorizing certain minor activities in specific geographic areas within Alabama (Mobile District jurisdiction) and Florida (Jacksonville District jurisdiction); or (3) an individual permit, which must be applied for if your project exceeds the scope of the nationwide and regional permits.

Before building or buying a home, you should ask six basic questions:

1. Is the community I'm locating in covered by the NFIP program? If not, why?
2. Is my building site above the 100-year flood level plus added wave height?
3. Is my building or community in a COBRA or CBIA zone?
4. What are the structural requirements for my building?
5. What are the limits of coverage?
6. What is the town's Community Rating? What is the town doing to improve its rating?

Coastal Zone Management Act

The federal Coastal Zone Management Act of 1972 (CZMA) established a national initiative for coastal management and encouraged states to develop coastal management programs. Key requirements of the CZMA are coastal land-use planning and protection of critical environments. Both Alabama and Florida participate in the program, but in contrasting styles.

Alabama Coastal Management Plan

Alabama participates in the federal Coastal Zone Management Program (CZM) via the Alabama Coastal Area Management Plan (ACAMP). ACAMP is administered by the Alabama Department of Economic and Community Affairs and is implemented by the Alabama Department of Environmental Management. ACAMP addresses issues such as erosion, dune protection, urban development, hazard management, and the establishment of the coastal construction control line (CCCL).

Some fundamental tenets of ACAMP are the following:

1. Property owners are *not* required to disclose hazards to potential buyers.
2. Hard stabilization is generally not permitted unless it is constructed landward of the CCCL, is necessary to protect and ensure the structural integrity of an existing or previously permitted structure, and there are no other feasible alternatives.
3. Primary dunes cannot be removed or altered; the only acceptable structures on primary dunes are walkovers, utility pipe lines, sand fencing, and approved conduits.
4. No new structures and no substantial improvements to existing structures lying between the mean high-tide line and the CCCL are allowed.

5. Select areas of unique or important habitat are designated Geographic Areas of Particular Concern (GAPCS).

The Florida Beach and Shore Preservation Act

Regulations applying to the coastal environment of Florida are found in legislation ranging from marine animal protection to the state building code. Perhaps the most important part of the Florida Statutes for coastal residents is chapter 161, "The Beach and Shore Preservation Act and the Coastal Zone Protection Act of 1985." The complete statutes should be available from most city halls and/or libraries. A complete and searchable copy of the Florida Statutes is available on-line at http://www.dep.state.fl.us/water/beaches. The following brief summary of some important aspects of Florida's coastal regulations is not a substitute for a thorough reading of the state and local regulations. Always check with the local building inspector before starting any project, as the statutes may have changed since the time of this writing and local ordinances may be stricter. Remember always to use federal, state, and local standards as minimum requirements, and exceed them whenever possible.

Coastal Construction Control Line (CCCL)

The cornerstone for state coastal regulation in Florida is the establishment of the coastal construction control line. Establishing fixed setback lines involves a minimum specified distance from a reference feature. Usually, the setbacks are based on physical reference features such as the seaward toe of the primary dunes, the vegetation line limit, the edge of an eroding bluff, a mean high-water mark, or a specified elevation contour. Setbacks can also be based on coastal processes rather than physical reference points. For example, Michigan and North Carolina use the average annual erosion rate, while Florida has adopted the inland reach of the 100-year storm to determine the setback line. Because these limits move with erosion, the setback position must be recalculated periodically.

Initiated in 1970 with a construction prohibition line for sandy shorelines only, Florida's CCCL established a setback line 50 feet landward of the mean high-water line. Modified and adopted the following year as the coastal construction setback line (CCSL), this control line was established based on the consideration of a number of factors, including erosion, elevation, and construction type. In 1978, the CCCL was adopted not as a line of prohibition, as was the CCSL, but as a line of jurisdiction. The CCCL is based on a computer model of expected flooding from a 100-year storm, and structures and construction seaward of this line are subject to specific rules and regulations.

The Coastal Zone Protection Act of 1985 (part 3 of the Beach and Shore Preservation Act) created a coastal building zone that expanded the state's construction jurisdiction to a line 1,500 feet landward of the CCCL. On Florida's barrier islands, the coastal building zone extends 5,000 feet landward of the CCCL or the entire width of the island, whichever is less. Structures located within this zone must comply with the specific rules in the state building code and be in compliance with NFIP regulations. In addition, mobile homes in the coastal building zone are required to meet the specifications of either the Federal Mobile Home Construction and Safety Standards or the Uniform Standard Code.

The CCCL is not a true setback because construction is not prohibited seaward of this line. Variances can be obtained through a permit process, and the construction must follow certain standards. Factors considered in permit approval include structure footprints, ability to withstand a 100-year storm, proximity to the shoreline, erosion rate, shoreline-parallel coverage, and vegetation disturbance. State law also requires (with minor exceptions) single-family dwellings to be set back a distance equal to 30 times the annual erosion rate; multifamily dwellings are prohibited seaward of the 60-year erosion line.

The establishment of the coastal building zone created the necessary space for a new setback provision. This setback rule prohibits new construction and regulates rebuilding from the seasonal high-water mark landward to a line equal to 30 times the historic erosion rate. Along vegetated coastlines where a CCCL has not been established, a 50-foot prohibitive setback exists. Although states are effectively using setbacks for new construction, they have not been very specific in determining what to do when buildings within the setback limit are threatened by erosion, or what happens when structures built following current setback guidelines are lost.

Critical Eroding Areas

In 1988, the state mandated that critical eroding areas be designated for the purpose of implementing long-term erosion management plans. These areas are broadly defined as sites where erosion poses a threat to the recreational beach, structures or buildings, wildlife and/or wildlife habitat, or cultural features. Thus, a coastline with a 15-foot-per-year erosion rate on an uninhabited island would not necessarily be considered a critical eroding area. This designation by the state is the trigger needed to initiate erosion mitigation programs such as hard stabilization or renourishment. The presence of development or man-made structures along the coast ought to be used to establish the best management practice to deal with erosion along specific shore segments instead of being the leading factor in the definition of erosion problem areas. The result of this approach is that critically eroding areas are rapidly expanding as uninhabited beaches become developed. For example, about 135 miles of Florida beaches were classified as critical eroding areas in 1985, while 222 miles were critically eroding in 1993 according to the Florida Department of Environmental Protection (FDEP), representing an increase of 64 percent in 8 years!

Determination of critical eroding areas is the responsibility of the Bureau of Beaches and Coastal Systems, which is part of the FDEP. Most of the barrier coastline of Florida has erosion data going back some 20 years, and many reaches have some historical shoreline data for the last 100-plus years. The critical eroding areas are updated periodically.

Florida's coastal laws and regulations are numerous and complex. Again, the short overview presented here is not intended to replace a thorough reading of the statutes. A more extensive examination reveals a system that, although well intended and implemented, can often fall on the side of preserving buildings rather than beaches, through loopholes, variances, and the influence of local developers. Unlike some states where legislative efforts have attempted to preserve beaches despite development, Florida's efforts sometimes have the effect of preserving beaches *for* development.

A comprehensive coastal management plan should include the following:

1. A statewide inventory of erosion problem areas (EPAS)
2. Priorities of protection based on state needs
3. A long-term erosion mitigation plan for erosive areas
4. Funding sources for coastal protection
5. Guidelines for planned occupation along undeveloped shores and measures to be taken when developed areas are in danger
6. A standardized monitoring study to be accomplished for every protection project

Florida's beach erosion program, however, is administered by the FDEP as a grant-in-aid to local governments and has not been able to effectively manage beach erosion despite significant shore protection efforts. At present, the state depends on the initiative of local governments to submit shore protection projects for approval. Thus, erosion control projects are implemented not on the basis of statewide needs, but on coastal communities' perception of beach erosion. Highly developed communities lead the search for shore protection support (i.e., lower Gulf and southeastern coastal segments); meanwhile, other EPAS have not been protected and may expose larger areas to erosion threats with time. Additionally, funding sources to ensure beach protection along Florida's beaches are based on general revenue appropriations on a year-to-year basis and on interest earnings, and have been insufficient to promote a comprehensive coastal management plan.

The current system encourages inefficiency because shore management is segmented in the sense that adjacent coastal communities may respond to beach erosion differently, based solely on their perceived problems, without concern that their activities may cause or accelerate erosion in neighboring communities. As the health of any shoreline is dictated by updrift processes, the coast must be viewed regionally, or over reasonably long reaches that are not restricted by political boundaries. A major legislative change is necessary to improve the state's role in coastal protection if a comprehensive coastal management plan is to be implemented in Florida.

Coastal management in undeveloped areas is not a difficult task, although the best management practice can be established only on the basis of comprehensive knowledge of coastal processes. Natural processes should be allowed to dominate undeveloped or partially developed shores where retreat may be the most feasible response. Such areas should be subject to this type of beach erosion response because any other approach would be too costly to be implemented. However, erosion should be monitored to determine the potential risk it will pose to adjoining areas, and evaluated according to the cost and future need of mitigation.

Legislative measures are very important in regulating land occupation along eroded shorelines to avoid increasing costs due to land and structure loss on a long-term basis. Beachfront acquisition by local or state governments is an effective way to prevent development in erosion problem areas, maintain the beach's public use, and preserve natural habitats. Costs may be high at the beginning, but such areas may become a revenue source based on their recreational use (i.e., entrance and parking fees). Other suggested legislative measures include restrictions on reconstruction of damaged buildings or protective structures within the setback zone (as in Texas and South Carolina), restricting flood insurance availability (Coastal Barrier Resources Act), tax incentives to beachfront owners who develop property for uses compatible with beach preservation (e.g., the Delaware Beaches 2000 plan), and consideration of sea-level rise in engineering projects (e.g., San Francisco Bay Conservation and Development Commission).

Coastal Regulation: Yesterday, Today, and Tomorrow

The recognition of the need for coastal zone management is as old as human occupation and development within the coastal high-hazard zone.

The consequences of unfettered development and overutilization of resources that are of greater value when left undisturbed demonstrate the need for management. Modern management was and is, for better or for worse, influenced by changing styles of government and politics. However, as our knowledge and experience of coastal dynamics and change increase, so do the levels of regulation. Proper management of the coastal zone is vital not just to natural Gulf environments and resources, but also to the Gulf economy, the welfare and safety of its population, and the investment in its coast.

New and existing development in the coastal zone must meet or exceed the minimum requirements of prudent management. Whether you are a developer or an individual planning to build/live in the coastal zone, you must seek the necessary permits. Expect stricter enforcement of existing regulations in the near future, and new, "tighter" regulations in the years to come as more and more people choose to live with the west Florida and Alabama Gulf shore.

Appendix A.   Hazard Safety Checklists

Natural disasters such as those described in this book can strike at any time, often without warning. Even with modern hurricane and flood prediction and warning capabilities, it is impossible to make perfect watch, warning, and evacuation calls every time. For example, Hurricane Opal in 1995 changed strength and forward speed so often that the residents of the Florida Panhandle and Alabama coasts were unsure what to do. A great disaster was narrowly averted when Opal weakened at nearly the last minute. In 1989, Hurricane Hugo's forward speed and absolute strength grew so rapidly during the few short hours before landfall that the coast from Virginia to Florida was still preparing for a category 3 storm when Hugo rammed Charleston, South Carolina, as a category 4 storm.

With respect to the uncertainties involved in preparing for natural disasters, we include in this appendix several safety checklists that give guidelines for preparing for, riding out, and recovering from natural disasters. Some precautions and preparations are the same for all disasters, and these are included as the "General Disaster Preparation Guide." Specifics for hurricanes, floods, and earthquakes follow the general information. Keep these checklists handy for protection of family and property.

Inland dwellers may be at risk, too. There is always a possibility of heavy rains and flooding inland when a hurricane strikes the coast; the widespread inland wind damage associated with Hurricane Opal and the flooding from Tropical Storm Alberto are cases in point. Unfortunately for inland residents whose property was damaged by Opal, many construction people had gone to the coast to repair and rebuild. Power, water, and telephone services were interrupted for a longer time in some inland areas than at the coast. Be prepared.

General Disaster Preparation Guide

Find out which natural hazards are likely to affect your community (or vacation rental site). Check your phonebook for the local evacuation route, or call the nearest town, township, or county office. Learn the evacuation route. Have a plan.

Do hurricanes occur here? Tornadoes? Are earthquakes possible? Are they likely? Are you located on a floodplain, and have heavy rains been predicted or have they recently occurred? Have you moved your family into your dream vacation home right on the oceanfront just as a tropical disturbance is forming or intensifying out to sea? Keep tabs on the weather via television, radio, or NOAA weather radio.

You should have a disaster supply kit already put together that contains the essentials needed for any emergency from power outages to hurricanes.

Stock adequate supplies:

— battery-powered radio
— weather radio with alarm function for direct National Weather Service broadcasts
— cellular telephone
— fresh batteries
— flashlights
— portable halogen lamp (you'll need more light than just the emergency flashlight when the power goes off)
— hammer
— boards (for securing windows and doors against hurricanes)
— pliers
— hunting knife
— tape
— first-aid kit
— prescribed medicines
— candles
— matches
— nails
— ax (to cut an emergency escape opening if you go to the upper floor or attic of your home)
— rope (for escape to the ground when water subsides)
— plastic drop cloths, waterproof bags, and ties
— containers of water
— canned food, juices, and soft drinks
— enough food for at least 3 days and enough water for more than 3 days (select food that does not require cooking or refrigeration)
— water purification tablets
— insect repellent
— chewing gum, candy
— life jackets
— charcoal bucket, charcoal, and charcoal lighter
— buckets of sand
— disinfectant
— hard-top headgear

— fire extinguisher

— can openers and utensils (knives, forks, spoons, cups)

Make sure you know how to shut off electricity, gas, and water at main switches and valves. Know where the gas pilots are and how the heating system works. Be ready and able to secure your property before you leave so your belongings won't cause harm to others and you will be able to reenter your home safely.

Make a record of your personal property. Photograph or videotape your belongings, and store the record in a safe place.

Keep insurance policies, deeds, property records, and other important papers in a safe place away from your home.

Hurricane Safety Checklist

When (or before) a Hurricane Threatens

— Most important, know the *official evacuation route* for your area. You will not be asked to evacuate unless your life is in danger, so *evacuate as directed* by local emergency preparedness officials. Do not react to rumors.

— Many local telephone books contain community information about hurricane preparedness and evacuation. Check to see if the information is there and make sure everyone in the house is familiar with it.

— Read your newspaper and listen to radio and television for official weather reports and announcements.

— Secure reentry permits if necessary. Some communities allow only property owners and residents with proper identification or tags to return in the storm's immediate wake.

— Pregnant women, the ill, and the infirm should call a physician for advice.

— Be prepared to turn off gas, water, and electricity where it enters your home.

— Make sure your car's gas tank is full.

— Secure your boat. Use long lines to allow for rising water.

— Secure movable objects on your property:

— doors and gates

— outdoor furniture

— shutters

— garden tools

— hoses

— garbage cans

— bicycles or large sports equipment

— barbecues or grills

— other

— Board up or tape windows, glassed-in areas, and glazing. Close storm shutters. Draw drapes and window blinds across windows and glass doors, and remove furniture in their vicinity.

— Check mobile home tie-downs.
— Your primary line of defense is *early evacuation*. If you are unable to evacuate, you should also do the following:
  — Know the location of the nearest emergency shelter. Go there if directed by emergency preparedness officials.
  — When a flood or hurricane is imminent, fill tubs and containers with water enough for 1 week (a minimum of 1 quart per person per day).

Special Precautions for Apartments/Condominiums

— Designate one person as the building captain to supervise storm preparations.
— Know your exits.
— Count stairs on exits: you may be evacuating in darkness.
— Locate the safest areas for occupants to congregate.
— Close, lock, and tape windows.
— Remove loose items from your terrace (and from your absent neighbors' terraces).
— Remove (or tie down) loose objects from balconies or porches.
— Assume other trapped people may wish to use the building for shelter.

Special Precautions for Mobile Homes

— Pack breakables in padded cartons and place on floor.
— Remove bulbs, lamps, and mirrors, and put them in the bathtub (you are leaving, so the bathtub will not be a water reservoir).
— Tape windows.
— Turn off water, propane gas, and electricity.
— Disconnect sewer and water lines.
— Remove awnings.
— *Leave.* Don't stay inside for *any* reason unless you can absolutely ascertain that the hazards from rising floodwaters are greater than those from wind.

Special Precautions for Businesses

— Take photographs of your building and merchandise before the storm.
— Assemble insurance policies.
— Move merchandise away from plate glass.
— Move merchandise to the highest location possible.
— Cover merchandise with tarps or plastic.
— Remove outside display racks and loose signs.
— Take out file drawers, wrap them in trash bags, and store them in a high place.
— Sandbag spaces that may leak.
— Take special precautions with reactive or toxic chemicals.

If You Remain at Home

— *Never* remain in a mobile home; go to an official shelter.
— Stay indoors. Remember, the first calm may be the hurricane's eye. Do not attempt to change your location during the eye unless absolutely necessary. Remain indoors until an official all-clear is given.
— Stay on the *downwind* side of the house. Change your position as the wind direction changes.
— If your house has an inside room (away from all outdoor walls), it may be the most secure part of the structure. Stay there.
— Monitor official information on radio and television continuously.
— Keep calm. Your ability to meet emergencies will help others.

If Evacuation Is Advised

— Leave as soon as you can. Follow official instructions only. Ignore rumors.
— Follow predesignated evacuation routes unless those in authority direct you to do otherwise.
— Take these supplies:
    — reentry permit
    — change of warm, protective clothes
    — first-aid kit
    — baby formula
    — identification tags: include name, address, next of kin (wear them!)
    — flashlight
    — food, water, gum, candy
    — rope
    — hunting knife
    — waterproof bags and ties
    — can opener and utensils
    — disposable diapers
    — special medicine
    — blankets and pillows, in waterproof casings
    — battery-powered radio
    — cellular telephone
    — fresh batteries (for radio and flashlight)
    — bottled water
    — purse, wallet, valuables
    — life jackets
    — games and amusements for children
— Disconnect all electric appliances except the refrigerator and freezer; their controls should be turned to the coldest setting and the doors kept closed.
— Leave food and water for pets. Seeing-eye dogs are the only animals allowed in the shelters.

— Shut off water at the main valve (where it enters your home).
— Lock windows and doors.
— Keep important papers with you:
  — driver's license and other identification
  — insurance policies
  — property inventory
  — Medic Alert or other device to convey special medical information

During the Hurricane

— Stay indoors and away from windows and glassed areas.
— If you are advised to evacuate, do so at once.
— Listen for weather bulletins and official reports.
— Use your telephone only in an emergency.
— Follow official instructions only. Ignore rumors.
— Keep a window or door *open* on the side of the house opposite the storm winds.
— Beware the eye of the hurricane. A lull in the winds does not necessarily mean the storm has passed. Remain indoors unless emergency repairs are necessary. Be cautious. Winds may resume suddenly, in the opposite direction and with greater force than before. Remember, if the wind direction does change, the open window or door must be changed accordingly.
— Be alert for rising water. Stand on furniture if necessary.
— If electric service is interrupted, note the time. Take the following steps when the electricity goes out:
  — Turn off major appliances, especially air conditioners.
  — Do not disconnect refrigerators or freezers. Their controls should have been turned to the coldest setting and the doors kept closed to preserve food for as long as possible.
  — Keep away from fallen wires. Report location of such wires to the utility company.

If You Detect Gas

— Do not light matches or cigarette lighters or turn on electrical equipment, not even a flashlight.
— Extinguish all flames.
— Shut off gas supply at the meter. Gas should be turned back on only by a gas service professional or licensed plumber.

Water

— The only *safe* water is the water you stored before it had a chance to come in contact with floodwaters.

— Should you require more water, be sure to boil it for 30 minutes before using it.
— If you are unable to boil water, treat it with water purification tablets. These are available at camping stores.

Note. An official announcement will proclaim tap water safe. Boil or treat all water except stored water until you hear the announcement.

After the Hurricane Has Passed

— Listen for official word that the danger has passed. Don't return to your home until officially directed to do so.
— Watch out for loose or hanging power lines as well as gas leaks. People have survived storms only to be electrocuted and burned. Fire protection may be nonexistent because broken power lines and fallen debris in the streets are blocking access.
— Walk or drive carefully through storm-damaged areas. Streets will be dangerous because of debris, undermining by washout, and weakened bridges. Traffic lights may not work; street signs may have been blown down. Approach every intersection as if it had a stop sign.
— Watch out for animals that may act irrationally after being driven out by floodwaters.
— Looting may be a problem in certain areas. Police protection may be nonexistent. Do not participate in such illegal acts and do not try to stop others. Wait for police, National Guard, or other officials to arrive.
— Eat nothing and drink nothing that has been touched by floodwaters.
— Place spoiled food in plastic bags and tie them securely.
— Dispose of all mattresses, pillows, and cushions that have been in floodwaters.
— Contact relatives as soon as possible.
— If you use an electric generator for home power, make sure your house's main circuit breaker switch is OFF. This will prevent your home-generated electricity from "leaking" out to the main power lines. After Hurricane Hugo in 1989, several power line repairers were electrocuted by electricity from the home generators of thoughtless individuals. Save a life! Make sure your main circuit breaker is off!

Note. If you are stranded, signal for help by waving a flashlight at night or white cloth during the day. If you have no cloth to wave, wave both arms (waving just one arm is an "OK" greeting).

Riverine and Flash Flood Safety Checklist

What to Do before a Flood

— Know the terminology:
  — *Flood watch: flooding is possible.* Stay tuned to NOAA weather radio or commercial radio or television.

- *Flash flood watch: flash flooding, which can result in raging waters in just a few minutes, is possible.* Move to higher ground, a flash flood could occur without any warning. Stay tuned to radio or television.
- *Flood warning: flooding is occurring, or will occur soon.* If evacuation is advised, do so immediately.
- *Flash flood warning: flash flood is occurring.* Seek higher ground on foot immediately.

— Find out from your local emergency management office whether your property is in a flood-prone area. Learn the elevation of your area. Learn about the likely flooding scenario of your lot/neighborhood/community.
— Identify dams in your area and determine if they pose a hazard.
— Purchase flood insurance (flood losses are not covered under your home-owner's insurance policy); it is widely available through the NFIP. Your local private insurance agent can direct you to find proper coverage. Have your agent advise you on complete insurance coverage even if you do not live on a river floodplain.
— Prepare a family plan:
    — Have a portable radio, flashlight, and emergency supplies.
    — Be prepared to evacuate.
    — Learn local evacuation routes.
    — Choose a safe area in advance.
    — Plan a family meeting place in case you are separated and cannot return home.

During a Flood

— Flood watch (2–3 days for flood; 2–12 hours for flash flood)
    — *If you have time,* bring outdoor garden equipment and lawn furniture inside or tie it down.
    — *If you have time,* move furniture and other items to higher levels (for flood).
    — Fill your car's gas tank (for flood).
    — Listen to radio or TV for up-to-the-minute information.

— Flood warning (24–48 hours for flood; 0–1 hour for flash flood)
    — Evacuate, if necessary, when flood warning indicates, and follow instructions.
    — Do not walk or drive through floodwaters.
    — Stay off bridges covered by water.
    — Heed barricades blocking roads.
    — Keep away from waterways during heavy rain; if you are driving in a low area and hear a warning, get out of your car and get to high ground immediately.
    — Keep out of storm drains and irrigation ditches.
    — Listen to radio or TV for up-to-the-minute information.

After a Flood

— Stay away from floodwaters, they could be contaminated.
— Stay away from moving water.

Earthquake Safety Checklist

Before an Earthquake

— Have a plan of action, and know what to do afterward.
— Have a family reunion plan.
— Have an out-of-state family contact.
— Have supplies on hand such as water, a flashlight, a portable radio, food, a fire extinguisher, and tools.
— Bolt down bookshelves and water heaters, secure cabinets.

During an Earthquake

— Get under a heavy table or desk and hold on, or sit or stand against an inside wall.
— Keep away from windows.
— If you are indoors, stay indoors.
— If you are outdoors, stay outdoors, away from falling debris, trees, and power lines.
— If you are in a car, stay in the car.
— Don't use elevators.

After an Earthquake

— Expect aftershocks.
— Check gas, water, and electrical lines and appliances for damage.
— Use a flashlight (not a match!) to inspect for damage. *Do not use even a flashlight if you smell gas!*
— Turn off main gas and electricity valves.
— Don't venture into damaged areas.
— Don't use telephones except in emergencies.
— Don't use vehicles except in emergencies.
— Use a portable radio for information.

Postdisaster Recovery

Both coastal and inland residents should prepare an emergency handbook or plan for postdisaster recovery: what to do and how to do it. Start with a disaster addendum to your phone book. List contact numbers not just of relatives and disaster agencies, but also the names of contractors you will need to do repair work (e.g., utilities, water, house repairs, tree clearance, etc.).

Unfortunately, the postdisaster period is a time of social "hazards." People are dazed, confused, and in need of help that is in short supply. Unscrupulous individuals may appear at your door in the guise of construction or clearance contractors. Numerous people, particularly the elderly, are bilked after each hurricane or other natural disaster. Do not accept bids for work unless the contractor provides evidence that the company is bonded and insured (it's best to have established contact with known contractors in advance).

Your telephone service is likely to be out. Keep your cellular telephone handy. Know in advance where you might go to find a public phone that is in service (e.g., there's usually a public phone at or near fast-food restaurants or quick-marts). Have enough gasoline to get there (gas stations generally do not have mechanical pumps; when the electricity is off, so are the pumps). When communications are out, rumor takes over. Word-of-mouth rumors spread misinformation, and people feel out of touch. Don't listen to or act on rumors. Get the "official" word. A limited number of radio or TV stations may be in service after the disaster. Make sure you have a portable radio or TV with fresh batteries.

Water may be your greatest need. Store water before the storm (see checklists above) and know in advance where emergency supplies are likely to be available. Power outages and flooding may result in contaminated water supplies for days. In the case of flooding, everything that has come in contact with the floodwater is likely to be contaminated (i.e., household furniture and other belongings may not be salvageable).

Debris clearance and disposal is one of the biggest poststorm problems. Victims often expect government help in the cleanup, but the U.S. Army Corps of Engineers and FEMA cannot go on private property to remove debris. Most likely, there will be no place immediately available for private individuals to put debris. Expect the cleanup to take weeks, more likely months, after the storm or flood.

Finally, people are not the only creatures displaced by these events. You may have to deal with some unwanted invaders. Be particularly cautious in regard to poisonous snakes, fire ants, bees, and other venomous, poisonous, or stinging animals. Dogs and cats also are more likely to bite or scratch when displaced, frightened, and disoriented.

Appendix B. A Guide to Local, State, and Federal Agencies Involved in Coastal Development

Numerous agencies at all levels of government are engaged in planning, regulating, permitting, or studying coastal development and resources. These agencies, listed below alphabetically by category, provide information on development to the homeowner, developer, or planner, and issue permits for various phases of construction and information on particular topics.

Aerial Photography, Coastal Construction Control Line Maps, Orthophoto Maps, and Remote Sensing Imagery

Alabama Department of Environmental Management (ADEM)
ADEM Montgomery Office
1400 Coliseum Boulevard
Montgomery, AL 36110-2059
Information: (334) 271-7700
http://www.adem.state.al.us
Mailing address:
P.O. Box 301463
Montgomery, AL 36130-1463

Bureau of Beaches and Coastal Systems
Florida Department of Environmental Protection
Majory Stoneman Douglas Building
3900 Commonwealth Boulevard
Tallahassee, FL 32399-3000
(850) 487-4469 or (850) 487-1262
http://www.dep.state.fl.us/water/beaches
Environmental Permitting
(850) 487-4471
Research Analysis and Policy:
(850) 487-4469
Beach and Coastal Ecosystem Management: (850) 487-1262
Coastal Protection and Engineering:
(850) 487-4475

Earth Science Information Center
U.S. Geological Survey
12201 Sunrise Valley Drive
Reston, VA 22092
Phone: (703) 860-6045; for book and map sales, (703) 648-6892
http://info.er.usgs.gov

Surveying and Mapping Office
Aerial Survey Section
Lafayette Building
605 Suwannee Street, MS 5-L
Tallahassee, FL 32399-0450
(850) 488-2250

U.S. Geological Survey, Florida District
Office
227 North Bronough Street, Suite 3015
Tallahassee, FL 32301
(850) 942-9500

Nautical charts in several scales contain
navigation information on Florida's and
Alabama's coastal waters. A nautical
chart index map is available from:

Coastal Zone Studies
Department of Government
University of West Florida
11000 University Parkway
Pensacola, FL 32514
(904) 474-2337

Distribution Branch N/CG 33
National Ocean Service
National Oceanic and Atmospheric
Administration
Riverdale, MD 20737-1199
(301) 436-6990

Local county or municipal governments also have maps. Address your
correspondence in care of the planning,
zoning, or building department.

Beach Erosion

Information on barrier beach erosion,
inlet migration, and erosion control alternatives is available from the following agencies:

Alabama Department of Environmen-
tal Management
ADEM Montgomery Office
1400 Coliseum Boulevard
Montgomery, AL 36110-2059
Information: (334) 271-7700
http://www.adem.state.al.us
Mailing address:
P.O. Box 301463
Montgomery, AL 36130-1463

Bureau of Beaches and Coastal Systems
Florida Department of Environmental
Protection
Majory Stoneman Douglas Building
3900 Commonwealth Boulevard
Tallahassee, FL 32399-3000
(850) 487-4469 or (850) 487-1262
http://www.dep.state.fl.us/water/
beaches

Coastal Zone Studies
Department of Government
University of West Florida
11000 University Parkway
Pensacola, FL 32514
(904) 474-2337

National Oceanic and Atmospheric
Administration
Office of Ocean and Coastal Resource
Management
1305 East-West Highway
Silver Spring, MD 20910
(301) 713-3115

University of Florida Coastal Engineering Archives
Department of Coastal and Oceanographic Engineering
433 Weil Hall
University of Florida
Gainesville, FL 32611
(352) 392-2710

U.S. Army Corps of Engineers
Jacksonville District Office
400 West Bay Street
Jacksonville, FL 32232
(904) 232-2234 or (800) 291-9405

U.S. Army Corps of Engineers
Mobile District
109 St. Joseph Street
Mobile, AL 36628
(344) 694-4444

Also correspond with local county or
municipal governments care of planning or engineering departments.

Bridges and Causeways

The U.S. Coast Guard has jurisdiction
over issuing permits to build bridges or
causeways that will affect navigable waters. Information for peninsular Florida from Fernandina Beach to St. Marks
River (near Panama City) is available
from:

Commander, 7th Coast Guard District
909 S.E. First Avenue, Room 954
Miami, FL 33130-3050
(305) 536-4108

For areas west of the St. Marks River
(near Panama City), contact:

Commander, 8th Coast Guard District
501 Magazine Street
New Orleans, LA 70130
(504) 589-6298

Building Codes, Planning, and Zoning

Most communities have adopted comprehensive plans and building codes
under the Southern Standard Building

Code, and in some cases under the improved South Florida Building Code.
Check with your county or city building department for permitted uses and
building codes. If you intend to build
on barrier islands, we advise you to obtain and follow all local and state codes.

Alabama Department of Environmen-
	tal Management
ADEM Montgomery Office
1400 Coliseum Boulevard
Montgomery, AL 36110-2059
Information: (334) 271-7700
http://www.adem.state.al.us
Mailing address:
P.O. Box 301463
Montgomery, AL 36130-1463

Coastal Construction Building Code
	Guidelines
Bureau of Beaches and Coastal Systems
Florida Department of Environmental
	Protection
Majory Stoneman Douglas Building
3900 Commonwealth Boulevard
Tallahassee, FL 32399-3000
(850) 487-4469 or (850) 487-1262
http://www.dep.state.fl.us/water/
	beaches

South Alabama Regional Planning
	Commission
651 Church Street
P.O. Box 1665
Mobile, Alabama 36633
Phone: (334) 433-6541
Fax: (334) 433-6009
http://www.sarpc.org

Coastal Regulations

Complete Florida Statutes available
online: http://www.leg.state.fl.us/

Complete Alabama Statutes available online: http://www.adem.state.al.us/

Coastal Zone Planning and Management Program

Florida adopted the Coastal Management Program (CMP) pursuant to the Florida Coastal Zone Management Act of 1978 (Chapter 380, Florida Statutes) and the Federal Coastal Zone Management Act of 1972. Florida's CMP did not create any new agency but provides for coordination and consistency in the implementation of the federal and state programs affecting coastal areas and barrier islands. For information on the CMP and designated barrier islands, contact:

Florida Coastal Management Program
Department of Community Affairs
2555 Shumard Oak Boulevard
Tallahassee, FL 32329-2100
(850) 922-5438

Construction

American Society of Civil Engineers
1801 Alexander Bell Drive
Reston, VA 20191-4400
(800) 548-2723
http://www.pubs.asce.org

Dredging, Filling, and Construction in Coastal Waters

Florida laws require that all those who wish to dredge, fill, or otherwise alter wetlands, marshes, estuarine bottoms, or tidelands apply for a permit from the appropriate state, federal, and local governments. For information, write or call the agencies listed below. For the standard state permit on dredging and filling, contact:

Florida Department of Environmental Protection
Division of Environmental Resource Permitting
Twin Towers Building
2600 Blair Stone Road
Tallahassee, FL 32301
(850) 488-0130
http://www.dep.state.fl.us/

For short-form dredge-and-fill application permits, contact the appropriate district office of the Florida Department of Environmental Protection.

For erosion control structures and coastal construction control line permits, write or call:

Bureau of Beaches and Coastal Systems
Florida Department of Environmental Protection
Majory Stoneman Douglas Building
3900 Commonwealth Boulevard
Tallahassee, FL 32399-3000
(850) 487-4469 or (850) 487-1262
http://www.dep.state.fl.us/water/beaches

Easements and submerged land leases for docks, piers, etc., must be obtained from:

Alabama Department of Environmental Management
ADEM Montgomery Office
1400 Coliseum Boulevard
Montgomery, AL 36110-2059
Information: (334) 271-7700
http://www.adem.state.al.us
Mailing address:

P.O. Box 301463
Montgomery, AL 36130-1463

or

Division of State Lands
Florida Department of Environmental
  Protection
Majory Stoneman Douglas Building
3900 Commonwealth Boulevard
Tallahassee, FL 32399-3000
(850) 487-4469 or (850) 487-1262
http://www.dep.state.fl.us/water/
  beaches

Federal law requires any person who
wishes to dredge, fill, or place any
structure in navigable water (almost
any body of water) to apply for a permit from the U.S. Army Corps of
Engineers — Permit Branch.

U.S. Army Corps of Engineers
Jacksonville District Office
400 West Bay Street
Jacksonville, FL 32232
(904) 232-2234 or (800) 291-9405

The Army Corps of Engineers has 10
additional field offices in Florida; 3 of
these field offices are located on the Gulf
coast. Consult your area telephone di-
rectory for the U.S. government listing
in the white pages.

The American Shore and Beach Preservation Association publishes a quar-
terly journal, *Shore and Beach,* that features articles concerned with dredging
and construction along the U.S. coasts.
For more information, write:

American Shore and Beach Preservation Association
1724 Indian Way
Oakland, CA 94611
http://www2.ncsu.edu/ncsu/cil/
  ncsu_kenan/shore_beach

Dune Alteration and Vegetation Removal

Florida laws prohibit the destruction,
damaging, or removal of sea grasses,
sea oats, or sand dunes and berms. Individual counties or cities may also
have ordinances pertaining to dune
alteration and vegetation removal. Permits for certain work and alteration
may be obtained from local county or
city planning and building departments. For permits to clear or alter
dunes or beaches seaward of the coastal
construction control line, write or call:

Alabama Department of Environmen-
  tal Management
ADEM Montgomery Office
1400 Coliseum Boulevard
Montgomery, AL 36110-2059
Information: (334) 271-7700
http://www.adem.state.al.us
Mailing address:
P.O. Box 301463
Montgomery, AL 36130-1463

Bureau of Beaches and Coastal Systems
Florida Department of Environmental
  Protection
Majory Stoneman Douglas Building
3900 Commonwealth Boulevard
Tallahassee, FL 32399-3000
(850) 487-4469 or (850) 487-1262
http://www.dep.state.fl.us/water/
  beaches

Geologic Information

Coastal Education and Research Foundation
P.O. Box 21087
Royal Palm Beach, FL 33421
(561) 753-7557

Earth Science Information Center
U.S. Geological Survey
12201 Sunrise Valley Drive
Reston, VA 22092
(703) 860-6045

Health, Sanitation, and Water Quality

All concerns about septic systems should be directed to:

Division of Water Facilities
Florida Department of Environmental
    Protection
2600 Blairstone Road
Tallahassee, FL 32399-2400
(850) 488-4524

Water Management Division
U.S. Environmental Protection Agency
345 Courtland Street, N.E.
Atlanta, GA 30365
(404) 347-4450

A permit for any discharge into navigable waters must be obtained from the U.S. Environmental Protection Agency. Recent judicial interpretations of the Federal Water Pollution Control Amendments of 1972 extend federal jurisdiction above the high-water mark for protection of wetlands. Federal permits may now be required to develop land that is occasionally flooded by water draining indirectly into a navigable waterway. Information may be obtained from:

Water Management Division
U.S. Environmental Protection Agency
Region IV
345 Courtland Street, N.E.
Atlanta, GA 30365
(404) 347-4450

History and Archaeology

If you suspect that your property may have an archaeological or historical site, write or call:

Bureau of Archaeological Research
Division of Historical Resources
500 South Bronough Street
Tallahassee, FL 32399-0250

Hurricane Information and Planning

The National Oceanic and Atmospheric Administration is the best agency to contact for information on hurricanes. NOAA storm-flood evacuation maps are prepared for vulnerable coastal areas. For details, call or write:

National Hurricane Center
1320 South Dixie Highway, Room 631
Coral Gables, FL 33146
(305) 536-5547
http://www.nhc.noaa.gov/aboutnhc.
    html

National Oceanic and Atmospheric
    Administration
Office of Ocean and Coastal Resource
    Management
1305 East-West Highway
Silver Spring, MD 20910
(301) 713-3115

Hurricane Evacuation and Disaster Assistance

Contact your local county or city civil defense or Disaster Preparedness office for hurricane evacuation and hurricane shelter information. Local radio and television stations provide hurricane warnings and evacuation bulletins when storms threaten an area. For information on hurricane disaster response, recovery, and assistance, contact:

American National Red Cross
Washington, DC 20006
(202) 728-6400

Federal Emergency Management
  Agency
Region IV
3003 Chamblee Tucker Road
Atlanta, GA 30341
(770) 220-5200
http://www.fema.gov/Reg-IV/

FEMA Disaster Services
(800) 262-9029

FEMA Main Office
(202) 646-2500 or (800) 427-4661

Florida Department of Community
  Affairs
Division of Emergency Management
Bureau of Preparedness and Response
2225 Shumard Oak Boulevard
Tallahassee, FL 32399-9900
(850) 413-9900
http://www.state.fl.us/comaff/DEM

The Bureau of Recovery and Mitigation and the Office of Policy and Planning are also in the Florida Department of Community Affairs, Division of Emergency Management.

U.S. Department of Housing and Urban Development Services
Washington, DC
(202) 708-1422

Insurance

In coastal areas, special building requirements must often be met to obtain flood or windstorm insurance. To find out the requirements in your area, check with your local building department and insurance agent. Further information is available from:

Federal Emergency Management
  Agency
National Flood Insurance Program
(800) 427-4661
http://www.fema.gov/nfip/index.htm

Federal Insurance Administration
National Flood Insurance Program
Department of Housing and Urban
  Development
500 C Street S.W.
Washington, DC 20472
(202) 646-2500

Florida Department of Insurance
The Capitol
Tallahassee, FL 32399-0301
(850) 922-3100
http://www.doi.state.fl.us/index.htm

For V-zone coverage or structure rating, contact:

National Flood Insurance Program
Attn: V-Zone Underwriting Specialist
P.O. Box 6468
Rockville, MD 20849-6468
(800) 638-6620

For flood maps, etc., contact:

Federal Emergency Management
  Agency
Flood Map Distribution Agency
6930 (A-F) San Thomas Road
Baltimore, MD 21227-6627
(800) 358-9616

Other agencies:

FEMA Disaster Services
(800) 262-9029

FEMA Main Office
(202) 646-2500 or (800) 427-4661

U.S. Department of Housing and Urban Development Services
(202) 708-1422

Property loss information is available
from:

Institute for Business and Home Safety
  (IBHS) (formerly the Insurance Institute for Property Loss
  Reduction)
73 Tremont Street, Suite 510
Boston, MA 02108-3910
(617) 722-0200

Land Planning and Land Use

Local county and municipal governments have adopted comprehensive
land-use plans and zoning and building codes under state law. It is advisable
to contact these agencies, preferably
before you buy land on a barrier island
or coastal area. For additional information, contact:

Division of Community Planning
Florida Department of Community
  Affairs
2555 Shumard Oak Boulevard
Tallahassee, FL 32399-2100
(850) 487-4545
http://www.state.fl.us/comaff/RPM/
  index.htm

Land Preservation

Several barrier beaches are being
considered by the state of Florida for
public acquisition under three state
programs: the Environmentally Endan-
gered Lands Program, the Save Our
Coast Program, and the Conservation
and Recreational Lands Program. If
you own large parcels of environmentally sensitive land on barrier islands
or coastal areas and want to preserve
it for future generations to enjoy, contact one of these agencies. On the other
hand, if you plan to buy barrier island
property, it would be advisable to contact the local government agency as
well as the following state agencies to
determine if there could be development and permitting problems.

Land Purchase and Sales

When acquiring a property or condominium — whether in a subdivision or
not — consider the following: (1) Owners of property next to dredged canals
should make sure that the canals are
designed for adequate flushing to keep
waters from becoming stagnant. Requests for federal permits to connect
extensive canal systems to navigable
waters are frequently denied. (2) Descriptions and surveys of land in
coastal areas are very complicated.
Old titles granting fee-simple rights

to property below the high-tide line may not be upheld in court; titles should be reviewed by a competent attorney before they are transferred. A boundary described as the high-water mark may be impossible to determine. (3) Ask about the provision of sewage disposal and utilities including water, electricity, gas, and telephone. (4) Be sure any promises of future improvements, access, utilities, additions, common property rights, etc., are in writing. (5) Be sure to visit the property and inspect it carefully before buying it.

Land Sales — Subdivisions

Subdivisions containing more than 50 lots and offered in interstate commerce must be registered with the Office of Interstate Land Sales Registration (as specified by the Interstate Land Sales Full Disclosure Act). Prospective buyers must be provided with a property report. This office also produces a booklet entitled *Get the Facts . . . before Buying Land* for people who wish to invest in property. Information on subdivision property and land investment is available from:

Office of Interstate Land Sales Registration
U.S. Department of Housing and Urban Development
451 7th Street S.W., Room 9146
Washington, DC 20410
(202) 708-0502
http://www.hud.gov

Florida office:
U.S. Department of Housing and Urban Development
1320 South Dixie Highway, 5th Floor
Coral Gables, FL 33146

Marine and Coastal Zone Information

National Sea Grant Depository
Pell Library Building
University of Rhode Island
Narragansett Bay Campus
Narragansett, RI 02882-1197
(401) 792-6114

Coast Alliance
210 D Street, S.E.
Washington, DC 20003
(202) 546-9554

Water Supply and Pollution Control

If your plan involves draining of land or a large water supply system, contact the appropriate area water management district for rules and permit process. Construction of any sewage or solid waste disposal facilities requires permits from the Florida Department of Environmental Protection. Contact appropriate district office of the FDEP. (See *Dredging, Filling, and Construction in Coastal Waters* for addresses.)

Wildlife and Habitat Protection

For the conservation and protection of fish and wildlife species and their habitat, contact the office of the Game and Fresh Water Fish Commission in your area. Also contact:

U.S. Fish and Wildlife Service
Department of the Interior
1360 U.S. Highway 1, Suite 5
Vero Beach, FL 32960
(561) 562-3909

Appendix C. 101 Useful References and Other Resources

The following publications are listed by subject and arranged in the approximate order in which they appear in the text. Sources are included for those readers who would like more information on a particular subject. Many of the references listed are either inexpensive or free. For scientific literature (books and journal articles), university libraries are the best source. Popular books should be available at general bookstores, or your local bookstore should be able to locate them for you. Government publications are available from the agency or from the U.S. Government Printing Office (Superintendent of Documents, P.O. Box 371954, Pittsburgh, PA 15250; phone: (202) 512-1800; www.access.gpo.gov/su_docs). See appendix B for other addresses. Another source of information is the "information superhighway." More and more agencies and organizations are creating their own home pages on the World Wide Web.

The original west Florida (*Living with the West Florida Shore*, by Larry Doyle and others, 1984) and Alabama (*Living with the Alabama-Mississippi Shore*, by Wayne Canis and others, 1985) books were published by the Duke University Press, Durham, N.C. Each contained an appendix that listed several classic references concerning pioneering work along the Gulf coast, works about barrier island processes in general, and references of historical interest that are not listed here. Although out of print, the books are available in libraries.

Floridians who wish to delve into the more detailed literature are referred to the outstanding library of the Department of Coastal Engineering at the University of Florida in Gainesville. This may well be one of the world's greatest repositories of coastal literature. Other important sources include the U.S. Army Corps of Engineers' district offices in Jacksonville and Mobile, offices of the Federal Emergency Management Agency, and various state agency offices concerned with marine affairs.

Abbreviations

ACAMP   Alabama Coastal Area Management Plan
ACOE   U.S. Army Corps of Engineers
ADEM   Alabama Department of Environmental Management
ASCE   American Society of Civil Engineers
BFE   Base Flood Elevation
CBRS   Coastal Barrier Resources System
CERC   Coastal Engineering Research Center
CZMP   Coastal Zone Management Program
FDEP   Florida Department of Environmental Protection
FEMA   Federal Emergency Management Agency
FIA   Federal Insurance Administration
FIRM   Flood Insurance Rate Map
HUD   U.S. Department of Housing and Urban Development
NFIP   National Flood Insurance Program
NHRAIC   Natural Hazards Research and Applications Information Center
NIST   National Institute of Standards and Technology
NOAA   National Oceanic and Atmospheric Administration
NRC   National Research Council
NTIS   National Technical Information Service
USGS   U.S. Geological Survey

History and Geology

1. *A History of Florida,* by Charlton W. Tebeau, 1971, discusses natural events such as hurricanes, droughts, and floods and their influence on the state's history. From the earliest Spanish exploration through the twentieth-century land booms and busts, natural hazards have played a significant role in altering the course of the state's history. The 502-page book, published by the University of Miami Press, is available through your library.

2. *Florida's Geological History and Geological Resources,* by the Florida Geological Survey, Special Publication 35, 1994, is a short (64 pp.) introduction to a wide variety of geologic topics. Of particular interest is the section by Ed Lane and K. M. Campbell on geologic hazards, including global warming and the sea level rise. Available from the Florida Geological Survey, Gunter Building, MS 720, 903 W. Tennessee St., Tallahassee, FL 32304.

3. *The Geomorphology of the Florida Peninsula,* by W. A. White, 1970, is a 164-page document published by the Florida Bureau of Geology, Tallahassee, as Geological Bulletin No. 51. White discusses barrier islands, headlands, sand, and Florida geology and geomorphology in general.

4. *Sinkhole Type, Development, and Distribution in Florida,* by W. C. Sinclair and J. W. Stewart, 1985, is a map that shows the distribution of four categories of bedrock type and cover thickness, and the associated sinkhole types for the

state. Although not a risk map, the information conveys a general regional sense of where collapse sinkholes are likely. Map Series 110 is available from the Bureau of Geology, FDEP.

Hurricanes and Storms

5. *Hurricane Frederic Post-Disaster Report,* by the U.S. Army Corps of Engineers, Mobile District, 1981, contains a great deal of information concerning the physical, social, and economic effects of Hurricane Frederic on the Mississippi, Alabama, and Florida coasts. A series of maps shows the areas flooded by storm surge. Anyone contemplating buying property in the coastal zone should review this publication. Copies are available through the U.S. Army Corps of Engineers, Mobile District, P.O. Box 2288, Mobile, AL 36628. Local planning offices also may have copies for inspection.

6. Additional hurricane-related reports produced by the ACOE, Mobile District, and available through that office include *After Action Report on Hurricane Camille,* 1970; *Hurricane Camille,* 1970; *Report on Hurricane Survey of Alabama Coast,* 1972; *Post-Disaster Report: Hurricane Eloise, 16–23 September,* 1975, 1976; and *Feasibility Report for Beach Erosion Control and Hurricane Protection — Mobile County, AL,* 1978 (includes Dauphin Island).

7. *Executive Summary of Draft Report: Coastal Flood Studies of the Florida Panhandle,* 1997, is a 12-page report that summarizes the results of studies of storm surge and wave effects resulting from Hurricane Opal. Data shown on/in FIRMs and FISs were compared with actual data compiled by various agencies during and after Opal to determine, for example, whether Opal's high-water elevations were within the range of the base flood elevations given on the maps. Graphs and tables show flood recurrence curves, hurricane wave heights, and new proposed BFEs for six Panhandle counties, Escambia through Gulf. This report was prepared by Dewberry and Davis, 8401 Arlington Blvd., Fairfax, VA 22031, for the Federal Emergency Management Agency, as publication FEMA-DR-1069-FL. The phone number for Dewberry and Davis is (703) 849-0100.

8. *Florida Hurricanes and Tropical Storms,* revised edition, by John M. Williams and Iver W. Duedall, 1997, presents a summary of the hurricanes and tropical storms that have struck Florida between 1871 and 1996, organized by historical periods. Technical Paper TP-71 of the Division of Marine and Environmental Systems, Florida Institute of Technology, Melbourne, Fla. Available from the Florida Sea Grant College Program.

9. *Hurricane! A Familiarization Booklet,* by NOAA, 1993, is a descriptive and nontechnical overview of U.S. hurricanes. It includes sections on hurricane anatomy, storm surge, forecasting, and lists of the most intense and destructive hurricanes through 1992, plus a hurricane checklist. The 36-page document, NOAA PA 91001, is available through NOAA.

10. *The Weather Book,* by Jack Williams, second edition, 1997, explains weather phenomena in easily understood language with many diagrams and photo-

graphs. Completely revised and updated from the first edition. Published by Vintage Books, Random House, New York.

11. *The Deadliest, Costliest, and Most Intense United States Hurricanes of This Century (and Other Frequently Requested Hurricane Facts)*, by Paul J. Hebert and Glenn Taylor, 1988 (updated in 1997), is NOAA Technical Memorandum NWS-TPC-1. This pamphlet contains a discussion of hurricane facts and several tables summarizing deaths, costs, and hurricane intensities. Available from NOAA, National Weather Service.

12. *Hurricane Opal: Poststorm Beach and Dune Recovery Strategic Management Plan for the Panhandle Coast of Florida*, FDEP, Bureau of Beaches and Coastal Systems, February 1996, revised March 1996. This excellent 27-page report with appendixes A–G was prepared by engineers in the Bureau of Beaches and Coastal Systems: Mark Leadon, Ralph Clark, Emmett Foster, Alfred Devereaux Jr.; Robert Dean of the University of Florida, Coastal and Oceanographic Engineering Department, and others. The plan recommends procedures for repairing beach and shoreline damage caused by Hurricane Opal and gives cost estimates for the work and for long-term management of the areas in a county-by-county format. Topics include beach and dune erosion, structural damage, overwash effects and inlet-related problems, remedies such as debris removal, and dune and beach sand restoration. Detailed descriptions are given for seven Panhandle counties, Escambia through Franklin.

13. *Impact of Hurricanes on Pinellas County, Florida, 1985* is a Florida Sea Grant College Publication, Technical Paper 51, written by R. A. Davis Jr. and M. Andronaco and published in 1987. It discusses growth on the county's barriers and gives details of the major storms of 1985 — Tropical Storm Juan and Hurricane Elena — and the damage resulting from them.

14. "Nor'easters," by Robert E. Davis and Robert Dolan, is one of the best and most thorough treatments of winter storms available. It includes a scale for ranking these storms patterned somewhat after the Saffir/Simpson scale for hurricanes, information on storm formation and tracking, and good historical accounts. Published in *American Scientist*, vol. 81 (1993), pp. 428–439.

15. Ralph Clark, an engineer with the FDEP, Bureau of Beaches and Coastal Systems, has written several documents regarding the effects of Hurricane Opal on the Florida Panhandle and beach conditions in the entire state. His "Post-Opal Beach/Dune Recovery Plan" (FDEP Memorandum with Attachments A–C, January 4, 1996) gives a detailed description of Opal and the damage it left behind along the Panhandle beaches. Several other FDEP memos by Clark provide details on coastal erosion problem areas in the state, particularly "Gulf Coast Critical Erosion Areas," January 15, 1998; "Gulf Coast Erosion Areas," February 11, 1998; "Critical Erosion Areas — Status Update for Gulf Coast," May 7, 1998; and those listed in reference 53 below.

16. "Hurricane Opal: Erosional and Structural Impact to Florida's Gulf Coast," by Mark Leadon, FDEP, Bureau of Beaches and Coastal Systems, Tallahassee, was published in the scientific journal *Shore and Beach*, October 1996. This article

provides an overview of Opal's characteristics and parameters, plus descriptions and summaries of the storm's impact on beaches, dune systems, and structures. Examples of beach and dune erosion are shown in graphic illustrations. Leadon concludes that in terms of erosion and structural damage, Hurricane Opal may have been the most destructive storm ever to strike the coast of Florida.

17. "Property Damage Mitigation Lessons from Hurricane Opal," by Craig A. Webb, David M. Bush, and Robert S. Young, 1997, is a photo essay and short report published in the *Journal of Coastal Research*, vol. 13, no. 1, pp. 246–252.

Barrier Islands and Beaches

18. *Geology of Holocene Barrier Island Systems*, 1994, edited by Richard A. Davis Jr., is a technical reference to barrier systems of the United States. Chapter 1: "Barrier Island Systems — a Geologic Overview" (pp. 1–46), written by Davis, gives a lot of background information on the geology and dynamics of barrier islands. Chapter 5: "Barriers of the Florida Gulf Peninsula" (pp. 167–206), also by Davis, provides an excellent, well-illustrated treatment of Florida's west-central barrier chain. Published by Springer-Verlag, New York, 464 pp.

19. *Quaternary Geology and Sedimentology of the Barrier Island and Marshy Coast, West-Central Florida, U.S.A.*, by Richard A. Davis Jr. and Albert C. Hine, 1989, is a field trip guide from Mullet Key, Pinellas County, to Crystal River, Florida. Field Trip Guidebook T375, American Geophysical Union, 2000 Florida Ave., N.W., Washington, DC 20009.

20. *America's Best Beaches*, 1998, by Stephen P. Leatherman, a.k.a. "Dr. Beach," includes a discussion of the Gulf coast. Several of west Florida's beaches have been listed on Dr. Leatherman's Top 10 Best Beaches list. His best beaches are usually in front of parklands rather than developed shorelines, suggesting that development and beaches do not coexist well. Available through bookstores, or contact www.topbeaches.com.

21. *Florida's Sandy Beaches: An Access Guide*, 1985, is a compilation by the Beach Access Project, Office of Coastal Studies, University of West Florida.

22. *Islands of the South and Southeastern United States*, by Sarah Bird Wright, 1989, is not comprehensive, but it does cover several Florida beaches.

23. *Quaternary Coasts of the United States: Marine and Lacustrine Systems*, 1992, edited by C. H. Fletcher III and J. F. Wehmiller, is a collection of technical papers that includes four pertinent to the Alabama-Florida Gulf coast. Published as Special Publication 48 by the Society for Sedimentary Geology, Tulsa, Okla. Of particular interest is a section entitled "Gulf of Mexico Coastal Systems," which includes six papers, including "Holocene Coastal Development of the Florida Peninsula," by Richard A. Davis Jr., Albert C. Hine, and Eugene A. Shinn, pp. 194–212; and "Quaternary Evolution of the Apalachicola Coast, Northeastern Gulf of Mexico," by Ervin G. Otvos, pp. 221–232.

24. "Sikes Cut," Glossary of Inlets Report No. 7, Florida Sea Grant College Report No. 35, August 1980. This 39-page report by T. A. Zeh tells the story of Sikes Cut on St. George Island, Franklin County, Florida. It discusses the controversy surrounding the digging of the artificial pass: fishermen wanted an outlet to the Gulf, but the oyster fishery feared that the pass would increase the salinity in Apalachicola Bay and damage the fishery.

25. "Historic Shoreline Changes in Southwest Florida," by Emmett R. Foster and Rebecca J. Savage, 1989, presents a brief tour of the barrier islands of Manatee, Sarasota, and Charlotte Counties, describing shoreline changes over the years between the 1850s and 1988. The authors discuss coastal geology, coastal processes involved with changing the shoreline, and characteristic coastal features of the area. One finding is that the nearshore and underlying limestone topography influences the shoreline profile in this region. *Coastal Zone '89*, pp. 4420–4433.

26. "Development and Stratigraphy of Three Rooker Bar, a Recently Emergent Barrier Island, Pinellas County, Florida," by Ann E. Gibbs and Richard A. Davis Jr., of the Department of Geology at the University of South Florida in Tampa, is an interesting account of the emergence over the past 22 years of a brand-new barrier island in the west-central Florida peninsula chain. Three Rooker Bar, which lies north of Honeymoon Island and south of Anclote Key, emerged in 1969 and has been growing ever since. Gibbs and Davis describe the various sediments found in cores taken from the island and propose the manner in which the island came into being. GCSSEPM [Gulf Coast Section of the Society for Sedimentary Geology] *Foundation 12th Annual Research Conference Program and Abstracts*, December 5, 1991, pp. 84–90.

27. "Florida," by William F. Tanner, a professor in the Geology Department at Florida State University, is a chapter (pp. 163–167) in *The World's Coastline*, edited by Eric C. F. Bird of the University of Melbourne, Australia, and Maurice L. Schwartz of Western Washington University, published in 1985 by Van Nostrand Reinhold, New York. The chapter contains a general description of the geology of Florida's shoreline, including the effects of wave energy and littoral drift, formation and location of beach ridges on islands, and descriptions of reef types and mangroves.

28. *The Gulf Coast of Florida: Overview of Physiography, Geology, and Historical Shoreline Change*, by J. H. Balsillie and R. R. Clark, 1992, is a pamphlet published by the Florida Department of Natural Resources, Division of Beaches and Shores, Tallahassee, 19 pp.

29. *Against the Tide: The Battle for America's Beaches*, by Cornelia Dean, science editor for the *New York Times*, 1999, is a "must" read that illustrates how we rescue building at the expense of beaches, and gives the problem a national perspective. Published by Columbia University Press, New York.

30. *Using Common Sense to Protect the Coasts*, by Michael Weber, 1990. This brief document (24 pp.) contains basic information on the geology and ecology of barrier islands, the destructive effects of development on these areas, and leg-

islation passed concerning their protection and management. Produced and distributed by the Coast Alliance.

31. *At the Sea's Edge: An Introduction to Coastal Oceanography for the Amateur Naturalist*, by W. T. Fox, 1983, is an excellent nontechnical, richly illustrated introduction to coastal processes, meteorology, environments, and ecology, published by Prentice-Hall, Englewood Cliffs, NJ, 07632.

32. *Coastal Environments — An Introduction to the Physical, Ecological and Cultural Systems of Coastlines*, by R. W. G. Carter, 1988, is an excellent text for almost all aspects of the coastal zone, although management of coastal environments is its emphasis. Published by Academic Press, New York.

33. *Coasts: An Introduction to Coastal Geomorphology*, by Eric C. F. Bird, third edition, 1984. This introduction to coastal types and their classifications discusses tides, waves, and currents; changing levels of the sea; cliffed coasts; beaches, spits, and barriers; coastal dunes; estuaries and lagoons; deltas; and coral reefs and atolls. Published by Basil Blackwell of London.

34. *Waves and Beaches*, by Willard Bascom, 1964, is a discussion of beaches and coastal processes based on research dating to World War II designed to assist amphibious landings. This classic may be the original coastal text. Updated periodically, it is a "must read" for beginners. Published by Anchor Books/ Doubleday, Garden City, NY 11530.

35. *The Coastal Almanac for 1980 — The Year of the Coast*, by Paul L. Ringold and John Clark, 1980, is a comprehensive tabulation of the state of the U.S. shoreline in total and by state as of 1980. Included is such information as length of the shoreline, water temperatures, environmental and pollution data, energy production, resources, recreation, and hurricanes. This 172-page book was published by W. H. Freeman and Company and is available at university libraries.

36. "Multiple Sediment Sources and a Cellular, Non-integrated, Longshore Drift System: Northwest Florida and Southeast Alabama Coast, USA," by G. W. Stone, F. W. Stapor, J. P. May, and J. P. Morgan, was published in *Marine Geology*, 1992, vol. 105, pp. 141–154.

Recreation and Nature

37. *The Audubon Society Field Guide to North American Seashells*, by Harold A. Rehder, 1995, is published by Alfred A. Knopf of New York. This well-illustrated reference is an excellent handbook for the serious shell collector.

38. *A Field Guide to Southeastern and Caribbean Seashores: Cape Hatteras to the Gulf Coast, Florida, and the Caribbean*, by Eugene H. Kaplan, 1988. One of the Peterson Field Guide Series, sponsored by the National Audubon Society and the National Wildlife Federation, this 425-page guide probably describes most of the wildlife you would encounter in Florida. Published by Houghton Mifflin of Boston.

39. *The Audubon Society Field Guide to North American Fishes, Whales, and Dol-*

phins, by H. Boschung, J. Williams, D. Gotshall, D. Caldwell, and M. Caldwell, 1983, provides detailed species accounts for the fishes and marine mammals of North America. Published by Alfred A. Knopf, New York.

40. *The Audubon Society Field Guide to North American Seashore Creatures*, by N. Meinkoth, 1995, gives detailed species descriptions and an overview of the taxonomy of the major shore animals of North America. Illustrated with color photographs. Published by Alfred A. Knopf, New York.

Shoreline Engineering and Beach Replenishment

41. *The Corps and the Shore*, by Orrin H. Pilkey and Katherine L. Dixon, 1996, delves into the role of the U.S. Army Corps of Engineers in U.S. beach management, including beach nourishment, and points out the need for external checks on Corps activities. Published by Island Press, Washington, D.C., 272 pp.

42. *The Effects of Seawalls on the Beach*, edited by Nicholas C. Kraus and O. H. Pilkey Jr., 1988, appeared as Special Issue 4 of the *Journal of Coastal Research*. This technical volume explores the nature of the impacts on the beach associated with seawalls. See the paper by Pilkey and Wright titled "Seawalls versus Beaches," which discusses the impact that seawalls have on the narrowing of beaches and clearly demonstrates that the problem is not whether or not seawalls destroy beaches, but how it happens.

43. "An Analysis of Replenished Beach Design Parameters on U.S. East Coast Barrier Islands," by Lynn Leonard, Tonya Clayton, and Orrin Pilkey, 1990. This scientific paper published in the *Journal of Coastal Research,* vol. 6, no. 1, p. 15–36, concludes that replenished beaches north of Florida generally have life spans of less than 5 years; storm frequency is a major factor. The authors document overestimates of beach life by the ACOE. See the Duke University Program for the Study of Developed Shorelines web site for updates of this study: http://www.geo.duke.edu/Research/psds/psds_tables.htm.

44. "A 'Thumbnail Method' for Beach Communities: Estimation of Long-Term Beach Replenishment Requirements," by Orrin H. Pilkey, 1988. This short paper demonstrates that current methods of estimating long-term volume requirements for replenished beaches are inadequate. The long-term volume required can be estimated by assuming that the initial restoration volume must be replaced at prescribed intervals depending on location. Published in *Shore and Beach*, vol. 56, no. 3, pp. 23–31.

45. "Redington Shores Breakwater: Beach Response," 1991, by Yen-hai Chu and others, discusses the effects of the detached breakwater constructed at Redington Shores in 1986. A summary of the breakwater parameters and beach nourishment in the area is presented, and the initial, postconstruction, and postnourishment shoreline responses (sand volume changes and contour changes) are described. *Coastal Sediments '91*, pp. 1770–1784.

46. *Citizen's Guide to Geologic Hazards,* by Edward B. Nuhfer and others, 1993, was written for the general public and discusses geologic hazards in understandable terms. Available from the American Institute of Professional Geologists, 7828 Vance Drive, Suite 103, Arvada, CO 80003-2124, (303) 431-0831.

47. *Coastal Hazards: Perception, Susceptibility, and Mitigation,* edited by Charles W. Finkl Jr., 1995, is Special Issue 12 of the *Journal of Coastal Research.* It features coastal hazard issues such as hazard recognition and evaluation, sea-level rise, storms, tsunamis, effects of humans on coastal environments, effects of coastal hazards on natural features, and hazard mitigation. Published by the Coastal Education and Research Foundation.

48. *Living by the Rules of the Sea,* by David M. Bush, Orrin H. Pilkey, and William J. Neal, 1996, is the umbrella volume for the Living with the Shore series. This 179-page book discusses coastal hazards, risk assessment, and property damage mitigation. If you are interested in what your community can do now to reduce the impact of the next storm, we recommend this guide. See other books in the series if you have family or friends in other coastal states or plan vacations or retirement there. Published by Duke University Press, Box 90660, Durham, NC 27708-0660.

49. *Disasters by Design: A Reassessment of Natural Hazards in the United States,* by Dennis S. Mileti, 1999, presents the conclusions of the National Assessment of Research and Applications on Natural Hazards. It discusses building disaster-resistant or sustainable communities as a basis for mitigation. Available from the National Academy Press, 2101 Constitution Avenue, N.W., Washington DC 20418, (800) 624-6242. It can be ordered on-line at a 20 percent discount at http://www.nap.edu.

50. *Coastline at Risk: The Hurricane Threat to the Gulf and Atlantic States, 1992, Excerpts from the 14th Annual National Hurricane Conference,* printed 1992. Published by FEMA, but compiled by and available from Lawrence S. Tait, National Hurricane Conference, 864 East Park Avenue, Tallahassee, FL 32301, (904) 561-1163. This 102-page booklet has five sections, including a report by Bob Sheets, former director of the National Hurricane Center, on the hurricane problem in the United States.

51. FEMA *Flood Insurance Studies* provide historic flood data, flood levels, and general information about the counties and towns involved in each study. Several FIS publications were used as source material in this book: Destin (1988); Escambia County, Florida (1987); Wakulla County (1986); Cinco Bayou (1985); Citrus County (1984); Holmes Beach and Bradenton (1983); Port Richey Supplement (1983); Port St. Joseph (1982); Gulf County (1982); and Port Richey (1981).

General

52. "Hurricane Opal Damages Which Could Have Been Prevented along Bay County, Florida, Shoreline with a Beachfill Project," by Cheryl P. Ulrich, 1997, is a short report on a U.S. Army Corps of Engineers beach-fill project at Panama City. The author maintains that the project would have paid for itself in one storm (had it been in place), by saving an estimated $49 million in damage repair costs. The report also briefly describes simulation methods used by the Corps to formulate beach-fill projects and quantify storm damage from shoreline recession, flooding, and wave damage to structures. *Coastal Zone '97 Conference Proceedings*, vol. 1, pp. 471–473.

53. *Beach Conditions in Florida: A Statewide Inventory and Identification of Beach Erosion Problem Areas in Florida*, December 1993, Beaches and Shores Technical and Design Memorandum 89-1, 5th edition, pp. 1–17, 50–61; and "Beach Conditions in Florida: A Statewide Inventory and Identification of the Beach Erosion Problem Areas in Florida for Beach Management Planning," 1989, in *Proceedings of Beach Preservation Technology '89*, Tampa, Florida, pp. 219–228. These detailed reports and revisions (1990, 1991, 1992) were written by Ralph R. Clark of the FDEP Bureau of Beaches and Coastal Systems. The reports systematically identify the beach erosion areas in all open-water coastal counties along the Atlantic and the Gulf of Mexico. Beach erosion problem areas are classified as either "critical" or "non-critical" according to whether or not substantial development or recreational interests onshore are threatened. Beach lengths affected by erosion are given in miles on a county-by-county and island-by-island basis, and beaches affected by inlets are also noted. These reports are important tools for coastal engineers, public planners and managers, and anyone interested in the state of the coast.

54. *Florida Assessment of Coastal Trends — FACT*, prepared by the Florida Center for Public Management, G. T. Bergquist Jr., project director, 1997, is loaded with summary data on population growth, urban development, infrastructure, disruption of coastal processes, coastal impacts and hazards, changes and trends in ecosystems, water resources, recreational value, and related topics. Data are presented for the entire state without any breakdown by county or by Atlantic or Gulf coast. The general trends, however, are sobering because more people and property are at risk, and at the expense of the natural environments and resources that are the basis of Florida's economy. This document is available on the Internet at http://www.fsu.edu/-cpm/FACT/index.html.

55. *Introduction to Coastal Management*, by Timothy Beatley, David J. Brower, and Anna K. A. Schwab, 1994, is a reference book for anyone working or interested in coastal management. Published by Island Press, Washington, D.C., 210 pp.

56. *Coastal Zone Management Handbook*, by John R. Clark, is a very detailed manual and reference source for coastal resources planners and managers. Published in 1996 by CRC Press, 2000 Corporate Blvd., N.W., Boca Raton, FL

33431, (800) 272-7737. You will find everything you want to know about the coast in this 694-page book, from development impacts to beach management to biotoxins to sewage treatment. Not for the casual reader, but recommended for your local coastal community's reference library.

57. *Managing Coastal Erosion*, by the Committee on Coastal Erosion Zone Management for the NRC, 1990, is a 182-page report on coastal erosion and its management written by a blue-ribbon panel of experts. Chapters include "Coastal Erosion: Its Causes, Effects, and Distribution"; "Management and Approaches"; "The National Flood Insurance Program"; "State Programs and Experiences"; and "Predicting Future Shoreline Changes." Available from the National Academy of Sciences, National Academy Press, in Washington, D.C.

Storm Damage Mitigation

58. "Hurricanes Gilbert and Hugo Send Powerful Messages for Coastal Development," by E. R. Thieler and D. M. Bush, 1991, compares the characteristics and impacts of Hugo and Gilbert and discusses how the types and designs of buildings contributed to the damage. Published in the *Journal of Geological Education*, vol. 39, pp. 291–299.

59. *Catastrophic Coastal Storms: Hazard Mitigation and Development Management*, by D. R. Godschalk, D. J. Brower, and T. Beatley, 1989, contains extensive information on mitigation and development management in at-risk coastal locations. Published by Duke University Press.

60. "Florida's History of Beach and Coast Preservation: The Early Years, 1910–1974," by James H. Balsillie of the Florida Geological Survey, 1996, is an interesting in-depth report of beach and coast preservation activities in Florida that covers much of the twentieth century. Balsillie includes historical accounts of coastal work that was accomplished in other states, such as New Jersey; by various federal, state, and local agencies; and by associations such as the Florida Shore and Beach Preservation Association, which was established in the 1950s. He also describes the steps leading up to the establishment of coastal construction setback lines and lists the dates they were established for each county. Published in *Proceedings of the 9th National Conference on Beach Preservation Technology*, Florida Shore and Beach Preservation Association, pp. 350–368.

Coastal Law and Public Involvement

61. *Florida Coastal Program Guide, and Reference Book, 1997 Revision*, by Florida Coastal Management Program, Department of Community Affairs, Tallahassee, outlines various programs relative to management and pertinent statutes.

62. *Projected Impact of Relative Sea Level Rise on the National Flood Insurance Program*, by FEMA, 1991, concludes that coastal flood hazard areas will require periodic mapping to stay abreast of the impact of the sea-level rise, but that elevation requirements of the present NFIP program provide at least a 10-year cushion (to 2010) for study and adjustment of those construction elevation requirements. The short (72-page) report includes projections of numbers of households in the coastal floodplains through the year 2100. Produced by the Federal Emergency Management Agency, Federal Insurance Administration, Washington, D.C.

63. *How to Use a Flood Map to Protect Your Property: A Guide for Interested Private Citizens, Property Owners, Community Officials, Lending Institutions, and Insurance Agents*, December 1994. This 22-page tabloid-sized publication is designed to help readers understand FIRMS, which establish the extent of flood hazards within a flood-prone community. Available from FEMA as publication FEMA-258.

64. *Questions and Answers on the National Flood Insurance Program*, by FEMA, publication FIA-2, 1983 (updated March 1992), explains the basics of flood insurance and provides addresses of FEMA offices.

Coastal Construction

Design, General

65. *Building Construction on Shoreline Property* (undated) is a checklist by C. A. Collier. Homeowners and prospective buyers of coastal property will find this pamphlet a handy guide for evaluating location, elevation, building design and construction, utilities, and inspection. Available from either the Marine Advisory Program, G022 McCarty Hall, University of Florida, Gainesville, FL 32611; or the Florida Department of Environmental Protection, Beaches and Coastal Systems, 3900 Commonwealth Blvd., Tallahassee, FL 32399.

66. *Free of Obstruction: Requirements for Buildings Located in Coastal High Hazard Areas*, FIA Technical Bulletin No. 5-93, considers the prevention of damage to coastal buildings resulting from obstructions underneath the buildings. Complies with National Insurance Program Requirements. Available from FEMA.

67. *Corrosion Protection for Metal Connections in Coastal Areas*, NFIP Technical Bulletin No. 8, provides guidance on selection, installation, and maintenance of metal connectors. Available from FEMA.

68. *Hurricane-Resistant Construction for Homes*, by Todd L. Walton Jr. and Michael R. Barnett, 1991, gives guidelines for wood frame, masonry, and brick construction; pole houses; and special considerations such as roofs, doors, glass, shutters, and siding. Available as Bulletin 16 (MAP-16) from Florida Sea Grant College Program, University of Florida, Gainesville, FL 32611.

69. *Coastal Construction Manual*, by FEMA, 2000. This revised and expanded

three-volume reference provides construction guidelines for one- to four-family residential buildings. Available from FEMA.

70. *Structural Failures: Modes, Causes, Responsibilities*, 1973. See especially the chapter entitled "Failure of Structures Due to Extreme Winds," pp. 49–77. Available from the Research Council on Performance of Structures, American Society of Civil Engineers, 345 East 47th Street, New York, NY 10017.

71. *Building Performance: Hurricane Andrew in Florida; Observations, Recommendations, and Technical Guidance*, 1992, by FEMA and the Federal Insurance Administration, inludes background information about the storm, on-site observations of the damaged area, and recommendations for reducing future damage. Available from FEMA as publication FIA-22.

72. *Building Performance Assessment: Hurricane Fran in North Carolina; Observations, Recommendations, and Technical Guidance*, 1997, by FEMA, contains an assessment of the problems that occurred during Hurricane Fran in North Carolina. Particularly useful are the recommendations on how to avoid the problems in the future. Available from FEMA as document FEMA 290.

73. *Building Performance Assessment Report: Hurricane Georges in the Gulf Coast; Building on Success — Observations, Recommendations, and Technical Guidance*, 1999, is another report similar to the one listed above. Of particular note are the separate treatments of each state affected and the detailed illustrations. FEMA 338, 110 pp., free from FEMA.

Wind Resistance

74. *Connectors for High Wind-Resistant Structures: Retrofit and New Construction*, 1992, Simpson Strong-Tie Company, Inc., Kell Dublin Corporate Center, 4120 Dublin Blvd., Suite 400, Dublin, CA 94568.

75. *Hurricane Resistant Construction Manual*, 1988, Southern Building Code Congress International, Inc., Birmingham, Ala.

76. *Wind and the Built Environment: U.S. Needs in Wind Engineering and Hazard Mitigation*, report of the Panel on the Assessment of Wind Engineering Issues in the United States for the Committee on Natural Disasters, NRC, 1993, 110 pp., is a state-of-the-art report on wind hazards by a panel of experts. Chapters include "The Nature of Wind," "Wind Engineering Research Needs," "Mitigation, Preparedness, Response, and Recovery," "Education and Technology Transfer," and "Cooperative Efforts." Available from National Academy Press, 2101 Constitution Avenue, N.W., Box 285, Washington, DC 20055.

77. *Against the Wind*, is a six-page brochure with summary information about protecting your home from hurricane wind damage. Developed jointly by the American Red Cross, FEMA, Home Depot, the National Association of Home Builders of the United States, and the Georgia Emergency Management Agency, and published in December 1993, it briefly discusses roof systems, exterior doors and windows, garage doors, and shutters. Available from the American Red Cross (publication ARC-5023) and FEMA (publication FEMA-247).

78. "Wind Conditions in Hurricane Hugo and Their Effect on Buildings in Coastal South Carolina," by P. R. Sparks, 1991 is a contribution to the *Journal of Coastal Research,* Special Issue 8, on Hurricane Hugo, pp. 12–24. Insured property owners should read this paper because the author gives a good evaluation of how and why buildings failed in Hurricane Hugo, and why the Standard Building Code's wind-resistance requirements were inadequate. Available through university libraries.

79. *Wind-Resistant Design Concepts for Residents,* by Delbart B. Ward. Vivid sketches and illustrations explain construction problems and methods of tying structures to the ground. This pamphlet offers recommendations for relatively inexpensive modifications that will increase the safety of residences subject to severe winds. Available as TR-83 from the Civil Defense Preparedness Agency, Department of Defense, The Pentagon, Washington, DC 20301; or from the Civil Defense Preparedness Agency, 2800 Eastern Boulevard, Baltimore, MD 21220.

80. *Interim Guidelines for Building Occupant Protection from Tornadoes and Extreme Winds,* TR-83A, and *Tornado Protection-Selecting and Designing Safe Areas in Buildings,* TR-83B, are supplements to ref. 79 and are available from the same address.

81. "Glazed Opening Design for Windborne Debris Impact," by J. Minor, in *Proceedings of the Conference on Natural Disaster Reduction,* 1996, American Society of Civil Engineers, 345 E. 47th St., New York, NY 10017-2398.

82. "Progress of the ASTM Standard on Fenestration Relative to Windstorms and Its Relationship to Building Codes," by D. Hattis, in *Proceedings of the Conference on Natural Disaster Reduction,* 1996, American Society of Civil Engineers, 345 E. 47th St., New York, NY 10017-2398.

Flooding

83. *Retrofitting and Flood Mitigation in Florida,* 1995. Available from the Florida Department of Community Affairs, State Assistance Office for the National Flood Insurance Program.

84. *Design Guidelines for Flood Damage Reduction,* was prepared by the American Institute of Architects for FEMA, 1981, to encourage appropriate design and construction practices in flood-prone areas. It is FEMA publication FEMA-15.

85. *Minimum Design Loads for Buildings and Other Structures,* 1995, American Society of Civil Engineers, Standard ASCE 7-95, contains criteria for calculating flood loads and for combining these with other loads. This standard meets, and in some cases exceeds, the National Flood Insurance Program requirements. Builders and design engineers should be familiar with this highly technical set of standards for construction. Available from the American Society of Civil Engineers, 345 E. 47th St., New York, NY 10017-2398.

86. *Coastal Construction Manual,* prepared by Dames & Moore and Bliss & Nyitray, Inc., for FEMA, 1986, is a guide to the coastal environment with rec-

ommendations on site and structure design relative to the National Flood Insurance Program. Discusses the program, building codes, coastal environments, and examples. The second edition includes a chapter on the design of large structures at the coast and recommends that pilings be embedded to a depth of 10 feet below mean sea level. Appendixes include design tables, bracing examples, design worksheets, equations and procedures, construction costs, and a list of references. Also includes engineering computer program listings and a sample construction code for use by coastal municipalities. Available from the U.S. Government Printing Office as publication FEMA-55 and from FEMA offices.

87. *Mitigation of Flood and Erosion Damage to Residential Buildings in Coastal Areas*, by FEMA, 1994. This report on flood-proofing investigations includes some case studies and is a good starting point to review flood-proofing techniques; includes additional reading list. Available as FEMA-257.

88. *Manufactured Home Installation in Flood Hazard Areas*, prepared by the National Conference of States on Building Codes and Standards for FEMA, 1985, is a 110-page guide to design, installation, and general characteristics of manufactured homes with respect to coastal and flood hazards. Anyone contemplating buying a manufactured home or already living in one should read this publication and follow its suggestions to lessen potential losses from flood, wind, and fire. Available from the U.S. Government Printing Office as publication 1985-529-684/31054; or from FEMA as FEMA-85.

89. *Flood Resistant Design and Construction Practices*, 1997, ASCE, Standard. This standard provides recommendations for design and construction of buildings that will resist flood loadings and meet or exceed the minimum requirements of the National Flood Insurance Program. Available from ASCE, 345 E. 47th St., New York, NY 10017-2398.

Building Codes

90. Several building codes, with varying jurisdictions, are important guidelines for helping to reduce potential damage. Four of importance in the Alabama and west Florida coastal areas include the South Florida Building Code, 1988 edition, Board of County Commissioners, Metropolitan Dade County, Miami, Fla. (see also http://www.buildingcodeonline.com); the Standard Building Code, 1988, Southern Building Code Congress International, Inc. Birmingham, Ala.; the Uniform Building Code, 1991, one of the commonly applied building codes in the United States, available from International Conference of Building Officials, 5360 S. Workman Mill Road, Whittier, CA 90601; and the Uniform Building Code with 1993 Supplement, by the International Conference of Building Officials, 5360 Workman Mill Road, Whittier, CA 90601-2298.

91. *Elevated Residential Structures*, prepared by the American Institute of Architects Foundation (1735 New York Avenue N.W., Washington, DC 20006) for FEMA, 1984, is an excellent outline of coastal and riverine flood hazards and the need for proper planning and construction. Discusses the National Flood Insurance Program, site analysis and design, design examples, and construction techniques. Includes illustrations, glossary, references, and worksheets for estimating building costs. Available as FEMA-54 from FEMA offices.

92. *Pole House Construction and Pole Building Design.* Available from the American Wood Preservers Institute, 1651 Old Meadows Road, McLean, VA 22101.

Mobile Homes

93. *A Study of Reaction Forces on Mobile Home Foundations Caused by Wind and Flood Loads*, by Felix Y. Yokel and others, 1981. This technical report from the National Bureau of Standards (not the National Institute of Standards Technology) emphasizes that diagonal ties resist wind forces while vertical ties are more effective for resisting flood forces. NBS Building Science Series 132, available from the U.S. Government Printing Office in Washington, D.C.

94. *Suggested Technical Requirements for Mobile Home Tie Down Ordinances*, prepared by the Civil Defense Preparedness Agency, 1974, as TR-73-1, should be used in conjunction with TR-75, below. Available from the U.S. Army Publications Center, Civil Defense Branch, 2800 Eastern Blvd. (Middle River), Baltimore, MD 21220.

95. *Protecting Mobile Homes from High Winds*, TR-75, prepared by the Civil Defense Preparedness Agency, 1974. This excellent 16-page booklet outlines methods of tying down mobile homes and means of protection such as positioning and windbreaks. It is publication 1974-0-537-785, available from the U.S. Government Printing Office; or from the U.S. Army Publications Center, Civil Defense Branch, 280 Eastern Blvd. (Middle River), Baltimore, MD 21220.

96. "Manufactured Home Construction and Safety Standards," 1992, 24 Code of Federal Regulations, chapter 20, pt. 3280, pp. 196–233.

97. *Wind Load Provisions of the Manufactured Home Construction and Safety Standards — A Review and Recommendations for Improvement*, 1993, contains the results of a study supported by the U.S. Department of Housing and Urban Development (HUD) and performed by the National Institute of Standards and Technology (NIST). Wind-load design criteria for manufactured homes were studied based on the effects of Hurricane Andrew (1992). Manufactured homes built after the Manufactured Home and Construction and Safety Standards and accompanying HUD labels were issued experienced less damage than did units constructed prior to these standards. In general, conventional residential homes fared better than manufactured homes, including those

with HUD labels. The report concludes that ASCE Standard 7-95 is the most logical reference to provide a basis for wind-load design criteria. Authored by R. D. Marshall, this report is available from the National Technical Information Service (NTIS), NISTIR 5189.

98. *Manufactured Homes — Probability of Failure and the Need for Better Windstorm Protection through Improved Anchoring Systems,* 1994, contends that a dominant failure mode is due to the anchoring system. The anchor system load capacity implied by the current standards for the installation of manufactured homes is rarely achieved in practice. This report, written by R. D. Marshall, is available from NTIS as NISTIR 5370.

99. *Recommended Performance-Based Criteria for the Design of Manufactured Home Foundation Systems to Resist Wind and Seismic Loads,* 1995, is another NIST report that questions whether the current practice for anchor systems for manufactured homes is adequate for wind-load protection. Prepared by R. D. Marshall, it is available from NTIS as NISTIR 5664.

Earthquake-Resistant Construction

100. *The Home Builder's Guide for Earthquake Design,* 1992. Available from FEMA as publication FEMA-232.

101. *Reducing the Risks of Nonstructural Earthquake Damage: A Practical Guide,* available from FEMA, is publication FEMA-74.

Other Publications and Newsletters

Publications List, Coastal Engineering Research Center and Beach Erosion Board, by the U.S. Army Corps of Engineers, is a list (updated periodically) of published research by the U.S. Army Corps of Engineers. Free from the ACOE. Lists of earlier publications are available from the same library.

FEMA Publications Catalog, by FEMA, February 1999, is a booklet listing more than 300 publications available from FEMA to assist everyone from individual property owners to emergency managers. Request publication FEMA-20.

Publications of the Natural Hazards Research and Applications Information Center (NHRAIC), in Boulder, Colorado. The center is a national clearinghouse of research and public policy on hazards. Visit their web site at http://www. colorado.edu/hazards. Hundreds of publications are available — most for a very nominal charge — covering all aspects of natural hazard preparedness, response, mitigation, and planning. A monthly magazine, *Natural Hazards Observer,* has a wealth of information. A new publication, the *Natural Hazards Informer,* contains peer-reviewed reports. Contact the NHRAIC Publications Clerk, Campus Box 482, University of Colorado, Boulder 80309-0482, (303) 492-6818.

Living on the Edge is 60-minute VHS video with a *Coastal Risk Assessment Field Guide* produced by Environmental Media in association with the Duke University Department of Geology. *Living on the Edge* is a video consumer guide to the special problems inherent in buying and owning property on the shoreline. To order, contact Environmental Media, P.O. Box 99, Beaufort, SC 29901, (800) 368-3382 or (803) 986-9034; http://www.envmedia.com.

The Beaches Are Moving is a one-hour VHS video providing an introductory course in barrier island geology by Orrin Pilkey, professor of geology and director of the Program for the Study of Developed Shorelines at Duke University. To order, contact Environmental Media, P.O. Box 99, Beaufort, SC 29901, (800) 368-3382 or (803) 986-9034; http://www.envmedia.com.

A House Built on Sand: Common Sense Rules for Buying and Building in Florida's Coastal High-Hazard Area, 1997, Florida Department of Community Affairs, Florida Coastal Management Program.

Against the Tide: When Permanent Structures Encounter a Moving Shoreline, 1997, Florida Department of Community Affairs, Florida Coastal Management Program.

Andrew! Savagery from the Sea! by the staff of the *Sun-Sentinel*, Fort Lauderdale, Fla. Tribune Publishing, P.O. Box 1100, Orlando, FL 32802-1100, ISBN 0-941263-71-1; $9.99.

Hurricane Andrew, August 24, 1993, As It Happened. WTVJ-4 News, Miami. Contact Bryan Norcross (800) 551-1010.

Alabama Coastal Hazards Assessment is a CD-ROM that contains comprehensive hazard-related data in one package. Complicated computer software is not needed to access information about flood hazard areas, demographics, flood loss data, hurricane storm surge hazards, emergency evacuation routes, historical disaster data, laws and policies, shelter locations, and growth trends. Available from NOAA Coastal Services Center, 2234 South Hobson Ave., Charleston, SC 29405-2413, (803) 974-6251. Publication NOAA CSC/10-97/001.

Index